First World War
and Army of Occupation
War Diary
France, Belgium and Germany

4 DIVISION
Headquarters, Branches and Services
Royal Army Medical Corps
Assistant Director Medical Services
19 July 1917 - 29 January 1919

WO95/1462

The Naval & Military Press Ltd
www.nmarchive.com
Published in association with The National Archives

Published by

The Naval & Military Press Ltd

Unit 10 Ridgewood Industrial Park,

Uckfield, East Sussex,

TN22 5QE England

Tel: +44 (0) 1825 749494

www.naval-military-press.com

www.nmarchive.com

This diary has been reprinted in facsimile from the original. Any imperfections are inevitably reproduced and the quality may fall short of modern type and cartographic standards.

© Crown Copyright
Images reproduced by permission of The National Archives, London, England, 2015.

Contents

Document type	Place/Title	Date From	Date To
Heading	4th Division Medical A.D.M.S July to September 1917		
War Diary	St Nicholas	19/07/1917	20/07/1917
Miscellaneous	R.A.M.C Orders By Lieut. Colonel. D. Ahern, D.S.O., R.A.M.C., A/A.D.M.S. 4th. Divn.	25/06/1917	25/06/1917
War Diary	St Nicholas	01/00/1917	31/00/1917
Miscellaneous	Addendum To R.A.M.C. Orders Dated 27. June, 1917.	02/07/1917	02/07/1917
Miscellaneous	R.A.M.C Orders By Lieut. Colonel, D. Ahern, D.S.O., R.A.M.C., A/A.D.M.S., 4th. Division	02/07/1917	02/07/1917
Miscellaneous	R.A.M.C. Orders By Colonel, J. Grech D.S.O. A.M.S. A.D.M.S. 4th Division	28/07/1917	28/07/1917
Miscellaneous	A Form Messages And Signals		
Heading	War Diary of A.D.M.S 4th Division From 1.8.1917 To 31.8.1917		
War Diary	St.Nicholas	01/08/1917	31/08/1917
Miscellaneous	R.A.M.C. Order By Col. J. Grech. D.S.O., A.M.S., A.D.M.S. 4th. Division.	17/08/1917	17/08/1917
Miscellaneous	Amendment To R.A.M.C. Order Dated 17-8-1917.	22/08/1917	22/08/1917
Miscellaneous	Amendment To R.A.M.C. Order Dated 17-8-1917	22/08/1917	22/08/1917
Map	Map		
Miscellaneous	Summary Of Medical War Diaries For 4th Divn. 14th Corps, 5th Army	20/09/1917	20/09/1917
Miscellaneous	4th Divn. 14th Corps. 5th Army. A.D.M.S		
Miscellaneous	Summary Of Medical War Diaries For 4th Divn.14th Corps, 5th Army	20/09/1917	20/09/1917
Miscellaneous	4th Divn. 14th Corps. 5th Army A.D.M.S		
Heading	War Diary of A.D.M.S 4th Divn For Period 1.9.17 To 30.9.17		
War Diary	St Nicholas	01/09/1917	08/09/1917
War Diary	Basseux	09/09/1917	20/09/1917
War Diary	Proven	21/09/1917	28/09/1917
War Diary	Welsh Farm Beside Elverdinghe	29/09/1917	29/09/1917
War Diary	Welsh Camp	29/09/1917	30/09/1917
War Diary	Welsh Farm	30/09/1917	30/09/1917
Miscellaneous	R.A.M.C. Order By Colonel J. Grech, D.S.O., A.M.S., A.D.M.S. 4th. Division.	03/09/1917	03/09/1917
Miscellaneous	Warning Order By Colonel J. Grech. D.S.O., A.M.S., A.D.M.S. 4th. Division.	14/09/1917	14/09/1917
Miscellaneous	Amendment To R.A.M.C. Warning Order Dated 23-9-17.	23/09/1917	23/09/1917
Miscellaneous	Warning Order By Col. J. Grech. D.S.O. A.M.S., A.D.M.S 4th. Division.	23/09/1917	23/09/1917
Miscellaneous	Medical Arrangements, 4th. Division	23/09/1917	23/09/1917
Miscellaneous	Amendment To 4th. Division R.A.M.C. Order Dated 25-9-1917.	26/09/1917	26/09/1917
Miscellaneous	R.A.M.C. Order By Col. J. Grech. D.S.O. A.M.S. A.D.M.S. 4th. Division.	25/09/1917	25/09/1917
Miscellaneous	R.A.M.C. Order By Colonel J. Grech. D.S.O., A.M.S., A.D.M.S. 4th. Division.	28/09/1917	28/09/1917
Heading	4th Division Medical A.D.M.S October to December 1917		

Heading	Summary Of Medical War Diaries For 4th Divn.14th Corps, 5th Army. 18th Corps From 15/10/17. 17th Corps From 17/10/17.		
Miscellaneous	4th Divn. 14th Corps 5th Army A.D.M.S Col. J. Grech D.S.O. 17th Corps from 17/10/17		
Heading	Summary Of Medical War Diaries For 4th Divn. 14th Corps, 5th Army. 18th Corps From 15/10/17. 17th Corps From 17/10/17.		
Miscellaneous	4th Divn. 14th Corps 5th Army. A.D.M.S. Col. J. Grech D.S.O.		
War Diary	Welsh Farm	01/10/1917	13/10/1917
War Diary	Proven	14/10/1917	14/10/1917
War Diary	Poperinghe	15/10/1917	16/10/1917
War Diary	Duisans	17/10/1917	24/10/1917
War Diary	Arras	25/10/1917	31/10/1917
Miscellaneous	Addendum No.1 To R.A.M.C. Order Dated 25-9-17.	01/10/1917	01/10/1917
Miscellaneous	R.A.M.C. Order By Colonel J. Grech. D.S.O., A.M.S. A.D.M.S. 4th Division.	07/10/1917	07/10/1917
Miscellaneous	Amendment To 4th Division R.A.M.C. Order Dated 7th. October, 1917.	08/10/1917	08/10/1917
Miscellaneous	Addendum No. 2 To 4th Division R.A.M.C. Order Dated 7th. October, 1917.	08/10/1917	08/10/1917
Operation(al) Order(s)	R.A.M.C. Order No.36 by Colonel J. Grech D.S.O. A.M.S A.D.M.S 4th Division	11/10/1917	11/10/1917
Operation(al) Order(s)	R.A.M.C. Order No.37 by Colonel J. Grech D.S.O. A.M.S A.D.M.S 4th Division	11/10/1917	11/10/1917
Miscellaneous	Table Of Moves		
Miscellaneous	Addendum To R.A.M.C. Order No.37 Dated 11th. October, 1917.	13/10/1917	13/10/1917
Operation(al) Order(s)	R.A.M.C. Order No.38 by Colonel J. Grech D.S.O. A.M.S A.D.M.S 4th Division	13/10/1917	13/10/1917
Operation(al) Order(s)	R.A.M.C. Order No.39 by Colonel J. Grech D.S.O. A.M.S A.D.M.S 4th Division	16/10/1917	16/10/1917
Miscellaneous	R.A.M.C. Warning Order By Colonel J. Grech. D.S.O. A.M.S., A.D.M.S. 4th. Division.	16/10/1917	16/10/1917
Miscellaneous	R.A.M.C. Order No.40 By Colonel J. Grech D.S.O. A.M.S A.D.M.S 4th Division	20/10/1917	20/10/1917
Miscellaneous	Map 1		
Map	Langemarck		
Map	Map		
War Diary	Arras	01/11/1917	30/11/1917
Operation(al) Order(s)	R.A.M.C. Order No.42 by Colonel J. Grech D.S.O. A.M.S A.D.M.S 4th Division	16/11/1917	16/11/1917
Operation(al) Order(s)	R.A.M.C. Order No.43 by Colonel J. Grech D.S.O. A.M.S A.D.M.S 4th Division	25/11/1917	25/11/1917
Operation(al) Order(s)	R.A.M.C. Order No.44 by Colonel J. Grech D.S.O. A.M.S A.D.M.S 4th Division	28/11/1917	28/11/1917
Map	Airy Corner Trench Map		
War Diary	Arras	01/12/1917	31/12/1917
Operation(al) Order(s)	Addendum No.1 To R.A.M.C. Order No.44 by Colonel J. Grech D.S.O. A.M.S A.D.M.S 4th Division	01/12/1917	01/12/1917
Miscellaneous	Supplementary Medical Arrangements	11/12/1917	11/12/1917
Map	Map		
Heading	4th Division Medical A.D.M.S January to April 1918		
Miscellaneous	On His Majesty's Service.		
War Diary	Arras	01/01/1918	31/01/1918

Type	Description	Date From	Date To
Map	Medical Services		
Operation(al) Order(s)	R.A.M.C. Order No.45 by Colonel J. Grech D.S.O. A.M.S A.D.M.S 4th Division	03/01/1918	03/01/1918
Miscellaneous	A.D.M.S. 4th. Division No.10/66	10/01/1918	10/01/1918
Miscellaneous	4th Division Medical Arrangements In Connection With 4th Division Defence Scheme	15/01/1918	15/01/1918
Operation(al) Order(s)	R.A.M.C. Order No.46 by Colonel J. Grech D.S.O. A.M.S A.D.M.S 4th Division	31/01/1918	31/01/1918
Miscellaneous	Addenda to 4th Divisional Medical Arrangements	26/01/1918	26/01/1918
Heading	A.D.M.S 4th Div Feb 1918		
War Diary	Arras	01/02/1918	28/02/1918
Miscellaneous	Administrative Instructions In Connection With R.A.M.C. Order No.46	02/02/1918	02/02/1918
Miscellaneous	Amendment No. 1 To R.A.M.C. Administrative Instructions	04/02/1918	04/02/1918
Miscellaneous	4th Division Medical Arrangements in Connection with Reserve Division Defence Scheme	16/02/1918	16/02/1918
Miscellaneous	Addendum To 4th Division Medical Arrangements In Connection With Reserve Division Defence Scheme	21/02/1918	21/02/1918
War Diary	Arras	01/03/1918	26/03/1918
Operation(al) Order(s)	R.A.M.C. Order No.51 by Colonel N. Faichnie A.M.S A.D.M.S 4th Division	26/03/1918	26/03/1918
War Diary	Arras	26/03/1918	26/03/1918
War Diary	Etrun	26/03/1918	31/03/1918
Operation(al) Order(s)	R.A.M.C. Order No.50 by Colonel N. Faichnie A.M.S A.D.M.S 4th Division	25/03/1918	25/03/1918
Miscellaneous	4th Division Medical Arrangements In Connection With 4th Division (Reserve Division) Defence Scheme (No.2)	02/03/1918	02/03/1918
Miscellaneous	Amendment No.1 To 4th Division Medical Arrangements In Connection With 4th. Division (Reserve Division) Defence Scheme No.2	02/03/1918	02/03/1918
Miscellaneous	Correction To 4th Division Medical Arrangements In Connection With 4th Division (Reserve Division) Defence Scheme No.2	03/03/1918	03/03/1918
Miscellaneous	Amendment No.2 To 4th Division Medical Arrangements In Connection With 4th Division (Reserve Division) Defence Scheme No.2	05/03/1918	05/03/1918
Miscellaneous	4th Division Medical Arrangements In Connection With 4th Division (Reserve Division) Defence Scheme No.3	03/03/1918	03/03/1918
Operation(al) Order(s)	R.A.M.C Order No.47 by Lieut Colonel R.P Lewis R.A.M.C. A.D.M.S 4th Division	08/03/1918	08/03/1918
Miscellaneous	4th Division Medical Arrangements In Connection With 4th Division (Reserve Division) Defence Scheme No.2	06/03/1918	06/03/1918
Miscellaneous	Amendment No.1 To 4th Division Medical Arrangements In Connection With 4th Division Defence Scheme	08/03/1918	08/03/1918
Miscellaneous	Ref 4th Division Medical Arrangements No.2 In Connection With 4th Division (Reserve Division) Defence Scheme	09/03/1918	09/03/1918
Miscellaneous	4th Division Medical Arrangements No.1 In Connection with Reserve Division Defence Scheme	10/03/1918	10/03/1918
Miscellaneous	A.D.M.S 4th Division No.31/126	11/03/1918	11/03/1918
Miscellaneous	O.C. 10.11.12 F. Amb	11/03/1918	11/03/1918

Type	Description	Start	End
Miscellaneous	Addendum No.2 To 4th Division Medical Arrangements No.2 In Connection With Reserve Division Defence Scheme	11/03/1918	11/03/1918
Miscellaneous	A.D.M.S 4th. Division No.17/12	11/03/1918	11/03/1918
Miscellaneous	A.D.M.S 4th Division No.31/126	11/03/1918	11/03/1918
Miscellaneous	4th Division Medical Arrangements No.3 (a) In Connection With 4th. Division (Reserve) Defence Scheme and 4th. Division G.A.4/73/G	11/03/1918	11/03/1918
Operation(al) Order(s)	R.A.M.C. Order No.48 by Lieut Colonel N. Faichnie R.A.M.C. A/A.D.M.S. 4th Division	18/03/1918	18/03/1918
Miscellaneous	4th Division Medical Arrangements In Connection With R.A.M.C. Order 48	18/03/1918	18/03/1918
Miscellaneous	Reference 4th. Division Medical Arrangements In Connection With R.A.M.C. Order No.48 Dated 18-3-18	20/03/1918	20/03/1918
Miscellaneous	4th Division Medical Arrangements In Connection With The Left Division Defence Scheme	21/03/1918	21/03/1918
Operation(al) Order(s)	R.A.M.C Order No.49 by Lieut Colonel N. Faichnie R.A.M.C. A/A.D.M.S. 4th Division	23/03/1918	23/03/1918
Miscellaneous	Amendments to 4th. Division Medical Arrangements In Connection With Left Division Defence Scheme	24/03/1918	24/03/1918
Heading	War Diary of A.D.M.S 4th Division For Period April 1st 1918 To April 30th 1918		
War Diary	Etrun	01/04/1918	08/04/1918
War Diary	Fosseux	09/04/1918	12/04/1918
War Diary	Bas Rieux	12/04/1918	30/04/1918
Miscellaneous	Diary		
Map	Map		
Operation(al) Order(s)	R.A.M.C. Order No.52 by Lieut Colonel N. Faichnie A.M.S.A.D.M.S. 4th Division	01/04/1918	01/04/1918
Operation(al) Order(s)	R.A.M.C. Order No.53 by Lieut Colonel N. Faichnie A.M.S.A.D.M.S. 4th Division	02/04/1918	02/04/1918
Miscellaneous	4th Division Medical Arrangements In Connection With R.A.M.C. Order No.53	02/04/1918	02/04/1918
Operation(al) Order(s)	R.A.M.C. Order No.54 by Lieut Colonel N. Faichnie A.M.S.A.D.M.S. 4th Division	07/04/1918	07/04/1918
Miscellaneous	Addendum No.1 To R.A.M.C. Order No.54 Dated 7-4-18	08/04/1918	08/04/1918
Miscellaneous	Medical Arrangements in Connection With 4th Division Order No.108 of 14-4-18	14/04/1918	14/04/1918
Operation(al) Order(s)	R.A.M.C. Order No.56 by Lieut Colonel N. Faichnie A.M.S.A.D.M.S. 4th Division	15/04/1918	15/04/1918
Operation(al) Order(s)	R.A.M.C. Order No.57 by Lieut Colonel N. Faichnie A.M.S.A.D.M.S. 4th Division	16/04/1918	16/04/1918
Miscellaneous	4th Division Medical Arrangements In Connection With R.A.M.C. Order 57	16/04/1918	16/04/1918
Miscellaneous	4th Division Arrangements For Collection Of Sick	16/04/1918	16/04/1918
Miscellaneous	Amendment No.1 To 4th Division Medical Arrangements	16/04/1918	16/04/1918
Operation(al) Order(s)	R.A.M.C. Order No.58 by Lieut Colonel N. Faichnie A.M.S.A.D.M.S. 4th Division	25/04/1918	25/04/1918
Miscellaneous	4th Division Medical Arrangements In Connection With R.A.M.C. Order No.58	26/04/1918	26/04/1918
Operation(al) Order(s)	R.A.M.C. Order No.59 by Lieut Colonel N. Faichnie A.M.S.A.D.M.S. 4th Division	29/04/1918	29/04/1918
Heading	4th Division Medical A.D.M.S May to August 1918		
Heading	140/2973		

Type	Description	Start	End
War Diary	Bas Rieux	01/05/1918	31/05/1918
Operation(al) Order(s)	4th Division R.A.M.C. Order No.60	10/05/1918	10/05/1918
Miscellaneous	4th Division Revised Medical Arrangements in Connection With R.A.M.C. Orders Nos. 58,59 & 60	14/05/1918	14/05/1918
Miscellaneous	Amendment No.1 Revised Medical Arrangements	17/05/1918	17/05/1918
Heading	War Diary of A.D.M.S Headquarters 4th Division For Period From 1st June 1918 To 30th June 1918		
War Diary	Bas. Rieux	01/06/1918	30/06/1918
Operation(al) Order(s)	4th Division R.A.M.C. Order No.61	12/06/1918	12/06/1918
War Diary	Bas Rieux	01/07/1918	31/07/1918
Miscellaneous	A.D.M.S. 4th. Division No. 17/12	17/07/1918	17/07/1918
Miscellaneous	4th Division Medical Arrangements No.2	17/07/1918	17/07/1918
Miscellaneous	Amendments to 4th Division Medical Arrangements No.2	27/07/1918	27/07/1918
Miscellaneous	Addendum No.1 To 4th Division Medical Arrangements No.2	27/07/1918	27/07/1918
War Diary	Bas Rieux	01/08/1918	23/08/1918
War Diary	Bomy	24/08/1918	24/08/1918
War Diary	Hautecloque	25/08/1918	25/08/1918
War Diary	Villers Au Bois	26/08/1918	27/08/1918
War Diary	Arras	28/08/1918	31/08/1918
Miscellaneous	4th Division Medical Arrangements No.3	09/08/1918	09/08/1918
Miscellaneous	Amendments to 4th Division Medical Arrangements No.3	11/08/1918	11/08/1918
Miscellaneous	Amendments (2) To 4th Division Medical Arrangements No.3	11/08/1918	11/08/1918
Miscellaneous	4th Division R.A.M.C. Warning Order, In Connection with 4th Div. Warning Order	20/08/1918	20/08/1918
Operation(al) Order(s)	4th Division R.A.M.C. Order No.62	21/08/1918	21/08/1918
Operation(al) Order(s)	4th Division R.A.M.C. Order No.63	21/08/1918	21/08/1918
Miscellaneous	Arrangements for Collection & Registration of Sick in New Area	21/08/1918	21/08/1918
Miscellaneous	A.D.M.S 4th Division No.17/154	22/08/1918	22/08/1918
Miscellaneous	4th Division R.A.M.C. Warning Order	24/08/1918	24/08/1918
Operation(al) Order(s)	4th Division R.A.M.C. Order No.64	24/08/1918	24/08/1918
Miscellaneous	To Accompany 4th Division R.A.M.C. Order 64		
Miscellaneous	Collection & Registration of Sick	24/08/1918	24/08/1918
Operation(al) Order(s)	4th Division R.A.M.C. Order No.65	27/08/1918	27/08/1918
Operation(al) Order(s)	4th Division R.A.M.C. Order No.66	29/08/1918	29/08/1918
Miscellaneous	Amendments to R.A.M.C. Order No.66	29/08/1918	29/08/1918
Heading	4th Division Medical A.D.M.S September to December 1918		
Heading	September 1918 A.D.M.S Div IV		
War Diary	Arras	01/09/1918	04/09/1918
War Diary	Villers Chatel	06/09/1918	19/09/1918
War Diary	Arras	20/09/1918	29/09/1918
War Diary	Les Fosses Farm	30/09/1918	30/09/1918
Operation(al) Order(s)	4th Division R.A.M.C. Order No.67	01/09/1918	01/09/1918
Operation(al) Order(s)	4th Division R.A.M.C. Order No.68	03/09/1918	03/09/1918
Operation(al) Order(s)	4th Division R.A.M.C. Order No.69	17/09/1918	17/09/1918
Miscellaneous	Amendments to 4th Division R.A.M.C. Order No.69	18/09/1918	18/09/1918
Miscellaneous	Amendments No 2 To 4th Division R.A.M.C. Order No.69	19/09/1918	19/09/1918
Miscellaneous	Amendments No.3 To 4th Div R.A.M.C. Order No.69	20/09/1918	20/09/1918
Miscellaneous	4th Division Medical Arrangements No.1	21/09/1918	21/09/1918

Miscellaneous	Amendments No.1 To 4th Division Medical Arrangements No.1	24/09/1918	24/09/1918
Operation(al) Order(s)	4th Division R.A.M.C. Order No.70	29/09/1918	29/09/1918
Miscellaneous	A.D.M.S. 4th Division	29/09/1918	29/09/1918
Heading	A.D.M.S 4th Division Oct 1918		
War Diary	Les Fosses Farm	01/10/1918	06/10/1918
War Diary	Warlus	07/10/1918	13/10/1918
War Diary	Escadoeuvres	17/10/1918	18/10/1918
War Diary	Naves	19/10/1918	21/10/1918
War Diary	Avesnes Le Sec	23/10/1918	31/10/1918
Miscellaneous	4th Division Medical Arrangements No.2	01/10/1918	01/10/1918
Operation(al) Order(s)	4th Division R.A.M.C. Order No.71	04/10/1918	04/10/1918
Operation(al) Order(s)	4th Division R.A.M.C. Order No.72	05/10/1918	05/10/1918
Miscellaneous	Collection of Divisional Sick	05/10/1918	05/10/1918
Operation(al) Order(s)	4th Division R.A.M.C. Order No.73	09/10/1918	09/10/1918
Operation(al) Order(s)	4th Division R.A.M.C. Order No.74	11/10/1918	11/10/1918
Operation(al) Order(s)	4th Division R.A.M.C. Order No.76	17/10/1918	17/10/1918
Miscellaneous	4th Division Medical Arrangements In Connection With R.A.M.C. Order No.76	18/10/1918	18/10/1918
Operation(al) Order(s)	4th Division R.A.M.C. Order No.77	18/10/1918	18/10/1918
Operation(al) Order(s)	4th Division R.A.M.C. Order No.78	20/10/1918	20/10/1918
Miscellaneous	4th Division Medical Arrangements In Connection With R.A.M.C. Order No.78	20/10/1918	20/10/1918
Miscellaneous	Addendum No.1 To 4th Division Medical Arrangements In Connection With R.A.M.C. Order 78	21/10/1918	21/10/1918
Miscellaneous	4th Division No.2 Provisional Medical Arrangements		
Miscellaneous	4th Division No.1 Provisional Medical Arrangements	14/10/1918	14/10/1918
Operation(al) Order(s)	4th Division R.A.M.C. Order No.75	12/10/1918	12/10/1918
Miscellaneous	4th Division Medical Arrangements in Connection With 4th Division Order No.169	23/10/1918	23/10/1918
Operation(al) Order(s)	4th Division R.A.M.C. Order No.80	27/10/1918	27/10/1918
Heading	War Diary of ADMS 4th Division From 1-11-18 To 30-11-18		
War Diary	Avesnes Le Sec	01/11/1918	01/11/1918
War Diary	Haspres	02/11/1918	02/11/1918
War Diary	Avesnes Le Sec	03/11/1918	10/11/1918
War Diary	Preseau	11/11/1918	19/11/1918
War Diary	Valenciennes	20/11/1918	25/11/1918
Operation(al) Order(s)	4th Division R.A.M.C. Order No.81	02/11/1918	02/11/1918
Operation(al) Order(s)	4th Division R.A.M.C. Order No.82	05/11/1918	05/11/1918
Operation(al) Order(s)	4th Division R.A.M.C. Order No.83	10/11/1918	10/11/1918
War Diary	Valenciennes	01/12/1918	31/12/1918
Miscellaneous	O.C. No.11 Field Ambulance	12/12/1918	12/12/1918
Miscellaneous	A.D.M.S 4th Division No.17/250	30/12/1918	30/12/1918
Heading Miscellaneous	BEF 4 Division ADMS 1919 Jan-1919 Feb Box-1141		
Heading	War Diary of A.D.M.S 4th Division From 1-1-1919 To 31-1-1919		
War Diary	Binche	30/01/1919	31/01/1919
Heading	War Diary of Medical 4th Division HdQrs February 1st To 28th 1919		
War Diary	Binche	01/02/1919	28/02/1919
War Diary	Valenciennes	01/01/1919	05/01/1919
War Diary	Binche	06/01/1919	29/01/1919

4th Division

Medical

A. D. M. S.

July to September

1917

WAR DIARY
or
INTELLIGENCE SUMMARY.

(Erase heading not required.)

Army Form C. 2118.

Place	Date	Hour	Summary of Events and Information	Remarks and references to Appendices
ST NICHOLAS			BLANGY PARK Camp.	
	19th	7.30a	Wounded horse to A.T.n.i.S XVII Corps.	29.
		6.70p	Wounded horse to A.T.n.i.S XVII Corps.	30.
		6.70p	Battle Casualties Return to A.T.n.i.S XVII Corps.	31.
			Two Officers one N.C.O and 20 other ranks joined from the base as reinforcements.	
		1.45p	Instructions to F.As re horses attached to 4. Div. for training.	32.
			A.D.M.S attended Conference at Corps H.Q. and presided 11.7.A.	
			D.A.D.M.S inspected Camp of 3/10th Middlesex Regt.	
	20th	7.30a	Wounded horse to A.T.n.i.S XVII Corps.	33
		6.0p.	Wounded horse to A.T.n.i.S XVII Corps.	34.
		6.0p.	Battle Casualties Return to A.T.n.i.S XVII Corps.	35.
			One Officer and 40 other ranks joined from the base as reinforcements. A report on a suspected case of diphtheria.	
			A.D.M.S. visited Officers hospital AUBIGNY. Very heavy rain during the evening, shower lasting about 2 hours.	36.

Copy No. 14

R.A.M.C. ORDERS

by

Lieut. Colonel, D. AHERN, D.S.O., R.A.M.C., a/A.D.M.S. 4th. Divn.

Map Refs: Trench Maps, 1/10,000.
PLOUVAIN. BOIRY-NOTRE-DAME.   25th. June, 1917.

The XVIIth. Corps will take over the Left Divisional Front of the VIth. Corps at 12, noon, July 1st. and will take over the VIth. Corps front as far South as the ARRAS-CAMBRAI Road exclusive, by 6 a.m. on July 2nd.

The 4th. Division will hold the line from I.14.c.6.2. to the junction of BIT LANE and SNAFFLE Trench, (I.31.d.9.1.).

To carry out the above adjustments of front the following reliefs will be carried out:-

(a). On 26th. inst and night of 26th/27th., the 52nd. Inf. Brigade, (17th. Division), will take over from the 10th. Inf. Brigade as far South as I.14.c.6.2.

(b). On night 26th/27th. inst. the 10th. Inf. Brigade will take over from the 11th. Inf. Brigade as far South as the River SCARPE.

(c). On night 27th/28th. inst. one Battalion of the 12th. Inf. Brigade will relieve the 11th. Inf. Brigade South of the River SCARPE.

(d). On night of 28th/29th. inst. the 12th. Inf. Brigade will take over from the 35th. Inf. Brigade, (12th. Division), as far South as I.31.d.9.1.

On completion of the above Reliefs Inter-Divisional boundaries East of ARRAS will be as follow:-

Between 17th. and 4th. Divisions:
I.14.c.6.2.-I.13.d.95.25.(to 4th. Division)-Junction of CUSP and CORFU Trenches(to 17th. Division)-CORFU (to 17th. Division) to junction with CRUMP-Railway Bridge over SCARPE in H.24.a.(to 4th. Division)- thence the River SCARPE (to 4th. Division). The SCARPE will be a common waterway to both Divisions.

Between 4th. and 12th. Divisions:
I.31.d.9.1.(to 4th. Division) thence the Southern Grid Line of the "I" square as far as I.31.c.35.65., thence ORANGE STREET(to 12th. Division), as far as H.36.d.55.20- H.36.d.0.0., thence Southern Grid Line of the "H" square as far as junction with ARRAS-CAMBRAI Road, thence the road (to 12th. Division).

I. (a). 10th. Field Ambulance will continue to clear the new front of the 4th. Division, (consisting of one Battalion North of the River and two Battalions South of it).
O.C. 10th. Field Ambulance will hand over to the 17th. Division, the Medical Post in FAMPOUX, (H.17.d.7.9.), on the night of 26th/27th. He will continue to keep a Relay Post in the SINGLE ARCH, (to carry back casualties from the Battn. North of the River), and a Loading Party for the Pontoons at the TRIPLE ARCH.

/The

-2-

The arrangements at FAMPOUX LOCK will remain as they are at present.
O.C. 10th. Field Ambulance will deal with cases of the 17th. Division arriving at FAMPOUX LOCK in the same way as cases of our own Division: if the number of such cases is excessive, personnel from 17th. Division to assist at FAMPOUX LOCK are available and should be asked for through the A.D.M.S., 4th. Division.

(b). The arrangements for clearing the Battalion on the immediate South of the River will continue as they are at present.

(c). O.C. 10th. Field Ambulance will arrange to evacuate the casualties from the Battalion on the Right of the Line, from their Regimental Aid Post at H.36.b.2.1.

Details as to Relay Posts to be taken over, routes of evacuation to be followed, etc., will be given later.

II. As soon as the Pontoon Evacuation starts again, the pontoons will be taken to BLANGY LOCK and unloaded there into motor ambulances for conveyance of wounded to the M.D.Stn.
O.C. 10th. Field Ambulance will move, as soon as necessary, the party from ATHIES LOCK to BLANGY LOCK, for unloading the pontoons.

III. ACKNOWLEDGE.

Headquarters,   Captain,
4th. Division.   for A.D.M.S. 4th. Division.

Issued at: 6.30 p.m.

Copies to: 10th.,11th.,12th. Infantry Brigades.
              10th.,11th.,12th. Field Ambulances.
              4th. Division, "G".
              4th. Division, "Q".
              C.R.E., 4th. Division.
              D.D.M.S., XVIIth. Corps.
              A.D.M.S. 12th. Division.
              A.D.M.S. 17th. Division.
              Diary.
              File.

WAR DIARY
or
INTELLIGENCE SUMMARY.

Army Form C. 2118.

A.D.M.S. 4th Army MEDICAL

Place	Date	Hour	Summary of Events and Information	Remarks and references to Appendices
ST. NICHOLAS	1st	7.5a	Wounded horse to Armies XVII Corps.	1.
		6.25p	Wounded horse to Armies XVII Corps.	2.
		6.25p	Battle Casualties Review to Armies XVII Corps	3.
	2nd	7.15a	Wounded horse to Armies XVII Corps	4.
		6.15p	Wounded horse to Armies XVII Corps.	5.
		6.15p	Battle Casualties Review to Armies XVII Corps.	6.
			Addendum (to Order issued by Armies dated 27.6.17) giving location of 107A Hosp.	A
			Orders by Armies re the taking over of the HOPITAL ST JEAN, ARRAS by 12.7A.	B
	3rd	7.0a	Wounded horse to Armies XVII Corps.	7.
		6.20p	Wounded horse to Armies XVII Corps.	8.
		6.20p	Battle Casualties Review to Armies XVII Corps.	9.
	4th	7.10a	Wounded horse to Armies XVII Corps.	10.
		6.15p	Wounded horse to Armies XVII Corps.	11.
		6.15p	Battle Casualties Review to Armies	12.
			The ADMS visited 11 & 12 F.A. and attended a conference at Corps HQ.	
			Mess detaining M.O. to temporary duty with 35th F.A. Rear Sec., WARLUS.	12A.

WAR DIARY
or
INTELLIGENCE SUMMARY.

(Erase heading not required.)

Army Form C. 2118.

Place	Date	Hour	Summary of Events and Information	Remarks and references to Appendices
ST. NICHOLAS.	5th.	7.20 a.	Manned wire to Armies XVII Corps.	13
		4.0 p.	Phonemes from return to Armies XVII Corps.	14
		6.20 p.	Wounded wire to Armies XVII Corps.	15
		6.30 p.	Battle Casualties Return to Armies.	16
	6th.	6.45 a.	Manned wire to Armies XVII Corps.	17
		6.30 p.	Manned wire to Armies XVII Corps.	18
		6.30 p.	Battle Casualties Return to Armies XVII Corps. The S/Armies and Districts visited the A.A. Stn. and inspected M.A.T. of the Right Sec.	19
			A.Armies returns from leave in U.K. and Lt. Col. Ahern D.S.O. resumes command of 117. A.	20
	7th.	7.0 a.	Manned wire to Armies XVII Corps.	21
		6.25 p.	Wounded wire to Armies XVII Corps.	22
		6.25 p.	Battle Casualties Return.	23
	8th.	7.30 a.	Manned wire to Armies XVII Corps.	24
		6.15 p.	Wounded wire to Armies XVII Corps.	

WAR DIARY
or
INTELLIGENCE SUMMARY.
(Erase heading not required.)

Army Form C. 2118.

Place	Date	Hour	Summary of Events and Information	Remarks and references to Appendices
St Nicholas	8th	6.15p	Battle Casualties Return	25
	(cont'd)	6.18p	Prisoner of war return to Acting Corps.	26
			A very heavy thunderstorm during the early morning.	
	9th	7.45a	Wounded wire to Acting XVII Corps	27
		3.20p	Prisoner of war return to Acting	28
		6.15p	Wounded horse to Acting XVII Corps	29
		6.15p	Battle Casualties Return	30
			A.D.M.S. attended a conference at Corps H/Qrs.	
	10th	7.0a	Wounded wire to Acting XVII Corps	31
		4.40p	Prisoner of war return	32
		6.10p	Wounded him to Acting XVII Corps	33
		6.16p	Battle Casualties Return	34
			D.A.D.M.S. visited RIFLE Camp.	
	11th	7.10a	Wounded wire to Acting XVII Corps.	35
		6.15p	Prisoner of war return.	36
		6.16p	Wounded him to Acting XVII Corps	37

Army Form C. 2118.

WAR DIARY
or
INTELLIGENCE SUMMARY.
(Erase heading not required.)

Place	Date	Hour	Summary of Events and Information	Remarks and references to Appendices
ST. NICHOLAS	11th (cont)	6.15p.	Battle Carnoy-etin Ravine	38
	12th	7.10a.	Wounded mine to Atrnig XVIj Corps	39
		5.15p.	Prisoners of war return	40
		6.0p.	Wounded mine to Atrnig XVIj Corps	41
		6.0p.	Battle Carnoy-etin Ravine	42
	13th	7.10a.	Wounded mine to Atrnig XVIj Corps	43
		4.15p.	Prisoners of war return	44
		6.10p.	Wounded mine to Atrnig XVIj Corps	45
		6.10p.	Battle Carnoy-etin Ravine	46
			The 11th Inf. Bde relieved the 12th Inf. Bde in the right Subsector of the line, the relief to be completed by the night of 14th/15th. The D.A.A.M.G. visits the A.D.S.rs. of FAMPOUX	
	14th	6.20a.	Wounded mine to Atrnig XVIj Corps	47
		4.0p.	Prisoners of war return to Atrnig XVIj Corps	48
		6.10p.	Wounded mine to Atrnig XVIj Corps	49
		6.10p.	Battle Carnoy-etin Ravine	50

WAR DIARY
or
INTELLIGENCE SUMMARY.

Army Form C. 2118.

Place	Date	Hour	Summary of Events and Information	Remarks and references to Appendices
Ft. MENDOLAS	15th	7.30a.	Wounded wire to D.D.M.S XVII Corps.	51.
		4.30p.	Prisoners from return.	52.
		6.0p.	Wounded wire to D.D.M.S XVII Corps.	53.
		6.0p.	Battle Casualties Return.	54.
	16th	7.15a.	Wounded wire to D.D.M.S XVII Corps.	55.
		5.0p.	Prisoners from return.	56
		6.15p.	Wounded wire to D.D.M.S XVII Corps.	57.
		6.15p.	Wounded wire to D.D.M.S XVII Corps. Battle Casualties Return.	58
			One N.C.O. joins from the base as a reinforcement and is posted to No.16. F. Amb.	
			The A.D.M.S. visited WILDERNESS Camp with O.C. 3rd Sanitary Section, Hdqtrs No.16. F.A and the barge relanding post at BLANGY. M.234 Machine Gun Coy joins the Division and is billeted in FIFE Camp.	
	17th	7.30a.	Wounded wire to D.D.M.S XVII Corps.	59.
		4.0p.	Prisoners from return.	60
		6.15p.	Wounded wire to D.D.M.S XVII Corps.	61

WAR DIARY
or
INTELLIGENCE SUMMARY.
(Erase heading not required.)

Army Form C. 2118.

Place	Date	Hour	Summary of Events and Information	Remarks and references to Appendices
St NICHOLAS	17th (ctd)	6.10p.	Battle Casualties Raine	62
	18th	7.10a.	The ADMS attended a conference at Corps HQrs.	63
		4.45p.	The ADMS visited the A.D.S4 at FEUCHY.	64
		6.15p.	Wounded wire to ADMS XVII Corps	65
		6.10p.	Prisoners from rhine	66
			Wounded wire to ADMS XVII Corps	
			Battle Casualties Raine	
	19th	6.30a.	The ADMS inspected BALMORAL, DINGWALL and BAROSSA Camps	67
		5.0p.	Wounded wire to ADMS XVII Corps	68
		6.25p.	Prisoners from rhine	69
		6.x.p.	Wounded wire to ADMS XVII Corps	70
			Battle Casualties Raine	71
	20th	7.15a.	Wounded wire to ADMS XVII Corps	72
		6.0p.	Wounded wire to ADMS XVII Corps	73
		6.0p.	Battle Casualties Raine	
			A.D.M.S. visited the A.A.S. FEUCHY and inspected RIFLE Camp.	

Army Form C. 2118.

WAR DIARY
or
INTELLIGENCE SUMMARY.
(Erase heading not required.)

Instructions regarding War Diaries and Intelligence Summaries are contained in F.S. Regs., Part II. and the Staff Manual respectively. Title pages will be prepared in manuscript.

Place	Date	Hour	Summary of Events and Information	Remarks and references to Appendices
St. MARCUS	21st	6.40a.	Wounded him to 8 Staing XVII Corps.	74.
		4.0p.	Prisoners & men return.	75.
		6.15p.	Wounded him to 8 Staing XVII Corps	76.
		6.15p.	Battle Casualties Return	77.
	22nd	7.0a.	Wounded him to 8 Staing XVII Corps.	78.
		5.0p.	Prisoners & men return.	79.
		6.35p.	Wounded him to 8 Staing XVII Corps.	80.
		6.40p.	Battle Casualties Return	81.
			The 16th F.A. Hosp. was shelled during the morning, one direct hit on the Officers' mess Kitchen accounted for all the casualties. Some further hits only with much difficulty recovered from the mass of debris which resulted. The neighbourhood of 4 Div. Hosp. was also shelled from about 8.0 am onwards; one shell of large calibre actually landed within the enclosure of the camp, but fortunately inflicted no casualties. A.D.M.S. visited Hosp. No 10 & No 11 F.A. and c/o.	

WAR DIARY or INTELLIGENCE SUMMARY

Army Form C. 2118.

Place	Date	Hour	Summary of Events and Information	Remarks and references to Appendices
St. NICHOLAS	23rd	7.0a.	Wounded him to 8thno XVII Corps.	82
		4.0p.	Prisoners from rhins.	83
		6.25p.	Wounded him to 8thno XVII Corps.	84
		6.28p.	Battle Casualties Raino.	85
	24th	6.30a.	Wounded him to 8thno XVII Corps.	86
		4.0p.	Prisoners from rhins.	87
		4.0p.	Battle Casualties Raino.	88
		6.16p.	Wounded him to 8thno XVII Corps.	89
	25th	6.30a.	Wounded him to 8thno XVII Corps.	90
		4.0p.	Prisoners from rhins.	91
		6.0p.	Battle Casualties Raino.	92
		6.0p.	Wounded him to 8thno XVII Corps.	93
			A.A.D.M.S. visited the regimental aid posts of the three battalions in the line, also inspected A.D. Stns at FAMPOUX LOCK and FEUCHY. Owing to a leak in the "CRINAN" the motor launch service has been temporarily suspended, the service being continued from ATHIES down river by hand towing.	

Army Form C. 2118.

WAR DIARY
or
INTELLIGENCE SUMMARY.
(Erase heading not required.)

Instructions regarding War Diaries and Intelligence Summaries are contained in F. S. Regs., Part II. and the Staff Manual respectively. Title pages will be prepared in manuscript.

Place	Date	Hour	Summary of Events and Information	Remarks and references to Appendices
ST NICHOLAS	26th	7.30a.	Wounded men to ARRAS XVII Corps.	94.
		4.0p.	Prisoners from rhine.	95.
		6.30p.	Wounded home to ARRAS XVII Corps.	96.
		6.30p.	Battle Casualties Ravine	97.
			The tube Camoufle 'CRINAN' is in working order again.	
	27th	7.25a	Wounded men to ARRAS XVII Corps	98
		4.0p.	Prisoners from rhine.	99
		6.15p.	Battle Casualties Ravine	100
		6.15p.	Wounded home to ARRAS XVII Corps.	101
	28th	7.5a.	Wounded men to ARRAS XVII Corps.	102
		4.30p.	Prisoners from rhine.	103
		6.0p.	Wounded home to ARRAS XVII Corps.	104
		6.0p.	Battle Casualties Ravine	105
			Order by A.D.M.S. re the evacuation of casualties by motor as far as ARRAS begin, instead of unloading cases at BLANGY as heretofore. This new arrangement to come into operation on 29th inst at 10 a.m.	

Army Form C. 2118.

WAR DIARY
or
INTELLIGENCE SUMMARY.
(Erase heading not required.)

Place	Date	Hour	Summary of Events and Information	Remarks and references to Appendices
ST. NICHOLAS	28th		D.A.D.M.S. visited A.D.M.S. 17th Div. to confer on the evacuation of Casualties in the SCARPE river as far up as ARRAS basin.	
	29th	7.a.	D.A.D.M.S. also visited No.11 Res. Ambce. and inspected STIRLING Camp.	
		7.a.	Wounded were to D.Dns. XVII Corps	106
		4.p.	Prisoner of War return	107
		6.p.	Battle Casualties Return.	108
		6.p.	Wounded men to D.Dns.	109
			The D.A.D.M.S. visited 11 & 12 F. Ambs. & also the front in ARRAS for evacuating the forward cases of wounded.	
	30th	7.20.a.	Wounded were to D.Dns. XVII Corps	110
		4.30.p.	Prisoner of War return	111
		6.p.	Wounded sent to D.Dns. XVII Corps	112
		6.45.p.	Battle Casualties Return.	113
	31st	2.10.a.	Wounded were to D.Dns. XVII Corps	114
		4.15.p.	Prisoners of War return	115
		6.15.p.	Wounded were to D.Dns. XVII Corps	116

Army Form C. 2118.

WAR DIARY
or
INTELLIGENCE SUMMARY.
(Erase heading not required.)

Instructions regarding War Diaries and Intelligence Summaries are contained in F. S. Regs., Part II. and the Staff Manual respectively. Title pages will be prepared in manuscript.

Place	Date	Hour	Summary of Events and Information	Remarks and references to Appendices
ST. NICHOLAS	31st	6.15p.	Battle Casualties Return.	117
			The A.D.M.S. visits Officer Conf~ Res. Stn. at WARLUS	
			The D.A.D.M.S. visited 11 F. Amb.	
			Map of line held by Division showing the month is on for June.	

Seul ewts / Capt
/u A.D.M.S, 6. M.

 Copy No. 29.

ADDENDUM
to

R.A.M.C. ORDERS DATED 27th. JUNE, 1917.

Map ref: 51b.N.W.

2nd. July, 1917.

* *

1. The Headquarters of No. 10 Field Ambulance and Transport have now been established at G.23.d.2.5.

Headquarters,
4th. Division.

D.AHERN.
Lieut. Colonel,
a/A.D.M.S. 4th. Division.

Copies to all recipients of Orders dated 27-6-17.

Copy No. 16

R.A.M.C. ORDERS

by

Lieut.Colonel, D.AHERN, D.S.O., R.A.M.C., a/A.D.M.S., 4th. Division.

2nd. July, 1917.

* *

1.   12th. Field Ambulance (less personnel at Rest Station, BERLETTE) will move to-morrow to HOPITAL ST JEAN, ARRAS and take over from the 2/1st. London Field Ambulance.

All details of taking over to be arranged between the Os.C. concerned.

Move to be completed by midnight 3/4th.

Completion of move to be reported by wire to this office.

II.   ACKNOWLEDGE.

[signature]
for
Captain,
A.D.M.S., 4th.Division.

Issued at 5.30 p.m.

Copies to :-

10, 11 & 12 Infantry Brigades.
10, 11 & 12 Field Ambulances.
A.D.M.S., 58th. Division.
D.D.M.S., XVIIth. Corps.
4th. Division "G".
4th. Division "Q".
C.R.E., 4th. Division.
O.C., 4th. Divisional Train.
O.C., 4th. Div'nl. Signal Coy.
D.A.D.V.S., 4th. Division.
Diary.
File.

Copy No. 7

D.A.M.S. ORDER

by

Colonel J.GREEN, D.S.O., A.M.S., A.D.M.S. 4th. Division.

28th. July, 1917.

1. In accordance with instructions received from the D.D.M.S., XVIIth. Corps, the evacuation of casualties by barge and motor launch will be carried out to ARRAS BASIN and cases will be unloaded there for transport by motor ambulances to the M.D.S. instead of unloading at BLANGY as has been done up to the present.

The change will take place at 10 a.m. on the 29th. inst., by which hour O.C. No. 11 Field Ambulance will establish an unloading party consisting of at least 1 N.C.O. and 4 O.R. with one motor ambulance adjacent to the unloading wharf at ARRAS BASIN.

At 9 a.m. on the 29th. inst., O.C. No. 10 Field Ambulance will recall his unloading party with motor ambulance from BLANGY.

2. PLEASE ACKNOWLEDGE.

Issued at 10 a.m.

Captain,
for A.D.M.S. 4th. Division.

Copies to :-

10 and 11 Field Ambulances.
D.D.M.S. XVIIth. Corps.
A.D.M.S. 17th. Division.
Inland Water Transport.
Diary.
✓ File.

"A" Form.
MESSAGES AND SIGNALS.

Army Form C.2121 (in pads of 100).

TO: D.D.M.S. 14th Corps

Sender's Number: M1656
Day of Month: 1st

AAA Wounded admitted since 8 AM. AAA Officers nil Other Ranks 1

From: Medical 4th Division
Time: 4.5 PM

MEDICAL

Confidential
War Diary
of
A.D.M.S. 5th Division.

from 1.8.1917 to 31.8.1917.

Army Form C. 2118.

WAR DIARY
or
INTELLIGENCE SUMMARY.
(Erase heading not required.)

Instructions regarding War Diaries and Intelligence Summaries are contained in F. S. Regs., Part II. and the Staff Manual respectively. Title pages will be prepared in manuscript.

Place	Date	Hour	Summary of Events and Information	Remarks and references to Appendices
ST. NICHOLAS	1st	7.20a.	Wounded wire to D.D.M.S. XVII Corps.	1
		4.10p.	Prisoners of War return	2
		6.15p.	Battle Casualties Return	3
		6.15p.	Wounded wire to D.D.M.S. XVII Corps.	4
	2nd	7.20a.	The A.D.M.S. v D.A.D.M.S. visited 11 v 12 F. Ambts	5
		4.30p.	Wounded wire to D.D.M.S. XVII Corps.	6
		6.35p.	Prisoners of War return	7
		6.35p.	Battle Casualties Return	8
		6.30p.	Wounded wire to D.D.M.S. XVII Corps. The 1/1R First Frontiers left the Division 6.1.0 to join the 3rd Army, their place in the 10th Bde being taken by the 3/10 Middlesex Regt.	9
"	3rd	7a.	Wounded wire to D.D.M.S. XVII Corps.	10
		4.45p.	Prisoners of War return	11
		6.30p.	Battle Casualties Return	12
		6.30p.	Wounded wire to D.D.M.S. XVII Corps. The D.A.D.M.S. visited 10, 11, 12 F. Amb & the Camps of the 3/10 Middlesex, the 1/Rwt Lancs & the 11/Somerset L. Infantry	

Army Form C. 2118.

WAR DIARY
or
INTELLIGENCE SUMMARY.

(Erase heading not required.)

Instructions regarding War Diaries and Intelligence Summaries are contained in F. S. Regs., Part II. and the Staff Manual respectively. Title pages will be prepared in manuscript.

Place	Date	Hour	Summary of Events and Information	Remarks and references to Appendices
ST. NICHOLAS	4ᵗʰ	7.20a.	Wounded wire to D.D.M.S.	13
		4.10p.	Prisoner of War return	14
		6 p.	Battle Casualties Return	15
		6 p.	Wounded wire to D.D.M.S.	16
	5ᵗʰ		The D.A.D.M.S. visited the A.D.S.'s at FAMPOUX & FEUCHY & the two M.D. Sta of the Inf. Bdes. in the Line.	
		7a.	Wounded wire to D.D.M.S.	17
		4.p.	Prisoner of War return	18
		6.p.	Battle Casualties Return	19
		6.p.	Wounded wire to D.D.M.S.	20
			D.M.Dept. visited 11 F. Amb. & looked for suitable [?] for ARRAS.	
			& F. Amb. & outskirts of ARRAS.	
	6ᵗʰ	7.20a.	Wounded return to D.D.M.S.	21
		4.10p.	Prisoner of War return	22
		4.p.	Particulars of two cases of dysentery	23
		6.15p.	Battle Casualties Return	24
		6.15p.	Wounded wire to D.D.M.S.	25

Army Form C. 2118.

WAR DIARY
or
INTELLIGENCE SUMMARY.
(Erase heading not required.)

Instructions regarding War Diaries and Intelligence Summaries are contained in F.S. Regs., Part II. and the Staff Manual respectively. Title pages will be prepared in manuscript.

Place	Date	Hour	Summary of Events and Information	Remarks and references to Appendices
ST. NICHOLAS	7	7a	Wounded) return 6- D.R.m.s.	26
		4.20p.	Prisoners of War return	27
		6.p.	Wounded return 4- D.R.m.s.	28
		6.p.	Battle Casualties Return	29
			the Divisional Arts had had 8th Hay.	
			the D.R.m.s. units 10, 11 & 12 J. Amb.	
	8	7.10a.	Wounded wire 1 D.R.m.s.	30
		4.10p.	Prisoners of War return	31
		6.p.	Wounded wire 4 D.R.m.s.	32
		6.p.	Battle Casualties Return	33
			the D.R.m.s. units 10 & 11 J. Amb.	
	9	7.a.	Wounded wire 4 D.R.m.s.	34
		1.10p.	Correction to wire no 31	35
		4.p.	Prisoners of War return	36
		6.15p.	Battle Casualties Return	37
		6.15p.	Wounded wire 6 D.R.m.s.	38

Army Form C. 2118.

WAR DIARY
or
INTELLIGENCE SUMMARY.
(Erase heading not required.)

Place	Date	Hour	Summary of Events and Information	Remarks and references to Appendices
ST. NICHOLAS	9"		The 12" Bn. carried out a raid at 7.45 p.m. but it was not successful as casualties were heavy. The Regimental Aid Posts & Relay posts on the front involved were reinforced by bearers from 10 F. Amb. for this raid.	
"	10	7.10 a.	Wounded arr. b. D.D.M.S.	39
		4.25 p.	Prisoners } War return	40
		6.40 p.	Battle Casualties Return	41
		6.40 p.	Wounded arr. b. D.D.M.S.	42
"	11"	6.45 a.	A.D.M.S. D.D.M.S. visited 12 F. Amb. & their two trains.	
			Wounded arr. b. D.D.M.S.	43
		4. p.	Prisoners } War return	44
		6 p.	Battle Casualties Return	45
		6. p.	Wounded arr. b. D.D.M.S.	46
"	12"	6.30 a.	The A.D.M.S. D.D.M.S. visited A.D.S.s at FAMPOUX & FEUCHY & The R.A.P's of the two battalions in the right.	
			Wounded arr. b. A.D.M.S. XVII Corps	47

Army Form C. 2118.

WAR DIARY
or
INTELLIGENCE SUMMARY.
(Erase heading not required.)

Instructions regarding War Diaries and Intelligence Summaries are contained in F. S. Regs., Part II. and the Staff Manual respectively. Title pages will be prepared in manuscript.

Place	Date	Hour	Summary of Events and Information	Remarks and references to Appendices
ST. NICHOLAS	12th (cont)	4.25p	Prisoner from return	48
		6.5p	Wounded home to Scarpe XVII Corps	49
		6.5p	Battle Casualties Returns	50
	13th	7.0a	Wounded home to Scarpe XVII Corps	51
		4.25p	Prisoner from return	52
		6.0p	Wounded home to Scarpe	53
		6.0p	Battle Casualties Returns	54
			D.A. Drus visited 1/Rifle Bde in Tilloy Camp.	
	14th	7.15a	Wounded home to Scarpe XVII Corps	55
		4.20p	Prisoner from return	56
		6.10p	Battle Casualties Returns	57
		6.10p	Wounded home to XVII Corps	58
	15th	6.30a	Wounded home to Scarpe XVII Corps	59
		4.0p	Prisoner from return	60
		6.5p	Battle Casualties Returns	61
		6.5p	Wounded home to Corps	62

Army Form C. 2118.

WAR DIARY
or
INTELLIGENCE SUMMARY.
(Erase heading not required.)

Place	Date	Hour	Summary of Events and Information	Remarks and references to Appendices
ST. NICHOLAS	15th (cont'd)		accompanied by the A.D.M.S. the D.M.S. inspected the A.D. Shns at FAMPOUX & FEVCHY. In the afternoon the M.D. Shn and 1.3.7.A. in ARRAS were also inspected by them.	
			D.A.D.M.S. visited R.A.P. & refg. Pn.	
	16th	6.40a	Wounded down to stations XVII Corps.	63
		4.45p	Prisoners from returns	64
		6.20p	Wounded home to stations	65
		6.20p	Battle casualties Return	66
	17th	6.30a	Wounded home to stations XVII Corps.	67
		4.20p	Prisoners from returns	68
		6.0p	Battle casualties Return	69
		6.0p	Wounded home to XVII Corps.	70
			Revise orders issued by XVIIth concerning the evacuation of casualties from the proposed extension of the 4. Divisional front. The right of the 4 Div. will be extended South taking over a portion of the line at present occupied by the 15th Division	A.

Army Form C. 2118.

WAR DIARY
or
INTELLIGENCE SUMMARY.
(Erase heading not required.)

Instructions regarding War Diaries and Intelligence Summaries are contained in F. S. Regs., Part II. and the Staff Manual respectively. Title pages will be prepared in manuscript.

Place	Date	Hour	Summary of Events and Information	Remarks and references to Appendices
ST. NICHOLAS	18th.	7.15a.	Wounded men to ADS in XVII Corps.	71.
		5.30p.	Prisoners from return.	72.
		4p.	Wounded men to Corps.	73.
		6.0p.	Battle Casualties Return.	74.
	19th.	7.5a.	Wounded men to ADS in XVII Corps	75.
		4.0p.	Prisoners from return.	76.
		6.15p.	Battle Casualties Return.	77.
		6.15p.	Wounded men to ADS.	78.
			The Division of the Divisional front is relief (The northern portion of the Div. Div. has now been completed. The southern (right) boundary rests on the north edge of northern TWIN COPSE. (O. 216 Scheme).	
	20th.	7.30a.	Wounded men to ADS in XVII Corps.	79.
		5.0p.	Prisoners from return.	80.
		6.15p.	Wounded men to XVII Corps.	81.
		6.15p.	Battle Casualties Return.	82.
			D.ADMS visited No. 11 & 12. Fd Ambs.	

Army Form C. 2118.

WAR DIARY
or
INTELLIGENCE SUMMARY.
(Erase heading not required.)

Place	Date	Hour	Summary of Events and Information	Remarks and references to Appendices
ST. NICHOLAS	21st	6.30a.m.	Wounded mine to St Anne XVII Corps.	83.
		3.58p	Prisoner from return.	84.
		6.0p	Battle Casualties Return	85.
		6.0p	Wounded mine to Corps.	86.
	22nd	7.5.a.	Wounded mine to St Anne XVII Corps.	87.
		4.30p	Prisoner from return	88.
		6.40p	Wounded mine to St Anne	89.
		6.40p	Battles Casualties Return	90.
			Amendment to A.D.M.S's order of 17-5-17. The relay post is now stationed in MUSKET RESERVE. ST. NICHOLAS. Valid No. 17 Feb. hands in ARRAS.	
	23rd	7.0.a.	Wounded mine to St Anne XVII Corps.	91.
		4.30p	Prisoner from return	92.
		6.15p	Wounded mine to St Anne	93.
		6.15p	Battle Casualties Return	94.
	24th	7.15a	Wounded mine to St Anne XVII Corps.	95.

Army Form C. 2118.

WAR DIARY
or
INTELLIGENCE SUMMARY.
(Erase heading not required.)

Place	Date	Hour	Summary of Events and Information	Remarks and references to Appendices
ST NICHOLAS	24th (cont)	5.30p	Prisoners from returns	96
		6.20p	Battle Casualties Ravine	97
		6.20p	Wounded horse to Corps	98
			A.A.D.M.S. visited the R.A.P's of the line battn of the right Bde, also the Ravine relay post in MUSKET RESERVE.	
	25th	6.30a	Wounded horse to 38thrig XVII Corps.	99.
		4.30p	Prisoners from returns	100
		6.15p	Battle Casualties Ravine	101
		6.K.p	Wounded horse to Corps.	102
			A.A.M.S & D.A.D.M.S. inspected STIRLING, WILDERNESS & SCOTT'S Camps.	
			They also visited 3d San Sectn in St. SAUVEUR.	
	26th.	7.0a.	Wounded horse to 38thrig XVII Corps	103.
		4.15p	Prisoners from returns	104.
		6.30p	Wounded horse to Corps.	105
		6.20p	Battle Casualties Ravine	106.
			A.A.D.M.S. inspected R.A.P of left battn of left Bde also A.D.Stns at FAMPOUX & FEUCHY.	

Army Form C. 2118.

WAR DIARY
or
INTELLIGENCE SUMMARY.
(Erase heading not required.)

Place	Date	Hour	Summary of Events and Information	Remarks and references to Appendices
St NICOLAS	27th	7.10a.	Wounded were to Advice XVII Corps.	107 / 108
		4.0p.	Prisoners from return.	109
		6.30p.	Battle Casualties Review	110
		6.30p.	Wounded were to Corps.	111
	28th	7.15a.	Wounded were to Advice XVII Corps.	112
		4.10p.	Prisoners from return.	113
		6.15p.	Wounded were to Corps.	114
		6.15p.	Battle Casualties Review	
			Owing to the rough weather many large trenches have been blown into the SCARPE. The main evacuation from FAMPOUX has consequently been temporarily suspended, cases now being brought back by road in motor ambulances, through FEUCHY to the M.D. Stn at TIRRAS.	
	29th	7.10a.	Wounded were to Advice XVII Corps.	115
		4.20p.	Prisoners from return.	116
		6.0p.	Battle Casualties Review	117 / 118
		6.0p.	Wounded were to Advice	

WAR DIARY
or
INTELLIGENCE SUMMARY.

Army Form C. 2118.

Place	Date	Hour	Summary of Events and Information	Remarks and references to Appendices
ST. NICHOLAS.	30th	7.10a	Wounded hus to Stonie XVII Corps.	119.
		4.30p	Prisoner from Milion.	120
		6.10p	Wounded hus to Corps.	121
		6.10p	Battle casualties Review.	122
			The mini SCARPE is now clear of debris and the barges for the Evacuation of casualties are now running as usual.	
	31st	7.15a	Wounded hus to Stonie XVII Corps.	123
		4.30p	Prisoner from Milion.	124
		6.10p	Wounded hus to Corps.	125
			Battle casualties Review.	126
			A.D.M.S visited DINGWALL & MIDDLESEX camps.	127
			Attached Map indicates formed Ravine position; together with routes formed in the Evacuation of casualties from the front line.	C.

John Murphy
Capt. A.D.M.S.
b.A.Divis.
H.Q.

Copy No. 13

R.A.M.C. ORDER
by
COL. J. GRECH. D.S.O.; A.M.S., A.D.M.S. 4th. Division.

Map Refs: 1/10000 Trench Map.   17th. August, 1917.
PLOUVAIN sheet.

On night of 18th./19th. August, the Right of the 4th. Division will be extended up to, and inclusive of, O.2/6 Trench in relief of 12th. Division.

SOUTHERN BOUNDARY.

O.2/6 Trench, North edge of Northern TWIN COPSE - Southern Corner of ARROWHEAD COPSE - Junction of ORCHARD Reserve and BRIDOON LANE, thence along ORCHARD Reserve, to the present boundary line.
ORCHARD Reserve and ORANGE AVENUE will be inclusive to 12th. Division but 4th. Division will have a right of way through them.

BRIGADE BOUNDARY.

I.25/1 - SCABBARD ALLEY - Battalion H.Qrs (H.30.d.1.3.) - railway crossing at H.23.b.65.35 (all incl. to left Brigade).
LANCER and JOHNSON AVENUES will be common to both Brigades.

1. (a). Evacuation of wounded N. & S. of the River will be carried out as it is at present along the same routes, with the exception that in the new area the carry from the new Trench becomes longer.

    (b). The R.A.P. at H.36.a.2.2. will be shared by the two Right Battalions, the two M.O's working together.

    (c). To shorten the carry from the extreme right, a Relay Post will be formed in Rifle Support.
    For this purpose, O.C. 10th. Field Ambulance will place one bearer squad at the disposal of the Regtl. M.O. of the Right Battalion, who will chose a suitable shelter in the Trench mentioned above.
    The squad will report to the Regtl. M.O. at the R.A.P. at H.36.a.2.2. with two days' rations on the evening of the 18th. inst. not later than 6 p.m. From the 21st. inclusive they will be rationed by the Battalion to which they are attached.
    They will carry between the Relay Post and the Regtl. Aid Post and will be relieved by another squad from 10th. Field Ambulance when the Battalion is relieved.

2. Later on, if considered necessary, the route will be changed, and a Relay Post established in ORANGE AVENUE or ORCHARD Reserve, and the evacuation will be carried out along route: BRIDOON LANE - ORCHARD Reserve - ORANGE AVENUE - R.A.P. (H.36.a.2.2.).

3. ACKNOWLEDGE.

Colonel,
A.D.M.S. 4th. Division.

Issued at 8.0 p.m.
Copies to:-   10, 11, 12 Field Ambulances.
                 10, 11, 12 Infantry Brigades.
                 4th. Division "G".
                 4th. Division "Q".
                 D.D.M.S. XVIIth. Corps.
                 A.D.M.S. 12th. Division.
                 C.R.E. 4th. Division.
                 Diary.
                 File.

Copy No. 12

R.A.M.C. ORDER

by

COL. J. GRECH. D.S.O., A.M.S., A.D.M.S. 4th. Division.

Map Refs: 1/10000 Trench Map.
PLOUVAIN sheet.

17th. August, 1917.

On night of 18th./19th. August, the Right of the 4th. Division will be extended up to, and inclusive of, O.2/6 Trench in relief of 12th. Division.

SOUTHERN BOUNDARY.

O.2/6 Trench, North edge of Northern TWIN COPSE - Southern Corner of ARROWHEAD COPSE - Junction of ORCHARD Reserve and BRIDOON LANE, thence along ORCHARD Reserve, to the present boundary line.

ORCHARD Reserve and ORANGE AVENUE will be inclusive to 12th. Division but 4th. Division will have a right of way through them.

BRIGADE BOUNDARY.

I.25/1 - SCABBARD ALLEY - Battalion H.Qrs (H.30.d.1.3.) - railway crossing at H.23.b.65.35 (all incl. to left Brigade). LANCER and JOHNSON AVENUES will be common to both Brigades.

1. (a). Evacuation of wounded N. & S. of the River will be carried out as it is at present along the same routes, with the exception that in the new area the carry from the new Trench becomes longer.

   (b). The R.A.P. at H.36.a.2.2. will be shared by the two Right Battalions, the two M.O's working together.

   (c). To shorten the carry from the extreme right, a Relay Post will be formed in Rifle Support.

   For this purpose, O.C. 10th. Field Ambulance will place one bearer squad at the disposal of the Regtl. M.O. of the Right Battalion, who will chose a suitable shelter in the Trench mentioned above.

   The squad will report to the Regtl. M.O. at the R.A.P. at H.36.a.2.2. with two days' rations on the evening of the 18th. inst. not later than 6 p.m. From the 21st. inclusive they will be rationed by the Battalion to which they are attached.

   They will carry between the Relay Post and the Regtl. Aid Post and will be relieved by another squad from 10th. Field Ambulance when the Battalion is relieved.

2. Later on, if considered necessary, the route will be changed, and a Relay Post established in ORANGE AVENUE or ORCHARD Reserve, and the evacuation will be carried out along route: BRIDOON LANE - ORCHARD Reserve - ORANGE AVENUE - R.A.P. (H.36.a.2.2.).

3. A C K N O W L E D G E.

Colonel,
A.D.M.S. 4th. Division.

Issued at 8.0 p.m.
Copies to:-   10, 11, 12 Field Ambulances.
              10, 11, 12 Infantry Brigades.
              4th. Division "G".
              4th. Division "Q".
              D.D.M.S. XVIIth. Corps.
              A.D.M.S. 12th. Division.
              C.R.E. 4th. Division.
              Diary.
              File.

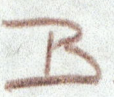

Copy No. 12

AMENDMENT TO R.A.M.C. ORDER DATED 17-8-1917.

Map refs: 1/10000, Trench Map,
PLOUVAIN Shoot.   22nd. August, 1917.

* *

Reference R.A.M.C. Order, dated 17th. August, 1917:

(a).   Evacuation of wounded North of the River will be carried out as before.

South of the River: By BRIDOON ALLEY, ORCHARD RESERVE, ORANGE AVENUE and R.A.P., H.36.a.2.2.

(b).   A Relay Post is formed in MUSKET RESERVE at I.31.c.3.8.

This cancels Para. 1, (c) of Order mentioned above.

J. Rinkingham
Capt. for
Colonel,
A.D.M.S. 4th. Division.

Issued at 11.0 a.m.

Copies to all recipients of R.A.M.C. Order of 17-8-1917.

B

Copy No. 13

AMENDMENT TO R.A.M.C. ORDER DATED 17-8-1917.

Map refs: 1/10000, Trench Map,
PLOUVAIN Shoot.   22nd. August, 1917.

* *

Reference R.A.M.C. Order, dated 17th. August, 1917:

(a).   Evacuation of wounded North of the River will be carried out as before.

South of the River: By BRIDOON ALLEY, ORCHARD RESERVE, ORANGE AVENUE and R.A.P., H.36.a.2.2.

(b).   A Relay Post is formed in MUSKET RESERVE at I.31.c.3.8.

This cancels Para. 1, (c) of Order mentioned above.

Capt. for
Colonel,
A.D.M.S. 4th. Division.

Issued at 11.0 a.m.

Copies to all recipients of R.A.M.C. Order of 17-8-1917.

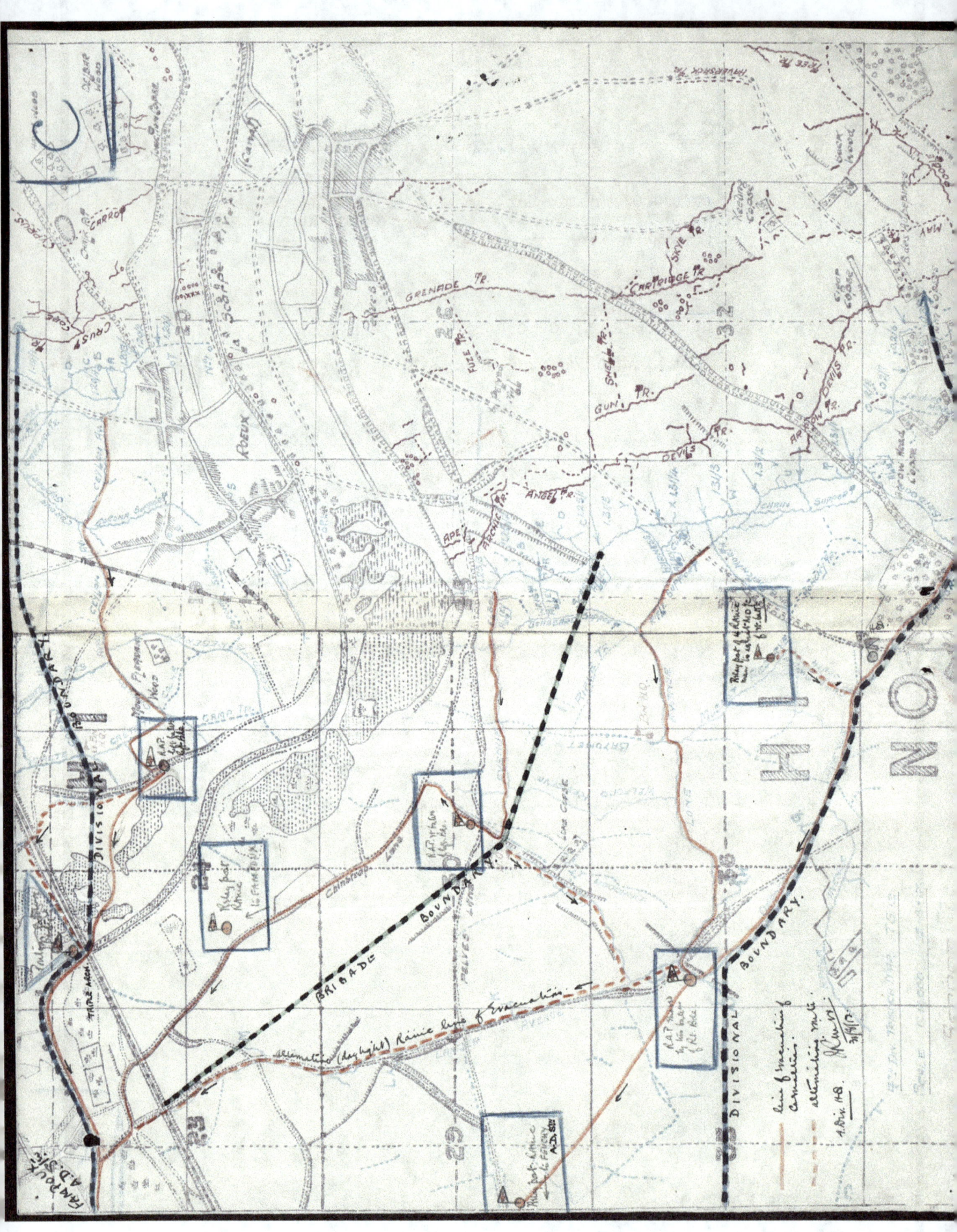

B.E.F.

SUMMARY OF MEDICAL WAR DIARIES FOR
4th Divn. 14th Corps, 5th Army.   from 20.9.17.

WESTERN FRONT Sept. 1917.

A.D.M.S.

D.A.D.M.S.

SUMMARISED UNDER THE FOLLOWING HEADINGS.

Phase "D" 1. Passchendaele Operations, July-Nov. 1917.
(a) Operations commencing 1/7/17.

B.E.F.   1.

4th Divn. 14th Corps, 5th Army.   WESTERN FRONT.
A.D.M.S.   September 1917.

Phase "D" 1. Passchendaele Operations July-Nov. 1917.
(a) Operations commencing 1/7/17.

1917.   Headquarters. At Proven (Central Camp.)

Sept. 20th.   Moves and Transfer. To Proven on transfer to 14th Corps
                from 6th Corps 3rd Army.
                Moves Field Ambulances:-
                11th Field Ambulance from Houpoutre to Priory Camp.
                12th   "   "   " Pesel Hoek to Singapore Camp.
                10th   "   "   " Proven to Panama Camp.

28th.   Moves Bde. 12th Inf. Bde. took over Reserve line from
                20th Divn.
                11th Inf. Bde. moved into Reserve Area by Canal Bank.
                Medical Arrangements: 12th Field Ambulance took over
                working of the line and 11th Field Ambulance took
                over Divisional and Corps W.W. Posts.

29th.   Moves: Military Situation: To Welsh Farm. Command
                of line taken over from 20th Divn.
                Medical Arrangements: Appendix F (Marked paras.)
                Attached. (Put back in diary.
                Operations Enemy. Whole area West of Ypres Canal
                bombed.

30th.   Area again bombed A.D.S. on canal bank damaged.
                Casualties R.A.M.C. 1 and 2 of 12th Field Ambulance
                wounded.

4th Divn. 14th Corps, 5th Army. WESTERN FRONT.
A.D.M.S. Sept. 1917.

Phase "D" 1. (a) (Cont.)

1917.
Sept.

Appendices:-

D. Warning O.   d/ 23/9/17.
E. Med. Arr. 4th Div.   23/9/17.
F. R.A.M.C. Op. O.   25/9/17.
G. R.A.M.C. Op. O.   28/9/17.

B.E.F.

SUMMARY OF MEDICAL WAR DIARIES FOR

4th Divn. 14th Corps, 5th Army. from 20.9.17.

WESTERN FRONT Sept. 1917.

A.D.M.S.
D.A.D.M.S.

SUMMARISED UNDER THE FOLLOWING HEADINGS.

Phase "D" 1. Passchendaele Operations, July-Nov. 1917.

(a) Operations commencing 1/7/17.

B.E.F.   1.

4th Divn. 14th Corps, 5th Army.   WESTERN FRONT.
A.D.M.S.   September 1917.

Phase "D" 1. Passchondaele Operations July-Nov. 1917.
   (a) Operations commencing 1/7/17.

1917.   Headquarters. At Proven (Central Camp.)

Sept. 20th.   Moves and Transfer. To Proven on transfer to 14th Corps
                from 6th Corps 3rd Army.
                Moves Field Ambulances:-
                11th Field Ambulance from Houpoutre to Priory Camp.
                12th   "   "   " Pesel Hook to Singapore Camp.
                10th   "   "   " Proven to Panama Camp.

28th.   Moves Bde. 12th Inf. Bde. took over Reserve line from
                20th Divn.
                11th Inf. Bde. moved into Reserve Area by Canal Bank.
                Medical Arrangements: 12th Field Ambulance took over
                working of the line and 11th Field Ambulance took
                over Divisional and Corps W.W. Posts.

29th.   Moves: Military Situation: To Welsh Farm. Command
                of line taken over from 20th Divn.
                Medical Arrangements: Appendix F (Marked paras.)
                Attached. *Put back in diary.*
                Operations Enemy. Whole area West of Ypres Canal
                bombed.

30th.   Area again bombed A.D.S. on canal bank damaged.
                Casualties R.A.M.C. 1 and 2 of 12th Field Ambulance
                wounded.

4th Divn. 14th Corps, 5th Army.   WESTERN FRONT.
A.D.M.S.   Sept. 1917.

Phase "D" 1. (a) (Cont.)

1917.
Sept.
    Appendices:-
    D. Warning O.   d/   23/9/17.
    E. Med. Arr. 4th Div.   23/9/17.
    F. R.A.M.C. Op. O.   25/9/17.
    G. R.A.M.C. Op. O.   28/9/17.

MEDICAL.

WAR DIARY
OF
A.D.M.S. 4th DIVN.
FOR PERIOD.
1.9.17 to 30.9.17

CONFIDENTIAL

Army Form C. 2118.

WAR DIARY
or
INTELLIGENCE SUMMARY.
(Erase heading not required.)

Instructions regarding War Diaries and Intelligence Summaries are contained in F. S. Regs., Part II. and the Staff Manual respectively. Title pages will be prepared in manuscript.

Place	Date	Hour	Summary of Events and Information	Remarks and references to Appendices
ST MESLOUPS	Sept. 1st	7.0 a	Wounded man to Amms XVii Corps.	1
		4.15p	Prisoner of war return	2
		6.20p	Wounded man to Corps	3
		6.20p	Battle casualties Return	4
	2nd	7.10 a	Wounded man to Amms XVii Corps.	5
		4.0p	Prisoner of war return	6
		6.20p	Battle casualties Return	7
		6.20p	Wounded man to Corps.	8
	3rd	7.10 a	Wounded man to Amms XVii Corps.	9
		4.0p	Prisoner of war return	10
		6.15p	Wounded man to Corps.	11
		6.5p	Battle casualties Return	12
			Riviere relieved by Adinfer indicating the move of the 2 mules to the ADINFER (Vii Corps) area on the occasion of the 4th Div. being relieved by the 15th Div. This relief is to take place during the night to the next. A.D.M.S. notified No 12 Fd Amb.	A.

Army Form C. 2118.

WAR DIARY
or
INTELLIGENCE SUMMARY.
(Erase heading not required.)

Instructions regarding War Diaries and Intelligence Summaries are contained in F. S. Regs., Part II. and the Staff Manual respectively. Title pages will be prepared in manuscript.

Place	Date	Hour	Summary of Events and Information	Remarks and references to Appendices
ST. MICHOLAS.	4th	7.10a.	Wounded home to 8th Divis XVII Corps.	13
		4.15p.	Prisoner from return.	14
		6.20p.	Battle casualties Revue	15
		6.20p.	Wounded home to Corps.	16
			8th Divis relieved the 6th Corps H.Q and arranged for the clearing of sick in the new area	
	5th	7.30a.	Wounded men to 8th Divis XVII Corps.	17
		4.30p.	Prisoner from return.	18
		6.20p.	Wounded home to Corps.	19
		6.15p.	Battle casualties Revue	20
		6.55a.	No. 11 sub butler proceeded to BERLES-AU-BOIS. 11th Ahr march to the new area.	21
			Wounded home to XVII Corps.	
	6th	4.15p.	Prisoner from return.	22
		6.10p.	Wounded home to Corps.	23
		6.15p.	Battle casualties Revue	24
			The 10th Inf Bde relieved in the line by the 45th Inf Bde, 15th Division. The 8/10 R Warwickshire Regt and the 2/10 Br Indn Regt move to the new area.	

Army Form C. 2118.

WAR DIARY
or
INTELLIGENCE SUMMARY.
(Erase heading not required.)

Place	Date	Hour	Summary of Events and Information	Remarks and references to Appendices
ST. NICHOLAS.	7th.		The 10th Inf Bde (less two Batns) move to the new area.	
			The 12th Inf Bde arrived in the PELVES sector by the 46th Inf Bde; the 1/King's Own and 7/W. Riding regiment march to new area.	
			No.10 Fd Ambce having handed over all his vacal posts to 46 F. Ambce, proceed to BAILLEULMONT. A.D.M.S. inspected No.10 & No.11 Fd Ambce in their new billet.	
		7.20.a.	Wounded horse to DAn'ie XVII Corps.	25
		4.0.p	Prisoners from Nelnin.	26
		6.15p	Wounded horse to Corps.	27
		6.15p	Battle casualties Return.	28
		7.25a.	Wounded horse to DAn'ie XVII Corps.	29
		1.0 p	Location horse to VI Corps.	30
			The 12th Inf Bde Hqtrs, 2/Essex Regt and 2/Lancashire Fus march to the new area.	
			The 10th F. Ambce move to HENDECOURT.	
			The 4th DIV. Hqtrs move to the new area, BASSEUX.	
BASSEUX	9th	Noon	A.D.M.S. inspected the billets at BELLACOURT which had been reoccupied by	

Army Form C. 2118.

WAR DIARY
or
INTELLIGENCE SUMMARY.
(Erase heading not required.)

Place	Date	Hour	Summary of Events and Information	Remarks and references to Appendices
BASSEUX	9th (Sun)		Troops who had been in earlier with difficulties taken and the billets were satisfactory. Every precaution has been taken and the billets were satisfactory.	
	10th		A.D.M.S. visited BAILLEUVAL, BERLES and BIENVILLERS, and inspected the bathing arrangements for the troops billeted there.	
	11th			
	12th		D.A.D.M.S. inspected M.12 Fd. Amb., 2/W. Riding and 2/Suffolks at HENDECOURT. The B.O.C. who had an accident whilst riding has to be evacuated to No 2 C.C.S. BOISLEUX as the result of the spinal injuries received.	
	13th		A.D.M.S. visited HENDÉCOURT.	
	14th		A.D.M.S. visited the 3/10 Bn. Man. Regt. at BELLACOURT. Morning order by A.D.M.S. issued with reference to the evacuation of the Division on the 19th inst.	B.
	15th			
	16th			
	17th		Addendum to A.D.M.S. order dated 3-9-17 concerning the disposal of sick.	A'.

Army Form C. 2118.

WAR DIARY
or
INTELLIGENCE SUMMARY.
(Erase heading not required.)

Place	Date	Hour	Summary of Events and Information	Remarks and references to Appendices
BASSEUX	18th		A.D.M.S. visited D.M.S. 3rd Army.	
	19th		11th Fd. Ambulance move to MONDICOURT for entrainment.	
			The Motor ambulance cars of No. 10 & No. 11 F. Ambces. proceed under charge of Capt. J.R.M. Whigham to the new area via DOULLENS – FREVENT – ST. POL – LILLERS – ST. VENANT – HAZEBROUCK – POPERINGHE – PROVEN.	
			No. 10 F. Amb. entrains at SAULTY-L'ARBRET & No. 11 at MONDICOURT and No. 12 at BEAUMETZ-RIVIERE.	
	20th	12.15a	No. 11 Fd. Amb. detrains at HOUPOUTRE at 12.15 a.m. and proceed to PRIORY CAMP.	
		6.30p	No. 12 Fd. Amb. detrains at PESEL HOEK at 6.30 p.m. and proceed to SINGAPORE Camp.	
		9.58p	No. 10 Fd. Amb. detrains at PROVEN at 9.50 p.m. and proceed to PANAMA Camp.	
			The Motor ambulance cars & cycles of No. 12 Fd. Amb. proceed to the new area under charge of A.A.D.M.S.	
		2pm	A. Div. H.Q. closed at BASSEUX and opens at CENTRAL Camp, PROVEN in the new area.	
		7.50p	4. Div. is transferred from THIRD Army (VI Corps) to FIFTH Army (XIV Corps). Location wire to Details XIV Corps.	31.

Army Form C. 2118.

WAR DIARY
or
INTELLIGENCE SUMMARY.

(Erase heading not required.)

Place	Date	Hour	Summary of Events and Information	Remarks and references to Appendices
PROVEN.	21st		1/Lt P.G. HAMLIN. U.S.M.O.R.C. joins No 10 70 Aunts from the base as reinforcement.	32
			A case of C.S.M. reported in 2/W. Riding Regt.	33
		4.30 p.	Daily state home to D.M.S. 5th Army.	34
		5.20 p.	Wounded home to A.D.M.S. XIV. Corps.	35.
		7.16 a.	Wounded home to D.D.M.S. II. Corps.	
			A.D.M.S. inspected the camps reoccupied by the three Field Ambulances and Rest'd Corps & Army Hosp'ls.	C 36
			Copy of the medical arrangements for the present area.	37
	22nd	2.30p.	Daily state home to D.D.M.S. XIV Corps.	38
		2.30p.	Daily state home to D.M.S. V. Army.	39.
		6.30p.	Wounded home to D.D.M.S. XIV Corps.	40
	23rd	2.28p.	Daily state home to D.M.S. V Army	
		2.25p.	Daily State home to D.D.M.S. XIV. Corps	
			Warning order (and amendment) by A.D.M.S. re relief of 10th Division in the line.	D
			Copy of medical arrangement for dealing with casualties in present area	E

Army Form C. 2118.

WAR DIARY
or
INTELLIGENCE SUMMARY.
(Erase heading not required.)

Instructions regarding War Diaries and Intelligence Summaries are contained in F. S. Regs., Part II. and the Staff Manual respectively. Title pages will be prepared in manuscript.

Place	Date	Hour	Summary of Events and Information	Remarks and references to Appendices
PROVEN.	24th.	1.30p.	Daily State sent to D.D.M.S. XIV. Corps.	41.
		2.70p.	A.D.S. hours to D.D.M.S. 5th Army.	42
			A.D.M.S. visited the 20th Divn. in the line and was informed as to the existing medical arrangements for evacuation of casualties.	
26th.	1.05p.	Daily State sent to D.D.M.S. 5th Army, repeated to D.D.M.S. XIV. Corps.	43
	1.45p.	Daily State sent to D.D.M.S. XIV Corps.	44
	5pm.	Wire detailing 2 Medical Officers & 1st Sub-division for duty with 46 C.C.S.	45
			Révise order by A.D.M.S. re the relief of the 20th Division in the line on the 27th, 28th & 29th inst.	F
26th.	2.70p.	Daily State sent to D.D.M.S. 5th Army, repeated D.D.M.S. XIV Corps.	46
		Daily State sent to D.D.M.S. XIV. Corps.	47
		Amendment to A.D.S. Revise order dated 25/9/17.	F1.
27th.		Daily State sent to D.D.M.S. XIV Corps.	48
		Daily State sent to D.D.M.S. 5th Army, repeated D.D.M.S. XIV Corps.	49
		A case of diphtheria from 2/Suffolks reported.	50

WAR DIARY
or
INTELLIGENCE SUMMARY.
(Erase heading not required.)

Army Form C. 2118.

Place	Date	Hour	Summary of Events and Information	Remarks and references to Appendices
PROVEN	28	1p.	Daily state wire to D.D.M.S. XIV Corps	51
		1.15p	" " " D.M.S. V Army repts Corps	52
		3.5p	Wire to D.D.M.S. XIV Corps re two cases of diphtheria	53
		3.10p	Wire to D.D.M.S. VI Corps re above two cases of diphtheria	54
		6p.	G. Division return to D.D.M.S. XIV Corps.	55
			the A.D.M.S. 32nd Divs. visited 10 F. Amb. & the 2/F. sports	G.
			Orders issued by A.D.M.S. re Counter-Btk coming operations	
			12 Bg. Bde took over the Division East nights from the 20 Div.	
			11 Bg. Bde moved into Reserve area by Canal Bank.	
			F. Amb. took over the working of the line & 11 F. Amb. took over	
			the Divisional Corps Walking Wounded Post	
WELSH FARM	29	7.30a.	Orders to F. Amb. re evacuation of sick respirators	56
		7.50a.	Wire to D.Dns. XIV Corps	57
ENVER ELVERDINGHE		2.1.	Wire to D.D.M.S. XIV Corps warnertriangleray	58
		2.45p	Wire to D.D.M.S. XIV Corps reports Divs V Army	59
		5.35p.	Wire to D.D.M.S. XIV Corps.	60

Army Form C. 2118.

WAR DIARY
or
INTELLIGENCE SUMMARY.
(Erase heading not required.)

Place	Date	Hour	Summary of Events and Information	Remarks and references to Appendices
WELSH CAMP	29 (cont)	10.10p.	Orders for the three F. Ambs. & 12th F. Amb. re-drawing of C. station. The 12th F. Amb. Bde took over the lines last night from the 20th Div. The 11th F. Amb. Bde moved into support & the 10th F. Amb. Bde moved into Reserve. 10th F. Amb. took over the Corps. Main Dressing Sta. Div. Hd. Qrs. moved to WELSH FARM & G.O.C. took over command of the line from 20th Div. The whole area west of the YPRES Canal was indiscriminately bombed by hostile aeroplanes during the night.	61
	30th	6.30a.	Wire to D.Ds.M.S. XIV Corps.	62
		11.a.	Veterinary arrangement from F. Ambs.	63
		3.p.	Wire to D.Dns. XIV Corps.	64
		3.p.	Wire to D.Dns. XIV Corps reports to D.M.S. 5th Army	65
		5.35p.	Wire to D.Dns. XIV Corps.	66
		7.30p.	Casualty wire to "A" Div. A. The D.A.D.M.S. inspected the arrangements to be in force for the deep and walking wounded.	67

Army Form C. 2118.

WAR DIARY
or
INTELLIGENCE SUMMARY.
(Erase heading not required.)

Place	Date	Hour	Summary of Events and Information	Remarks and references to Appendices
WELSH FARM	30th	cont.	The area West of the Canal was again bombed at night & the A.D.S. on the Canal bank was damaged & Capt. Simpson & 2 O.R. of 12th F. Amb. were wounded. An acct. of the Canea fighting the third week by the Division will be forwarded with next months diary.	

S. W. Bowater
Capt. for
A.D.M.S.

Copy No. 18

R.A.M.C. ORDER
by
Colonel J. GRECH, D.S.O., A.M.S., A.D.M.S. 4th. Division.

Map Refs: Lens, 11.　　　　　　　　　　　　3rd. September, 1917.

The 4th. Division, (less Artillery), will be relieved by the 15th. Division during the period 5th. to 8th. September.

MOVES:
1. Field Ambulances will move with their Brigade Groups under orders of B.G.C.

   (a). No. 11 Field Ambulance will proceed to BERLES-AU-BOIS on the 5th. inst.

   (b). No. 10 Field Ambulance will hand over all Medical Posts to 46th. Field Ambulance, 15th. Division on the night of 6th./7th. inst. and be ready to proceed to BAILLEULMONT on the morning of the 7th. inst.

   (c). No. 12 Field Ambulance will act as Main Dressing Station from 6 p.m. 4th. inst., and be ready to move to HENDECOURT on the morning of the 8th. inst.

Billeting Officers will be sent to the respective villages early on dates of departure of Units.
The handing over of the various Medical Posts will be arranged by O's C. Field Ambulances concerned.

COLLECTION OF SICK IN NEW AREA:
2. For purposes of collection, the new area will be divided into two by a line drawn through BASSEUX and MONCHY AU-BOIS. No. 11 Field Ambulance will collect West and No. 12 Field Ambulance East of that line. Both villages will be inclusive to 12 Field Ambulance.

No. 10 Field Ambulance will remain closed for the present. Later if considered necessary, it will be opened for the reception of sick from the other Field Ambulances.

Until the arrival of No. 12 Field Ambulance in HENDECOURT, No. 11 Field Ambulance will collect from the whole area.

FODEN LORRY.
3. The Foden Lorry will proceed to BASSEUX on the evening of the 5th. inst. and be ready to commence the disinfection of dirty clothing on the 6th.

4. Completion of handing over, and arrivals in the new area to be reported by wire to the A.D.M.S.

5. Office of the A.D.M.S. will close at G.16.b.7.7. and open at BASSEUX at 10.15 a.m. on 8th. inst.

6.   ACKNOWLEDGE.

                                        [signature]
                                            Capt
                                        для
Issued at 11.0 a.m.   A.D.M.S. 4th. Division.

Copies to: No. 10 Field Ambulance.
             No. 11 Field Ambulance.
             No. 12 Field Ambulance.
             10th. Infantry Brigade.
             11th. Infantry Brigade.
             12th. Infantry Brigade.
             4th. Division "G".
             4th. Division "A".
             D.D.M.S., XVII Corps.
             D.D.M.S. VI Corps.
             A.D.M.S. 15th. Division.
             A.D.M.S. 17th. Division.
             A.D.V.S. 4th. Division.
             O.C. 4th. Divisional Train.
             O.C. 4th. Division Signals.
             C.R.E. 4th. Division.
             Diary.
             File.

B. Copy No. 15

WARNING ORDER
by
Colonel J. GRECH. D.S.O., A.M.S., A.D.M.S. 4th. Division.

Map Refs: LENS. 11.   14th. September, 1917.

* * * * * * * * * * * * * *

The 4th. Division, (Less Artillery), will be prepared to entrain on 19th. September, 1917 on transfer to the Fifth Army.

Entraining Stations will be:-

BEAUMETZ-RIVIERE.......... 12th. Inf. Bde. Group.
SAULTY-LARBRET............ 10th. Inf. Bde. Group.
MONDICOURT................ 11th. Inf. Bde. Group.

11th. Infantry Brigade Group will move to MONDICOURT area on 18th. inst.

Detailed orders for entrainment will be issued by "Q", 4th. Division.

1.   Field Ambulances (less Motor Transport), will move with their Brigade Groups. Orders for Motor Transport will be issued later.

2.   A C K N O W L E D G E.

                                  [signature]
                                      Capt.
                           for Colonel,
                         A.D.M.S. 4th. Division.

Issued at 2.0 p.m.

Copies to:
       10th. Inf. Bde.
       11th. Inf. Bde.
       12th. Inf. Bde.
       10th. Field Ambulance.
       11th. Field Ambulance.
       12th. Field Ambulance.
       4th. Division, "G".
       4th. Division, "A".
       D.D.M.S. VIth. Corps.
       C.R.E. 4th. Division.
       A.D.V.S. 4th. Division.
       4th. Divisional Train.
       4th. Division Signals.
       Diary.   File. ✓

AMENDMENT TO R.A.M.C. WARNING ORDER
DATED 23-9-17.

September 23rd., 1917.

Reference R.A.M.C. Warning Order of to-day's date:

The following will be substituted for the words "So as to be completed by the morning of the 27th. inst";

"So as to be completed by the morning of the 29th. inst".

[signature]

Captain,
for A.D.M.S. 4th. Division.

Copies to all recipients of Warning Order dated 23-9-17.

D

Copy No. Diary

WARNING ORDER
by
COL. J. GRECH. D.S.O., A.M.S., A.D.M.S. 4th. DIVISION.

23rd. September, 1917.

The 4th. Division will relieve the 20th. Division in Right Sector of the XIVth. Corps.

The 12th. Infantry Brigade will be in the Front Line with the 10th. Infantry Brigade in Support and the 11th. Infantry Brigade in Reserve.

The relief will probably begin on the 26th. inst. so as to be completed by the morning of the 29th. inst.

1. The 12th. Field Ambulance will carry out the collection and evacuation of casualties in the Forward Area.

2. A C K N O W L E D G E.

[signature]
Captain,
for A.D.M.S. 4th. Division.

Issued at 11.30 a.m.

Copies to:-   10th. Field Ambulance.
              11th. Field Ambulance.
              12th. Field Ambulance.
              10th. Infantry Brigade.
              11th. Infantry Brigade.
              12th. Infantry Brigade.
              4th. Division, "G".
              4th. Division, "A".
              A.D.M.S. 20th. Division.
              D.D.M.S. XIVth. Corps.
              4th. Divisional Signals.
              C.R.E. 4th. Division.
              4th. Divisional Train.
              Diary.
              File.

E

Copy No.

MEDICAL ARRANGEMENTS, 4th. DIVISION.

Map Refs: Sheet 28, 1/40000. 23rd. September, 1917.

1. **PERSONNEL.**
   Regimental Stretcher Bearers will be doubled, (i.e. made up to 32 per Battalion.)
   Eight R.A.M.C. bearers will be attached to each Battalion for temporary duty under the Regimental Medical Officer.
   No. 12 Field Ambulance will carry out the evacuation of wounded from the Forward Area.

2. **POSITIONS OF MEDICAL UNITS.**

   (a). REGIMENTAL AID POSTS.
   1. Right Battalion.   LANGEMARCK (U.29.a.4.9.)
   2. Left Battalion.   AU BON GITE (U.28.d.2.9.)
   3. Support Battalion.   CEMENT HOUSE (U.28.c.1.3.)
   4. Reserve Battalion.   CORK HOUSE (C.3.a.2.5.)

   (b). FIELD AMBULANCE RELAY POSTS & A.D.STNS.
   1. Forward A.D.Stn.   CEMENT HOUSE (U.28.c.1.3.)
   2. Relay Posts: CHIEN FARM (U.28.c.7.7.)
                           CORNER HOUSE (C.2.c.6.6.)
                           GALLWITZ FARM (C.8.a.8.5.)
   3. A.D.STN. & H.Q. 12 Fd. FUSILIER (Canal Bank,
      Ambulance.   C.13.c.1.3.)

   (c). DIVISIONAL COLLECTING POST (Walking Wounded).
                           CHEAPSIDE (B.17.b.9.2.)

   (d). BEARER CAMP. (For reserve bearers).
                           PELISSIER FARM (B.21.a.3.0.)

   (e). DECAUVILLE UNLOADING POST. SOLFERINO FARM. (B.22.b.8.3.)

   (f). CORPS MAIN DRESSING STATION. CANADA FARM (A.18.a.1.7.).

   (g). CORPS SICK COLLECTING POST. Hut adjoining CANADA FARM
                           (A.12.c.4.2.)

   (h). CORPS COLLECTING POST. (Walking Wounded).
                           MOUTON FARM (B.14.a.2.9.)

3. **EVACUATION.** (a).
   1. By hand to CEMENT HOUSE, thence,
   2. By Decauville to SOLFERINO FARM and Corps Main Dressing Station.
   3. In the event of the Decauville not being available, by trolley to GALLWITZ FARM and FUSILIER A.D.Stn., or,
   4. By Ford cars, wheeled stretchers or Horsed Ambulance wagons, by PILCKEM-LANGEMARCK Road and Wooden Road to FUSILIER A.D.STN.
   5. In the event of heavy shelling on GALLWITZ ROAD it may be necessary to evacuate from CORNER HOUSE by track to TAMWORTH STATION (C.7.d.2.5.)

   (b). Walking Wounded. As many as possible by Decauville to about 400 yards South of CHEAPSIDE (B.18.c.4.4.) thence to CHEAPSIDE and by Busses to Corps Walking Wounded Post (MOUTON FARM) B.14.a.2.9.

   (c). Sick. To Sick Collecting Post near Corps Main Dressing Station.
   Lying sick to be treated as lying wounded.

AMENDMENT TO 4th. DIVISION R.A.M.C. ORDER
DATED 25-9-1917.
===

Reference R.A.M.C. Order dated 25th. inst:

On page 1, para. 1. (a)., line 3;

For "Sixteen" read "Eight".

26th. September, 1917.

Capt
/t
Colonel,
A.D.M.S. 4th. Division.

F.

Copy No.

R.A.M.C. ORDER
by
Col. J.GRECH. D.S.O., A.M.S., A.D.M.S. 4th. DIVISION.

Map Refs: Sheets 20 and 28,   25th. September, 1917.
     1/40000.
Trench Maps, BROEMBEEK & LANGEMARCK,
     1/10000.

The 4th. Division (less Artillery), will relieve the 20th. Division (less Artillery), on 27th., 28th., 29th. inst.

1. **PERSONNEL:**

    (a). The number of Regimental Stretcher Bearers will be doubled, i.e. made up to 32 per Battalion.
    Eight ~~Sixteen~~ extra stretchers will be drawn by Regimental Medical Officers from their respective Field Ambulances on 26th. inst.

    (b). Eight R.A.M.C. bearers will be attached to each Battn. for temporary duty under the Regimental Medical Officer.
    These bearers will be provided by No. 11 Field Ambulance as follows:-

    For 12th. Brigade, on night of 29th/30th. in the line. O.C. 12th. Field Ambulance to be responsible for the transfer.

    For 11th. Brigade, on morning of 27th. inst. To report to the Staff Captain.

    For 10th. Brigade, on morning of 28th. inst. To report to Staff Captain.

    These attached bearers will be rationed up to the 29th. inst. inclusive, after which date they will be rationed by the Regiment to which they are attached.
    These bearers must not be used in front of Regimental Aid Posts.

2. **RELIEFS.**
    The following Medical Posts will be taken over from the 20th. Division on dates and at times specified below:-

    12th. Field Ambulance:
    All Medical Posts East of the YPERLEE on the night of 27th/28th. inst.

        PELISSIER FARM: Evening of 26th. inst.

        Advanced Parties: Night 26th/27th. inst.

    Reliefs to be completed by the morning of the 28th. inst.

<u>OVER.</u>

- 2 -

    <u>11th. Field Ambulance</u>:
        Corps Walking Wounded Post, MOUTON FARM, midday on 28th. inst.

        CHEAPSIDE and Decauville Unloading Post, SOLFERINO FARM, at 9 a.m. on 28th. inst.

        Advanced Parties on afternoon of 26th. inst.

    <u>10th. Field Ambulance</u>:
        Corps Main Dressing Station, CANADA FARM, midday on 29th. inst.

        Advanced parties on afternoon of 27th. inst.

3. MOVES:

(a). Advanced parties will proceed to the new area under arrangements made by the Ambulance Commanders.
    Remainder of personnel will move by train with their Brigade Groups under orders of G.O.C. Brigade.

(b). O.C. No. 11 Field Ambulance will, on the morning of the 28th. inst., send 1 Tent Sub-Division composed of 2 Officers and 19 Other Ranks, to 46 Casualty Clearing Station, MENDRINGHEM, in relief of a Tent Sub-Division of the 20th. Division.

(c). O.C. No. 10 Field Ambulance will send his Bearer Division less 12 Other Ranks to PELISSIER FARM on the evening of the 28th. inst.

(d). O.C. 12th. Field Ambulance will send 1 Tent Sub-Division to SOLFERINO FARM by 9 a.m. on 28th. inst.(This Tent Sub-Division will be temporarily attached to 11th. Field Ambulance).

4. DUTIES.

(a). O.C. 12th. Field Ambulance will be responsible for the evacuation of sick and wounded East of the YPERLEE. He will have his Headquarters at PELISSIER FARM, but will move to FUSILIER Advanced Dressing Station during Active Operations.
    He will have under his control the reserve bearers, motor ambulance cars and horsed ambulances, and during his absence Lieut. & Quartermaster Tilbrook, R.A.M.C., will assume command of PELISSIER.

(b). O.C. No. 11 Field Ambulance will be responsible for the evacuation of casualties West of the YPERLEE, and will have under his charge CHEAPSIDE, SOLFERINO and MOUTON FARM.

(c). O.C. 10th. Field Ambulance will, if senior, assume command of the Corps Main Dressing Station.

5. POSITION OF MEDICAL POSTS.

(a). Regimental Aid Posts. The position of these will vary from time to time; at present they are situated as follows:-

                                              OVER.

- 3 -

    Right Battalion.   PUFF HOUSE. (U.29.b.40.95).

    Left Battalion.   LANGEMARCK. (U.29.a.50.65).

    Right Support Battn.   AU BON GITE.(U.28.d.3.7).

    Left Support Battn.   PIG & WHISTLE. (U.28.b.4.3.)

(b). <u>Relay Posts</u>.

    AU BON GITE.   U.28.d.3.7.

    PIG & WHISTLE.   U.28.b.4.3.

    CEMENT HOUSE.   U.28.c.1.3.

    CORK HOUSE.   C.3.a.2.5.

    CORNER HOUSE.   C.2.c.6.6.

    GALLWITZ FARM.   C.8.a.8.5.

(c). <u>Advanced Dressing Station</u>.

    FUSILIER, (Canal Bank). C.13.c.1.3.

(d). <u>Divisional Collecting Post.(Walking Wounded)</u>.

    CHEAPSIDE.   B.17.b.9.2.

(e). <u>Bearer Camp</u>.

    PELISSIER FARM. B.21.a.3.0.
         Reserve bearers, ambulance cars, and horsed ambulance wagons will be kept here.

(f). <u>Decauville Unloading Post</u>.

    SOLFERINO FARM. B.22.b.8.3.

(g). <u>Corps Main Dressing Station</u>.

    CANADA FARM.   A.18.a.1.7.

(h). <u>Corps Sick Collecting Post</u>.

    Hut adjoining CANADA FARM. (A.12.c.4.2.)

(i). <u>Corps Walking Wounded Collecting Post</u>.

    MOUTON FARM.   B.14.a.2.9.

6. EVACUATION.

    I.(a). By hand to CEMENT HOUSE.

       (b). Thence by Decauville, loading at WEEDON, to SOLFERINO, where cases will be dressed if necessary, and by motor ambulance to Corps Main Dressing Station.

<u>OVER</u>.

- 4 -

    (c). In the event of the Decauville not being available, by trolley to GALLWITZ FARM and FUSILIER Advanced Dressing Station.

    (d). If unable to use Decauville or Trolley, evacuation will be carried out by hand and wheeled stretcher along the PILCKEM-LANGEMARCK road to the CORNER HOUSE and along the track in C.2.c. to TAMWORTH JUNCTION at C.7.d.2.4.
        If the CORNER HOUSE is at the time heavily shelled, the track starting about C.2.b.6.2. and running through C.2.d. to C.2.c.8.0. and on to TAMWORTH will be used, or route via GALLWITZ to FUSILIER.

    (e). 2 Ford cars and 2 Horsed ambulances will be waiting at TAMWORTH JUNCTION to convey wounded to FUSILIER.

II.(a). <u>Walking Wounded</u>. As many walking wounded as possible will be carried by Decauville to about 400 yards South of CHEAPSIDE, (B.18.c.4.4.) Thence by busses to MOUTON FARM.

    (b). If the Decauville is not running they will be directed along the PILCKEM-LANGEMARCK road, branching off along duckboarded German Trench leading direct to GALLWITZ FARM, and directed via CACTUS PONTOON to CHEAPSIDE.

    (c). <u>Sick</u>. Lying sick will be treated as lying wounded. Walking sick will follow the same route as mentioned above for walking wounded.
        All cases will be evacuated to Corps Sick Collecting Post (CANADA FARM).

<u>N.B.</u> Severe lying cases after being dressed will be taken direct in motor ambulances to Casualty Clearing Station.
    For this purpose 10 M.A.C. cars carrying red discs on the radiator will collect from the A.D.Stn. If there are no suitable cases for transfer they must at once be loaded and despatched to Corps Main Dressing Station. Orders to that effect must be given in writing to the driver.

7. <u>Divisional Stretcher Bearers.</u>
    200 Divisional stretcher bearers will report at PELISSIER FARM on the morning of the 27th. inst.
    They will come under the charge of O.C. 12th. Field Ambulance and will be utilised according to his discretion. They will be rationed by their Units up to 28th. inst. inclusive.

8. <u>STRETCHERS & AMBULANCES</u>. All wheeled stretchers, motor and horsed ambulances will be pooled, and come under the charge of O.C. No. 12 Field Ambulance.
    4 Wheeled stretchers, 4 ambulance cars and 2 horsed ambulances per Field Ambulance will report to Lieut. & Quartermaster Tilbrook, R.A.M.C. at PELISSIER FARM on the morning of the 28th. inst. Remainder of cars and ambulance wagons will report at the same place on the afternoon of the 29th. inst.

9. Completion of reliefs to be reported by wire to A.D.M.S. 4th. Division.

<u>OVER</u>.

10. Office of A.D.M.S. will close at PROVEN at 10 a.m. on the 29th. inst., and reopen at WELSH FARM at the same hour.

11. A C K N O W L E D G E.

Issued at 8.30 p.m.

Colonel,
A.D.M.S. 4th. Division.

Copies to:-

10th. Field Ambulance.
11th. Field Ambulance.
12th. Field Ambulance.
10th. Infantry Bde.
11th. Infantry Bde.
12th. Infantry Bde.
4th. Division, "G".
4th. Division, "A".
D.D.M.S. XIVth. Corps.
A.D.M.S. 29th. Division.
A.D.M.S. 51st. Division.
C.R.E. 4th. Division.
O.C. Div. Signals.
A.D.V.S. 4th. Division.
4th. Divisional Train.
All Regimental Medical Officers.
Diary (2).
File.

SECRET

G.

Copy No. 33

R.A.M.C. ORDER
by
COLONEL J. GRECH. D.S.O., A.M.S., A.D.M.S. 4th. DIVISION.

Map Refs: BROEMBEEK } 1/10000.
LANGEMARCK   }   28th. September, 1917.

The Second and Fifth Armies are continuing the attack on Z day.
The objective of the XIVth. Corps will be captured by the 4th. and 29th. Divisions on the right and left respectively. The boundary between the Divisions will be the line U.23.central- U.18.b.5.0.

The 4th. Division will attack at Zero hour with two Brigades in the front line and one in Reserve:
    11th. Infantry Bde. will be on the right.
    10th. Infantry Bde. will be on the left.
    12th. Bde. will be in reserve.

The boundary between Brigades will be the line U.23.b.8.0.- V.13.c.0.5.

1. (a). The Regimental Aid Posts at LANGEMARCK (U.29.a.4.9.) and PUFF HOUSE (U.29.b.5.9.) will be moved up to EAGLE TRENCH during Y/Z night so as to be in position at Z-2 hours.
    These two posts will then become Relay Posts for the Right and Left Brigades.

    (b). O.C. 12th. Field Ambulance will on Y/Z night send sufficient personnel to the two posts mentioned above, and form Relay Posts.
    A small stretcher and blanket dump will be kept at both places and also in EAGLE TRENCH. These will be replenished from CEMENT HOUSE (U.28.c.1.3.)

    (c). Other Medical Posts will be as mentioned in R.A.M.C. Order dated 25-9-1917.

    (d). Reinforcement of the various posts will be left to the discretion of O.C. No. 12 Field Ambulance.

2.   Routes of evacuation will be as laid down in R.A.M.C. Order dated 25-9-1917. Ford cars will if possible, be sent as far as CORK HOUSE.

3.   On Z day, CHEAPSIDE (B.17.b.9.2.) will be opened as a Divisional Walking Wounded Collecting Post, and SOLFERINO (B.22.b.8.5.) reinforced if it is found that the Decauville is running on that day.
    Details as to personnel, equipment, etc., will be left to O.C. 11th. Field Ambulance.

4.   O.C. 10th. Field Ambulance will send one Motor Cycle on Z day to the A.D.Stn. at FUSILIER (C.13.c.1.3.) for temporary duty with No. 12 Field Ambulance.

5.   Z day and Zero hour will be notified later.

6.   A C K N O W L E D G E.

Colonel,
A.D.M.S. 4th. Division.

Issued at 7.30 p.m.

Distribution:-

Copy No. 1 to 10th. Field Ambulance.
        2.   11th. Field Ambulance.
        3.   12th. Field Ambulance.
        4.   10th. Infantry Brigade.
        5.   11th. Infantry Brigade.
        6.   12th. Infantry Brigade.
        7.   4th. Division, "G".
        8.   4th. Division, "Q".
        9.   D.M.S. Fifth Army.
      10.   D.D.M.S. XIVth. Corps.
      11.   A.D.M.S. 29th. Division.
      12.   A.D.M.S. 20th. Division.
      13.   C.R.E. 4th. Division.
      14.   Regimental Medical Officers.
    to 30.
    31 & 32 Diary.
    33.   File.

4th Division

Medical

A.D.M.S.

October to December

1914

B.E.F.

SUMMARY OF MEDICAL WAR DIARIES FOR

4th Divn. 14th Corps, 5th Army.
18th Corps from 15/10/17.
17th Corps from 17/10/17.

———

WESTERN FRONT Oct. 1917.

———

A.D.M.S. Col. J. Grech D.S.O.
D.A.D.M.S.   ?

SUMMARISED UNDER THE FOLLOWING HEADINGS
Phase "D" 1. Passchendaele Operations July-Dec. 1917.
(b) Operations commencing 1/10/17.
Canadians attacked Passchendaele Oct. 30th.
Canadians took Passchendaele Nov. 6th.

B.E.F. 1.

4th Divn. 14th Corps 5th Army.   WESTERN FRONT.
A.D.M.S. Col. J. Grech D.S.O.   Oct. 1917.

Phase "D" 1. Passchendaele Operations July-Dec. 1917.

(b) Operations commencing 1/10/17.
Canadians attacked Passchendaele Oct. 30th
Canadians took Passchendaele Nov. 6th.

1917.
Oct. 4th.   Headquarters. At Welsh Farm.

Operations. 10th and 11th Inf. Bgdes. attacked at 6 a.m. All objectives taken by 10 a.m.

Medical Arrangements. Appendix A (Para. 2) *(Put back into Diary)* Attached and Map 1.

Evacuation. Worked well. Decauville Railway worked all day with about three breaks owing to line being damaged by shell fire.

Casualties. 12 and 357 wounded 4th Divn.
0 and 58 wounded other Formations.

Casualties R.A.M.C. 0 and 2 wounded 11th Field Ambulance.

0 and 1 wounded 12th Field Ambulance.

5th.   Casualties. 19 and 385 wounded 4th Divn.
3 and 21 wounded other Formations.

Ps. O.W. 0 and 1 wounded.

Casualties Gas. 1 and 0 4th Divn. since 4th-10-17.
1 and 5 other Formations.

Casualties R.A.M.C. 0 and 1 wounded 10th Field Ambulance. 1/Lt. P.G. Halin U.S.M.O.R.C. wounded.

0 and 3 wounded 11th Field Ambulance.

0 and 2 wounded 12th Field Ambulance.

6th.   Weather. Heavy rain during night, bitterly cold during day.

B.E.F. 2.

4th Divn. 14th Corps, 5th Army.   WESTERN FRONT.
A.D.M.S. Col. J. Grech D.S.O.   Oct. 1917.

Phase "D" 1. (b) (Cont).

1917.

Oct. 6th (Cont.)   Military Situation. 11th Inf. Bde. and 1 Battn. 29th Divn. took over line from 10th Inf. Bde.

Casualties. 4 and 103 wounded 4th Divn.

1 and 9 wounded Other Formations.

Casualties R.A.M.C:-

0 and 1 wounded 10th Field Ambulance.

0 and 2 killed. 11th Field Ambulance.

0 and 2 wounded 12th Field Ambulance.

      7th.   Military Situation. 12th Inf. Bde. took over line/from 11th Inf. Bde.

Weather. Wet cleared up towards night.

Casualties R.A.M.C. 0 and 1 wounded 10th Field Ambulance.

Casualties. 1 and 83 wounded 4th Divn.

0 and 4 wounded Other Formations.

      8th.   Medical Arrangements. Appendix B. (Paras. 4) Attached. (Put back into Diary)

D.W.W.P. established at Stray Farm.

Weather. Heavy rain.

Casualties. 1 and 35 wounded 4th Divn.

0 and 5 wounded Other Formations.

Casualties R.A.M.C. 0 and 5 wounded 11th Field Ambulance.

0 and 1 wounded 12th Field Ambulance.

      9th   Operations: Medical Arrangements. Assistance. Put back into Diary
App.B.(para. 1.2.5.6.) App.C.D. also Map Attached.
Attack commenced 5.20 a.m. first objective gained

B.E.F.

4th Divn. 14th Corps, 5th Army.   WESTERN FRONT.
A.D.M.S. Col. J. Grech D.S.O.   Oct. 1917.

Phase "D" 1. (b) (Cont.)

1917.
Oct. 9th. (Cont.)   Operations: Medical Arrangements: Assistance (Cont.)
by 4th Divn. attack then held up. Large number of
Germans captured who helped to evacuate wounded.
Evacuation: Terrain. On account of long carries
and mud, forward evacuation was slow, but always
steady, wounded evacuated by Decauville from
A.D.S. Cement House. Trains worked steadily
and without a hitch.
Casualties.   11 and 205 wounded 4th Divn.
1 and 2 wounded Other Formations.
1 and 70 wounded Ps. O.W.
Casualties R.A.M.C.   0 and 1 wounded 10th Field
Ambulance.

10th.   Evacuation. Very satisfatory from A.D.S. Cement
House. Congestion at one time at 2nd Essex R.A.P.
which was cleared by sending up 8 squads.
Casualties:-
10 and 204 wounded 4th Divn.
0 and 2 wounded Other Formations.
2 and 27 wounded Ps. O.W.
Casualties R.A.M.C.   0 and 6 wounded 11th Field
Ambulance;   0 and 2 wounded 12th Field Ambulance.

11th.   Casualties.   8 and 85 wounded 4th Divn.
0 and 7 wounded Other Formations.
0 and 5 wounded Ps. O.W.

B.E.F. 4.

<u>4th Divn. 14th Corps, 5th Army.</u>   <u>WESTERN FRONT.</u>
<u>A.D.M.S. Col. J. Grech D.S.O.</u>   <u>Oct. 1917.</u>
<u>18th Corps from 15/10/17.</u>

<u>Phase "D" 1. (b) (Cont.)</u>

1917.

Oct. 11th. (Cont.)   <u>Casualties R.A.M.C.:-</u>
0 and 1 wounded 11th Field Ambulance.
0 and 1 wounded 12th Field Ambulance.

12th.   <u>Operations.</u> Appendix E. (Less Paras. 5 and 6) also Map 3. Attached. (Put back into Diary.)
<u>Medical Arrangements.</u> 4th Divn. attacked at 5.25 a.m. Attack successful except on extreme right.
<u>Casualties: Evacuation: Terrain.</u> Evacuation of casualties which were not heavy, carried out quickly and well considering very bad state of ground, and length of carries. By night battle front practically cleared.
8 and 174 wounded 4th Divn.
and 29 wounded Ps. O.W.
<u>Casualties R.A.M.C.</u> 0 and 1 wounded 11th Field Ambulance.

13th.   <u>Casualties.</u> 2 and 127 wounded 4th Divn.
0 and 2 Other Formations.
0 and 4 Ps. O.W.
<u>Casualties R.A.M.C.</u> 0 and 1 wounded 10th Field Ambulance.

14th.   <u>Military Situation: Medical Arrangements.</u> Appendix F.(a,c and I.) Also Table Attached. (Put back into Diary)
<u>Moves.</u> To Proven.

15th.   <u>Moves and Transfer.</u> To 18th Corps and moved to Poperinghe.

B.E.F. 5.

<u>4th Divn. 18th Corps, 5th Army.</u>   <u>WESTERN FRONT.</u>
<u>A.D.M.S. Col. J. Grech D.S.O.</u>   <u>Oct. 1917.</u>
<u>17th Corps from 17/10/17.</u>

<u>Phase "D" 1. Passchendaele Operations July-Dec. 1917.</u>

 (b) Operations commencing 1/10/17.
  Canadians attacked Passchendaele Oct. 30th.
  Canadians took Passchendaele Nov. 6th.

1917.   <u>Headquarters.</u> At Poperinghe.

Oct. 15th. <u>Moves and Transfer.</u> To 18th Corps and moved to Poperinghe.

 <u>Moves Field Ambulance.</u> 10th Field Ambulance to St. Jan Der. Beezen.

 11th Field Ambulance to Poperinghe.

16th. <u>Moves Field Ambulance.</u> 12th Field Ambulance to St. Jan. Der. Beezen.

17th. <u>Moves and Transfer.</u> To 17th Corps, 3rd Army.
 Moved to Duisans.

 <u>Appendices:-</u>

 A1. File of Field Messages giving casualties etc.
 A. Addendum to R.A.M.C.O./of 25-9-17. d/1/10/17
 B. R.A.M.C. Order 35 d/ 7/10/17.
 C. Amendment to R.A.M.C. Order 35 d/ 8/10/17
 D. Addendum No.2. to R.A.M.C. O. 35. 8/10/17.
 E. R.A.M.C. O. 36 11/10/17.
 F. do. 37 11/10/17.
 G. do. 38 14/10/17.
 H. do. 39 16/10/17.
 Maps. 1,2. and 3.

B.E.F.

SUMMARY OF MEDICAL WAR DIARIES FOR

4th Divn. 14th Corps, 5th Army.
18th Corps from 15/10/17.
17th Corps from 17/10/17.

WESTERN FRONT Oct. 1917.

A.D.M.S. Col. J. Grech D.S.O.
D.A.D.M.S.   ?

SUMMARISED UNDER THE FOLLOWING HEADINGS
Phase "D" 1. Passchendaele Operations July-Dec. 1917.

(b) Operations commencing 1/10/17.
Canadians attacked Passchendaele Oct. 30th.
Canadians took Passchendaele Nov. 6th.

B.E.F.   1.

4th Divn. 14th Corps 5th Army.   WESTERN FRONT.
A.D.M.S. Col. J. Grech D.S.O.   Oct. 1917.

Phase "D" 1. Passchendaele Operations July-Dec. 1917.

(b) Operations commencing 1/10/17.
Canadians attacked Passchendaele Oct. 30th
Canadians took Passchendaele Nov. 6th.

1917.
Oct. 4th.

Headquarters. At Welsh Farm.

Operations. 10th and 11th Inf. Bgdes. attacked at 6 a.m. All objectives taken by 10 a.m.

Medical Arrangements. Appendix A (Para. 2) Attached and Map 1.

Evacuation. Worked well. Decauville railway /worked all day with about three breaks owing to line being damaged by shell fire.

Casualties. 12 and 357 wounded 4th Divn. 0 and 58 wounded other Formations.

Casualties R.A.M.C. 0 and 2 wounded 11th Field Ambulance.

0 and 1 wounded 12th Field Ambulance.

5th.

Casualties. 19 and 385 wounded 4th Divn.
3 and 21 wounded other Formations.
Ps. O.W. 0 and 1 wounded.

Casualties Gas. 1 and 0 4th Divn. since 4th-10-17.
1 and 5 other Formations.

Casualties R.A.M.C. 0 and 1 wounded 10th Field Ambulance. 1/Lt. P.G. Halin U.S.M.O.R.C. wounded.
0 and 3 wounded 11th Field Ambulance.
0 and 2 wounded 12th Field Ambulance.

6th.

Weather. Heavy rain during night, bitterly cold during day.

B.E.F. 2.

4th Divn. 14th Corps, 5th Army.   WESTERN FRONT.
A.D.M.S. Col. J. Grech D.S.O.   Oct. 1917.

Phase "D" 1. (b) (Cont).

1917.

Oct. 6th (Cont.) Military Situation. 11th Inf. Bde. and 1 Battn.
29th Divn. took over line from 10th Inf. Bde.
Casualties. 4 and 103 wounded 4th Divn.
1 and 9 wounded Other Formations.
Casualties R.A.M.C:-
0 and 1 wounded 10th Field Ambulance.
0 and 2 killed. 11th Field Ambulance.
0 and 2 wounded 12th Field Ambulance.

7th. Military Situation. 12th Inf. Bde. took over line from 11th Inf. Bde.
Weather. Wet cleared up towards night.
Casualties R.A.M.C. 0 and 1 wounded 10th Field Ambulance.
Casualties. 1 and 83 wounded 4th Divn.
0 and 4 wounded Other Formations.

8th. Medical Arrangements. Appendix B. (Paras. 4) Attached.
D.W.W.P. established at Stray Farm.
Weather. Heavy rain.
Casualties. 1 and 35 wounded 4th Divn.
0 and 3 wounded Other Formations.
Casualties R.A.M.C. 0 and 3 wounded 11th Field Ambulance.
0 and 1 wounded 12th Field Ambulance.

9th Operations; Medical Arrangements; Assistance.
App.B.(para. 1.2.5.6) App.C.D also Map Attached.
Attack commenced 5.20 a.m. First objective gained

4th Divn. 14th Corps, 5th Army.   WESTERN FRONT.
A.D.M.S. Col. J. Grech D.S.O.   Oct. 1917.

Phase "D" 1. (b) (Cont.)

1917.

Oct. 9th. (Cont.)   Operations: Medical Arrangements; Assistance (Cont.)
by 4th Divn. attack then held up. Large number of
Germans captured who helped to evacuate wounded.
Evacuation; Terrain. On account of long carries
and mud, forward evacuation was slow, but always
steady, wounded evacuated by Decauville from
A.D.S. Cement House. Trains worked steadily
and without a hitch.
Casualties.   11 and 205 wounded 4th Divn.
1 and 2 wounded Other Formations.
1 and 70 wounded Ps. O.W.
Casualties R.A.M.C.   0 and 1 wounded 10th Field
Ambulance.

10th.   Evacuation. Very satisfatory from A.D.S. Cement
House. Congestion at one time at 2nd Essex R.A.P.
which was cleared by sending up 8 squads.
Casualties:-
10 and 204 wounded 4th Divn.
0 and 2 wounded Other Formations.
2 and 27 wounded Ps. O.W.
Casualties R.A.M.C.   0 and 6 wounded 11th Field
Ambulance. 0 and 2 wounded 12th Field Ambulance.

11th.   Casualties.   8 and 85 wounded 4th Divn.
0 and 7 wounded Other Formations.
0 and 5 wounded Ps. O.W.

B.E.F. 4.

4th Divn. 14th Corps, 5th Army.   WESTERN FRONT.
A.D.M.S. Col. J. Grech D.S.O.   Oct. 1917.
18th Corps from 15/10/17.

Phase "D" 1. (b) (Cont.)

1917.

Oct. 11th. (Cont.)   Casualties R.A.M.C.:-

0 and 1 wounded 11th Field Ambulance.

0 and 1 wounded 12th Field Ambulance.

12th.   Operations. Appendix E. (Less Paras. 5 and 6) also Map 3. Attached.

Medical Arrangements.   4th Divn. attacked at 5.25 a.m. Attack successful except on extreme right.

Casualties; Evacuation; Terrain. Evacuation of casualties which were not heavy, carried out quickly and well considering very bad state of ground, and length of carries. By night battle front practically cleared.

8 and 174 wounded 4th Divn.

2 and 29 wounded Ps. O.W.

Casualties R.A.M.C. 0 and 1 wounded 11th Field Ambulance.

13th.   Casualties. 2 and 127 wounded 4th Divn.

0 and 2 Other Formations.

0 and 4 Ps. O.W.

Casualties R.A.M.C. 0 and 1 wounded 10th Field Ambulance.

14th.   Military Situation; Medical Arrangements. Appendix F.(a,c and I.) Also Table Attached.

Moves.   To Proven.

15th.   Moves and Transfer. To 18th Corps and moved to Poperinghe.

B.E.F.   5.

4th Divn. 18th Corps, 5th Army.   WESTERN FRONT.
A.D.M.S. Col. J. Grech D.S.O.   Oct. 1917.
17th Corps from 17/10/17.

Phase "D" 1. Passchendaele Operations July-Dec. 1917.

(b) Operations commencing 1/10/17.
Canadians attacked Passchendaele Oct. 30th.
Canadians took Passchendaele Nov. 6th.

———

1917.   Headquarters.   At Poperinghe.

Oct. 15th.   Moves and Transfer.   To 18th Corps and moved to Poperinghe.

Moves Field Ambulance.   10th Field Ambulance to St. Jan Der. Beezen.

11th Field Ambulance to Poperinghe.

16th.   Moves Field Ambulance.   12th Field Ambulance to St. Jan. Der. Beezen.

17th.   Moves and Transfer.   To 17th Corps, 3rd Army.
Moved to Duisans.

Appendices:-

A1. File of Field Messages giving casualties etc.
A. Addendum to R.A.M.C. O/ of 25-9-17.   d/1/10/17
B. R.A.M.C. Order 35   d/ 7/10/17.
C. Amendment to R.A.M.C. Order 35   d/ 8/10/17
D. Addendum No.2. to R.A.M.C. O. 35.   8/10/17.
E. R.A.M.C. O. 36   11/10/17.
F.   do.   37   11/10/17.
G.   do.   38   14/10/17.
H.   do.   39   16/10/17.

Maps. 1,2. and 3.

Army Form C. 2118.

WAR DIARY
or
INTELLIGENCE SUMMARY.
(Erase heading not required.)

Place	Date	Hour	Summary of Events and Information	Remarks and references to Appendices
WELSH FARM	1st	6.10a.	Wire to D.Dms. XIV Corps	1
		1.50p.	Wire to D.Dms. XIV Corps repeater Dnr. 5th Army	2
		2.p.	Wire to D.D.M.S. XIV Corps	3
		5.20p.	Do. Do.	4
		2.10p.	Casualty wire to "A" (RAMC)	5
			Addendum to Op Orders issued by A.D.M.S.	A.
			The D.A.D.M.S. visits the D.Dms. XIV Corps + arranges about extra blankets to be needed for forthcoming Operations.	
	2nd	6.20a	Wire to D.Dms. XIV Corps	6
		1.6p.	Do. Do.	7
		2.35p	Do to D. Dms. 5th Army repts D.Dms. XIV Corps	8
		5.5p	Do. to D.Dms. XIV Corps	9
		5.20p.	RAMC Casualty return to "A"	10
			The A.D.M.S. D.A.D.M.S. visited the A.D.S. on the Canal Bank + the forward A.D.S. at CEMENT HOUSE — the A.D.M.S. attended a Conference at Corps H.Q. on	

Army Form C. 2118.

WAR DIARY
or
INTELLIGENCE SUMMARY.
(Erase heading not required.)

Place	Date	Hour	Summary of Events and Information	Remarks and references to Appendices
WELSH FARM	2nd (ctd)		The D.D.M.S. visited H.Q. 2nd 12th F. Amb.	
			The 12th Inf. Bde. came out of the line & the 10th & 12th Inf. Bdes. moved in preparatory to the offensive operations forthcoming.	
	3rd	6.a.	Wire to D.Dns. XIV Corps.	11
		1.5.p.	Wire to D.Dns. XIV Corps.	12
		1.30.p.	Wire to D.M.S. 5th Army repeats D.D.M.S. XIV Corps.	13
		1.55.p.	Received Enemy report D.Dns. XIV Corps	14
		5.20.p.	Wire to D.Dns. XIV Corps	15
			All bearers moved up to their relay posts on Taxis down in A.D.M.S's orders ready to take part in the attack at 6 a.m. on the 4th inst.	
	4th		The 10th & 11th Inf. Bdes. assaulted at 6 a.m. & all objectives were taken by about 10 a.m. Then the lights on the Eff. Bde. front varied & many varied reports came in as to result but in the evening the situation was reported as alright. The A.D.M.S. visited Corps Main Dressing Stn., Corps Walking Wounded Post	

WAR DIARY or INTELLIGENCE SUMMARY

Army Form C. 2118.

Place	Date	Hour	Summary of Events and Information	Remarks and references to Appendices
WELSH FARM	4 (Cont)		Divisional Dressing Stn. Finished Walking Wounded Post. The D.A.D.M.S. proceeded to the Forward A.D.S. at CEMENT HOUSE at Zero hour (6 a.m.) & remained there until 1 p.m. & saw the evacuation of Casualties up there. The relays worked well & the Bearers worked all along with about three breaks owing to the line being damaged by Shell fire: these breaks were quickly mended. At 9 p.m. a phone message was received from 11th Inf. Bde saying that their area was not clear of wounded; on receipt of this message all available stretcher bearers at our disposal (9's) were sent off to 11th Bde to try to clear them.	
		6.30 a.m.	Casualty wire to D.D.M.S. XIV Corps	16
		10.50 a.m.	Orders to 12th F. Amb. to reinforce Squad at CORNER HOUSE	17
		1.55 p.m.	Routine Casualty return	18
		1.55 p.m.	Casualty wire to D.M.S. 5th Army	19
		1.55 p.m.	Casualty wire to D.D.M.S. XIV Corps	20
		5.55 p.m.	Casualty wire to D.D.M.S. XIV Corps	21

Army Form C. 2118.

WAR DIARY
or
INTELLIGENCE SUMMARY.
(Erase heading not required.)

Instructions regarding War Diaries and Intelligence Summaries are contained in F. S. Regs., Part II and the Staff Manual respectively. Title pages will be prepared in manuscript.

Place	Date	Hour	Summary of Events and Information	Remarks and references to Appendices
WELSH FARM	5th		The enemy continued shelling the battlefield all night. An aeroplane flew definitely shots over lines on our objectives.	
		6.30a	Casualty report to D.D.M.S. XIV Corps	22
		10.a.	Wire to 11 Lt. Bde. re regimental aid post	23
		10.45a	Report for Covers for railway trucks for wounded carriage	24
		1.p.	Rain. Casualty return L-"A".	25
		1.p.	Report of Officer sick casualty to D.D.M.S. XIV Corps	26
		2.30p	Casualty report to D.D.M.S. 5th Army	27
		2.30p	Casualty report to D.D.M.S. XIV Corps	28
		3.p	Orders from G. re Stretcher bearers attached from Warwicks	29
		5.40p	Casualty report to D.D.M.S. XIV Corps	30
		5.45p	Order to F. Ambs. to place material excess of mob. equip. the A.D.H.Q. accompanied the D.D.M.R. XIV Corps to the Corps Walking Wounded Post & Main Dressing Stn & Wrecking Wounded Post.	31
		11.p.	Report of Officer casualty in 12th F. Amb.	32

Army Form C. 2118.

WAR DIARY
or
INTELLIGENCE SUMMARY.
(Erase heading not required.)

Instructions regarding War Diaries and Intelligence Summaries are contained in F.S. Regs., Part II. and the Staff Manual respectively. Title pages will be prepared in manuscript.

Place	Date	Hour	Summary of Events and Information	Remarks and references to Appendices
WELSH FARM	6th	6.30 a.	Casualty wire to D.Dm.S. XIV Corps	33
		2.30 p.	Ration Casualties to "A"	34
		2.30 p.	Message to 11th Div. re Casualties	35
		3.25 p.	Casualty report to D.m.S. 5th Army re D.Dm.S. XIV Corps	36
		3.30 p.	Casualty report to D.Dm.S. XIV Corps	37
		3.30 p.	Message to J. Amb. re maps	38
		3.45 p.	Casualty report to D.Dm.S. XIV Corps	39
		6. p.	Orders from C.in.C. that the XIV Corps will continue the attack. The A.Dm.S. visited D.Dm.S. XIV Corps. The A.Dm.S. had a conference with A.Q.M.G. 29th Div re the /11th- coming offensive. The D.A.D.M.S. visited the A.D.Sta. & Divl. Walking Wounded Pnt. Heavy rain fell last night - & it was bitterly cold throughout the day. The 11th Inf. Bde D a Batt. of the 29th Div. took over the line in relief of the 10th Inf. Bde who came out.	

2353 Wt. W 2544/1454 700,000 5/15 D. D. & L. A.D.S.S./Forms/C. 2118.

Place	Date	Hour	Summary of Events and Information	Remarks and references to Appendices
WELSH FARM	7²		Operation orders issued by A.D.M.S. for forthcoming operation of the 12ᵗʰ Inf. Bde. took over on the line from the 11ᵗʰ Inf. Bde. The A.D.M.S. held a conference of M.O.'s & representatives of the 12ᵗʰ Inf. Bde. The D.D.M.S. visited the Div. A.D. Stn., the Corps Walking Wounded Post & also the Corps A.D. Stn. being made by 10ᵗʰ F. Amb. The day was very hot normally but cleared up towards night but the going is very bad.	B.
		6.35a.	Casualty wire to D.D.M.S. XIV Corps	40
		10.30a.	French post relieved	41
		10.30a.	Congratulatory message to F. Amb.	42
		2.40p.	Return Battle Casualties 1-A²	43
		3p.	Casualty wire to Army Hdqtrs. Corps	44
		3p.	Casualty wire to Corps	45
		4.40p.	Request to O. for additional men to act on stretcher bearers	46
		5.30p.	Orders to F. Amb. re road traffic	47
		6.30p.	Casualty wire to Corps	48

Army Form C. 2118.

WAR DIARY
or
INTELLIGENCE SUMMARY.
(Erase heading not required.)

Place	Date	Hour	Summary of Events and Information	Remarks and references to Appendices
WELSH FARM	8		Queen Trent to O.B. Orders of 7² by A.D.M.S.	C.
			Addendum to Op. Orders of 7² by A.D.M.S.	D.
		6.30a	Casualty wire to D.Dr.S. XIV Corps	49
		2.15p	Movement report of 10th F. Amb. to Corps	50
		2.15p	Rain	51
		2.30p	Casualty report to Corps	52
		2.35p	Casualty report to D.M.S. 5th Army repeated Corps	53
		5.40p	Casualty report to Corps	54
		9.p	Message to F. Ambs re road traffic	55
			the 10th F. Amb. opened a Corps Advanced Dressing Pt at SOLFERINO (B.22.6.9.2) & a Divisional Walking Wounded Post was established by a place called STRAY FARM in the forward area. For A.Dr.S. D.A.Dr.S. visits 12th + 10th F. Amb. & the Corps Walking Wounded Post.	
			Heavy rain fell all day but the weather cleared up towards night.	

Army Form C. 2118.

WAR DIARY
or
INTELLIGENCE SUMMARY.
(Erase heading not required.)

Instructions regarding War Diaries and Intelligence Summaries are contained in F. S. Regs., Part II. and the Staff Manual respectively. Title pages will be prepared in manuscript.

Place	Date	Hour	Summary of Events and Information	Remarks and references to Appendices
WELSH FARM	9ᵗʰ		The Division attacked at 5.20 a.m. with the 11ᵗʰ Div on our right & the 29ᵗʰ Div on our left. The first objective was reached by 4ᵗʰ Div but the attack was then held up, & could not go any further. A large number of Germans were captured. These proved to the greatest use in helping to clear the casualties back. On account of the long carries for stretcher cases in the forward area, the removal to the mud the forward evacuation was a bit slow but it was always steady. When the cases arrived at the forward A.D.S. at CEMENT HOUSE they were evacuated from there by Decauville tram, of which three had been allotted for the conveyance of casualties. Have been worked steadily all the time without a hitch. The D.A.D.M.S. visited CEMENT HOUSE & saw the evacuation of Casualties proceeding during the action.	56 57 58
		6.35a.	Casualty report to Corps	
		2.40p.	Do Do	
		2.45p.	Do to Army & Corps	

Army Form C. 2118.

WAR DIARY
or
INTELLIGENCE SUMMARY.
(Erase heading not required.)

Place	Date	Hour	Summary of Events and Information	Remarks and references to Appendices
WELSH FARM (cont)	9.	3p.	Ravine Casualties	59
		5p.	Orders h. J. Amb & pack transport	60
		6p.	Casualty report to Corps	61
	10.		The D.A.D.M.S. visits CEMENT HOUSE. I am told the evacuation was getting on; it was very perfunctory except that there was a report that the 2/ bearer aid post was crumped. An officer was sent up with 6 squads to deal with this & later in the day the stretcher bearers reports cleared of Casualties. Orders received from "G" that the attack was to be continued on the 12th inst. Orders received from "G" that the 34th Div. (dism'd) relieves this Division in the line, the relief Infantry on the 12th inst. with the 11th Fd. Amb.	
		3.10 a.	Messages to XIV Corps, Light Rly Offices re ambulance trains	62
		6.50 a.	Casualty report to Corps	63
		10.6 a.	Message to Army & Corps asking for Ravine reinforcements	64
		2.17 p.	Ravine Casualty report to "A"	65

Place	Date	Hour	Summary of Events and Information	Remarks and references to Appendices
WELSH FARM	10 (cont)	3.5p.	Message to F. Amb. re relief	66
		5.12p.	Orders from "C" placing more men at our disposal as stretcher bearers	67
		5.35p.	Casualty report to Army reported to Corps	68
		5.48p.	Casualty report to Corps	69
		5.49p.	Do	70
			He R.A.M.C. stretcher bearers att. to the 10th & 11th Sy. Bdes went with Divn. to 12th F. Amb. today as there is not much likelihood of these Bdes being used in forthcoming operation	E
			Operation Orders issued by A.D.M.S. for forthcoming operation	F
"	11		Operation Orders for move viewed by A.D.M.S. to all concerned	71
		7.30a.	Casualty report to XIV Corps	72
		2.p.	R.A.M.C. Casualty report to "A"	73
		2.15p.	Congratulatory wire to J. Amb.	74
		2.45p.	Casualty report to XIV Corps	75
		5.30p.	Casualty report to 5th Army reported to Corps	76
		5.45p.	Casualty report to XIV Corps re movement of Light Rly ambulance trains	77
			Instructions from XIV Corps re movement of Light Rly ambulance trains	

Army Form C. 2118.

WAR DIARY
or
INTELLIGENCE SUMMARY.
(Erase heading not required.)

Place	Date	Hour	Summary of Events and Information	Remarks and references to Appendices
WELSH FARM	12		The 4th Div. attacked this morning again at 5.25 a.m. with the rest of the XIV Corps. Line: the B.G., 12th Inf. Bde carried out the attack with a composite Bde made up of two battns of the 10th Bde (Warwicks the Seaforth) with a battn of the 11th Bde & his battn of the 12th Bde. Except for one extreme right the attack was unsuccessful. The evacuation of casualties, which were not very heavy, was done quickly. Considering the very bad condition of the ground & the length of the carries (practically clear). From as practically cleared). Owns the evacuation presently is to forward the dressing area during the morning.	78
		2.15 a.m.	Casualty from to XIV Corps	79
		2 p.	Rame Casualty report to A.A.	80
		3.50 p.	Casualty report to XIV Corps	81
		3.50 p.	do to 5th Army report Corps	
		5.45 p.	do to XIV Corps.	82

Army Form C. 2118.

WAR DIARY
or
INTELLIGENCE SUMMARY.
(Erase heading not required.)

Place	Date	Hour	Summary of Events and Information	Remarks and references to Appendices
WELSH FARM	13		11th F. Amb. (cont'd) over to the 36th Div. to proceed to PROVEN area.	G.
			Operation orders by Hqrs. for further moves the 10th Inf. Bde. proceeds to PROVEN area. The 12th Inf. Bde. being relieved in the line to-night by the 36th Div. 10th F. Amb. was relieved by 36 Div at SOLFERINO (Corps A.D. Dressing Stn) 12th F. Amb. was relieved in the line by a 36th Div F. Amb.	
		8 a.	Casualty report to XIV Corps	£3
		10 a.	Congratulatory message from Corps Commander	£4
		2.20p.	Reinf. Casualty report to Corps.	£5
		2.15p.	Casualty report to Corps	£6
		4. p.	Casualty report to XIV Corps	£7
		6.5p.	So XIV Corps.	£8
PROVEN	16		10th & 12th F. Ambs proceeded to PROVEN Div. HQ. An moved to PROVEN 12th Inf. Bde. moved to PROVEN.	

WAR DIARY
or
INTELLIGENCE SUMMARY.

(Erase heading not required.)

Army Form C. 2118.

Place	Date	Hour	Summary of Events and Information	Remarks and references to Appendices
	14" (Aug)	7.25a	Casualty report to XIV Corps	89
		3.30p	Location report to XIV Corps	90
		4.40p	French front return to XIV Corps	91
		4.40p	Casualty report to XIV Corps	92
		4.40p	Do	93
		5.p	RauC Casualty report to "A"	94
		7.50p	Casualty report to XIV Corps	95
Poperinghe	15"		Div H.Q. Br. moved to ST VAN DER BEEZEN with 10" Inf. Bde.	
			10" F. Amb. moved to ST VAN DER BEEZEN with 10" Inf. Bde.	96
			11" F. Amb. moved to POPERINGHE with 11" Inf. Bde	97
		12.30p	Location wire to DDMS XVIII Corps	98
		A.F.	Orders to F. Amb. re collection & disposal of sick & wounded	
		11.30p	Casualty report to DDMS 5th Army	H.
"	16"	12. F. Amb. moved to ST VAN DER BEEZEN with 12" Inf. Bde.	J
			Operation orders for move to all concerned.	
			Warning order to all F. Ambs.	99
		2.25p	Casualty report to DDMS XVIII Corps	100
		2.30p	Do to DMS 5th Army report XVIII Corps	

WAR DIARY
or
INTELLIGENCE SUMMARY
(Erase heading not required.)

Army Form C. 2118.

Place	Date	Hour	Summary of Events and Information	Remarks and references to Appendices
DUISANS	17th		Div. H.Q. moved to DUISANS	
		1.45p	Orders to 12 F Amb. to detail an officer & 32nd Bde. R.F.A. to replace casualty	101
		3.50p	Casualty report to XVIII Corps	102
		3.50p	2nd Dvnl. 5th Army report to XVIII Corps	103
	18th			104
	19th	10 am	Location Return to Dvnl. XVIII Corps	
			W.O.s 10, 11 & 12 F. Amb. arrived in new area by train	
"	20th		Operation orders received from G. for this Division & titles and bns. from R.A. Div.	K
			Operation orders by A.D.M.S. made to 10, 11 & 12 F Amb.	
			The A.D.M.S. 13th Div. visited H.Q. & explained the medical arrangements in the line about to be taken over by 6th Div.	
"	21st		The dressings was taken over by A.D.M.S. 12th Div. & A.D.M.S. 12th Div. L relay posts & repeated aid posts & the different from the A.D.S., &c.	
			lines of evacuation	
	22nd		Four officer reinforcements arrived from the base main posts & F Ambulances	
"			The A.D.M.S. visited H.Q. 3rd Army	
			11th F. Amb. moved to ARRAS with 11th Inf. Bde.	
"	23rd		10th F. Amb. moved to ARRAS with 10th Inf. Bde.	
		10.55a	12 F. Amb. moved to WARLUS	105
			Orders for green not to serve as mess on account of a case of diphtheria	

Army Form C. 2118.

WAR DIARY
or
INTELLIGENCE SUMMARY.
(Erase heading not required.)

Instructions regarding War Diaries and Intelligence Summaries are contained in F. S. Regs., Part II. and the Staff Manual respectively. Title pages will be prepared in manuscript.

Place	Date	Hour	Summary of Events and Information	Remarks and references to Appendices
DUISANS	24		The A.D.M.S. visited the 2/1 Essex re the outbreak of diphtheria in that unit. The D.A.D.M.C. visited 10th & 11th F. Ambs. The 11th Inf. Bde took over the left Bde front last night from the 12th Div. putting two battalions in the line. The 11th F. Amb. took over the working of the line from a F. Amb. of the 12th Div.	
ARRAS	25		Div. A.D. Ord. moved to ARRAS	
		7.20 a	Casualty report to D.D.M.S., XVIII Corps	106
		12.30 p	Lousten report to XVII Corps	107
		5 p.	Prisoners of War returns	108
		6 p.	Casualty report to XVII Corps	109
			The A.D.M.S. visited units. 10th & 11th F. Ambs. The 10th Inf. Bde took over from the right Bde of the 12th Div. last night putting one batt. in the line.	
	26	5.0 a	Casualty report to D.D.M.S. XVIIth Corps	110
		9.15 a	Battle casualties returns to XVIIth Corps	111
		4.30 p	Prisoners of War returns	112

Army Form C. 2118.

WAR DIARY
or
INTELLIGENCE SUMMARY.
(Erase heading not required.)

Place	Date	Hour	Summary of Events and Information	Remarks and references to Appendices
ARRAS.	26/5	6.20p	Casualty report to Armies XVII Corps.	113
	(con⟨td⟩ 27/5)	7.45a	Casualty report to Armies XVII Corps.	114
		7.45a	Battle Casualties Return	115
		5.0p	Prisoners from Rhine	116
		6.0p	Casualty report to Armies XVII Corps.	117
			A case of diphtheria reported in ⟨?⟩ Regt. Admit'd & Armies noted No.11 ? Ambce who re-inoculating the lines. They also inspected the A.D.S.P., relay and regimental aid posts.	118
	28/5	6.20a	Casualty report to Armies XVII Corps.	119
		6.30a	Battle Casualties Return	120
		5.30p	Prisoners from Rhine	121
		6.0p	Casualty report to Armies XVII Corps.	122
	29/5	7.30a	Battle Casualties Return	123
		7.00a	Casualty report to Armies XVII Corps.	124
		4.58p	Prisoners from Rhine	125
		6.0p	Casualty report to Armies XVII Corps.	126

Army Form C. 2118.

WAR DIARY
or
INTELLIGENCE SUMMARY.
(Erase heading not required.)

Place	Date	Hour	Summary of Events and Information	Remarks and references to Appendices
ARRAS.	29th (contd)		The 12th Inf. Bde. leaves the Division to become attached temporarily to the 51st Divn. (VI Corps)	
	30th	7.0 a	Battle casualties Return	127
		7.0 a	Casualty report to ADMS XVII Corps.	128
		5.6 p	Prisoner of War return.	129
		6.0 p	Casualty report to ADMS XVII Corps.	130
	31st	7.30 a	Battle casualties Return	131
		7.0 a	Casualty report to ADMS XVII Corps.	132
		5.0 p	Prisoner of War return	133
		6.0 p	Casualty report to ADMS XVIII Corps	134
			Three trench maps L, M + N are included showing the disposition of the various medical posts during the periods of the 4th, 9th & 12th respectively.	L M N

John Murphy
Capt RAMC
for ADMS 46th Div HQ
31/10/17

Copy No. 33

ADDENDUM NO. 1 TO R.A.M.C. ORDER DATED 25-9-17.

1. **MEDICAL POSTS: (Amendment).**

With reference to R.A.M.C. Order dated 25th. September, 1917;
In para. 5:(a), For AU BON GITE substitute PIG & WHISTLE.

      (b). Delete AU BON GITE and CORNER HOUSE.
         Add WELLINGTON HOUSE (C.5.a.1.9.)

2. **EVACUATION:**

(a). As it is anticipated that the large majority of wounded from the front line will find it impossible to go through LANGEMARCK after Zero, evacuation should be carried out along the boarded track running through U.29.b., U.29.c. and U.28.d. to CEMENT HOUSE.

    A Relay Post will be formed (four squads) at WELLINGTON HOUSE (C.5.a.1.9.). Others further forward will be formed as the line advances, probably about U.23.d. and U.24.c.

N.B.   Wounded of the 29th. Division will in all probability also find their way along this boarded track. They will be dealt with exactly in the same way as are wounded of this Division.

    Similarly walking wounded of the 29th. Division will be conveyed by Light Railway to CHEAPSIDE with the walking wounded of this Division.

    For the purpose of helping in the evacuation, the A.D.M.S. 29th. Division will place at the disposal of O.C. 11th. Field Ambulance, 2 Officers and 19 Other Ranks; and 1 Officer and 51 Other Ranks at the disposal of O.C. 12th. Field Ambulance. The former will report at MOUTON FARM, and the latter at PELISSIER FARM at 5 p.m. on Y day.

(b). By Light Railway. Three trains of two trucks have been allotted for conveyance of wounded. The latter will be loaded at HANLEY (C.3.b.1.1.) by day, and at WEEDON by night. There will be an hourly service to SOLFERINO; first train to leave HANLEY with walking wounded for CHEAPSIDE at Zero plus 2 hours.

3. **SICK:**

(a). M.O's in charge of troops occupying SOULT, WOLFE, LEIPZIG, REDAN and SARRAGOSSA Camps will report to M.O. in charge of SOLFERINO Medical Post, before 9 a.m. daily the number of lying and sitting cases to be conveyed to Sick Hut near CANADA FARM. On receipt of message from M.O. in charge of SOLFERINO giving numbers required, M.O. in charge of PELISSIER FARM will send horsed ambulance wagons or ambulance cars to collect them.

(b). M.O. in charge of troops at BRIDGE CAMP will inform the M.O. in charge of PELISSIER FARM direct.

(c). Sick from CARIBOU and ROUSSOL FARMS will be sent direct to CANADA FARM if able to walk. If they require transport, O.C. 10th. Field Ambulance (CANADA FARM) will be asked to send horsed ambulance wagons.

    On Z day, no ambulance cars will be available for sick. Horsed ambulance wagons must be used.

                                                       Colonel,
                                               A.D.M.S. 4th. Division.

Issued at 6.0 p.m.

Distribution:
- 10th. Field Ambulance. 1.
- 11th. Field Ambulance. 2.
- 12th. Field Ambulance. 3.
- 10th. Inf. Brigade. 4.
- 11th. Inf. Brigade. 5.
- 12th. Inf. Brigade. 6.
- 4th. Division "G". 7.
- 4th. Division "A". 8.
- D.M.S. Fifth Army. 9.
- D.D.M.S. XIV Corps. 10.
- A.D.M.S. 11th. Division. 11.
- A.D.M.S. 17th. Division. 12.
- A.D.M.S. 29th. Division. 13.
- All Regimental M.O's. (Series 14-30).
- C.R.E. 4th. Division. 31.
- Diary. (32.
-   (33.
- File. 34.

B.

Copy No. 34

R.A.M.C. ORDER
by
COLONEL J. CRECH. D.S.O., A.M.S.
A.D.M.S. 4th. Division.

※※※※※※※※※※※※※※※※※※※※※※※※※※※※※※※※※※※※※

Map Refs: 1/10000 Trench Maps,
LANGEMARCK & BROEMBEEK.   7th. October, 1917.

1. (a). The enemy suffered severe losses on the 4th. inst.

   (b). The attack is being resumed over a very wide front on Z day.

   (c). The XIVth. Corps is attacking with 3 Divisions:
           4th. Division on the Right.
           29th. Division in the Centre.
           Guards Division on the Left.

   (d). The 32nd. Infantry Brigade, 11th. Division is attacking on the right of the 4th. Division.

2. The Division will attack with 12th. Inf. Bde. in the Front Line, 10th. Inf. Bde. in Support and 11th. Inf. Bde. in Reserve.

3. Unless orders are issued to the contrary the advance on Z day will be continued from the Green Line to the Purple Line at Zero plus 9 hours.

4. RELIEFS. (a). The 10th. Field Ambulance will be relieved at CANADA FARM by the 51st. Field Ambulance by noon on 8th. inst., and will proceed to the Corps Advanced Dressing Station at B.22.b.9.2. near SOLFERINO FARM.

   (b). The 4th. Division Advanced Dressing Station at SOLFERINO FARM will be withdrawn by No. 11 Field Ambulance at 8 p.m. on 8th. inst. and the Post taken over by No. 10 Field Ambulance as Corps Advanced Dressing Station.

   (c). The Advanced Dressing Station at CEMENT HOUSE, and the Relay Post at PIG & WHISTLE at present run by 12th. Field Ambulance, will be handed over to the 87th. Field Ambulance, 29th. Division, on the evening of the 9th. inst.

5. MEDICAL POSTS.

   Regimental Aid Posts. LOUIS FARM. (U.24.c.40.95).
                          U.23.d.9.0.
                          PUFF HOUSE. (U.23.d.2.2.)

   These will be pushed forward as the line advances, and will be as close as possible to Battalion Headquarters.
   Change of R.A.P. to be reported as soon as practicable to Bearer Officer at LOUIS FARM by first returning stretcher bearers.
   O.C. 12th. Field Ambulance will establish a Relay Post at LOUIS FARM as soon as the R.A.P. moves forward.

                                                    Relay Posts.

- 2 -

Relay Posts.   LANGEMARCK. (U.29.a.5.6).
                PIG & WHISTLE. (U.28.b.4.2.).
                CEMENT HOUSE. (U.28.c.1.3).
                WELLINGTON HOUSE. (C.5.a.1.9).
                CORNER HOUSE. (C.2.a.8.7).

Divisional Walking Wounded Post.
                HANLEY. (U.3. central). C3 c.c.c.

Corps Advanced Dressing Station.
                SOLFERINO FARM.

Corps Advanced Walking Wounded Post.
                CHEAPSIDE.

Decauville Railhead.
                HANLEY.

6. EVACUATION.

As laid down in R.A.M.C. Order dated 25th. September, 1917, with the exception that in the event of the Light Railway not being available, cases will be taken by motor ambulance from GALLWITZ to SOLFERINO A.D.Stn. or C.C.Stns. direct.

Para. 6 (o) of the above-mentioned Order is cancelled.

N.B.

Wounded of the 4th. Division will be attended to by the 29th. Division at CEMENT HOUSE.

Evacuation of wounded of 4th. and 29th. Divisions in rear of CEMENT HOUSE will be carried out by O.C. 12th. Field Ambulance.

7.   Zero Hour will be notified later.

8.   Acknowledge.

Issued at 2 p.m.

Colonel.
A.D.M.S. 4th. Division.

DISTRIBUTION.

Copy No.
1. D.D.M.S. Fifth Army.
2. A.D.M.S. XIVth. Corps.
3. A.D.M.S. Guards Divn.
4. A.D.M.S. 11th. Divn.
5. A.D.M.S. 29th. Divn.
6. 10th. Field Ambulance.
7. 11th. Field Ambulance.
8. 12th. Field Ambulance.
9. 4th. Division "G".
10. 4th. Division "A".
11. 10th. Inf. Brigade.
12. 11th. Inf. Brigade.
13. 12th. Inf. Brigade.
14. C.R.E. 4th. Division.
15 - 31 Regtl. M.O's.
32,33. Diary.
34. File.

SECRET

Copy No. 31

AMENDMENT TO
4th. Division R.A.M.C. ORDER DATED 7th. OCTOBER, 1917.

Map Refs: 1/10000, LANGEMARCK. 8th. October, 1917.

1. In para. 5 of R.A.M.C. Order dated 7th. October, 1917:
   For the position of Walking Wounded Post shown as at
   HANLEY (U.5.central) substitute C.3.c.0.0.

2. ACKNOWLEDGE.

   Colonel,
   A.D.M.S. 4th. Division.

Copies to: D.M.S. Fifth Army.
           D.D.M.S. XIV th. Corps.
           A.D.M.S. 29th. Division.
           10th. Field Ambulance.
           11th. Field Ambulance.
           12th. Field Ambulance.
           4th. Division "G".
           4th. Division "Q".
           C.R.E. 4th. Division.
           Regimental M.O's.
           Diary.
           File.

SECRET

ADDENDUM NO. 2
to
4th. Division R.A.M.C. Order dated 7th. October, 1917.

DECAUVILLE AMBULANCE TRAIN ARRANGEMENTS.

1. An ambulance train will leave HANLEY at Zero plus 2 hours and a regular service will be maintained after this of at least one train an hour.

The Medical Officer in charge of the Loading Post at HANLEY can order the train to go up further towards WEEDON to load if he thinks it safe.

The Decauville Train can be stopped at any place on route for SOLFERINO to pick up wounded, if there is room on the train.

Colonel,
A.D.M.S. 4th. Division.

8th. October, 1917.

 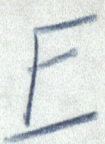

Copy No. 33.

R.A.M.C. ORDER NO. 36
by
COLONEL J. CRECH. D.S.O., A.M.S., A.D.M.S. 4th. DIVISION.
==

Map Refs: 1/10000 BROEMBEEK.   11th. October, 1917.

The attack will be resumed at a date which has been communicated to all concerned.

The XIVth. Corps is attacking with the 4th. Division on the Right, the 17th. Division in the Centre and Guards Division on the Left.

The 18th. Division is attacking on the Right of the 4th. Division.

The 12th. Infantry Brigade will carry out the attack.
Two Battalions of the 10th. Infantry Brigade will be attached to the 12th. Infantry Brigade for the attack.

The objective is the "Purple Line" which has been altered to a line about 200 yards beyond the Green Line.

1. POSITION OF MEDICAL POSTS:

   Regimental Aid Posts for Battns. in Front:-
      FERDAN HOUSE. (U.19.a.7.6).
      IMBROS HOUSE. (U.18.d.6.5).
   These will be advanced as Battn. H.Q. move forward, and their place taken as Relay Posts by O.C. 12th. Field Ambulance.

   Other Medical Posts remain as laid down in R.A.M.C. Order of 7th. October, 1917.

2. EVACUATION:

   By hand as far as LANGEMARCK Relay Post; thence if possible by Trolley to CEMENT HOUSE. Failing the Trolley Route, by hand to the PIG & WHISTLE where they will be taken over by the 17th. Division and passed on to CEMENT HOUSE. This latter post will be manned by, and under the control of 52nd. Field Ambulance, 17th. Division.
   Beyond CEMENT HOUSE the evacuation of the 4th. & 17th. Divisions will be carried out by O.C. 12th. Field Ambulance by Trolley, Light Railway and Motor Ambulance to SOLFERINO, Corps A.D.Stn.
   The walking wounded will, as far as circumstances permit, be conveyed to NUNEATON by Light Railway, and thence to CHEAPSIDE on foot.

3. DUTIES:

   O.C. 12th. Field Ambulance will detail an Officer for duty at LOUIS FARM and another at LANGEMARCK POST. The former will control the evacuation from the Regimental Aid Posts to PUFF HOUSE, and will establish Relay Posts at FERDAN HOUSE and

                                                    IMBROS.

IMBROS HOUSE as soon as those places are vacated by Regimental Medical Officers.

The Officer at LANGEMARCK will control the evacuation between PUFF HOUSE and the PIG & WHISTLE.

Close communication must be kept between the two by means of runners.

An Officer will also be detailed for duty at the Div. Walking Wounded Post. He will also supervise the evacuation by Trolley and Light Railway between CEMENT HOUSE and GALLWITZ.

4. BLANKETS & STRETCHERS:

Ample supply of Blankets and Stretchers must be kept at LANGEMARCK and LOUIS FARM, to be replenished from CEMENT HOUSE.

5. ZERO Hour will be notified later.

6. ACKNOWLEDGE.

Colonel,
Issued at 10 a.m. A.D.M.S., 4th. Division.

Copies to:
- D.M.S. Fifth Army.
- D.D.M.S. XIVth. Corps.
- A.D.M.S. 17th. Division.
- A.D.M.S. 18th. Division.
- 10th. Field Ambulance.
- 11th. Field Ambulance.
- 12th. Field Ambulance.
- 4th. Division "G".
- 4th. Division "A".
- 10th. Infantry Brigade.
- 11th. Infantry Brigade.
- 12th. Infantry Brigade.
- C.R.E. 4th. Division.
- Regimental Medical Officers.
- Diary (2).
- File.

 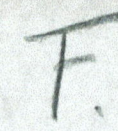

R.A.M.C. ORDER NO. 37   Copy No. 17
by
COLONEL J. GRECH, D.S.O., A.M.S., A.D.M.S. 4th. DIVISION.

Map Refs: BELGIUM, Sheet 27, 1/40000.
FRANCE & BELGIUM, Sheet 19 S.E., 1/20000.   11th. October, 1917.

* * * * * * * * * * * *

(a). The 4th. Division (Less artillery) will be relieved by the 34th. Division on the 12th, 13th and 14th. inst.

(b). All moves from and to the STRAY FARM area will take place in small parties at intervals of 100 yards.

(c). The G.O.C. 4th. Division will hand over command of the area to the G.O.C. 34th. Division at 10 a.m. on 14th. inst.

I. Field Ambulances will move to the new area according to the attached table.

II. O's.C. Field Ambulances will send by road an Advance Party to the places allotted to them in the new area, on the day before the Unit moves.
   In the case of the 11th. Field Ambulance this Advance Party should consist of 2 Officers, 10 O.Ranks, with 3 horsed ambulances and 2 motor ambulances. This party will collect and dispose of sick of the 11th. Infantry Brigade until the Field Ambulance moves in the next day.
   Rations for the complete units for the day following will be dumped in new area camps of units and will be taken over by these advance parties on the day of their arrival.

III. O.C. 12th. Field Ambulance will bring with his unit to the new area, all extra stretcher bearers from the other two Field Ambulances, and all the men lent by the Infantry Brigades to act as stretcher bearers. Orders will be issued later as to when these men will be returned to their Brigades.
   O.C. 12th. Field Ambulance will return to their units in the new area, all motor ambulances lent to him by 10th. and 11th. Field Ambulances.

IV. All details of reliefs to be arranged between O's.C. Field Ambulances concerned.
   All extra equipment to be handed over to relieving Units, receipts being obtained.

V. ACKNOWLEDGE.

Issued at 7.30 p.m.   /r. A.D.M.S. 4th. Division.   Colonel,

Copies to:-
    D.M.S. Fifth Army.
    D.D.M.S. XIVth. Corps.
    A.D.M.S. 34th. Division.
    A.D.M.S. 17th. Division.
    10th. Field Ambulance.
    11th. Field Ambulance.
    12th. Field Ambulance.
    4th. Division "G".
    4th. Division "A".
    C.R.E. 4th. Division.
    O.C. 4th. Div. Signals.
    O.C. 4th. Divisional Train.
    D.A.D.V.S. 4th. Division.
    10th. Infantry Brigade.
    11th. Infantry Brigade.
    12th. Infantry Brigade.
    Diary (2).
    File.

SECRET

TABLE OF MOVES.

Date.	Unit.	From.	To.	Route.	Relieving Unit.	Remarks.
13-10-17.	11th. Field Ambulance.	HOUTON FARM.	~~(will be notified later).~~ Pigeon Camp. F.14.a.	By Rail.	103rd. Field Ambulance.	(a). Relief to be completed by 10 a.m. on 13th. inst. (b). To entrain at FLUFFDINGHE at 1.30 p.m. (c). Relief of Tent Sub-Division at 44 C.C.S. will be arranged later.
14-10-17.	10th. Field Ambulance.	SOLFERINO.	~~ROUSBRUGGHE (N.1.d.4.1).~~ Purley Camp. (E.6.a.4.9).	By Road.	51st. Field Ambulance.	Will be relieved on morning of 14th. inst. and will move as soon as possible after completion of relief.
14-10-17.	12th. Field Ambulance.	PELISSIER, & Forward Posts.	~~PURLEY CAMP. (E.5.a.4.9).~~ Portsea Camp. (F.1.b.4.1).	By Rail.	104th. Field Ambulance.	(a). Advance parties of 104th. Fd. Amb. will arrive on night of 12/13. Relief to be complete by midnight, 13/14th.

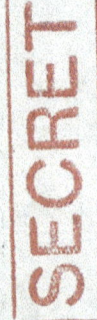

ADDENDUM TO

R.A.M.C. ORDER NO. 37 DATED 11th. OCTOBER, 1917.
****

1. The office of the A.D.M.S. 4th. Division will close at WELSH FARM at 10 a.m. on 14th. October, 1917 and re-open at the same hour at NORTH CAMP, PROVEN, (F.1.c.2.0.).

Colonel,
A.D.M.S. 4th. Division.

13th. October, 1917.

G   Copy No. 13

R.A.M.C. ORDER NO. 38
by
COLONEL J.GRECH, D.S.O., A.M.S., A.D.M.S. 4th. DIVISION.

13th. October, 1917.

The 4th. Division (less artillery) will move from the XIVth. Corps area into the XVIIIth. Corps,(POPERINGHE), area on the 15th. & 16th. October, 1917.

The 4th. Division (less artillery) will be transferred to the Third Army area by rail on the 17th. & 18th. October, under orders to be issued later.

1. Field Ambulances will move with their Brigade Groups under the orders of the B.G's. concerned.

2. The office of the A.D.M.S. will close at PROVEN at 11 a.m. on the 15th. inst., and will re-open at 6, Rue de PCTS, POPERINGHE, at the same hour.

3. ACKNOWLEDGE.

Colonel,
A.D.M.S. 4th. Division.

Issued at 6.30 p.m.

Copies to:
- 10th. Field Ambulance.
- 11th. Field Ambulance.
- 12th. Field Ambulance.
- D.M.S. Fifth Army.
- D.D.M.S. XIVth. Corps.
- D.D.M.S. XVIIIth. Corps.
- 4th. Division "G".
- 4th. Division "A".
- O.C. 4th. Div. Signals.
- C.R.E. 4th. Division.
- D.A.D.V.S. 4th. Division.
- O.C. 4th. Div. Train.
- Diary.
- File.

SECRET H Copy No. 19

R.A.M.C. ORDER NO. 39

by

COLONEL J. GRECH. D.S.O., A.M.S., A.D.M.S. 4th. DIVISION.

Map Refs: HAZEBROUCK 5a, 1/100000.
LENS 11, 1/100000.   16th. October, 1917.

The 4th. Division (Less Artillery & Pioneer Battalion) will be transferred from the XVIIIth. to the XVIIth. Corps, Third Army, and will move by rail on 17th., 18th., and 19th. inst.

Entraining Stations will be HOPOUTRE & PESELHOEK.
Detraining Stations will be ARRAS & AUBIGNY.

Brigade Groups on arrival will be located as follows:
10th. Brigade Group: DUISANS & "Y" Huts.
11th. Brigade Group: DAINVILLE, WARLUS & WANQUETIN.
12th. Brigade Group: GOUVES, MONTENESCOURT & HABARCQ.

1. Field Ambulances will move with their Brigade Groups under the orders of the B.G's. concerned.

2. On arrival in the new area, Field Ambulances will collect sick from their Brigade Group. The method of disposal of these sick will be notified later. Until such orders are received, cases requiring evacuation should be sent to the nearest C.C.Stn.

3. Orders re the move of the motor ambulances will be issued later.

4. The office of the A.D.M.S. will close at POPERINGHE at 2 p.m. on the 17th. inst. and re-open at DUISANS at the same hour.

5. ACKNOWLEDGE.

Issued at 1 p.m.

Captain,
for A.D.M.S. 4th. Division.

Copies to: D.M.S. Third Army.
D.M.S. Fifth Army.
D.D.M.S. XVIIth. Corps.
D.D.M.S. XVIIIth. Corps.
10th. Field Ambulance.   10 Inf. Bde
11th. Field Ambulance.   11 "   "
12th. Field Ambulance.   12 "   "
4th. Division "G".
4th. Division "A".
C.R.E. 4th. Division.
D.A.D.V.S. 4th. Division.
4th. Div. Signals.
4th. Divisional Train.
Diary(2).
File.

SECRET

Copy No. 17

R.A.M.C. WARNING ORDER.

by

COLONEL J. GRECH. D.S.O., A.M.S., A.D.M.S. 4th. DIVISION.

16th. October, 1917.

The 4th. Division will relieve the 12th. Division in the MONCHY Sector between the 22nd. and 25th. inst.

Probably the 10th. Infantry Brigade will be on the Right on a one battalion front and the 11th. Infantry Brigade on the Left on a two battalion front.

The Reserve Brigade will be in ARRAS.

1. The 11th. Field Ambulance will run the evacuation of cases from the Forward Area.

2. ACKNOWLEDGE.

Captain,
for A.D.M.S. 4th. Division.

Issued at 1 p.m.

Copies to:
D.M.S. Third Army.
D.M.S. Fifth Army.
D.D.M.S. XVIIth. Corps.
D.D.M.S. XVIIIth. Corps.
10th. Field Ambulance.   10th. Inf. Bde.
11th. Field Ambulance.   11th. Inf. Bde.
12th. Field Ambulance.   12th. Inf. Bde.
4th. Division "G".
4th. Division "A".
C.R.E. 4th. Division.
D.A.D.V.S. 4th. Division.
4th. Div. Signals.
4th. Divisional Train.
Diary (2).
File.

SECRET

Copy No. 15

R.A.M.C. ORDER NO. 40
by
COLONEL J. CRECH, D.S.O., A.M.S., A.D.M.S. 4th. DIVISION.

Map Ref's: LENS.11. 1/100000.
FRANCE, 51b. 1/40000.   20th. October, 1917.

* * * * * * * * * * * * *

The 4th. Division (less artillery) will relieve the 12th. Division (less artillery) in the Right Sector of the XVIIth. Corps Front.

1. Nos. 11 and 10 Field Ambulances will move to ARRAS, under the orders of G.O's.C. Brigades, on the 22nd. and 23rd. October respectively.

   (a). No. 10 Field Ambulance will take over the Main Dressing Station in the ECOLE NORMALE, ARRAS, from the 57th. Field Ambulance on the morning of the 24th. inst.
   Advance parties will be sent on 23rd. inst.

   (b). No. 11 Field Ambulance will carry out the evacuation of sick and wounded from the front line to the Main Dressing Station, and will relieve the 36th. Field Ambulance.
   Advance parties of 2 Officers and 50 Other Ranks will be sent on the night of 23rd/24th. inst., completing the relief of the Advanced Posts by the night of the 24th/25th. inst.
   Relief of all posts will be completed by 11 a.m. on the 25th. inst.
   The Headquarters of the Field Ambulance will be at TILLOY.

   (c). No. 12 Field Ambulance will take over the Corps Rest Station at PARLUS from the 58th. Field Ambulance by 10 a.m. on 23rd. inst.
   Advance parties consisting of the Second in Command and 1 Tent Sub-Division, will be sent on the 21st. inst.

   Details of relief's will be arranged between the O's.C. Field Ambulances concerned.

2. Completion of relief's will be reported by wire to the A.D.M.S. 4th. Division.

3. Field Ambulances will collect sick from their respective brigades up to the morning of the 23rd. inst, after which date No. 10 Field Ambulance will also collect the sick of the 12th. Brigade, in the HABARCQ area on the morning of the 24th., and afterwards in ARRAS.

4. The office of the A.D.M.S. will close at DUISANS at 10 a.m. on 25th. inst. and re-open in RUE DE LA PAIX, ARRAS at the same hour.

5. ACKNOWLEDGE.

Issued at 8 p.m.

Colonel,
A.D.M.S. 4th. Division.

Distribution:- Copy No. 1 to D.D.M.S. XVIIth. Corps.
- 2 - A.D.M.S. 12th. Division.
- 3 - 10th. Field Ambulance.
- 4 - 11th. Field Ambulance.
- 5 - 12th. Field Ambulance.
- 6 - 4th. Division "G".
- 7 - 4th. Division "A".
- 8 - 10th. Infantry Brigade.
- 9 - 11th. Infantry Brigade.
- 10 - 12th. Infantry Brigade.
- 11 - C.R.E. 4th. Division.
- 12 - O.C. 4th. Div. Signals.
- 13 - 4th. Divisional Train.
- 14 - D.A.D.V.S. 4th. Division.
- 15 - Diary.
- 16
- 17 - File.

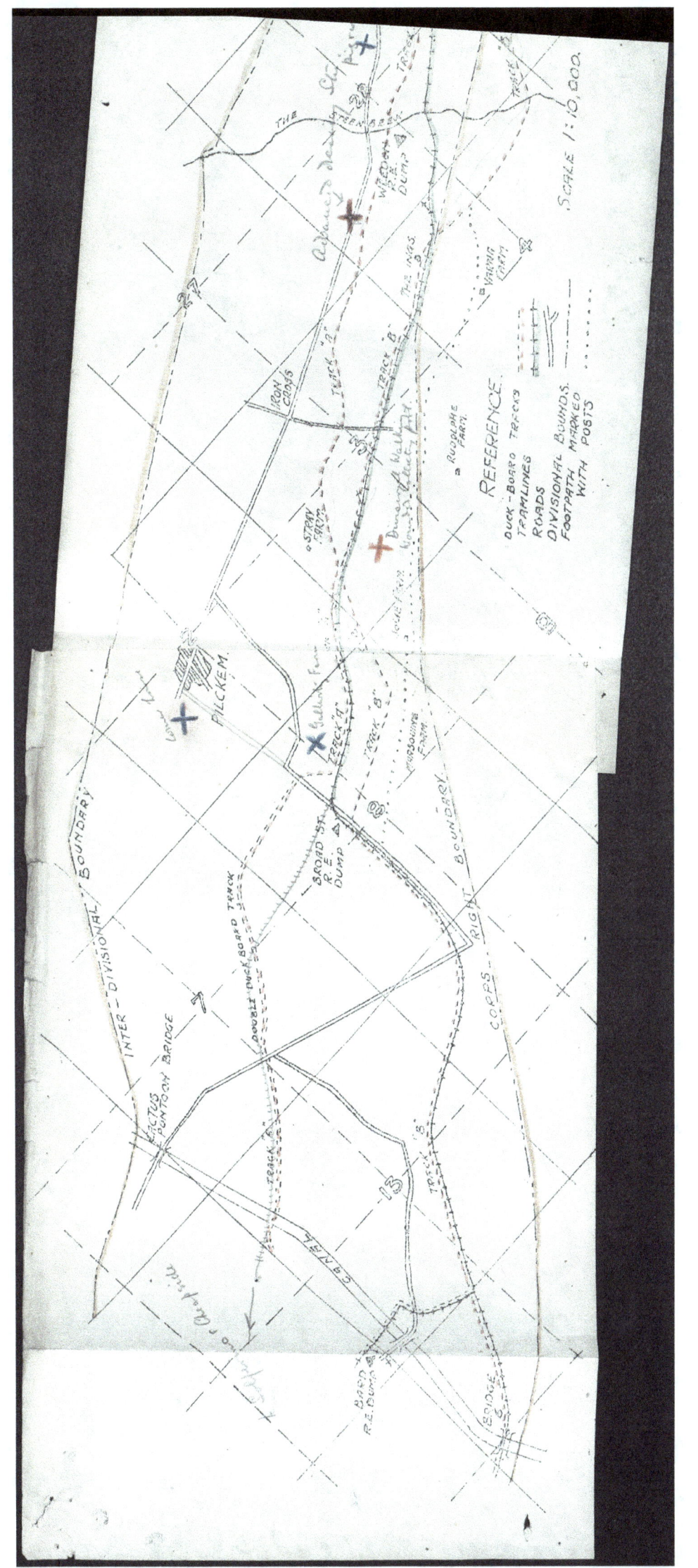

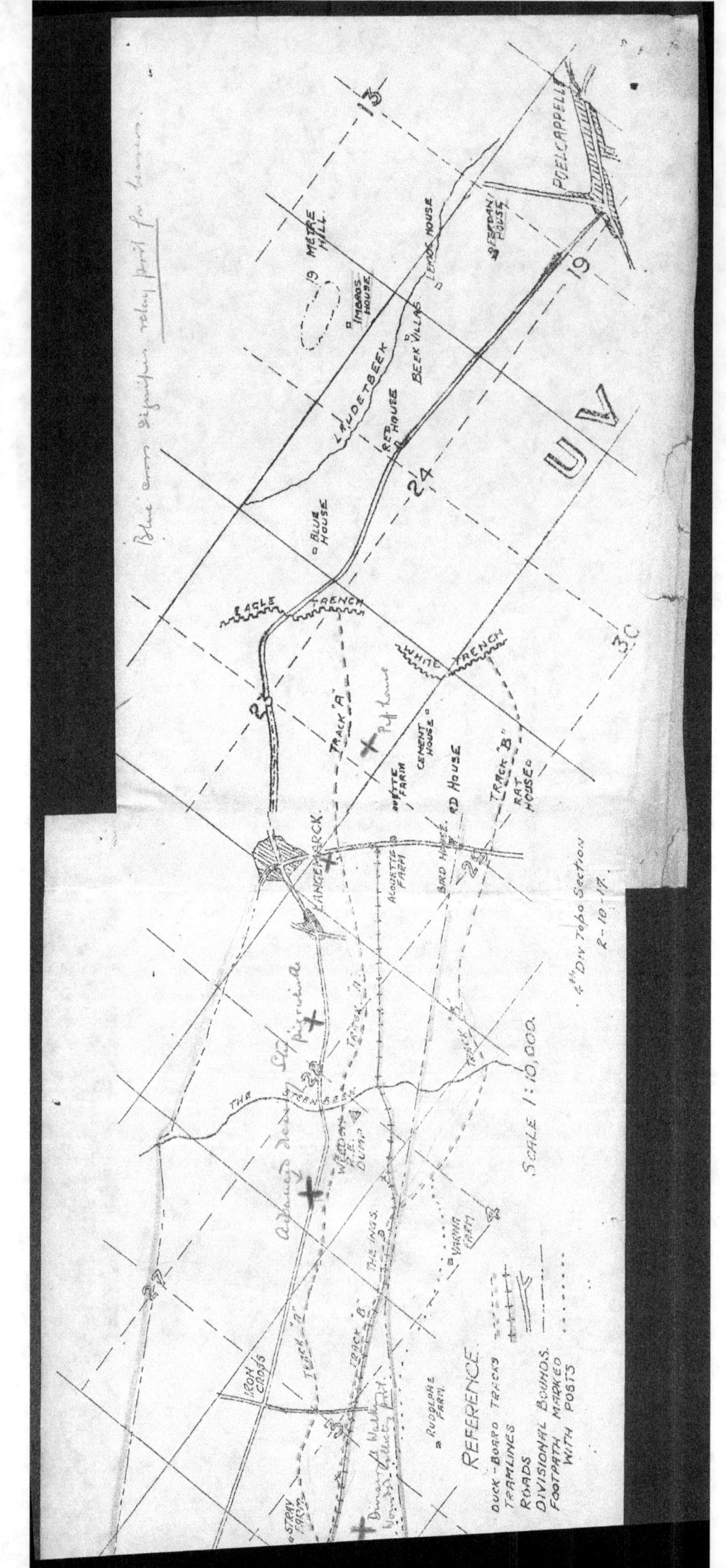

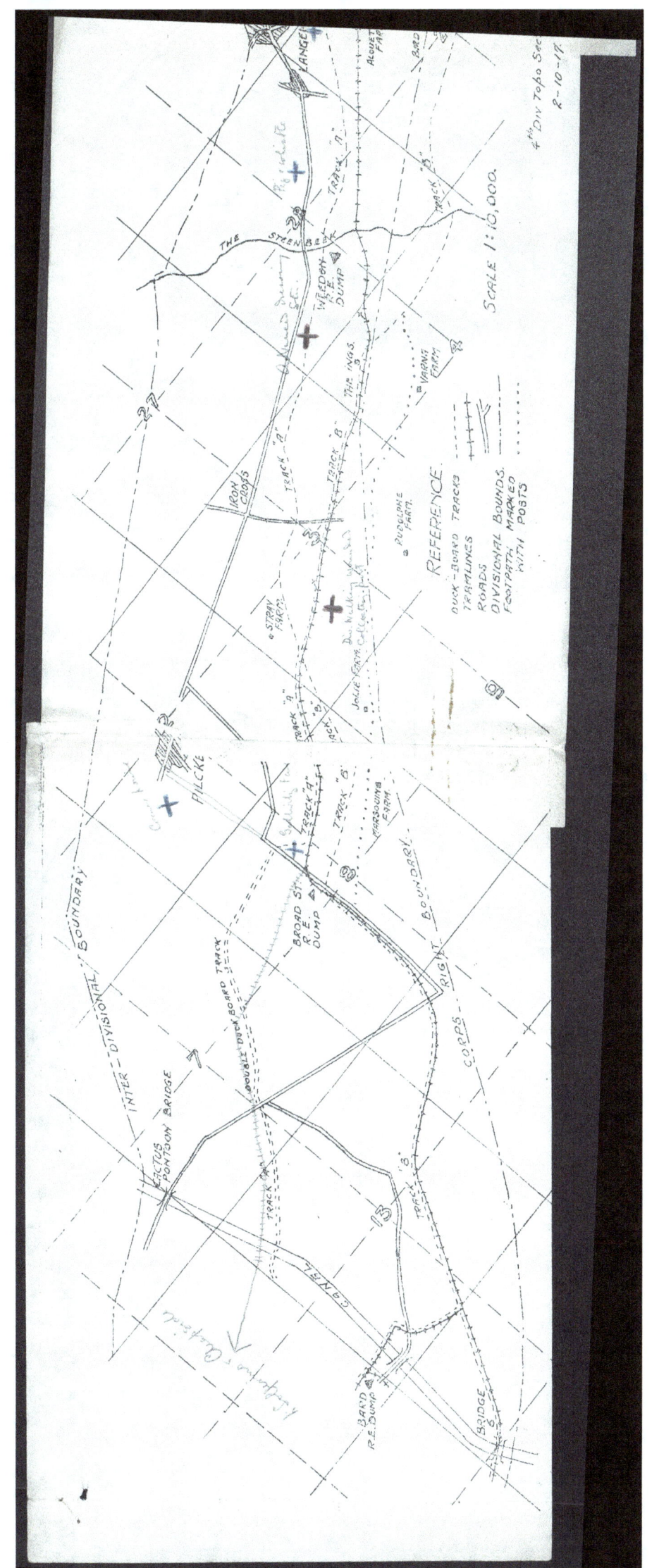

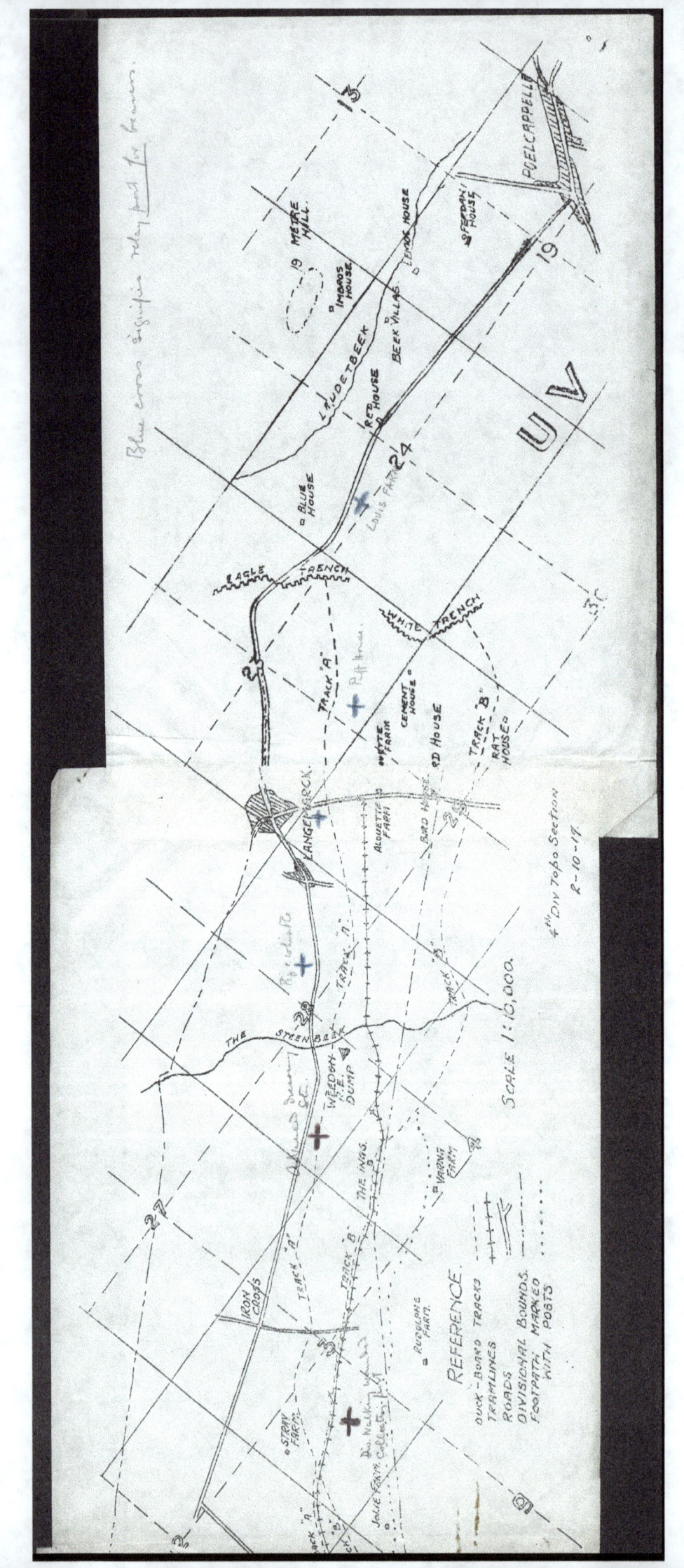

MEDICAL Army Form C. 2118.

WAR DIARY
or
INTELLIGENCE SUMMARY.
(Erase heading not required.)

Instructions regarding War Diaries and Intelligence Summaries are contained in F. S. Regs., Part II. and the Staff Manual respectively. Title pages will be prepared in manuscript.

Place	Date	Hour	Summary of Events and Information	Remarks and references to Appendices
ARRAS.	Nov 1st	7.0a	Battle casualties Renie	1.
		7.0a	Casualty report to ADMS XVII Corps.	2.
		4.0p	Prisoner of war return	3.
		6.0	Casualty report to ADMS XVII Corps.	4.
			ADMS visited No 11 Fd Amb TILLOY.	
	2nd	7.15a	Battle casualties Renie	5.
		7.15a	Casualty report to ADMS XVII Corps.	6.
			Arrangements thrown open for abandoned Fd Ambs	# 7
		4.15p	Prisoner of war return	8.
		6.0p	Casualty report to ADMS XVII Corps.	
			ADMS inspected the transport lines of 10th, 11th & 12th Bns at RONVILLE	
	3rd	7.15a	Battle casualties Renie	9.
		7.15a	Casualty report to ADMS XVII Corps	10.
		4.0p	Prisoner of war return	11.
		6.0p	Casualty report to ADMS XVII Corps	12.
			ADMS visited MONCHY & 11th Bde HQ.	

Army Form C. 2118.

WAR DIARY
or
INTELLIGENCE SUMMARY.
(Erase heading not required.)

Place	Date	Hour	Summary of Events and Information	Remarks and references to Appendices
ARRAS	3rd (cont'd)	7.0a	Army inspected the Corps Rest Stn. WARLUS. (No 12 Fd Ambce)	13
	4th	7.0a	Battle Casualties Ramé	14
		4.30p	Casualty report to Armie XVII Corps	15
		6.0p	Prisoners form return	16
		7.15a	Casualty report to Armie XVII Corps	17
	5th	7.15a	Casualty report to Armie XVII Corps	18
		6.0p	Battle Casualties Ramé	19
		6.0p	Prisoners form return	20
	6th	7.15a	Casualty report to Armie XVII Corps Army inspected Schramm Barracks	21
		7.15a	Casualty report to Armie XVII Corps	22
		5.0p	Battle Casualties Ramé	23
		6.0p	Prisoners form return	24
	7th	8.15a	Casualty report to Armie XVII Corps	25
		8.15a	Casualty report to Armie XVII Corps	26
		4p	Battle Casualties Ramé	26
			Prisoners of War return	27

Army Form C. 2118.

WAR DIARY
or
INTELLIGENCE SUMMARY.
(Erase heading not required.)

Place	Date	Hour	Summary of Events and Information	Remarks and references to Appendices
ARRAS	7 (a.s.)	6 p.	Casualty report to D.D.M.S XVII Corps	28
	8		The D.D.M.S visited SCHRAMM Barracks	29
		7. a	Battle casualties Return	30
		7. a	Casualty report to D.D.M.S. XVII Corps	81
		4.4 p.	Proposed of New return	32
		6 p.	Casualty report to D.D.M.S. XVII Corps	33
		6.30 p	Instructions to 2/1st of the cases of diphtheria	
			The D.D.M.S visited the Corps Rest Station	
			the Dep. ADS reported the Division from the YPRES area to the 21st M.Y.Rhen	
			Rpt. also reported from the same area	
	9	7. a	Battle Casualties Return	34
		7.a	Casualty report to D.D.M.S. XVII Corps	35
		5.15 p.	Proposed of New return	36
		6 p.	Casualty report to D.D.M.S. XVII Corps	37
	10		The D.D.M.S visited 11. F. Amb.	
			The 21st M. Yorks Regt arrived in ARRAS from the YPRES area.	

Army Form C. 2118.

WAR DIARY
or
INTELLIGENCE SUMMARY.
(Erase heading not required.)

Instructions regarding War Diaries and Intelligence Summaries are contained in F.S. Regs., Part II. and the Staff Manual respectively. Title pages will be prepared in manuscript.

Place	Date	Hour	Summary of Events and Information	Remarks and references to Appendices
ARRAS	10		Hd. A.D.S.S. rem'd to SCHRAMM Barracks & APPXS. to D.D.M.S. note)	
			11 J. Amb. the A.D.S.G.	38
			4ᵗʰ Div A/T completed the taking over the line from 12ᵗʰ Div. O.R. this evening	39
		7.30 a.	Battle casualties Ravine	40
		7.30 a.	Casualty report to D.D.M.S. XVII Corps	41
		5. p.	Prisoners of War return	42
		6. p.	Casualty report to D.D.M.S. XVII Corps	43
	11	3.15 a.	Battle casualties Ravine	44
		7.15 a.	Casualty report to D.D.M.S. XVII Corps	44¹
		4.15 p.	Prisoners of War return	45¹
		6. p.	Casualty report to D.D.M.S. XVII Corps XVII Corps	
	12		the Adjnt. units D.D.M.S. XVII Corps	46
		7. a.	Battle casualties Ravine	47
		7. a.	Casualty report to D.D.M.S. XVII Corps	48
		4.45 p.	Prisoners of War return	49
		6. p.	Casualty report to D.D.M.S. XVII Corps	

Army Form C. 2118.

WAR DIARY
or
INTELLIGENCE SUMMARY.
(Erase heading not required.)

Place	Date	Hour	Summary of Events and Information	Remarks and references to Appendices
ARRAS	12 (cont)		The A.D.M.S. attended a conference at XVII Corps H.Q.	50
			The A.D.M.S. with O.C. 3a Sam. Sect inspected the horse lines of the 29th & 32nd Bdes Div Artly	51
	13	7.a.	Battle Casualty Return	52
		7.a.	Casualty report to D.D.M.S. XVII Corps	53
		4.30p	Proaena of War return	
		6.p.	Casualty report to D.D.M.S. XVII Corps	
			The A.D.M.S. Divisional visited the Recreation Rm of the 10th & 11th & 13th Bns in the huts lately occupied by them	
	14	4pm	Capt. W.E. Aitken Raine (S.R.) assumed the appointment of D.A.D.M.S. 4th Division vice Capt. W. Younger Raine who proceeded to No. 5 Cmbrland Dpt S.R. for duty there in accordance with orders of D.G., M.S.	54
		7/30am	Battle casualty R.A.M.C.	55
		4/30am	Casualty report to D.D.M.S. XVII Corps	56
		10.45am	Seen 16 2nd Seaforths re inoculation of diphtheria contacts	

WAR DIARY
or
INTELLIGENCE SUMMARY

Army Form C. 2118.

Place	Date	Hour	Summary of Events and Information	Remarks and references to Appendices
ARRAS	14/Apr	4.30pm	Prisoners of War Returns	5-4 / 5
		6 pm	General report to D.D.M.S. XVII Corps	3-8
		9.45pm	Visit to 8th Seaforths re case of diphtheria	3-9
			A.D.M.S. visited XVII Corps Rest Station (12th Hornsly) at WARLUS.	
	15/Apr	7.30am	R.A.M.C. battle casualty prov.	60.
		7.30am	Battle casualty prov to DDMS XVII Corps	61
		6 p.m.	Sent do 10th inf. Bde re posting two Privates R.A.M.C. for duty with 14th R.F.C. Bde	62.
		1.15pm	Prisoners of war return to D.D.M.S. XVII Corps	63
		6 am	Battle casualty prov to D.D.M.S. XVII Corps	64
			A.D.M.S. and D.A.D.M.S. visited lilled of 1st Royal Warwicks in College Communal and killed of 4th Durham details in SCHRAMM Barracks.	
	16/Apr	7.15am	A.D.M.S. visited. D.D.M.S. XVII Corps	65
		7.15am	R.A.M.C. battle casualty prov	
		7.30am	Battle casualty prov to DDMS XVII Corps	66

Army Form C. 2118.

WAR DIARY
or
INTELLIGENCE SUMMARY.

(Erase heading not required.)

Instructions regarding War Diaries and Intelligence Summaries are contained in F.S. Regs., Part II. and the Staff Manual respectively. Title pages will be prepared in manuscript.

Place	Date	Hour	Summary of Events and Information	Remarks and references to Appendices.
ARRAS	16/April	4pm	Wire to D.D.M.S XVII Corps re prisoners of war.	67.
"	16.	6pm	Wire to O/C Sexforts re moving 8 Regimental Aid Post owing to case of diptheria having occurred among their stretcher bearers.	68. 69.
"	16.	11am	Battle casualty return D.O.M.S XVII Corps.	
"	16.		A.D.M.S. and D.A.D.M.S. visited 4th Divl. Signal Coys 4 Divisional Ammn Column, and 11th Field Ambulance.	A
"	"	7pm	Reply by R.A.M.C. order No 42. re posting of Medical Officers and personnel for temporary duty with No 20 and 29 C.C.S's	70. 71. 72. 73.
"	17.	4.35am	R.A.M.C. casualty return.	
"	"	11.15am	Battle casualty return to D.O.M.S XVII Corps	
"	"	4.10pm	Promotion of staff officer. A.D.M.S XVII Corps.	
"	"	6pm	Battle casualty return to D.O.M.S XVII C'ps	
"	"		A.D.M.S & D.A.D.M.S visited 12 & 13 Field Ambulance (XVII Corps C.S. Station) WARLUS.	

2353 Wt. W.3541/1434 700,000 5/15 D. D. & L.   A.D.S.S./Forms/C. 2118.

Army Form C. 2118.

WAR DIARY
or
INTELLIGENCE SUMMARY.
(Erase heading not required.)

Place	Date	Hour	Summary of Events and Information	Remarks and references to Appendices
ARRAS	18/Aug/	1 a.m.	R.A.M.C. Casualty wire.	74/45
		7.30 a.m	Battle casualty wire to D.D.M.S. XVII Corps	
		4 p.m	Sent to 3A Sanitary Section to inspect a lot (officers) at Duisans	46
			in BOIS-DES-BOEUFS Camp occupied by 2nd Seaforths	
		4.30 p.m	Prisoners of war return	74
		6 p.m	Battle casualty wire to D.D.M.S. XVII Corps	75
			ADMS & DADMS visited 2nd Seaforths in BOIS-DES-BOEUFS Camp	49
			and arrived re isolation of diphtheria contacts and inspected some previous methods for the internal	
			affects. Also 10% Fd Amb and inspected the whole of their billets inc. "ECOLE NORMALE"	
	19/Aug/-	1 a.m.	R.A.M.C. battle casualty wire	
		4 a.m	Battle casualty wire to D.D.M.S. XVII Corps	50
		11.33 a.m	Visited 4th Div. G. Horsfield Bn & 10th Ay Bde rs rec of RAP	81
			D 13.b.75 after horrowgh interview on arrival	
		4.10 p.m	Prisoners of war return to D.D.M.S. XVII Corps	82
		6 p.m	Battle Casualty wire to D.D.M.S. XVII Corps	83
			DADMS visited 10 Bde H Qrs and 29th Bde R.F.A.	

WAR DIARY or INTELLIGENCE SUMMARY

Army Form C. 2118.

Place	Date	Hour	Summary of Events and Information	Remarks and references to Appendices
ARRAS.	20/April	9.10am	R.A.M.C. battle casualty return	84
"	"	11.10am	Battle casualty return to D.D.M.S. XVII Corps	85
"	"	5.15pm	Return of mon then Battle casualty return	86
"	"	6 pm	A.D.M.S. visited 10 Fd Bde Headquarters, and 11 Fd Bde at TILLOY-LES-MAFFLAINES.	87
"	21/April	9.10am	R.A.M.C. battle casualty return	88
"	"	11.10am	Battle casualty return	89
"	"	4.15pm	Return of war men to D.D.M.S XVII Corps	90
"	"	6 pm	Battle casualty return	91
"			D.A.D.M.S. visited main army station (10th Fd Amb). Billets in College Communal and Schramm barracks when hygienic improvements as suggested by the A.D.M.S. are being executed. A.D.M.S. visited 12th Fd. Amb. at WARLUS.	
"	22/April	8.30am	R.A.M.C. battle casualty return	92

WAR DIARY or INTELLIGENCE SUMMARY

Army Form C. 2118.

Place	Date	Hour	Summary of Events and Information	Remarks and references to Appendices
ARRAS	Contd 22/4/17	8.55am	Battle casualty returns to D.D.M.S. XVII Corps	93
"		4 pm	Prisoners of war went to D.D.M.S XVII Corps	94
"		6 pm	Battle casualty returns to D.M.S expected Riwaki supply to divisional troops at ACHICOURT.	95
"	23/4/17	7.30 am	R.A.M.C Battle casualty return	96
"		1.30 am	Battle casualty went to D.D.M.S XVII Corps	97
"		4 pm	Prisoners of war went to D.D.M.S XVII Corps	98
"		6 pm	Battle casualty return to D.D.M.S XVII Corps	99
"			D.A.D.M.S visited 12th Inf Base and all trains arrived by Rev Y 11 th ant and arrived aveing Station	
"	24/4/17	11 am	A.D.M.S visited 12 Stationary Hospital and 19 C.C.S.	100
"		4 pm	R.A.M.C Battle casualty war	101
"			Battle casualty war	
"		4 pm	Prisoners of war	102
"		4.30 pm	Men to OC 19CCS to instruct 1st Lieut MAX MULLER A.O.C USA European Army, hon'y Lieut Kirr, how in rept to D.D.M.S study	103

ETABLES

Army Form C. 2118.

WAR DIARY
or
INTELLIGENCE SUMMARY.
(Erase heading not required.)

Instructions regarding War Diaries and Intelligence Summaries are contained in F. S. Regs., Part II. and the Staff Manual respectively. Title pages will be prepared in manuscript.

Place	Date	Hour	Summary of Events and Information	Remarks and references to Appendices
ARRAS	24/10/17	4.30 pm	June 16 XVII Corps reported 1st Army x Capt G.A.HARVEY R.A.M.C attached R Lan R wounded	104.
"	"	5pm	Recd K' 10th Fd Aml re relief of Capt G.A.HARVEY R.A.M.C wounded	105.
"	"	6pm	" K' 4th Div "A" re Capt G.A.HARVEY R.A.M.C wounded	106.
"	"	6pm	Battle casualty nurse	107.
"			Capt E.T. TATLOW R.A.M.C (T.F) reported for duty and posted to 12 Fd Aml.	
"			D.A.D.M.S accompanied O/c 11 Fd A y O/c 3A Sanitary section visited night sector trenches occupied by 10 Inf Bde y BOIS-DES-BOEUFS camp	
"			31 O.R. R.A.M.C reinforcements arrived for duty and posted as follows LZ to 10 Fd Aml 3, 4 to 11 " Fd Aml and 9, 10, 12 " Fd Aml	
"			A.D.M.S. visited XVII Corps Rest Station (17th Aml) and 19 C.C.S.	108.
"	25/10/17	11 am	R.A.M.C horse casualty	
"		11.45 am	Battle casualty nurse	109.

Army Form C. 2118.

WAR DIARY
or
INTELLIGENCE SUMMARY.
(Erase heading not required.)

Instructions regarding War Diaries and Intelligence Summaries are contained in F.S. Regs., Part II. and the Staff Manual respectively. Title pages will be prepared in manuscript.

Place	Date	Hour	Summary of Events and Information	Remarks and references to Appendices
ARRAS.	26 Jun	4.30pm	Prisoner of war	110
"	"	6 pm	Battle casualty returns	111
"	"	6 pm	Operation orders by Lt. Col. Perel. A.D.M.S.	B
"	"		A.D.M.S. and D.A.D.M.S. visited 12 Fd. Amb. MARIUS. A.D.M.S. visited 19 C.C.S.	
"	"		For M.O.R.C. U.S.A. officers reinforcements arrived. Posted as follows. 1st Lts C.D. BARKLEY & S.H. ADAMS to 10th Fd. amb. 1st Lts J.L. BEACH & T.S. MOWRY to 11th Fd. amb. 1st Lt J.E. AVELLONE to 12th Fd Amb.	112 113
"	26 Jun	7:30 am	R.A.M.C. battle casualty returns to D.D.M.S. XVII Corps	
"	"	7:30 am	Battle casualty returns	
"	"	9:30am	Sent 1st Lt 10th Fd. Amb. to relief an M.O. for temporary duty with 2nd Seaforths, replacing Capt G.H. BROWN. R.A.M.C. (T.C.) sick	114
"	"	4 pm	Prisoner of war returns	115
"	"	6 pm	Battle casualty returns	116
"	"		A.D.M.S. attended conference of A.D.M.Ss. at D.D.M.S. Office at 2.30 P.M.	

Army Form C. 2118.

WAR DIARY
or
INTELLIGENCE SUMMARY.
(Erase heading not required.)

Instructions regarding War Diaries and Intelligence Summaries are contained in F. S. Regs., Part II. and the Staff Manual respectively. Title pages will be prepared in manuscript.

Place	Date	Hour	Summary of Events and Information	Remarks and references to Appendices
ARRAS	27th	4.45am	R.A.M.C. intake casualty clear	118
		7.45am	Battle casualty rec'd to D.D.M.S. XVII Corps	119
		4pm	Enemy guns	
		6pm	Battle casualty rec'd	120
	"		A.D.M.S. held a conference of field ambulance commanders. A.D.M.S. & D A.D.M.S. visited 12 Fd Amb. and 10th Fd Amb (main Dressing Station).	
	28th	7.45am	R.A.M.C. battle casualty rec'd	121
		7.45am	Battle casualty rec'd	122
		4.10pm	Enemy's war sum	123
		6pm	Battle casualty sum	124
	"		A.D.M.S. interviewed O/C M.F.P. and visited his hospitals.	
			R.A.M.C. Operation order No. 44 conveyed on relief of 61st Division by 4 Div & 15 Div.	C

Army Form C. 2118.

WAR DIARY
or
INTELLIGENCE SUMMARY.
(Erase heading not required.)

Instructions regarding War Diaries and Intelligence Summaries are contained in F.S. Regs., Part II. and the Staff Manual respectively. Title pages will be prepared in manuscript.

Place	Date	Hour	Summary of Events and Information	Remarks and references to Appendices
ARRAS	29/11	8am	R.A.M.C. Battle Casualty	125
"	"	8am	Battle Casualty nom. roll D.D.M.S XVII Corps	126
"	"	4.10pm	Prisoners of War nom. roll	127
"	"	6pm	Battle casualty nom. roll	128
"	"		D.A.D.M.S. visited A.D.S. and 11th Fd. Amb. and 10th Fd. Amb.	
"	30/11	1/50am	R.A.M.C. Battle Casualty nom. roll D.D.M.S XVII Corps	129
"	"	1/50am	Battle casualty nom. roll D.D.M.S XVIII Corps	130
"	"	4.30pm	Prisoners of War nom. roll	131
"	"	6pm	Battle casualty nom. roll	132
"	"		A.D.M.S or D.A.D.M.S visited 12 Fd Amb (Corps Rest Station WARLUS) S.C.C.S. and D.D.M.S XVII Corps	

J G M Critchley
Capt R.A.M.C.
for O.C. A.D.M.S
4th Division

A5834 Wt.W4973/M687 750,000 8/16 D. D. & L. Ltd. Forms/C.2118/13.

Copy No. 9

R.A.M.C. ORDER NO. 42,

by

COLONEL J.GRECH, D.S.O., A.M.S., A.D.M.S. 4th. DIVISION.

16th. November, 1917.

4 Medical Officers, 4 N.C.O's. and 32 men, (including 5 nursing orderlies), will proceed to 20 and 29 Casualty Clearing Stations as follows:-

(a). 3 Medical Officers.   To 20 C.C.Stn.
     3 N.C.O's.   BOISLEUX.
     24 men (including 4 nursing orderlies)   (Map 51b, M.33.c.)

(b). 1 Medical Officer.   To 29 C.C.S.
     1 N.C.O.   GREVILLERS.
     8 men (including 1 nursing orderly)   (Map 57c, G.30)

Parties to arrive on 18th. inst.

O.C. No. 12 Field Ambulance will detail Capt. WARWICK, R.A.M.C. to assume Medical Charge of 1st. R.Warwick Regt., forthwith, vice 1/Lt. LITTLE, M.O.R.C.U.S.A., who will join No. 12 Field Ambulance on relief.
He will detail 1/Lt. HAYS, M.O.R.C.U.S.A., and 1/Lt. LITTLE, 2 N.C.O's. and 12 men (including 2 nursing orderlies), to proceed to 20 C.C.Stn., BOISLEUX, as in (a) for temporary duty.

O.C. No. 10 Field Ambulance will recall Lieut. NELSON, R.A.M.C., from the Depot Battalion forthwith, and transfer him to No. 11 Field Ambulance as a temporary measure.
He will detail 1 N.C.O. and 12 men (including 2 nursing orderlies) to proceed to BOISLEUX as in (a) for temporary duty.

O.C. No. 11 Field Ambulance will detail 1/Lt. JOYCE, M.O.R.C.U.S.A., to proceed to No. 10 Field Ambulance and join the party going to BOISLEUX; also 1 N.C.O. and 8 men (including 1 nursing orderly) to proceed to 29 C.C.Stn., GREVILLERS as in (b) above, for temporary duty.

The Medical Officer mentioned in (b), above, will be 1/Lt. MARXMILLER, M.O.R.C.U.S.A. (10th. Field Ambulance), who is at present doing temporary duty at 29 C.C.Stn.

Captain ELLIOTT and Lieutenant GAMBLE, R.A.M.C. will report at the Corps Rest Station on the morning of the 18th. inst., under orders of the D.D.M.S. XVIIth. Corps.

Field Ambulances will use their own ambulance cars for sending the parties mentioned above.

Completion of moves to be wired to the A.D.M.S., 4th. Division.

J.G.McCutcheon
Captain,
for A.D.M.S. 4th. Division.

Issued at 8 p.m.

Distribution:-

1. D.D.M.S. XVII Corps.
2. 10th. Field Ambulance.
3. 11th. Field Ambulance.
4. 12th. Field Ambulance.
5. 10th. Infantry Brigade.
6. 4th. Division "G".
7. 4th. Division "A".
8,9. Diary.
10. File.

SECRET

Copy No. 30

R.A.M.C. ORDER No. 43

by

COLONEL J. GRECH, D.S.O., A.M.S., A.D.M.S. 4th. DIVISION.

Map Refs: Sheet 51b. 1/40000.   25th. November, 1917.

****

1. **No. 11 Field Ambulance.**

On the enemy retiring to the DROCOURT-QUEANT Line, or intermediate position, and on receiving orders from the A.D.M.S. to move forward:

(a).   O.C. No. 11 Field Ambulance will send a party of 1 Officer and 15 Other Ranks to occupy the R.A.P. near CRATER SUBWAY, (O.13.b.5.9.) which will be called the "Forward Advanced Dressing Station".

(b).   He will withdraw all R.A.M.C. personnel from all Medical Posts N. of GORDON AVENUE with the exception of 9 men per battalion in the line, who will follow the advancing battalions as far as the new Regimental Aid Posts, where they will remain for duty between the R.A.P's. and 1st. Relay Posts.

(c).   He will send the requisite equipment for opening an A.D.Stn., by pack-horses to LA BERGERE. These will wait there until they are ordered to proceed forward.

(d).   He will send 1 Officer, 3 N.C.O's. and 20 Men behind the advancing troops, in order to reconnoitre and occupy a suitable position in the neighbourhood of O.9.b. This place is to be chosen with a view to establishing an A.D.Stn. as soon as practicable.

He will instruct the Officer to leave 1 N.C.O. and 4 Men to look after the place chosen, and then proceed with the remainder of the party to BOIRY, where he will establish a Relay Post of 1 N.C.O. and 8 Men about O.5. central, and another Relay Post of a similar number, about O.4.b.9.5. The Officer will then return to O.9.b. and take charge of the Post.

(e).   As soon as the O.C. No. 11 Field Ambulance has ascertained by personal reconnaissance that the Post at O.9.b. is fit to be used as an A.D.Stn., he will order the pack-horses from LA BERGERE and the M.O. and 8 Other Ranks from the Forward Advanced Dressing Station, to proceed to the new A.D.Stn.

The Forward A.D.Stn. will then become a Loading Post at the motor ambulance terminus.

N.B.

The A.D.Stn. at O.9.b. will only be established on the first day if conditions are favourable. If no suitable place is discovered near the road, a Relay Post with 1 M.O. in charge and sufficient personnel and equipment will be formed instead, and cases will be brought down by hand to the Forward A.D.Stn., (O.13.b.5.9)

Efforts will be made to open an A.D.Stn. forward the next day after further reconnoitring.

(f).   The Headquarters of No. 11 Field Ambulance and the remainder of the personnel will move to LA BERGERE.

(g).   The Transport will remain at TILLOY until further orders.

(h).   The various Medical Posts will be subsequently reinforced at the discretion of O.C. No. 11 Field Ambulance.

In the event of the enemy retiring to an intermediate position, the place chosen for an A.D.Stn. at O.9.3. will be a Relay Post, and the R.A.P. near CRATER SUBWAY will be the A.D.Stn.

2. Regimental Aid Posts.

These will be established in suitable places, probably in front of BOIRY.

Regimental M.O's will inform the O.C. No. 11 Field Ambulance by runner of their exact locality as soon as they have established themselves in their new Aid Posts, and they will at once get in touch with the first Relay Posts.

3. Evacuation.

Will be carried out by hand or wheeled stretcher to the A.D.Stn. (About O.9.b.); thence by hand or wheeled stretcher to the Loading Post at O.13.b.5.9.; thence by motor ambulance to ECOLE NORMALE, ARRAS; and by M.A.C. to C.C.Stn.

The light railway can also be used between GORDON AVENUE and LA BERGERE.

Motor ambulances will move up to the new A.D.Stn. as soon as the BOIRY road becomes practicable for transport.

4. Main Dressing Station.

No. 10 Field Ambulance, at ECOLE NORMALE.

5. Corps Rest Station.

No. 12 Field Ambulance, at WARLUS.

6. Casualty Clearing Stations.

For wounded: No. 19 C.C.Stn.) AGNEZ LES DUISANS.
For sick   : No. 8 C.C.Stn.)

7. The office of the A.D.M.S. will remain at 1, Place de la Prefecture, ARRAS.

8.   A C K N O W L E D G E.

Colonel,
A.D.M.S. 4th. Division.

Issued at 6.0 p.m.

Copies to:-   D.M.S. Third Army.
D.D.M.S. XVIIth. Corps.
10th. Field Ambulance.
11th. Field Ambulance.
12th. Field Ambulance.
4th. Division "G".
4th. Division "A".
10th. Infantry Brigade.
11th. Infantry Brigade.
12th. Infantry Brigade.
4th. Div. Signals.
Regimental M.O's.
Diary.
File.

SECRET

Copy No. 32

R.A.M.C. ORDER NO. 44,
by
COLONEL J. GRECH. D.S.O., A.M.S., A.D.M.S. 4th. DIVISION.

Map Refs: Sheet 51b. 1/40000.   28th. November, 1917.

* *

The following reliefs will be carried out:-

(a). 27th/28th.   10th. Inf. Bde. will extend Northwards and will relieve the Right Battalion of the 11th. Inf. Bde. which will move to Camp at BOIS DES BOEUFS.

(b). 28th.   10th. Inf. Bde. will again extend its left as far as CASE ALLEY (O.2.d.45.65) inclusive.

(c). 28th.   One Battalion 11th. Inf. Bde. to WILDERNESS CAMP. One Battalion 10th. Inf. Bde. from ARRAS to BOIS DES BOEUFS.

(d). 28th/29th.   11th. Inf. Bde. will extend its left to SCABBARD Trench exclusive, relieving the 44th. Inf. Bde. of 15th. Division.

On completion of the above reliefs the Division will be disposed as follows:-

Right Front Brigade.   2 Bns. front line.
                        1 Bn. support.
                        1 Bn. BOIS DES BOEUFS.

Left Front Brigade.   2 Bns. front line.
                        1 Bn. support.
                        1 Bn. WILDERNESS CAMP.

Reserve Brigade.   ARRAS.

1.   The disposition of Medical Posts will be as follows:-

   Regimental Aid Posts:

      Left Brigade:-
         (a). Right Battalion. SHRAPNELL TRENCH. (O.2.c.2.2.)
         (b). Left Battalion.   CURB SWITCH RESERVE.(I.31.c.3.3.)

      Right Brigade:-
         (a). Right Battalion. Near CRATER SUBWAY.(O.13.b.2.8.)
         (b). Left Battalion.   PICK CAVE.

   Relay Posts:
         (a). THE MOUND. (N.6.d.4.5.)
         (b). EAST TRENCH. (O.1.d.5.2.)

   Advanced Dressing Station:
         LA BERGERE.

Other Posts remain as before.

2. Evacuation: From R.A.P's.(PICK CAVE & O.2.c.2.2.) along VINE AVENUE, FORK RESERVE, PICK AVENUE, to LA BERGERE.

From O.13.b.2.8. along SPADE RESERVE, PICK AVENUE, or possibly along CAMBRAI ROAD, to LA BERGERE.

From CURB SWITCH RESERVE along tracks behind MONCHY to MOUND in N.6.d.4.5., to LA BERGERE.
Other route; ORCHARD RESERVE, EAST RESERVE, VINE AVENUE, or FORK RESERVE, PICK AVENUE.

3. O.C. No. 11 Field Ambulance will re-open the MOUND, (N.6.d.4.5.) as a Relay Post, and also attach two bearer squads to the R.A.P. in CURB SWITCH RESERVE.
He will also send one squad to occupy Post at H.36.c.1.7.

4. Times and details of relief will be arranged between officers concerned.

5. Office of A.D.M.S. remains at 1 Place de la Prefecture.

6. A C K N O W L E D G E.

Colonel,
A.D.M.S. 4th. Division.

Issued at 1 p.m.

Copies to:
D.M.S. Third Army.
D.D.M.S. XVIIth. Corps.
10th. Field Ambulance.
11th. Field Ambulance.
12th. Field Ambulance.
ALL Regimental M.O's.
4th. Division "G".
4th. Division "A".
10th. Inf. Bde.
11th. Inf. Bde.
12th. Inf. Bde.
C.R.E. 4th. Division.
4th. Div. Signals.
A.D.M.S. 15th. Division.
Diary(2).
File.

Army Form C. 2118.

WAR DIARY
or
INTELLIGENCE SUMMARY.
(Erase heading not required.)

Instructions regarding War Diaries and Intelligence Summaries are contained in F. S. Regs., Part II. and the Staff Manual respectively. Title pages will be prepared in manuscript.

Place	Date	Hour	Summary of Events and Information	Remarks and references to Appendices
ARRAS	1917 Dec.	7:30 am	R.A.M.C. Baths conveyed here to D.D.M.S. XVIIth Corps	1
"	"	7:30 am	Battle casualty van to D.D.M.S. XVIIth Corps	2
"	"	8:30 pm	Rumour B. war son to D.C. in S XVIIth Corps	3
"	"	6 pm	Battle casualty van	4
"	"		A.D.M.S. prepared dumped & depot totalizer 10 7st Cas.	A
"	"	8:30 pm	Rotterdam h. 1 to R.A.M.C. stores in action to 44 Divn.	5
"	2nd Dec.	7:30 am	R.A.M.C. Battle casualty van to D.D.M.S. XVIIth Corps	6
"	"	11 am	Battle trench son to Dtons XVIIth Cas.	
"	"	3 pm	" " to 10 s. the Gns the adjutant a k. off duty at dept both	7
"	"	4 pm	Prisoners B. war son	
"	"		T D.M.S. and D.A.D.M.S. waited in 7 A.dmt (Corps) Red station WARLUS) Carriacks	8
"	"		Out D.M.S. wales S.C. H. R.A.M.C.	
"	3 Dec.	7.30am	Battle casualty son	9
"	"	7:30 am	R.A.M.C. Battle casualty van to D.D.M.S. XVIIth Corps	10
"	"	4 pm	Rumour B. war son	11
"	"	6 pm	Battle casualty van to D.D.M.S. XVIIth Corps	12
			D.A.D.M.S. marked COLLEGE COMMUNAL	

Army Form C. 2118.

WAR DIARY
or
INTELLIGENCE SUMMARY.
(Erase heading not required.)

Place	Date	Hour	Summary of Events and Information	Remarks and references to Appendices
ARRAS	4 Dec	11 am	R.A.M.C. Battle casualty return 6 – D.D.M.S. XVII Corps	13
"	"	4 pm	Battle casualty return	14
"	"	6.5 pm	Progress of front line	15
"	"	6 pm	Battle casualty return	16
"	5 Dec	1 am	A.D.M.S. inspected ADSs & ARPs of all units forward Inspection of troops and morale extremely satisfactory	
"	"	9 am	A.D.M.S. Battle casualty return to D.D.M.S. XVII Corps	17
"	"	9/11 am	Battle casualty return	18
"	"	4.45 pm	Progress of front line	19
"	"	6 pm	Battle casualty return to D.D.M.S. XVII Corps	20

A.D.M.S. visits 10th Fd Amb Main dressing station etc
NORVALE.
D.A.D.M.S. visits Advance dressing station and all RAPs of front & support line — also relay posts of Nth Ash Rearparties

About 70 gas (shell) cases occurred, including one M.O., Matho from gas bombardment by trench mortars and shells by the Enemy at 1 am – See App. C

Army Form C. 2118.

WAR DIARY
or
INTELLIGENCE SUMMARY.

(Erase heading not required.)

Instructions regarding War Diaries and Intelligence Summaries are contained in F.S. Regs., Part II. and the Staff Manual respectively. Title pages will be prepared in manuscript.

Place	Date	Hour	Summary of Events and Information	Remarks and references to Appendices
ARRAS	6 Dec	10am	R.A.M.C. staff personnel met to D.D.M.S. XVIII Corps	21
"	"	10.30am	Border casualty visits to D.D.M.S. XVII Corps	22
"	"	11am	Conf. with A.D. to instruct a M.O. for duty with 3rd Bde.	23
"	"	4pm	referring Lt. A.J. HENDERSON R.A.M.C. general	24
"	"	6pm	Record of evacuations	25
"	"	9pm	Battle casualty visits	26
"	"		R.A.M.C. report — visits to 4 Div A.D.M.S. and D.A.D.M.S. visited 10 Fd. Amb. S.A. Sanitary Section, 12 Fd. Amb. (Corps rest station)	27
"	7 Dec	10am	R.A.M.C. battle casualty report	28
"	"	11am	Battle casualty report	29
"	"	4.30pm	Prisoners of war — D.D.M.S. XVIII Corps	30
"	"	6pm	Battle casualty report A.D.M.S. & P.A.D.M.S. visits 10 Fd. Amb. and 5 C.C.S. gone	
"	Ypres	noon	R.A.M.C. battle casualty — D.D.M.S. XVIII Corps	31
"	"		Battle casualty report	32

WAR DIARY
or
INTELLIGENCE SUMMARY.

Army Form C. 2118.

Place	Date	Hour	Summary of Events and Information	Remarks and references to Appendices
ARRAS	8 Dec 1916	4 pm	Prisoners of war sent to D.D.M.S. XVIII Corps	33
		6 pm	Battle casualty return to D.D.M.S. XVIII Corps	34
	9 Dec	9 am	D.A.D.M.S. visited SCHRAMM Barracks	
			R.A.M.C. nominal casualty return to D.D.M.S. XVIII Corps	35
		10 am	Battle casualty return	36
		11.30 am	Prisoners of war return	37
		6 pm	Battle casualty return	38
		"	Visit to O.C. 2nd Seaforths re case of diphtheria	29
			D.A.D.M.S. visited billets of personnel from ACHICOURT	
			R.A.M.C. Lieut. casualty return to D.D.M.S. XVIII Corps	40
	10 Dec	9 am	Battle casualty return	41
	"	"	Visit to O/C 2nd Seaforths re precaution	
	"	12.15 pm	R. anthrax serum sent to 2nd Seaforths	42
		4 pm	Prisoners of war return to D.D.M.S. XVIII Corps	43

Army Form C. 2118.

WAR DIARY
or
INTELLIGENCE SUMMARY.
(Erase heading not required.)

Instructions regarding War Diaries and Intelligence Summaries are contained in F.S. Regs., Part II. and the Staff Manual respectively. Title pages will be prepared in manuscript.

Place	Date	Hour	Summary of Events and Information	Remarks and references to Appendices
ARRAS	10th Dec 1917	6.15pm	Battle casualties sent to D.D.M.S. XVII Corps	44
			Hon Lt Col Gn H.S. WISHART (T.C.) arrived on the S. of	
			Hon Col & Gn A MORRISON 11th Fd Ambulance.	
			D.A.D.M.S. visited 10th Fd Amb (Main Dressing Station-ECOIVRES	45
			NORMALE) and 11 Fd Amb (A.D.S.) and 8 - C.C.S. June	46
	11th Dec	9am	R Amb After Convoys went to D.D.M.S. XVII Corps	4/7
	"	9am	Battle convoys run	4/5
	"	6.10pm	Running of war time	
	"	6pm	Battle convoys run	
			Supplementary medical arrangements for reinforcements of	
			Stretcher Bearers in case of necessity.	B
			D.A.D.M.S. visited 3 Canadian Stat. Hosp. (Officers hospital)	
			LUCHEUX.	June

Army Form C. 2118.

WAR DIARY
or
INTELLIGENCE SUMMARY.
(Erase heading not required.)

Instructions regarding War Diaries and Intelligence Summaries are contained in F. S. Regs., Part II. and the Staff Manual respectively. Title pages will be prepared in manuscript.

Place	Date	Hour	Summary of Events and Information	Remarks and references to Appendices
ARRAS	12th Dec	7.30am	RAMC notes cannot not to DDMS XVII Corps	49
	"	4.0am	Battle Casualty nil	50
	"	4 pm	Prisoners of war nil	51
	"	6 pm	Battle casualty nil	52
			DADMS visited SCHRAMM Barracks billets of 1st Somerset L.I. and 1st Rifle Bde. and 10th Fd Amb	
			Lt. Capt. J.R.M. WHIGHAM RAMC proceeded to 33rd Division on appointment as DADMS	
	13th Dec	9.30am	RAMC notes casualty nil	53
	"	1.30am	Battle casualty nil b DDMS XVII Corps	54
	"	4 pm	Prisoners of war nil	55
	"	6 pm	Battle casualty nil	56
			Hon Col. & Pn. T MORRISON RAMC proceeded for duty with 12 General Hospital. ADMS & DADMS visited 8 CCS & 10 Stat. Amb.	

A.5834 Wt.W4973/M687 750,000 8/16 D. D. & L. Ltd. Forms/C.2118/13.

Army Form C. 2118.

WAR DIARY
or
INTELLIGENCE SUMMARY.
(Erase heading not required.)

Place	Date	Hour	Summary of Events and Information	Remarks and references to Appendices
ARRAS	14 Dec	11.40am	R.A.M.C. ladder casualty nil — D.D.M.S. XVII Corps	5-7
"			Battle casualty nil	3-8
"		4pm	Prisoners of war nil	59
"		6pm	Battle casualty nil	60
"	15 Dec	7.30am	D.A.D.M.S visited R.A.P at FEUCHY-CHAPEL cross roads also H.Q of 315 Bde of Fd Artillery	
"		7.30am	R.A.M.C. ladder casualty nil — D.D.M.S. XVII Corps	61
"			Battle casualty nil	62
"		4pm	Prisoners of war nil	63
"		6pm	Battle casualty nil	64
"	16 Dec	7.30am	R.A.M.C. ladder casualty nil — D.D.M.S. XVII Corps	65
"		7.30am	Battle casualty nil	66
"		4pm	Prisoners of war nil	67

Army Form C. 2118.

WAR DIARY
or
INTELLIGENCE SUMMARY.

(Erase heading not required.)

Instructions regarding War Diaries and Intelligence Summaries are contained in F. S. Regs., Part II. and the Staff Manual respectively. Title pages will be prepared in manuscript.

Place	Date	Hour	Summary of Events and Information	Remarks and references to Appendices
ARRAS	16th Dec	6 pm	Battle enquiry sent to D.D.M.S XVIIth Corps. DADMS visited billets of COLLEGE COMMUNALE and 10th Fd Amb. ran along station	68
"	17 Dec 11:30am		R.A.M.C. Bone Research van to D.D.M.S XVII Corps. gone	69, 70
"	"	4pm	Battle casualty enquiry	71
"	"	6pm	Provisional training note	72
"	"		Battle casualty enquiry	
"	18 Dec 11:45am		Battle casualty enquiry van gone	73, 74, 75
"	"	4pm	R.A.M.C. training carpentry dept	
"	"	6pm	Enquiry re went now	
"	"		Wire to 10 Fd Amb to attend a party to assist in the making of a dug out separate from the A.D.S. but close to it, for the treatment of gas cases	76

Army Form C. 2118.

WAR DIARY
or
INTELLIGENCE SUMMARY.
(Erase heading not required.)

Instructions regarding War Diaries and Intelligence Summaries are contained in F.S. Regs., Part II. and the Staff Manual respectively. Title pages will be prepared in manuscript.

Place	Date	Hour	Summary of Events and Information	Remarks and references to Appendices
ARRAS	18th Dec	6.15 pm	Battle casualties were 30. D.D.M.S. XVII Corps	77
"			Lt Col. D. AHERN RAMC O/C No 11 F.A. will act as A.D.M.S. during the temporary absence on leave of Lt Col. J. CREECH A.M.S. D.S.O. from 19th Dec 17 to 2nd Jan 18.	
"			S.D.M.S. visited 12 Fd Amb, Corps Rest Station WARLUS	None
"	19th Dec	4.00 am	R.A.M.C. to the casualty evac	78
"	"		Battle casualties 1221	79
"	"	4.10 pm	Prisoners of war 1001	80
"	"	6 pm	Battle casualties 1000	81
"			D.A.D.M.S. visited 10th 27th A.C.C. (main dressing station)	None
"	20 Dec	7.30 am	R.A.M.C. Battle casualties sent to D.D.M.S. XVII Corps	82
"	"	7.30 am	Battle casualties	83

WAR DIARY
or
INTELLIGENCE SUMMARY.

Army Form C. 2118.

Place	Date	Hour	Summary of Events and Information	Remarks and references to Appendices
ARRAS	20 Dec 1917	4pm	Prisoners of war were to O.D.M.S. XVII Corps	84
			Prisoners escorts were	85
"		6pm	O/A.D.M.S. noted S.O.C. 16th Bde. R.A.P's in new and	
			sense truck. P.A.D.M.S. visited fields in SCHRAMM Bks.	
			and COMEDE COMMINALE	
"	21 Dec	9am		88
			R.A.M.C battle casualty were to D.D.M.S. XVII Corps	Ff
		8am	Battle casualty were	89
"		4pm	Prisoners of war were	
		6pm	Battle casualty were	
			H.A.D.M.S. visited A.D.S. and R.A.P at Pick Camp	
	22 Dec 1917	7.45am	R.A.M.C battle casualty were to D.D.M.S XVII Corps	90
"		4.15pm	Battle casualty were	91
			Prisoners of war were	92

WAR DIARY or INTELLIGENCE SUMMARY

Army Form C. 2118.

Place	Date	Hour	Summary of Events and Information	Remarks and references to Appendices
ARRAS	22nd cont	6pm	Battle casualty with D.D.M.S. XVII Corps	93
		—	A/D.M.S. visited conference ambulances and R.A.P. in HAPPY VALLEY and CURB SWITCH	94. 95.
	23rd	7:45am	R.A.M.C. battle casualty with D.D.M.S. XVII Corps	96
	"	7:45am	Battle casualty — nil	
	"	2:10pm	Prisoners of war — nil	
	"	6pm	Battle casualty — nil	97
	"		A/D.M.S. visited A.D.S. and 2/A Sanitary section	
	24th	7:45am	R.A.M.C. battle casualty with D.D.M.S. XVII Corps	98
	"	7:45am	Battle casualty — nil	99
	"	11:15am	W.O. re 10 awtd. and R. officers, 15 hid O.R. R.A.M.C. (wounded) attached 2nd Army	100

Army Form C. 2118.

WAR DIARY
or
INTELLIGENCE SUMMARY.
(Erase heading not required.)

Instructions regarding War Diaries and Intelligence Summaries are contained in F. S. Regs., Part II. and the Staff Manual respectively. Title pages will be prepared in manuscript.

Place	Date	Hour	Summary of Events and Information	Remarks and references to Appendices
ORRIS	24th Dec	4.10 pm	Prisoners of war sent to D.D.M.S. XVIII Corps	101
"	"	6 pm	Battle casualty wire	102
"	25 Dec	7.50 am	C/A.D.M.S. visited 11 Fd Amb and A.D.S.	
"	"	4.45 a.m	R.A.M.C. casualty wire to D.D.M.S. XVIII Corps	103
"	"		Battle casualty wire	104
"	"	4.10 pm	Prisoners of war wire	105
"	"	6 pm	Battle casualty wire	106
"	"		C/A.D.M.S. visited A.D.S.	
"	"		D.A.D.M.S. visited Wilderness Camp	
"	26 Dec	9.15 am	R.A.M.C. battle casualty wire to D.D.M.S. XVIII Corps	107
"	"	9.15 am	Battle casualty wire	108
"	"	4.15 pm	Prisoners of war wire	109
"	"	6 pm	Battle casualty wire D.O.M.S + D.A.D.M.S visited D.O.M.S Corps and arrived dept Battalion	110

Army Form C. 2118.

WAR DIARY
or
INTELLIGENCE SUMMARY.
(Erase heading not required.)

Instructions regarding War Diaries and Intelligence Summaries are contained in F. S. Regs., Part II. and the Staff Manual respectively. Title pages will be prepared in manuscript.

Place	Date	Hour	Summary of Events and Information	Remarks and references to Appendices
ARRAS	27 Dec	8.10 am	R.A.M.C. battle wastage war to D.D.M.S. XVII Corps	111
"		8.30 am	Barrels arrived war	112
"		6 pm	Rations from war	113
"		6 pm	Battle casualty war	114
"			A.D.M.S. noted if on Road and Rly pass at Rck Corp	
"			Sanitary of York & SPADE wars Court House	
"			CRESCENT	
"	28 Dec	8 am	R.A.M.C. battle casualty war 6.0.0 M.S. XVII Corps	115
"	"	8 am	Battle casualty war	116
"	"	4 pm	Rations from war	117
"	"	6 pm	Battle casualty war	118
"	"		D.A.D.M.S. visited the 32nd Div R.F.A. 1st L.f.Br Ad Bn and Coll Rones in R.A. PPJ VALLEY	

Army Form C. 2118.

WAR DIARY
or
INTELLIGENCE SUMMARY.
(Erase heading not required.)

Place	Date	Hour	Summary of Events and Information	Remarks and references to Appendices
ARRAS	29 Dec	8 am	R.A.M.C. Inspec "casualty" went to D.D.M.S. XVII Corps	119
"	"	7.30 am	Battle casualty" move	120
"	"	4.10 pm	Prisoners of war move	121
"	"	6.10 pm	Battle casualty move	122
			D/ADMS visited A.D.S. from stay posts at 37th Bde R.F.A. H.Q. R.A.P. in cool sented. Also sanitary inspection of J.F. Stores front and rear machine gun posts in the neighbourhood of 11th Jat Ambulance.	
			D/ADMS visited Corps Rest Station (12 th Fd Amb)	
			WARLUS	
ARRAS	30 Dec	7 am	R.A.M.C. Battle casualty" went to D.D.M.S. XVII Corps	123
"	"	7.10 am	Battle casualty move	124
"	"	4.10 pm	Prisoners of war move	125
"	"	6 pm	Battle casualty move	126
			D/ADMS visited transport lines 8, 12 by Bde.	

Army Form C. 2118.

WAR DIARY
or
INTELLIGENCE SUMMARY.
(Erase heading not required.)

Instructions regarding War Diaries and Intelligence Summaries are contained in F.S. Regs., Part II. and the Staff Manual respectively. Title pages will be prepared in manuscript.

Place	Date	Hour	Summary of Events and Information	Remarks and references to Appendices
ARRAS	3/Dec	7am	Rame home camels wint to D.D.M.S XVII Corps	12·7
"		8am	Rame comets ann	12·8
"		4pm	Browns B. has run	12·9
"			Battle camels 1 an	13·0
"		6pm	O/A DMS went to D L R&O CRATER SURWAY and BROWN line between	

JMC

ADDENDUM NO. 1 TO R.A.M.C. ORDER NO. 44

by

COLONEL J. GRECH. D.S.O., A.M.S., A.D.M.S. 4th. DIVISION.

Map.Refs: Sheet 51b. 1/40000.   1st. December, 1917.

* *

1. **MEDICAL POSTS:-**

    The Regimental Aid Post for the Right Battalion, Left Brigade in SHRAPNEL TRENCH, will be transferred to CURB SWITCH RESERVE forthwith, the latter becoming a combined R.A.Post for the Right and Left Battalions, and the former a Relay Post.

    The Relay Post at the MOUND, N.6.d.5.5. will be abandoned and two others formed, one at N.5.a.7.4. and the other at the end of ORANGE AVENUE.

2. **EVACUATION:-**

    Evacuation for the Left Brigade will be as follows:-
    North of TWIN COPSE to R.A.Post in CURB SWITCH RESERVE, along ORANGE AVENUE, by wheeled stretcher along tracks to Relay Post at N.5.a.7.4., and thence to one of the following Motor Ambulance Termini, the latter of which will be used when the track to the former is not practicable:
    (a). Near the tank on the CAMBRAI road.
    (b). FEUCHY CHAPEL CROSS-ROADS.
    From the Motor Ambulance Terminus cases will be conveyed to the Dressing Station of No. 11 Field Ambulance at TILLOY.

    South of TWIN COPSE to the Relay Post in SHRAPNEL trench, thence to the R.A.Post in PICK CAVE and to the A.D.Stn. at LA BERGERE.

    Other posts remain as before.

Issued at 4.50 p.m.

Colonel,
A.D.M.S. 4th. Division.

Copies to all recipients of R.A.M.C. Order No. 44.

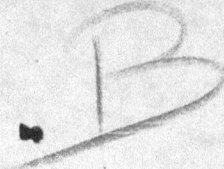

A.D.M.S. 4th. Division No. 17/12.

SUPPLEMENTARY MEDICAL ARRANGEMENTS.

1. O.C. No. 11 Field Ambulance, should the necessity for increased numbers of Stretcher-Bearers arise, will immediately notify the A.D.M.S.

2. O.C. No. 10 Field Ambulance will have 60 Stretcher-Bearers with stretchers detailed at once.

   They will "Stand to" and be ready to move to reinforce No. 11 Field Ambulance immediately on receipt of orders to that effect from this office.

3. Acknowledge.

11th. December, 1917.

Captain, for
A.D.M.S. 4th. Division.

Copies to 10th. Field Ambulance.
         11th. Field Ambulance.
         Diary (2).
         File.

4th Division

Medical

A. D. M. S.

January to April
1918

On His Majesty's Service.

Confidential

D.A.G
3rd Echelon

MEDICAL

Army Form C. 2118.

WAR DIARY
or
INTELLIGENCE SUMMARY.

(Erase heading not required.)

Instructions regarding War Diaries and Intelligence Summaries are contained in F. S. Regs., Part II. and the Staff Manual respectively. Title pages will be prepared in manuscript.

Place	Date	Hour	Summary of Events and Information	Remarks and references to Appendices
ARRAS	1/4/17	8 am	R.A.M.C. staff arrived here to D.D.M.S XVIIth Corps	1
		9 am	Baker reported sick	2
		4 pm	Brennan & war work	3
		6.10 pm	Batt'n casualty returns	4
			A/DDMS made R.T.P supply returns to Brown line	
			and 11 fold amb. DADMS S indes wells in SCHRAMM Bks	
				Jac
	2/4/17/1918		R.A.M.C staff carried over to D.D.M.S XVIIth Corps	5
		7.10 am	Battle casualty ret'n	6
		8.10 pm	Brennan & war work	7
		6.15 pm	Batt'n casualty ret'n	
			9/ADMS made R.K.P's right sector A.D.S. w/c includes	
			Sanitaria of YORK and SPADE Redoute	
			DADMS inspected billets in SCHRAMM Bks and dugout of	
			New Zealand Tunnellers in Happy Valley. No mail a case of	
			measles last evening.	

WAR DIARY
or
INTELLIGENCE SUMMARY.
(Erase heading not required.)

Army Form C. 2118.

Place	Date	Hour	Summary of Events and Information	Remarks and references to Appendices
ARRAS	3/May	4.45am	Battle casualty enquiry to DDMS XVII Corps	9
"	"	7.30am	RAMC collect casualty returns	10
"	"	3pm	Went to No 7th Fd Amb re on cases of diphtheria and	11
"	"		location of contacts	11a
"	"	4.10pm	Prisoners of war burial	12
"	"	6.30pm	Battle casualty return	13
"	"		RAMC (Hospital) order re Inspection of all water fronts	A
"	"		Col J CREECH ADMS ADMS returned from leave. Lt Col D	
"	"		AHERN RAMC o/c ADMS signed the count 11 until aal	
				Jmc
"	4/May	6am	RAMC battle casualty report	
"	"	8am	Battle casualty returns	14
"	"	4pm	Prisoners of war returns	15
"	"	6pm	Battle casualty returns to DDMS XVII Corps	16
				17
				Jmc

WAR DIARY or INTELLIGENCE SUMMARY

Army Form C. 2118.

Instructions regarding War Diaries and Intelligence Summaries are contained in F. S. Regs., Part II. and the Staff Manual respectively. Title pages will be prepared in manuscript.

(Erase heading not required.)

Place	Date	Hour	Summary of Events and Information	Remarks and references to Appendices
ARRAS.	5 Jan	7.30 am	R.A.M.C. troops casualty return to DDMS XVII Corps	18
"	"	9.30 am	Battle casualty return	19
"	"	11.30 am	Letter to K.O. 218th Rest Joes. (Powers) re attend to sick & sanitation of 39 A.A. Aircraft searchlight section	20
"	"	4.10 pm	Prisoners of war return	21
"	"	6.10 pm	Battle casualty return	22
			A.D.M.S. marks Surgeon General B, 3rd Army DPMS, marked 10 d A.A. A.D.C. Transport line gone	
ARRAS	6 Jan	9.40 am	R.A.M.C. cattle casualty return to DDMS XVII Corps	23
"	"	9.40 am	Battle casualty return	24
"	"	4.1 pm	Prisoners of war return	25
"	"	6 pm	Battle casualty return	26
"	"	7 pm	Letter to 3rd Lapaths re care of artillery	27

WAR DIARY
or
INTELLIGENCE SUMMARY.

Army Form C. 2118.

Place	Date	Hour	Summary of Events and Information	Remarks and references to Appendices
ARRAS	6/4/17 contd.	-	A.D.M.S. visits D.D.M.S. XVII Corps	
"	7/4/17	7.30am	R.A.M.C. "battle casualty" return to D.D.M.S. XVII Corps	28
"	"	7.30am	Baree casualty mse	29
"	"	4.10pm	Prisoners of war mse	30
"	"	6pm	Base casualty mse	31
"	"		D.A.D.M.S. visits 12 F.A. and (Corps Rest Station) marked XVII Corps	
"	"		A.D.M.S.	Jane
"	8/4/17	7.30am	R.A.M.C. "battle casualty" mse to D.D.M.S. XVII Corps	32
"	"	7.30am	Baree casualty mse	33
"	"	4.10pm	Prisoners of war mse	34
"	"	6.10pm	Baree casualty mse	35
			A.D.M.S. & D.D.M.S. XVII Corps visited 10 C.C.S. and ECOLE NORMALE and 11 F.A. and TILLOY	Jane

Army Form C. 2118.

WAR DIARY
or
INTELLIGENCE SUMMARY.
(Erase heading not required.)

Instructions regarding War Diaries and Intelligence Summaries are contained in F. S. Regs., Part II. and the Staff Manual respectively. Title pages will be prepared in manuscript.

Place	Date	Hour	Summary of Events and Information	Remarks and references to Appendices
ARRAS	9/9/17	7.55am	R.A.M.C. battle casualty evac to D.D.M.S. XVIII Corps	36
"	"	7.55am	Brance casualty nun	37
"	"	4.10pm	Brigdiers Dinner nun	38
"	"	6pm	Battle casualty nun	39
"	"	4.10pm	nun ten to 12 Fd Amb Relieving 1st Fd GK HAYS. MDRCUSA. for permanent duty with 2g W Ridings vice Capt A. CLIMIE. nto Etaples 6" ETAPLES for duty	40
"	"		A.D.M.S. y R.A.D.M.S. and O/C 3A Sanitary sectn visited transport lines vacated by "C" Bty, 315 Bde. R.F.A. at ST SAUVEUR also billets occupied by 6 Wagon details and Ammunition store in RONVILLE	
"	"	10pm	R.A.M.C. battle casualty evac to D.D.M.S XVII Corps same	41
"	"	7.45am	Battle casualty nun	42
"	"	4.10pm	Brance funeral nun	43

WAR DIARY
or
INTELLIGENCE SUMMARY.
(Erase heading not required.)

Army Form C. 2118.

Instructions regarding War Diaries and Intelligence Summaries are contained in F.S. Regs., Part II. and the Staff Manual respectively. Title pages will be prepared in manuscript.

Place	Date	Hour	Summary of Events and Information	Remarks and references to Appendices
ARHS	10th cont	6pm	Battle casualty win to D.O.M.S XVII Corps	44
"	"	"	A.D.M.S V D.A.D.M.S visited 4 Bn Debel Bn (Corps Rest Station) WARCUS Report to D.D.M.S XVII Corps on gas arrangements in this division. J.Smie	B
"	11pm 6am		R.A.M.C battle casualty win to D.D.M.S XVII Corps	45
"	6am		Battle casualty win	46
"	4.10pm		Prisoners of war win	47
"	6.10pm		Battle casualty win	48
"	8pm		4 Medical Officers "reinforcements" arrived from HAVRE and posted as follows:— Capt. DONALD CHARLES SCOTT R.A.M.C (SR) to 10 Fd Ambulance Capt. JOHN BRUCE LOW R.A.M.C (T.C) to 11 Fd Ambulance Capt. PERCIVAL C. LEEMAN R.A.M.C (T.C) to 12 Fd Ambulance Lieut EDWARD P.N. CREAGH R.A.M.C (SR) to 12 Fd Ambulance	

WAR DIARY
or
INTELLIGENCE SUMMARY.

Army Form C. 2118.

Place	Date	Hour	Summary of Events and Information	Remarks and references to Appendices
ARRAS	11th Feb 1917	—	A.D.M.S. visited D.G.M.S. HESDIN	
"	12th	9 am	RAMC Batts. consult. went to DDMS XVIIth Corps	49
"	"	10am	Batter consult. ans	50
"	"	4.10 pm	Prisoners of war ans	51
"	"	6.10 pm	Battle consult. ans	52
"	"		A.D.M.S. visited R.A.P. on CURB SWITCH Relay post at N 5 a 7.4 in the afternoon. A.D.M.S. attended a conference of A.D's M.S. at D.D.M.S. XVIIth Corps. office at 3 pm	
"	13 Feb 1917	8 am	Draw table Casualty wire to D.D.M.S. XVIIth Corps. 8 pm e	53

Army Form C. 2118.

WAR DIARY
or
INTELLIGENCE SUMMARY.
(Erase heading not required.)

Place	Date	Hour	Summary of Events and Information	Remarks and references to Appendices
ARRAS	13 Jan	8.0am	Battle casualty wire to DDMS XVII Corps	54
		4.15pm	Prisoners of war wire	55
		6.10pm	Battle casualty wire	56
			Capt McCutcheon RAMC DADMS proceeded on 14 days leave to UK. Capt Ballero is acting for him.	
		4.0pm	ADMS held a conference of MO's C in O of 12 Inf Bde J Service sprayers Semicetator J93	57
			Main points of Conference were (a) to J93	58
			Capt D.C. SCOTT ex 10 Field returned Capt MURPHY RAMC left returning the letter proceeded to England on expedition of contact J93	59
				60
14		7.40 am	Same battle casualty wire to ADMS XVII Corps	61
		9.40 am	Battle casualty wire	62
		4.15pm	Prisoners of war wire	63
		6.10pm	Battle casualty wire	
15		7.50am	Same battle casualty wire to DDMS XVII Corps	
		7.50am	Prisoners of war wire	
		4.10pm	Prisoners of war wire	

WAR DIARY
or
INTELLIGENCE SUMMARY.

Army Form C. 2118.

Place	Date	Hour	Summary of Events and Information	Remarks and references to Appendices
ARRAS	15	6.10pm	Battle casualty wire to DDMS XVII Corps	64
			"4 Div Medical arrangements in connection with 4 Div defence scheme" completed. Copy attached dated 15/1/18.	C
			ADMS visited SCARPMN BARRACKS. Huts are being installed which will improve the accommodation of medical units.	
	16	8am	Plane battle casualty wire to DDMS XVII Corps	65
		8am	Battle casualty wire	66
		4.10pm	Prisoners of war wire	67
		6.10pm	Battle casualty wire	68
			ADMS visited M.D.S. (1st D.F. Pk Ard) ECOLE NORMALE	JHB
	17	7.45am	Plane battle casualty wire to DDMS XVII Corps	69
		7.45am	Battle casualty wire	70
		4.10pm	Prisoners of war wire	71
		6.10pm	Battle casualty wire	72
			ADMS visited the 4 Div Depot Battalion also DDMS XVII Corps	JHB
	18	7.45am	Plane battle casualty wire to DDMS XVII Corps	73
		7.45am	Battle casualty wire 12 OR including 11 gassed (mustard shell)	74
		4.10pm	Prisoners of war wire	75

Army Form C. 2118.

WAR DIARY
or
INTELLIGENCE SUMMARY.
(Erase heading not required.)

Place	Date	Hour	Summary of Events and Information	Remarks and references to Appendices
ARRAS	18	6.10pm	Battle casualty wire to Dopes XVII Corps	76
			The last two days the Conditions of the trenches makes it impossible to keep stretcher cases through them. The old R.A.P at HAPPY VALLEY H.36.c.2.7. sheet 57B has been re-opened as an extra R.A.P	
			Condition of trenches is due to heavy rain directly after the thaw.	
	19	8.00 am	A.D.M.S batlle casualty wire to D.D.M.S XVII Corps	77
		8.0 am	Battle casualty wire	78
		4.10pm	Prisoners of war wire	79
		6.0 pm	Battle casualty wire.	80
			A.D.M.S visits 1st D.gn. Signal school at BEAURAINS where one Case of Diphtheria has recently occurred. All precautions are being taken. JHB	
	20	7.35 am	A.D.M.S (Battle casualty wire to D.D.M.S XVII Corps	81
		7.35 am	Battle casualty wire	82
		4.3 pm	Prisoners of war wire	83
		6.0pm	Battle casualty wire	84
			The trenches are still in very bad condition which tells to great extent on high sick admission JHB	

WAR DIARY or INTELLIGENCE SUMMARY.

Army Form C. 2118.

Place	Date	Hour	Summary of Events and Information	Remarks and references to Appendices
ARRAS	21	8.00am	Adv & battle casualty wire to DDMS XVII Corps	85
		9.00am	Battle casualty wire	86
		4.10pm	Prisoners of war wire	87
		6.0pm	Battle casualty wire	88
	22	8.50am	Adv & battle casualty wire to DDMS XVII Corps	89 JB
		9.50am	Battle casualty wire	90
		4.0pm	Prisoners of war wire	91
		6.0pm	Battle casualty wire	92
		11.0am	Conference of Reg. M.O. at this Office to discuss Sanitation and General Sanitation of trenches which is still very bad. Trench fever traced here to men overloaded	
		2.30pm	ADMS attend a conference of DDMS XVII Corps JB	
	23	7.400am	Adv & battle casualty wire to DDMS XVII Corps	93
		7.400am	Battle casualty wire	94
		4.10pm	Prisoners of war wire	95
		6.0pm	Battle casualty wire	96
	24	7.50am	Adv & battle casualty wire to DDMS XVII Corps	97
		7.50am	Battle casualty wire	98
		4.0pm	Prisoners of war	99
		6.0pm	Battle casualty wire ADMS attended conference with DDMS XVII Corps on Sanitation	100 JB

Army Form C. 2118.

WAR DIARY
or
INTELLIGENCE SUMMARY.
(Erase heading not required.)

Instructions regarding War Diaries and Intelligence
Summaries are contained in F.S. Regs., Part II.
and the Staff Manual respectively. Title pages
will be prepared in manuscript.

Place	Date	Hour	Summary of Events and Information	Remarks and references to Appendices
ARRAS	25	8.0am	Rawe battle casualty wire ADMS XVII corps	101
		8.0am	Battle casualty wire	102
		4.0pm	Prisoner of war wire	103
		6.0pm	Battle casualty wire	104
		6.0pm	ADMS visited the Brown line in Tilloy with OC Sanitary Section concerning (sic 3rd) & decided there should be wire in lieu of pit system in front of the line as a temporary measure for the pits have fallen in — ADMS selected site with OC's for A.D.S. in the start of the defence scheme having to be put into action. The new site is behind Tilloy & (the ones) in the start of later being the heavily shelled —	ad med. arrang. ads report sheet
	26	2.0am	Rawe battle casualty wire to DDMS XVIII corps	105
		8.0am	Battle casualty wire	106
		4.0pm	Prisoner of war wire	107
		6.0pm	Battle casualty wire	108
			ADMS visited DDMS XVIII corps during the morning & also 12 F/Amb who are at WARLUS during the corps rest station took H.B.	
	27	7.30am	Rawe battle casualty wire to DDMS XVIII corps	109
		7.30am	Battle casualty wire	110

A5834 Wt.W4973/M687 750,000 8/16 D.D. & L. Ltd. Forms/C.2118/13.

Army Form C. 2118.

WAR DIARY
or
INTELLIGENCE SUMMARY.
(Erase heading not required.)

Instructions regarding War Diaries and Intelligence Summaries are contained in F.S. Regs., Part II. and the Staff Manual respectively. Title pages will be prepared in manuscript.

Place	Date	Hour	Summary of Events and Information	Remarks and references to Appendices
PARIS	27	4.35pm	Previous Diary mis'd	111
		6.0pm	Battle casualty wire	112
	28	7.30am	Prev. battle casualty wire to D.D.M.S XVII Corps	113
		7.30am	Battle casualty wire	114
		4.0pm	Previous Q wire	115
		6.0pm	Battle casualty wire	116
			A.D.M.S. 10th Div. F.Amb. to see new area — D.D.M.S. decided not	
			Rec. O. & R. F.Amb. to S. of AVESNES - LE - COMTE	173
			11 F.Amb. should go to	
"	29	7.50am	R.A.M.C. battle casualty wire	117
	"	7.50am	Battle casualty wire	118
	"	2.50pm	Wire to 10" Inf Bde to detail M.O. for temp duty with	119
			Div Engineers in relief of their M.O. on leave	
	"	4.30pm	Previous Q wire	120
	"	6pm	Battle casualty wire	121
	"	7.30pm	Wire to 11" Inf Bde to detail M.O. for temp duty with 2" W.	
			Regts in relief of their M.O. sick	122

Capt McCUTCHEON DADMS returned from leave

Army Form C. 2118.

WAR DIARY
or
INTELLIGENCE SUMMARY.
(Erase heading not required.)

Place	Date	Hour	Summary of Events and Information	Remarks and references to Appendices
ARRAS	29/5		A.D.M.S. held a conference of R.M.O of 11th Bdes. Points of conversation were sanitation and prophylactic against venereal disease.	none
"	30 May	10 am		
"	"	11 am	R.A.M.C. batter exercise — were H.D.M.S XVIII Corps	123
"	"	4 pm	Ranks carried out without (G.R) Prisoners 9 ours own.	124
"	"	6 pm	Batter carried — nil.	12.5
"			A.D.M.S visited D.D.M.S XVII Corps and A.A.P.M.G XIII Corps	12.6
			A.D.M.S. delivered a lecture to regimental medical officers of XVIII Corps , School . Secondary to syllabus drawn up
			by D.D.M.S. Subject of Lecture. Duties of R.M.O in trench warfare.
			At the time there obviously to the C.O. and adjutant, declined
			of sick s/c.

A5834. Wt. W4973/M687 750,000 8/16 D.D. & L. Ltd. Forms/C.2118/13.

Army Form C. 2118.

WAR DIARY
or
INTELLIGENCE SUMMARY.
(Erase heading not required.)

Place	Date	Hour	Summary of Events and Information	Remarks and references to Appendices
ARRAS	31 May	7.00 am	R.A.M.C. Officer casualty sent to DDMS XVII Corps	127
"			Battle casualty sent	128
"		4 pm	Summary of [illegible] now	129
"		6 pm	Battle casualty now	130
"			Ops for 4th Div & in transfer of 1st E. LANCASHIRE Regt to 34th Div	131
"			R.A.M.C. # order to ADMS ~ which of division and collection in disposed [illegible] of after relief.	
"			4y 15th Div Division	
"			DADMS visited A.D.S. LA BERGERE, R.A.P.s in CRATER SUBWAY, 1 PICK CAVE and EUREE TRENCH. May got in EAST RESERVE. The sanitation of the forward area was found to was satisfactory that	D

Army Form C. 2118.

WAR DIARY
or
INTELLIGENCE SUMMARY.
(Erase heading not required.)

Instructions regarding War Diaries and Intelligence Summaries are contained in F. S. Regs., Part II. and the Staff Manual respectively. Title pages will be prepared in manuscript.

Place	Date	Hour	Summary of Events and Information	Remarks and references to Appendices
ARRAS	31/5/17	Cont	Supervision of sanitation as taking place	same

J Smith
Colonel AMS
A.D.M.S. 4th Division

8/6/17

SECRET

Copy No. 26

R.A.M.C. ORDER NO. 45.

by

COLONEL J. GRECH. D.S.O., A.M.S., A.D.M.S. 4th. DIVISION.

Map Refs: FRANCE, Sheet 51b, 1/40,000.   3rd. January, 1918.

Regimental Medical Officers will be responsible for the supervision of the various Water Points in their neighbourhood.

(a). In the "Brown Line": The M.O. of the Left Battalion will supervise the Water Points North of the ARRAS-CAMBRAI road, and the M.O. of the Right Battalion those South of that road.

(b). The M.O. occupying the Regimental Aid Post at PICK CAVE will supervise the Water Points at PICK CAVE and FORK RESERVE.

(c). The M.O. of the Battalion occupying the Left Sector will supervise the Water Point at H.36.a.0.7 in HAPPY VALLEY.

(d). The M.O. occupying the Aid Post at O.13.b.4.9. will be responsible for the Water Point at GORDON ALLEY.

(e). The Water Point at LES FOSSES FARM will be looked after by the M.O. occupying that Post.

(f). For the purpose of chlorinating the water, Regimental M.O's. will post one of their Water Duty Orderlies to the Water Points in LES FOSSES FARM, GORDON ALLEY, PICK CAVE, FORK RESERVE and HAPPY VALLEY, and give them full instruction in the nature of their duties.

A list of Water Points in the Forward Area is appended.

WATER POINTS IN THE FORWARD AREA.

WATER POINT.	CONTROL.
BOIS DES BOEUFS.	By Area Commandant, BOIS DES BOEUFS, who has attached to him 1 N.C.O. from Division and 1 man of Labour Company. (At MAISON ROUGE.) A N.C.O. from Sanitary Section is attached to Area Commandant, to supervise sanitation.
BROWN LINE: H.34.c.7.7. N.4.a.6.9. N.4.a.6.1. N.4.c.9.1. N.10.a.9.2. N.10.d.1.1.	
LES FOSSES FARM (N.11.b.9.3). GORDON ALLEY. PICK CAVE. FORK RESERVE. HAPPY VALLEY (H.36.a.0.7).	Supervised and provided with personnel by Regtl. M.O's. of Battalions in the line.

R.A.M.C. Order No. 41, dated 23rd. October, 1917 is cancelled.

Issued at 7.0 p.m.

Colonel,
A.D.M.S. 4th. Division.

Distribution:-

    4th. Division.
    4th. Division "A". (6 copies).
    10th. Infantry Brigade.
    11th. Infantry Brigade.
    12th. Infantry Brigade.
    M.O's. of 12 Infantry Battns.
    A.D.M.S. 15th. Division.
    3a Sanitary Section.
    Area Commandant, BOIS DES BOEUFS.
    Diary. (2 copies).
    File.

A.D.M.S. 4th. Division No. 10/66.

D.D.M.S.,
XVIIth. Corps.

With reference to your No. 28/28, dated 8-1-18:

The Divisional arrangements for dealing with Gas Cases are as follow:-

An elephant dugout has been placed facing, and in the same trench as, the A.D.Stn. at LA BERGERE. The dugout in height is 6 feet, length 24 feet, breadth 9 feet and head cover 7 feet. It has two entrances. Curtains are placed separating the passage from the dugout.

If the number of Gas Cases is small, they are changed in the passage and from there they proceed to the dugout where they are bathed and put into pyjamas.

From here they go through the other passage into the A.D.Stn. where they are treated and venesection is performed if considered necessary.

If the number is large, a certain number have to change in the dugout itself. The clothes are removed, sprayed and exposed to the air at once.

From the A.D.Stn. they are transferred as ordinary cases to the Main Dressing Station, ARRAS, where they are further treated and venesection is performed on cases that develop symptoms during the journey between the A.D.Stn. and ARRAS.

From here they are sent to the Cas. Clg. Stn.

The French system is excellent in my opinion, but it has to be carried out some distance behind the line, and it only varies in detail from that which we are at present following, and which in my opinion is superior, as it deals with the cases at a much earlier period.

A gas station could certainly be formed in ARRAS, but I think it would have to be a Corps Post and not run Divisionally and it must be prepared to receive "N.Y.D. Gas" cases instead of sending them to FREVENT.

I see no advantage in keeping light cases in ARRAS when the Cas. Clg. Stn. is so close.

Headquarters,
4th. Division.
10-1-1918.

J.GRECH.
Colonel,
AD.M.S. 4th. Division.

SECRET

Copy No. 12

4th. DIVISION MEDICAL ARRANGEMENTS.

IN CONNECTION WITH

4th. DIVISION DEFENCE SCHEME.

Map Refs: Sheet 51b. 1/40,000.   15th. January, 1918.

In the event of the enemy attacking this Divisional Front, the following alterations in the Medical Arrangements will take place -

1. If our present Front and Support Line are penetrated but we still hold SPADE and FORK RESERVE as our Front Line, the Regimental Aid Posts will be transferred from their present positions as follows:

(a). Right Sector to LA BERGERE. To work in conjunction with the A.D.Stn.

(b). Left Sector to a dugout which will shortly be made by the R.E. in ORANGE AVENUE at H.36.c.3.3.

The A.D.Stn. will remain at LA BERGERE.

Evacuation will then be carried out as follows,
(a). From the A.D.Stn. by wheeled stretcher to the motor ambulance car terminus which will be at some convenient spot on the ARRAS-CAMBRAI road, probably near N.4.d.3.4. Thence to TILLOY, Main Dressing Station and Cas. Clg. Stn. Cars will only stop at TILLOY and ARRAS if considered necessary. If no further dressing is required, ambulance cars will proceed direct from the ARRAS-CAMBRAI road to Cas. Clg. Stn.

(b). From the R.A.P. in H.36.c.3.3, by hand carriage or wheeled stretcher to the Relay Post at N.5.a.7.4. Thence either to the ambulance car terminus near N.4.d.3.4. or to FEUCHY CHAPEL cross roads, where other ambulance cars will be waiting.

2. If the Front Line is pushed back and has to occupy the Intermediate Line, the A.D.Stn. will at once be withdrawn to TILLOY, and LA BERGERE will only be used as a R.A.P. for the Right Sector.

The R.A.P. for the Left Sector will remain in H.36.c.3.3. and a Relay Post will be formed near N.4.d.3.4.

Ambulance cars will in all probability, be able to run as far as FEUCHY CHAPEL cross roads, in which case evacuation for the Right Sector will be carried out by hand or wheeled stretcher along the ARRAS-CAMBRAI road to FEUCHY CHAPEL cross roads, thence as mentioned in para. 1, above.

The evacuation for the Left Sector will be carried out as mentioned in para.1, with the exception that all cases will be taken to FEUCHY CHAPEL cross roads.

/The

The QUARRY dugouts in N.3.b.8.3. will be taken over to form a Divisional Walking Wounded Post, and also to provide shelter to ambulance car drivers.

The transfer of the A.D.Stn. from LA BERGERE to TILLOY may have to be very rapid, depending on the development of operations. As much material as possible will be taken to the new A.D.Stn., and the order to move must be left to the discretion of the O.C. No.11 Field Ambulance, who will also detail the necessary R.A.M.C. personnel to the R.A.P's. and Relay Posts as soon as he decides to move the A.D.Stn. If time permits, orders for the move will be issued by the A.D.M.S. as usual.

At TILLOY, the present elephant Dressing Room will be reinforced and made as strong as possible by sinking the elephant to the level of the ground and placing sufficient cover on top to make it moderately proof. The work will be commenced at once.

The reinforced concrete dugout and cellar at present in existence, will be used for patients and personnel.

The Headquarters and Transport of No. 11 Field Ambulance will move to the ECOLE NORMALE, ARRAS, sharing the School Building and horse standing with No. 10 Field Ambulance.

The motor ambulance cars of the three Field Ambulances will be at the disposal of the A.D.M.S. as soon as the enemy attack is developed.

3. In the event of a further retirement to the Corps Line, the R.A.P's. for the Right and Left Sectors will be in suitable places to be notified later.

A Relay Post will be formed in a dugout near MAISON ROUGE. Another will be formed near BOIS DES BOEUFS.

The QUARRY dugouts in N.3.b.8.3. will be used as a Relay and Collecting Post with a M.O. from No. 11 Field Ambulance in charge. This M.O. will keep in touch with the Regimental M.O's and have control of the evacuation of wounded as far as TILLOY A.D.Stn.

The A.D.Stn. will remain at TILLOY.

Evacuation will be carried out by hand and wheeled stretcher to TILLOY. An attempt will be made to send ambulance cars or horsed ambulances, or both, as far as BOIS DES BOEUFS by night.

The Divisional Walking Wounded Post will be at TILLOY

N.B. If it is considered necessary, the A.D.Stn. will be withdrawn still further to the GIRLS' SCHOOL, ST SAUVEUR; but this will not be done unless the Post at TILLOY proves to be untenable.

Colonel,
A.D.M.S. 4th. Division.

Issued at 12, noon.

SECRET   D   Copy No. 35

R.A.M.C. ORDER
No. 46
by
COLONEL J.GRECH. D.S.O., A.M.S., A.D.M.S. 4th. DIVISION.

Map refs: Sheet 51b. 1/40000.
         Lens,11. 1/100000.   31st. January,1918.

* *

The 4th. Division will be relieved by the 15th. Division between 5th. and 9th. February,1918.

(a).   The Artillery reliefs will begin on 7th. February, and will be completed by 6 a.m. 9th. February.

(b).   On completion of the relief, one Brigade, R.F.A. will be in HABARCQ and one Brigade in observation, South of the SCARPE.

1. MOVES:

(a).   No. 11 Field Ambulance will be relieved by No. 45 Field Ambulance of the 15th. Division. The Forward Medical Posts will be handed over on 5th., relief of all Posts to be complete by 9 a.m. on 6th. February.

Advanced parties of No. 11 Field Ambulance will be sent to No. 47 Field Ambulance at AVESNES-LE-COMTE on 5th. February, and H.Q. and remainder of No. 11 Field Ambulance will take over from 47 Field Ambulance at AVESNES-LE-COMTE on the evening of 6th. February. Relief to be completed by 6 p.m.

Details of relief to be arranged between O's.C. concerned.

Route: No. 11 Field Ambulance will proceed to AVESNES-LE-COMTE via DAINVILLE, WARLUS, WANQUETIN. To be clear of WARLUS by 11.15 a.m.

(b).   No. 10 Field Ambulance will remain at the ECOLE NORMALE, ARRAS.

(c).   No. 12 Field Ambulance will remain at WARLUS.

2. COLLECTION OF SICK:

(a).   No. 11 Field Ambulance will collect sick from Units billetted in WANQUETIN, FOSSEUX and HABARCQ.

Two horse ambulance wagons will be sent out, one to HABARCQ and the other to FOSSEUX and WANQUETIN daily. These will convey light sitting-up cases.

One motor ambulance car will be sent out daily to convey lying-down cases. It will call first at HABARCQ, and return via FOSSEUX.

(b). No. 10 Field Ambulance will collect sick from WARLUS, SIMENCOURT and BERNEVILLE, and from the Brigade stationed in ARRAS. For this purpose, O.C. No. 10 Field Ambulance will attach one horse ambulance wagon to No. 12 Field Ambulance for the collection from the above-mentioned places, exclusive of ARRAS.

He will send another daily to WARLUS to bring back the cases to the ECOLE NORMALE.

Cases collected will be sorted at WARLUS, and those requiring admission to the Corps Rest Station will be kept there, others being returned to ARRAS.

The horse ambulance wagon attached to No. 12 Field Ambulance will remain at WARLUS during the period the Division is in rest.

(c). A motor ambulance car will be sent by No. 12 Field Ambulance to collect lying down cases if any are reported by the returning horse ambulance wagon.

(d). Urgent cases must be collected with the least possible delay by the nearest Field Ambulance on receiving intimation.

3. No. 11 Field Ambulance will accommodate at least 50 light cases at AVESNES-LE-COMTE.

4. EVACUATION: Sick and wounded will be evacuated to Nos. 8 and 19 Casualty Clearing Stations at AGNEZ-LES-DUISANS.

5. SPECIAL CASES:

(a). Dental: Dental cases from the Brigade in ARRAS will be sent to No. 10 Field Ambulance (ECOLE NORMALE), at 9 a.m. on Mondays and Thursdays.
From WANQUETIN, FOSSEUX, SIMENCOURT, HABARCQ, at WARLUS, under arrangement between O.C. Corps Rest Station, (No. 12 Field Ambulance), and O.C. No. 11 Field Ambulance.

(b). Eye Cases: Cases of defective vision will be collected at No. 10 Field Ambulance on Thursdays. They will be sent to No. 3 C.C.Stn., GREVILLERS on Fridays, to arrive by 9 a.m. Not more than 6 cases to be sent on any Friday. Nominal roll in duplicate to accompany patients, A.B's. 64 to be taken.

(c). Ear, Throat and Nose Cases: From Brigade in ARRAS will be sent to No. 10 Field Ambulance on Sundays. Those from Units West of ARRAS will be sent to No. 11 Field Ambulance on Sundays. From both of these Units, parties will be sent to No. 12 Stationary Hospital, ST POL on Mondays, to arrive by 10 a.m. Nominal roll in duplicate to accompany parties. All men to carry one day's rations.

(d). N.Y.D.Gas Cases: These will be sent to C.C.Stn. as usual.

(e). N.Y.D.N. Cases: These will be evacuated as follows:-
Officers: To Officers' Hospital, LUCHEUX.
Other Ranks: To 3 Can. Stationary Hospital, DOULLENS.

(f). Infectious Cases: To No. 12 Stationary Hospital, ST POL.

6. <u>Mobile Laboratory</u>: Available for Pathological and Bacteriological examinations. No. 20 Mobile Laboratory, AGNEZ-LES-DUISANS.

7. <u>Sanitary Sections</u>:
   3a Sanitary Section, GIRLS' SCHOOL, ST SAUVEUR. Forward Area.
   5a Sanitary Section, c/o TOWN COMMDT, ARRAS. ARRAS.
   32 Sanitary Section, 92 Rue de DOULLENS, ARRAS. Back Area.

8. <u>Advanced Depot, Medical Stores</u>: No. 33, at SAVY.

9. Office of A.D.M.S. 4th. Division will remain at No. 1 Place de la Prefecture, ARRAS. Completion of all reliefs detailed above to be reported by wire to this Office.

10. ACKNOWLEDGE.

Issued at 3.30 p.m.

Colonel,
A.D.M.S. 4th. Division.

<u>Distribution</u>: Copy No. 1 to D.D.M.S. XVIIth. Corps.
2   No. 10 Field Ambulance.
3   No. 11 Field Ambulance.
4   No. 12 Field Ambulance.
5   4th. Division.
6   4th. Division "A".
7   10th. Infantry Brigade.
8   11th. Infantry Brigade.
9   12th. Infantry Brigade.
10 A.D.M.S. 15th. Division.
11 A.D.M.S. Guards' Division.
12 4th. Div. Arty.
13 C.R.E. 4th. Division.
14 4th. Div. Signals.
15 4th. Division Train.
16 D.A.D.V.S. 4th. Division.
17-33 Regimental Medical Officers.
34,35 War Diary.
36 File.

Distribution:-

Copy No.	1. to	D.D.M.S. XVIIth. Corps.
	2.	4th. Division.
	3.	No. 10 Field Ambulance.
	4.	No. 11 Field Ambulance.
	5.	No. 12 Field Ambulance.
	6.	4th. Division "A".
	7.	10th. Infantry Brigade.
	8.	11th. Infantry Brigade.
	9.	12th. Infantry Brigade.
	10.	C.R.E. 4th. Division.
	11.	4th. Div. Arty.
	12.) 13.)	Diary.
	14.	File.

ADDENDA

to

4th. DIVISIONAL MEDICAL ARRANGEMENTS
====================================

Dated 15th. January, 1918.

****

1. The elephant dressing room at TILLOY will not be sunk as mentioned in para. 2, but merely reinforced.

    A German dugout in G.36.b.5.5. will be cleared and repaired, and an 18 foot elephant placed in the existing trench, so as to form a Dressing Station. This will be used if the A.D.S. at TILLOY becomes untenable prior to finally withdrawing that A.D.S. to the GIRLS' SCHOOL in ST SAUVEUR, as mentioned in the note to para. 3.

2. In para. 3 the R.A.P. North of the CAMBRAI road will be at N.4.a.6.5. That South of the CAMBRAI road, at N.4.c.7.4.

26th. January, 1918.

Colonel,
A.D.M.S. 4th. Division.

COMMITTEE FOR THE
MEDICAL HISTORY OF THE WAR
Date -8 APR 1919

Army Form C. 2118.

WAR DIARY
or
INTELLIGENCE SUMMARY.
(Erase heading not required.)

Vol 43

Place	Date	Hour	Summary of Events and Information	Remarks and references to Appendices
ARRAS.	1/2/15	7.40am	R.A.M.C. battle peasants move to D.O.M.S. XVII Corps	1.
"	"	"	Battle casualty nil	2.
"	"	4 pm	Prisoners of war nil	3.
"	"	6 pm	Battle casualty nil	4.
"	"		A.D.M.S. visited XVII Corps 12th Fd Amb (Corps Rest Station WARLUS) some A
"	"		Ammunition fulfilm connection with R.A.M.C. Units n.6.	5.
"	2/2/15	7.40am	R.A.M.C. battle casualty nil	6.
"	"		Battle casualty nil	7 / 8 B
"	"	4.15 pm	Prisoners of war nil	
"	"	6 pm	Battle casualty nil	
"	"		Accident. No 1 to R.A.M.C. men to 4.6.	
"	"		S.A.D.M.S. visited 11th Fd Amb (Corps Rest Station WARLUS) some	
ARRAS.	3.2.18	7.25am	R.A.M.C. battle casualty nil	9
"	"	"	Battle casualty nil	10
"	"	4.30 pm	Prisoners of war nil	11
"	"	6 pm	Battle casualty nil	12
"	"		D.A.D.M.S. inspected billets of 4th Div R.E. and 11th Coy Bombing School (Rue Boulloni) some	

Army Form C. 2118.

WAR DIARY
or
INTELLIGENCE SUMMARY.
(Erase heading not required.)

Place	Date	Hour	Summary of Events and Information	Remarks and references to Appendices
ARRAS	4.7.16	1/1.20am	RAMC battle casualty nil	13
"	"		Battle casualty nil	14
"	"	4.30pm	Prisoners of war nil	15
"	"	6pm	Battle casualty nil	16
"	"		DADMS visited 11th Fd Amb. TILLOY. Medical board now held in Office 1 FDMS (authority DAG 3rd Echelon No CR 80049/A) to examine, classify & report on No 52831 Pte St. J. CHADWICK 2-1st (P) W. Yorks	
"	5.7.18	1/7.00am	RAMC battle casualty nil	17/18
"	"		Battle casualty nil	19
"	"	10.05am	Visit to XVII Corps re relief of Major SPACKMAN by Cpt STONER	20
"	"	4.30pm	Prisoners of war nil	21
"	"	6pm	Battle casualty nil	
"	"		Relief of 4 Dn by 15th Dvn. 10 Inf Bde relieves by 45th Inf Bde. 10th Trench Gunners by 45th Trench MG Coy. 10 Trench Mortar relieved by 45th Trench mortar Bty.	

WAR DIARY
or
INTELLIGENCE SUMMARY

Army Form C. 2118.

Place	Date	Hour	Summary of Events and Information	Remarks and references to Appendices
ARRAS	5.2.18 cont		16th Fd Bde K.B. ARRAS.	
			11th Cvy Bde to 45th Fd Amb 3 on Bh B	
			11th F.A. Bde H.Q. moved to WARLUS. 46th Cvy Bde	
			12th F.A. Bde relieves 44th Inf. Bde.	
			12th Inf Bde H.Q. to BERNEVILLE 6-0pm 11am on 6th	JSmC
	6.2.18	1/30am	R.A.M.C. battle casualty nil	2.2
	"	"	Battle casualty nil (2 guard still away)	2.3
	"	5pm	Prisoners of war nil	24
	"	6pm	Battle casualty nil	25
			11th Fd Amb on relief by 45th Fd Amb (15th Div) in the forward area and A.D.S. proceeded to relieve 47 Fd Amb AYSHES-LE-COMTE.	
			A.D.M.S & D.A.D.M.S inspected billets taken over by 11th Fd Amb units from 15th Div in SIMEN COURT, WANQUETIN and FOSSEUX.	
				JSmC

Army Form C. 2118.

WAR DIARY
or
INTELLIGENCE SUMMARY.
(Erase heading not required.)

Place	Date	Hour	Summary of Events and Information	Remarks and references to Appendices
ARRAS	7.12.15	9.45am	R.A.M.C. battle casualty nil	26
"	"		Battle casualty nil	27
"	"	4pm	Prisoners from nil	28
			Staff Officer T/Capt J. WALKER R.A.M.C. arrived from Base for duty and posted to 1st Hampshire Reg. in relief of Capt D.C. SCOTT RAMC (SR) who on relief was transferred to 11th Fd Ambulance for duty	29 & 29(A)
			A.D.M.S. & D.A.D.M.S. inspected billets taken over by 4th division in BERNEVILLE, FOSSEUX, and 11th Fd Ambulance AVESNES-LE COMTE.	
			Relief of 4th Div Art. commenced by 15th Div Art. commenced to be completed on the 8th. 29th Bde R.F.A going into billets at HABARQ. 32nd Bde R.F.A. in observation. 3/10 Middlesex left division for depot battalion to be disbanded have this Capt MILNE RAMC (TF) attached to 16th Amd for duty. Note	

WAR DIARY
or
INTELLIGENCE SUMMARY.

Army Form C. 2118.

Place	Date	Hour	Summary of Events and Information	Remarks and references to Appendices
ARRAS	6.2.18	-	DADMS visited SCHRAMM BARRACKS billets of 10th Fd Bde and 10th Inf Bde HQrs	
"	9.2.18	-	Routine BH Bn Arty completed. Routine	
"	10.2.18	-	Household Battalion disbanded their medical officer T Capt J.F.M. SLOAN being attached to 17 Fd Amb. ADMS & DADMS visited 17 Fd Ambulances and Camp occupied by 2nd Essex in BERNEVILLE.	
"	11.2.18	-	ADMS and DADMS visited Camp at HABARCQ occupied by 29th Bde RFA and 11 Fd Amb. & AVESNES-LE-COMTE.	
"		2pm	Visited 16 & 17 Fd Amb to detail MO for permanent duty with 32nd Bas. Rec T Capt Moffat A.B. RAMC who proceeds to England on expiration of contract.	30

WAR DIARY
or
INTELLIGENCE SUMMARY.

(Erase heading not required.)

Army Form C. 2118.

Place	Date	Hour	Summary of Events and Information	Remarks and references to Appendices
ADMS	12.2.18		ADMS worked off the Will Ops of the R.E's Dis Ammunition Columns, and 10th Fd Ambulance. DADMS visited 11th Fd Ambulance. DADMS visited 10th Fd Ambulance and arranged that pack of the Dis Horses Jos Bttn to be used daily.	
	13.2.18		ADMS & DADMS visited HENICOURT AREA and mainly front. DADMS visited 17th Ambulance (Corps Rest Station) range WARLUS.	
	16.2.18		ADMS & DADMS visited COLLEGE COMMUNALE, SCHRAM BKS and 15th Bn Headquarters. DADMS accompanied by OC 3A Sanitary Section visited COLLEGE COMMUNALE, SCHRAM BKS inspected all attention rooms, and rooms in SCHRAMM BKS & suggestions were made to OC SCHRAMM BKS as to the nature of improvements which should receive immediate attention.	

Place	Date	Hour	Summary of Events and Information	Remarks and references to Appendices
ARRAS	16.2.18		ADMS visited 4th Divisional Signal School BEAURAIN.	C
"	17.2.18		ADMS attended strategic exercise in which was shown the one A.D.[?] schemes and on Trench out division of 10 cwt ambulance, n WAILLY field range. The service was in the before an open battle, and an advancing party. B one brigade. D.D.M.S. visited 10 cwt ambulance	
"	19.2.18		ADMS visited XVII Corps DDMS D.A.D.M.S visited SCHRAMM B.Ks. live x hour of 4th Divisional Train	fair gave gave c. 31
"	20.2.18		A.D.M.S attended a conference of ADsMS & DDMS office XVII Corps	
"	19.2.18		A.D.M.S. lectured to Indian Officers under Corps arrangements - Subject: Duties of R.M.O., Sanitation etc.	gave

Army Form C. 2118.

WAR DIARY
or
INTELLIGENCE SUMMARY.
(Erase heading not required.)

Place	Date	Hour	Summary of Events and Information	Remarks and references to Appendices
ARRAS	21.2.18		ADMS inspected 1st Lot. and OVESNES-LES-COMTE and billets in WANQUETIN occupied by 1st Somerset L.I. DADMS visited The 2nd system area, choosing sites for R.A.P's.	32.
	22.2.18	4pm	Under instructions from 4th arm Q park 20 (O.R.s) Reinfs were detailed for work on fabrication of Hospital huts against bombs. ADMS + DADMS visited camp occupied by 1st Rfle Bde. at SIMON COURT. Medical board, President Col. T. CRECH A.M.S. members Lt Col LEWIS R.A.M.C. and Lt Col LANGRISHE, held in the office of the ADMS 4 Div, to examine PTE. MacPHERSON 14 (no C/23259) 2nd Seaforths, under maintenance from D.G.M.S. They found him fit for active service Class "A".	
	"	"	ADMS held a conference of all O's C. 4th Div Field Ambulances	

2353 Wt W2354/1454 700,000 5/15 D.D.&L. A.D.S.S./Forms/C. 2118.

Army Form C. 2118.

WAR DIARY
or
INTELLIGENCE SUMMARY.
(Erase heading not required.)

Place	Date	Hour	Summary of Events and Information	Remarks and references to Appendices
ARRAS	23.2.18 cont⁴		and discussed with them the medical arrangements of the 1st, 2nd & 3rd Defence Systems, also the posting of a reliable N.C.O. to supervise the loading of the wounded to ambulance and detect any shirkers during the fighting.	
"	24.2.18		ADMS & DADMS visited Camps occupied by 1st Cavalry Div at FOSSEUX. ADMS & DADMS made details and arrangements B. 29 - 2nd Life. R.F.A. at Hd Qrs BARCQ and found considerable improvement in the sanitation of the camps, chiefly in latrines and cook houses.	None
"	25.2.18		DMDMS visited 32ⁿᵈ Bde RFA & 1ˢᵗ Royal Warwicks. ADMS inspected 16 Fd Ambulance ECOLE NORMALE. ADMS & DADMS visited corps and billets of 1st Royal & 2nd Royal Fus at St Suspt in BERNEVILLE.	None None
"	26.2.18		DADMS visited 10ᵗʰ & 12ᵗʰ Fd Ambulance. Capt SLOAN I.F.M. struck off strength having proceeded to Y. Ambulance dept.	None None

WAR DIARY
or
INTELLIGENCE SUMMARY.

Army Form C. 2118.

Place	Date	Hour	Summary of Events and Information	Remarks and references to Appendices
ARRAS	2/2/16		ADMS and DADMS visited one of the field ambulances the well at ATHIES and inspected it with a view to establishing a working service for it. There is no reason ADMS attended a conference of ADSMS on the genes g DDMS XVII Corps.	

J M Curtis Capt
DADMS
for Coe ADMS
4th Bns
3.3.16

A.D.M.S. 4th. Division No. 17/12.

ADMINISTRATIVE INSTRUCTIONS
IN CONNECTION WITH
R.A.M.C. ORDER NO. 46, DATED 31-1-1918.

1. **SUPPLY RAILHEAD ARRAS.**

   The system of supply will be the same as at present, i.e. the Divisional Train will deliver to Units. (The O.M.Store).

2. **FUEL.**

   A fuel dump for Units West of ARRAS will be established at BERNEVILLE on 4-2-1918 so that Units can draw on 5-2-1918.
   The fuel dump for Units in ARRAS or East of the town will be at ACHICOURT on 5-2-1918.

3. **BAGGAGE WAGONS.**

   The baggage wagons will join their Units on the afternoon previous to the move. On completion of each Unit's move, baggage wagons of all Units will be sent to the Divisional Train, a loader to be sent with each wagon.

4. **STORES.**

   Trench and area stores will be handed over to relieving Units of the 15th. Division.
   Receipts will be obtained for all articles handed over and the detailed list of stores will accompany the receipts to be sent direct to 4th. Division "Q" 48 hours after completion of relief.
   In the case of Camps and the billets in ARRAS, each Unit will be responsible for handing them over with the Area Stores to the Area Commandant, or ARRAS Town Major in a thoroughly clean and sanitary condition, and will obtain a certificate to that effect from the Area Commandant or ARRAS Town Major. (Attention is called to 4th. Division No. A.3904/187 of 4-11-17).
   These certificates will be forwarded to 4th. Division "Q" as soon as possible after the completion of handing over of billets.

5. **ORDNANCE.**

   The Ordnance Dump will remain in ARRAS at G.21.c.8.6.
   Ordnance for Units in and West of WANQUETIN will be sent by lorry to WANQUETIN and drawn at 2 p.m. daily. (Units in HABARCQ will draw from WANQUETIN daily).

6. **VETERINARY.**

Officer.	Where Billeted.	Units Administered.
Capt. D.C.Greene.	4 Mob. Vet. Section.	10th. Field Ambce.
Capt. A.Jackson.	WANQUETIN.	11th. Field Ambce.
		12th. Field Ambce.

7. **CANTEENS.**
   (a). BERNEVILLE.   No. 2 Rue de Warlus.
   (b). WANQUETIN.   Adrian Hut.
   (c). ARRAS.   Rue de la Paix.

-2-

8. **R.E. STORES.**

Any material required for the improvement of billets will be demanded direct from the C.R.E.

9. **STORES.**

The following will be handed over to relieving Units:-
Soyers Stoves.
Water-carrying tins surplus to Mobile Reserve.
Huts.
Tents.
Ration Bags waterproof.

Chaff cutters will not be left behind.

10. ACKNOWLEDGE.

Headquarters,
4th. Division.
2nd. February, 1918.

Colonel,
A.D.M.S. 4th. Division.

AMENDMENT NO. 1

to

R.A.M.C. ADMINISTRATIVE INSTRUCTIONS

dated 2-2-1918.

Ref. this office No. 17/12 of 2nd. inst:

In para. 2 ;

    for "BERNEVILLE" substitute "WARLUS".

4-2-1918.   A.D.M.S. 4th. Division.
                                 Colonel,

Copies to: 10th. Field Ambulance.
            11th. Field Ambulance.
            12th. Field Ambulance.

SECRET

Copy No. 14 Diary

4th DIVISION MEDICAL ARRANGEMENTS.

IN CONNECTION WITH

RESERVE DIVISION DEFENCE SCHEME.

Map Ref's: Sheet 51b. 1/40,000.   16th February, 1918.

1.   The Division is to be prepared to take over at short notice the centre portion of Corps Front.

THE SOUTHERN BOUNDARY:-

'P' Sap (to Right Division) - MONCHY Trench as far as junction with CURL RESERVE (to Centre Division) - 'G' Post (to Right Division) - old trench H.35.c.6.3 (to Right Division) - thence a straight line to meet the CAMBRAI Road H.32.d.3.3. - thence the CAMBRAI Road (to the Right Division).

THE NORTHERN BOUNDARY:-

I.14.a.50.15 - junction of CROW ALLEY and CORONA Support - Railway crossing at I.13.c.95.85.- COLT Reserve at I.13.a.0.1 (all to Left Division) - QUARRY at H.18.a.2.5 - machine gun emplacement H.17.b.2.5.- trench junction H.16.d.5.8 - CAM Trench as far as H.16.a.0.0.(all to Centre Division)thence straight line to FEUCHY LOCK - thence the River SCARPE. The Division will take over this portion of the line with two Brigades in front and one in reserve.

2.   On receiving orders from A.D.M.S. No.10.Field Ambulance will take over from Field Ambulance of Left Division Medical Posts of their Right Sector North of SCARPE, with Headquarters at BLANGY, and will be responsible for the evacuation from the front line to Main Dressing Station. O.C.10.Field Ambulance will at once send 8 bearers per Battalion to the 10th and 12th Infantry Bdes. He will send sufficient personnel to form relay posts, and open A.D.S's at FAMPOUX LOCK and FEUCHY - the latter should only have sufficient personnel to act as reserve A.D.S. He will evacuate all sick unfit for duty from ECOLE NORMALE to C.C.S.

3.   No.11 Field Ambulance will take over ECOLE NORMALE as M.D.S. from No.10.Field Ambulance - for this purpose O.C.No.11.Field Ambulance on receipt of orders from A.D.M.S.will send all his available bearers to report to O.C.No.10.Field Ambulance for duty. As many as possible of these bearers will be dispatched by returning Motor Ambulances - the remainder going by road. One Tent Sub-division, less 1 officer, will be left at AVESNES-LE-COMTE. Only sufficient transport will be sent to ARRAS.

4.   The Tent Division of No.12.Field Ambulance will remain at WARLUS running the Corps Rest Station. On receipt of orders from A.D.M.S, O.C.No.12.Field Ambulance will send his Bearer Division to the ECOLE NORMALE, ARRAS.

5. Medical Posts will be as follows:-

    R.A.P.   <u>Right Brigade.</u>

                  1 and 2. H.30.d.2.8.

                 <u>Left Brigade.</u>

                  1.   H.24.b.8.2.
                  2.   I.13.a.2.2.

    Relay.   H.24.c.2.8.
                          H.24.a.5.7.
                          H.29.c.5.4.

    A.D.S.   1.   FAMPOUX LOCK. H.23.a.9.5.
              2.   FEUCHY.   H.21.c.9.5.

<u>Walking Wounded Posts.</u>

        1. for 1st and 2nd System. FEUCHY.
        2. for 3rd System.   BLANGY.

Busses will be sent to these places if possible to convey patients to WARLUS.

<u>Main Dressing Station.</u>

    ECOLE NORMALE, ARRAS.

6. <u>EVACUATION.</u>

(a) While the Division is holding the first system:- by hand carriage to FAMPOUX LOCK, via TRIPLE ARCH for Left Brigade, via CHIN STRAP LANE for Right Brigade. Thence by Barges and Motor Ambulances to M.D.Station.

(b) In the second system by hand carriage to FEUCHY. i.e. for the Left Brigade along FAMPOUX-FEUCHY road - for the Right Brigade over ORANGE HILL.

(c) In the third system FEUCHY will still be used as A.D.S. for the left battalion of the Right Brigade - The right battalion of Right Brigade will evacuate wounded through the Division on the right to A.D.S. at TILLOY.

The Left Brigade will evacuate wounded through the Division on the left with A.D.S. at L'ABBEYETTE.

(d) In the event of the enemy breaking through the third system the FEUCHY A.D.S. will be withdrawn to cellars in Rue de DOUAI, ARRAS, East of billet 52 and at billet 57.

Light railways will be used for all systems if available.

In the event of the Ambulance running the M.D.S. having to leave ARRAS, the wounded will be taken direct to C.C.S.

<u>Disposal of cases by detail.</u>

(a) Wounded, N.Y.D.N. severe, Gas severe, by Field Ambulance Cars and M.A.C. Cars to 8 and 19 C.C.S.

(b) Wounded trivial.   )
     N.Y.D.N. slight.   )
     Ordinary sick.   ) by Lorry and Bus to C.R.Station.
     Infectious cases.   )
     Gas slight.   )

Tallies must be clearly marked AGNES or WARLUS: not C.R.S. or C.C.S.

3. **CLERKING.**

O.C.No. 11 Field Ambulance will be prepared to send 9 clerks including 1 N.C.O. to the C.C.S. Clerks will be in possession of A. and D. Books and the Order of Battle of the Division.
Until orders to the contrary are given by the A.D.M.S. the clerking will be done at the M.D.S. and Walking Wounded Posts.

ADDENDUM to Para.2.
O.C.No.10 Field Ambulance will also take over from the Field Ambulance of right Division the Medical Posts South of the SCARPE within the Brigade Boundary.

Issued at 4.30 p.m.

Colonel,
A.D.M.S. 4th.Division.

Copies:- D.D.M.S.,XVIIth.Corps.
10th.Field Ambulance.
11th.Field Ambulance.
12th.Field Ambulance.
10th.Infantry Brigade.
11th.Infantry Brigade.
12th.Infantry Brigade.
4th.Division "G".
4th.Division "Q".
A.D.M.S.,Guards Division.
A.D.M.S.15th.Division.
C.R.E.,4th.Division.
O.C.,4th.Division Signals.
O.C.,4th.Division Train.
C.R.A.
Diary.
File.

SECRET

ADDENDUM TO 4th DIVISION MEDICAL ARRANGEMENTS IN CONNECTION WITH RESERVE DIVISION DEFENCE SCHEME, DATED 16th FEBRUARY, 1918.

In para 5 add:-

R.A.P. Right Brigade.

H.36.c.1.9.
H.28.c.4.8.

Left Brigade.

TRIPLE ARCH.
FAMPOUX LOCK.
H.16.d.1.9.
H.21.b.9.9.

In para 6. EVACUATION. For (a) (b) (c) substitute the following:-

(a) In the first system:-

Right Brigade: From Regimental Aid Posts at H.30.d.2.8. to FAMPOUX LOCK via CHIN STRAP LANE.
Left Brigade: From Regimental Aid Posts at H.24.b.8.2. and I.13.a.2.2. via TRIPLE ARCH to FAMPOUX LOCK.

(b) For the second system the Regimental Aid Posts will be as follows:-

Right Brigade: H.36.c.1.9. (double).
Left Brigade: TRIPLE ARCH, FAMPOUX LOCK. (A.D.S.).
From Regimental Aid Posts to FEUCHY over ORANGE HILL for Right Brigade, and along FAMPOUX-FEUCHY Road for Left Brigade.

(c) In third system the Regimental Aid Posts will be as follows:-

Right Brigade: H.28.c.4.8.
Left Brigade: H.16.d.1.9.
H.21.b.9.9.

Wounded of left battalion of Right Brigade will be evacuated to FEUCHY A.D.S, those of right battalion of the Right Brigade to A.D.S., TILLOY.
The Left Brigade will evacuate wounded to L'ABBAYETTE, the A.D.S. of the Division on the left.

21st February, 1918.

Colonel,
A.D.M.S., 4th Division.

Issued at 4-30 p.m.

Copies to all recipients of 4th Division Medical Arrangements dated 16th February, 1918.

MEDICAL
Army Form C. 2118.

A.D.M.S.
4 DIVISION

WAR DIARY
or
INTELLIGENCE SUMMARY.
(Erase heading not required.)

Place	Date	Hour	Summary of Events and Information	Remarks and references to Appendices
ARRAS	1.3.18		Wrote to 10th Bn to detail an M.O. for permanent duty with divisional machine gun battalion.	1
	2.3.18		T/Capt PLOWRIGHT RAMC posted for permanent duty with 2 Bn machine gun battalion.	
			A.D.M.S. & D.A.D.M.S. visited H.Q.s of VI & XVII Corps (the Corps on the right & left of 6th & XVII Corps) to consult re medical arrangements should 4 Divn be ordered to these Corps. System N & S of the river SCARPE & hence arrangements for 2 systems N & S of the river SCARPE	A
	3.3.18		Routine.	
	4.3.18		D.A.D.M.S. accompanied by O.C. 10th Fd Amb scouted the ground between ST.LAURENT.BLANGY, Railway Embankment and GAVRELLE road with a view to establishing medical posts should the 4 Division be ordered to counter attack there. Arr mediaral arrangements for division if sent to 6th or 7th Corps	B

Army Form C. 2118.

WAR DIARY
or
INTELLIGENCE SUMMARY.
(Erase heading not required.)

Instructions regarding War Diaries and Intelligence Summaries are contained in F.S. Regs., Part II. and the Staff Manual respectively. Title pages will be prepared in manuscript.

Place	Date	Hour	Summary of Events and Information	Remarks and references to Appendices
ARRAS	5.3.18		DADMS attended conference of ADs MS in Office of DDMS X VII Corps. Present No 2 & 4 and medical arrangements (Reserve divisional) Defence Scheme No 2.	
"	6.3.18		DADMS visited 11th Ambulance. C.C.J. CREECH D.S.O. A.M.S. appointed 2nd in Command. 9th Col R.P. LEWIS R.AM.C. O.C. 16th Fd Amb and became O/ADMS. O/ADMS attended a conference with G.O.C. 4th Division R.A.M.C. order No 47.	C
"	7.3.18		Lt Col N FAICHNIE R.A.M.C. arrived as O/ADMS. Lt Col RP LEWIS R.A.M.C. handed over and resumed his rival 10th Fd Amb. 10th Field Amb moved from Ecole Normale to Hospice St Jean and medical arrangements in connection with 3rd System Defence Scheme.	
"	8.3.18		ADMS, DADMS and OC 10th Fd Amb visited the 3rd System N+S of SCARPE ADSs. TILLOY, FEUCHY + LAGNETTE. ADMS + DADMS visited 10th Fd Ambulance HOSPICE ST JEAN.	D

Army Form C. 2118.

WAR DIARY
or
INTELLIGENCE SUMMARY.
(Erase heading not required.)

Instructions regarding War Diaries and Intelligence Summaries are contained in F. S. Regs., Part II. and the Staff Manual respectively. Title pages will be prepared in manuscript.

Place	Date	Hour	Summary of Events and Information	Remarks and references to Appendices
ARRAS	8.3.18 Contd		Amendment No 1 to hedical arrangements 4 Div Defence Scheme.	Issue.
"	9.3.18		ADMS & DADMS visited 11th Ambulance at AVESNES-LE-COMTE; 12th Fd Amb, Corps Rest Station WARLUS.	
			Amendment No 1 and addendum to medical arrangements 4 Div Defence Scheme	Issue.
"	10.3.18		Previous medical arrangements No 1 "cancelling" Note dated 16. Feb 1918	Issue.	E
"	11.3.18		ADMS & DADMS visited the DDMS XVII Corps and discussed with him medical arrangements for defence schemes.	
			Order to all MO's to carry standards on their stretchers	F
			Stand to order to Field ambulances	G
			Addendum to 4th Div medical arrangements No 2	H
			RAMC order re XVII Corps Main Dressing Station	I
			RAMC order to all MOs to draw certain supplies from 10 Fd Amb.	J

WAR DIARY
INTELLIGENCE SUMMARY

Army Form C. 2118.

Place	Date	Hour	Summary of Events and Information	Remarks and references to Appendices
ARRAS	11.3.18		4 Bde relieve arrangements No 3 @ in event of 4 Bde Recovery Reserve Division of VIth Corps.	K
"			ADMS visited DDMS VIth Corps and VIth Corps Reserve area	gone
"	12.3.18		All units in area ordered to hold themselves in "Constant Readiness" as from 3 am on the 13th	gone
"			ADMS visited 10 Fd Ambulance	gone
"	13.3.18		Usual office routine	gone
"	14.3.18		Usual office routine. State of "Constant readiness" cancelled.	gone
"	15.3.15		O/ADMS visited 2nd Seaforths and 1st R Warwicks billets in SCHRAMM BARRACKS.	gone
"	16.3.18		O/ADMS visited 3rd Army School of Sanitation (32 London Section)	gone
"	17.3.18		O/ADMS & DADMS inspected billets of 2nd Bn Duke of Wellington in College Communal	gone

Army Form C. 2118.

WAR DIARY
or
INTELLIGENCE SUMMARY.
(Erase heading not required.)

Instructions regarding War Diaries and Intelligence Summaries are contained in F.S. Regs., Part II. and the Staff Manual respectively. Title pages will be prepared in manuscript.

Place	Date	Hour	Summary of Events and Information	Remarks and references to Appendices
ARRAS	18.3.18	–	O/ADMS inspected billets of 2nd Hants Fusiliers in BAUDIMONT billet ARRAS. RAMC operation order 48	L
			revise arrangements in connection with op. order 48 applying to relief of 8 guards division by 4th Brit commencing 20th	
"	19.3.18		B Col N FAICHNIE RAMC appointed ADMS	gone
			ADMS v DADMS attended conference in office of DDMS XVIIth Corps	M
"	20.3.18		Amendment to Above medical arrangements.	gone
		6 pm	Relief of 8 Guards field ambulances completed	
		7.30am	Battle casualty rem to DDMS XVIIth Corps	2
		6 pm	Battle casualty " " "	3
"	21.3.18	5.30am	ARRAS heavily bombarded by long range guns. ADMS v DADMS visited 10, 11, v 12 Fd Ambulances and L'ABBAYETTE	gone
		6 pm	Battle casualty rem to DDMS XVIIth Corps	4 –
		6 pm	Battle " " " "	5 –
		6 pm	Prisoners of war " " "	6
			Medical arrangements in connection with Reff Division Defence Scheme	N

WAR DIARY or INTELLIGENCE SUMMARY

Army Form C. 2118.

Place	Date	Hour	Summary of Events and Information	Remarks and references to Appendices
ARRAS	22.3.18		4" Div H.Q. moved from Arras to rats' tunnel at ramparts (BASTION CAMP)	#0
		4/am	Came therewith order W.49 re hours of transport	4
		6 p.m	R.A.M.C. battle casualties sent to DDMS XVII Corps	8
		7:30 pm	Battle casualties -nil-	9
			Battle " "	
	23.3.18	1 am	ARRAS DADMS still intermittently shelled	10
		6:30 am	Battle casualties sent to DDMS XVII Corps	11
		—	R.A.M.C. battle casualties sent to DDMS XVII Corps	12
		6 p.m	Battle casualties sent to DDMS XVII Corps	13
		7:15 pm	Leave — cancelled	
			Small attack on 11 Bde front	
		1:30 am	bns: L" Hays & others rallying them from tanks	gone
	24.3.18	4:40 am	Battle casualties sent to DDMS XVII Corps	14
		8 am	R.A.M.C. battle casualties sent	15
		4 pm	Orders of next mov't Casualties sent to DDMS XVII Corps	16
		6.10 pm	Battle " " "	17

WAR DIARY or INTELLIGENCE SUMMARY

Army Form C. 2118.

Place	Date	Hour	Summary of Events and Information	Remarks and references to Appendices
ARRAS	24.3.18	Contd	Amendment to 4 Div medical arrangement; left division defence scheme. DADMS visited 4 Div Town and XVII Corps. ADMS visited the three field ambulances H.Qrs. Lt Col G. AHERN returned from leave. Arras not so heavily shelled.	R
"	25.3.18		RAMC order no 50 re posting of 4 RAMC Bearers to the front line and firsts.	Q 18 19 20 21
		6.30am	Battle casualty wire to DDMS XVIII Corps	
		4.10am	RAMC battle casualty wire " " "	
		4 pm	RAMC " " " to DDMS XVII Corps	
		4.45pm	Battle casualty wire to DDMS XVII Corps	
			ADMS and DADMS attended a conference of field ambulance commanders (10, 11, 12) in hospice St. Jean at 9.30 pm.	
"	26.3.18		4 Div H.Qrs moved to ETRON. RAMC operation order no 51 re allotting field ambulances to brigades. 3 Officers reinforcement reported for duty. 1/Lt J.W. ALDRIDGE. MORC USA posted to 12th ambulance.	R

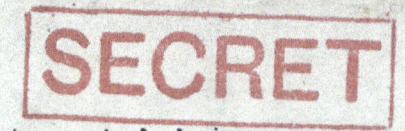 

Copy No. _____

R.A.M.C. ORDER NO. 51

by

COLONEL N. FAICHNIE, A.M.S., A.D.M.S. 4th. DIVISION.

==

Map Refs: 51b, 1/40000.   26th. March, 1918.
==

1.   All previous Medical Arrangements in connection with the front at present held by the 4th. Division are cancelled.

2.   From this date, Field Ambulances of the 4th. Division will become Brigade Units as under:
        No. 10 Field Ambulance will evacuate from 10th. Inf. Bde.
        No. 11 Field Ambulance will evacuate from 11th. Inf. Bde.
        No. 12 Field Ambulance will evacuate from 12th. Inf. Bde.
        Field Ambulances, until further orders will move with their respective Brigades.

3.   O.C. No. 11 Field Ambulance will take over from O.C. No. 10 Field Ambulance, all Medical Posts of the 11th. Inf. Bde. Sector, and will establish an A.D.S. at L'ABBAYETTE in conjunction with No. 12 Field Ambulance.

4.   Medical Posts, (i.e., Relay Posts, W.W.P's., etc.) will be established at the discretion of the Field Ambulance Commanders, for the evacuation of sick and wounded from their respective Brigade Sectors.
        Alteration of positions of Medical Posts or formation of new ones will be reported to this office at once, the map reference of the new site being given.

5.   The ECOLE NORMALE ceases to function as a C.M.D.S. from this date and the details of No. 11 Field Ambulance at present there will will rejoin their Unit at once.

6.   Each Field Ambulance will resume normal clerical work in connection with the evacuation of sick and wounded at once.
        The Daily State, 'Wounded Wires' and all routine returns and reports will be submitted to this office by each.

7.   Evacuation of sick and wounded will be as follows:-
        Wounded will all be evacuated to Nos. 7, 8 and 19 C.C.S's., AGNEZ LES DUISANS.
        Sick, Infectious Cases, N.Y.D.N. and 'Mustard Gas' Cases will continue to be sent to No. 48 Field Ambulance at HAUTE AVESNES.

8. The office of the A.D.M.S. 4th. Division is now open at HIRUN.

9. ACKNOWLEDGE.

[signature]
Colonel,
Issued at 5.30 p.m.   A.D.M.S. 4th. Division.

Copies to:-
- D.D.M.S., XVIIth. Corps.
- O.C., XVII Corps M.D.Stn.
- 10th. Field Ambulance.
- 11th. Field Ambulance.
- 12th. Field Ambulance.
- 4th. Division.
- 4th. Division "A".
- 10th. Infantry Brigade.
- 11th. Infantry Brigade.
- 12th. Infantry Brigade.
- XV M.A.C.
- A.D.M.S. 15th. Division.
- A.D.M.S. 62nd. Division.
- A.D.M.S. 56th. Division.
- C.R.E. 4th. Division.
- 4th. Division Signals.
- 4th. Divisional Train.
- A.P.M. 4th. Division.
- Diary (2).
- File.

WAR DIARY
or
INTELLIGENCE SUMMARY.

(Erase heading not required.)

Army Form C. 2118.

Place	Date	Hour	Summary of Events and Information	Remarks and references to Appendices
ARRAS	26.3.18 cont'd		Lt. C.O. MILLER (TC) and Lt. R.P.S. HANNON posted to 11 Fd Amb	
		5:30am	Battle casualty wire to DDMS XVII Corps	21, 22
		6:00am	R.A.M.C. battle casualty experiences. DDMS visited 4 tune field ambulances	23
ETRUN	4:15pm		Battle casualty wire to DDMS XVII Corps	24
			DADMS visited DDMS XVII Corps (NOYELLE-VION)	
ETRUN	27.3.18	7am	R.A.M.C. battle casualty wire to DDMS XVII Corps	25
		"	Battle casualty wire	26
		4pm	R.A.M.C. battle casualty wire	27
		"	Progress of war wire	28
		4pm	Battle casualty wire	29
			DADMS visited No 1 Heavy field ambulance Hqrs, also 9 F.A.	
ETRUN	28.3.18	4pm	Progress of war wire	
		4pm	R.A.M.C. battle casualty wire	30
		6:30pm	Battle casualty wire	31
			Heavy fighting 4 Div front. Our troops b'yield a little. Total casualties Officers 13	32
				O.R. 500 +

A5834 Wt.W4973/M687 750,000 8/16 D.D.&L.Ltd. Forms/C.2118/13.

Army Form C. 2118.

WAR DIARY
or
INTELLIGENCE SUMMARY.
(Erase heading not required.)

Place	Date	Hour	Summary of Events and Information	Remarks and references to Appendices
ETRUN	28.3.18	c/d	heavy fort at FAMPOUX & ATHIES Mill ave given up. 11 1/2 Fd ambulance hand to ST. CATHERINE G15 a & 4.	
			ADMS visited 11 & 12 Fd Ambulance H.Qrs	Jenie
			L'ABAYETTE ADS stored by 11 & 12 Fd Aml.	Jenie
	29.3.18	9.33am	Battle casualty rom to DDMS XVIIth Corps	33
		"	R.A.M.C. battle casualty rom	34
		5pm	" " "	35
		"	" " "	36
		6.15pm	Battle casualty rom	37
		"	Prisoners of war rom	
			fighting not so heavy. Evacuation of wounded proceeding satisfactorily	
"	30.3.18	6am	Battle casualty rom	38
		"	R.A.M.C. battle casualty rom	39
		5.30pm	Prisoners of war rom	40
		"	R.A.M.C. battle casualty rom	41
		7.30pm	Battle casualty rom	42
			fighting not so severe. ADMS & DADMs attend conference at DDMS Office	Jenie
			XVIIth Corps	Jenie

Army Form C. 2118.

WAR DIARY
or
INTELLIGENCE SUMMARY.
(Erase heading not required.)

Instructions regarding War Diaries and Intelligence Summaries are contained in F. S. Regs., Part II. and the Staff Manual respectively. Title pages will be prepared in manuscript.

Place	Date	Hour	Summary of Events and Information	Remarks and references to Appendices
ETRUN	31/3/18	1:noon	Battle Casualty returns to DDMS XVII Corps	43
"		"	RAMC Battle casualty returns	44
"		4pm	Prisoner of war returns	45
"		"	RAMC Battle Casualty returns to "A" DDMS XVII Corps	46
"		6.25pm	Battle casualty returns to DDMS XVII Corps	47
			Spent very much time visiting the three field ambulances	
			DADMS	

J Snow

J Brackette
Colonel AMS
ADMS
4 Division

1. 4. 18.

SECRET

R.A.M.C. ORDER NO. 30

by

COLONEL E.FAICHNIE, A.M.D., A.D.M.S. 4th. DIVISION.

26th. March, 1918.

1. O.C. Nos. 10 and 12 Field Ambulances will send 4 men to act as bearers between the R.A.P. and A.D.S., to each of the Battalions in the front line of their respective sectors of the Divisional front, as soon as possible.

2. These men will not be employed forward of the R.A.P's.

3. They will not be considered as permanently attached to any one Battalion, and will therefore, not accompany Battalions back on relief.
   They will however, be relieved as often as necessary by men of their own Units, and will return on relief to their own Units.

4. They will continue to be rationed by their own Units during the period of attachment to a Battalion.
   Rations will be drawn daily from respective A.D.S's.

5. O's.C. Nos. 10 and 12 Field Ambulance will notify the A.D.M.S. as soon as each Battalion in their respective Sectors' front lines have been provided with 4 men.

J.S.McCutcheon
Capt. for
Colonel,
A.D.M.S. 4th. Division.

Issued at 12.30 a.m.

Copies to:
    10th. Field Ambulance.
    12th. Field Ambulance.
    10th. Infantry Brigade.
    11th. Infantry Brigade.
    12th. Infantry Brigade.
    4th. Division.
    4th. Division "A".
    Diary.
    File.

SECRET

Copy No. 13.

4th DIVISION MEDICAL ARRANGEMENTS.

IN CONNECTION WITH

4th DIVISION (RESERVE DIVISION) DEFENCE SCHEME (No.2.)

Map Refs: Sheet 51b. 1/40,000.   2nd March, 1918.

(1). Should the Division be ordered to occupy the 3rd System between N.10.d.0.0. and the SCARPE, Brigades will be disposed as follows:-

    12th. Inf. Bde. (H.Q., N.1.a.6.5.)   N.10.d.0.0. to VINE AVE. (exclusive), N.5.a.8.0.

    11th. Inf. Bde. (H.Q., H.31.c.4.0.)   N.5.a.8.0. to H.35.a.7.8.

    10th. Inf. Bde. (H.Q., H.25.d.9.5.)   H.35.a.7.8. to SCARPE.

(2). Medical Arrangements will be as follows:-

  i. No. 10 Field Ambulance will undertake the evacuation of casualties from the front area.

  For this purpose, O.C. No. 10 Field Ambulance will send 8 bearers per Battalion to each of the three Brigades.

  These bearers will work between the Regimental Aid Posts and the first Relay Posts under the orders of the Regimental Medical Officers.

(3). Medical Posts:-

REGIMENTAL AID POSTS.

Left Brigade.   H.28.a. and c.

Centre Brigade.   N.3.b.8.8.
    FEUCHY CHAPEL CROSS ROADS. (N.3.b.8.1.)
    N.4.a.5.5.

Right Brigade.   N.4.d.8.3.
    N.4.d.3.5.

RELAY POSTS.

MAISON ROUGE, (N.3.a.5.7.)
BOIS DES BOEUFS. (H.32.c.7.3.)

ADVANCED DRESSING STATIONS.

TILLOY.   FEUCHY.

MAIN DRESSING STATIONS.

Deaf and Dumb Institute, ARRAS.
Ecole Normale, ARRAS.

(4). EVACUATION:- For the Right and Centre Brigades by hand and wheeled stretchers, to the A.D.Stn., TILLOY. Thence by horse and motor ambulance to the M.D.Stns.

    For the Left Brigade by hand and wheeled stretchers to FEUCHY. Thence by horse and motor ambulance to M.D.Stn. at the Ecole Normale.

-2-

(5). <u>Walking Wounded Post</u>: This will be at TILLOY. Busses will be sent forward as far as practicable to collect Walking Wounded and convoy them to Casualty Clearing Stations.

(6). <u>No. 11 Field Ambulance</u>: No. 11 Field Ambulance will be ready to move at short notice from their present billets to the Ecole Normale. Should the necessity arise, reinforcements for the forward posts will be provided by this Unit.

===

II.

(1). Should the Division be ordered to occupy the 3rd. System, bet-North of the SCARPE, Brigades will be disposed as follows:-

    12th. Inf. Bde. (H.Q., Railway Cutting). From SCARPE to H.10.d.9.3.
    10th. Inf. Bde. (H.Q., Railway Cutting). From H.10.d.9.3. to GAVRELLE Road.
    11th. Inf. Bde. ARRAS.

(2). As for the 3rd. System, South of the SCARPE, above.

(3). <u>MEDICAL POSTS</u>:-

REGIMENTAL AID POSTS.

<u>Left Brigade.</u>   H.9.a.5.7.
                        H.9.b.2.7.

<u>Right Brigade.</u>   H.3].b.9.8.
                        CAM VALLEY. (H.18.a.2.8.)

RELAY POST.

ATHIES.

ADVANCED DRESSING STATION.

L'ABBAYETTE.

MAIN DRESSING STATIONS.

Ecole Normale, ARRAS.
Hospice des Vieillards, ARRAS.

(4). EVACUATION: For Right Brigade, by hand or wheeled stretchers, along FAMPOUX Road to L'ABBAYETTE.

        For Left Brigade by hand or wheeled stretchers, via ATHIES to L'ABBAYETTE. Thence by horse or motor ambulance to M.D.Stns.

(5). <u>Walking Wounded Post</u>: This will be at L'ABBAYETTE. Busses will be sent forward as far as practicable to collect Walking Wounded and convoy them to Casualty Clearing Stations.

(6). As in (6) above.

===

III.

The following paras. will apply in both conditions set forth above:-

(1). The A.D.Stns. and M.D.Stns. of the Right and Left Divisions will be reinforced by the A.D.M.S., 4th. Division if necessary.

Motor ambulances will also be lent to neighbouring Divisions to help in the evacuation of wounded.

(2). Disposal of cases in detail, (for North and South of the SCARPE), will be as given in 4th. Division Medical Arrangements in Connection with Reserve Division Defence Scheme, dated 16th. February, 1918.

(3). The office of the A.D.M.S. 4th. Division will remain in its present position.

Colonel,
A.D.M.S. 4th. Division.

Issued at 7.0 p.m.

Distribution:
    D.D.M.S. XVIIth. Corps.
    4th. Division.
    4th. Division "A".
    10th. Field Ambulance.
    11th. Field Ambulance.
    12th. Field Ambulance.
    10th. Infantry Brigade.
    11th. Infantry Brigade.
    12th. Infantry Brigade.
    C.R.E. 4th. Division.
    O.C. 4th. Div. Signals.
    Diary.(2).

AMENDMENT NO. 1.

to

4th. DIVISION MEDICAL ARRANGEMENTS IN CONNECTION WITH 4th. DIVISION

(RESERVE DIVISION) DEFENCE SCHEME NO. 2.

Para. (6) is cancelled, and the following substituted:-

(6). On receipt of orders from the A.D.M.S. 4th. Division, the O.C. Nos 11 and 12 Field Ambulances will act in accordance with paras. 3 and 4 of "4th. Division Medical Arrangements in Connection with Reserve Division Defence Scheme" dated 16th. February, 1918.

Colonel,
A.D.M.S. 4th. Division.

2nd. March, 1918.

Copies to all recipients of 4th. Division Medical Arrangements in Connection with 4th. Division (Reserve Division) Defence Scheme No. 2.

CORRECTION TO

4th. DIVISION MEDICAL ARRANGEMENTS

IN CONNECTION WITH

4th. DIVISION (RESERVE DIVISION) DEFENCE SCHEME NO.2.
==

In Section II, para. (3), "Regimental Aid Posts, Right Brigade",
for CAM VALLEY, (H.18.a.2.8.) substitute CAM VALLEY, (H.15.a.2.8.)

[signature] McCutcheon

Captain,
for A.D.M.S. 4th. Division.

3rd. March, 1918.

Copies to all concerned.

AMENDMENT NO. 2

to

4th. DIVISION MEDICAL ARRANGEMENTS IN CONNECTION WITH 4th. DIVISION (RESERVE DIVISION) DEFENCE SCHEME NO.2.

==

Reference Para.(3): "REGIMENTAL AID POSTS."

The position of the former R.A.P. of the Right Brigade will not be as stated, (N.4.d.8.3.), but the Post will be established at N.4.c.9.3.

5th. March, 1918.

Captain,
for A.D.M.S. 4th. Division.

Copies to all recipients of "4th. Division Medical Arrangements in Connection with 4th. Division (Reserve Division) Defence Scheme No. 2".

 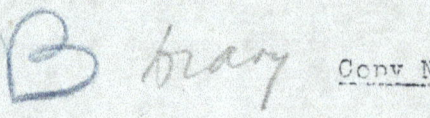 Copy No. 14

4th. DIVISION MEDICAL ARRANGEMENTS
IN CONNECTION WITH
4th. DIVISION (RESERVE DIVISION) DEFENCE SCHEME NO.3.

Map Refs: Sheet 51b, 1/40000.   3rd. March, 1918.

In case the left front of the VIth. Corps is attacked, the Reserve Division of the XVIIth. Corps will move by lorry and march route to the area North of MERCATEL.

The Division is to be prepared to move forward, using covered routes through positions of assembly in N.20.d. and N.17.b., to occupy 3rd. system in VIth. Corps area from about HENIN SUR COJEUL to boundary between VIth. and XVIIth. Corps.

Should this situation arise, Brigades will move to the following assembly areas.

    10th. Infantry Brigade, to Area, M.24.b.
    12th. Infantry Brigade, to Area, M.24.c.
    11th. Infantry Brigade, to Area, M.29.a. and b.

From these positions of assembly, the Division may be ordered to occupy the 3rd. system from HENIN to N.10.d.0.0.
In this case, the Brigades will probably move as follows:-

11th. Infantry Brigade to the Right from No. 32.d.0.8. to N.27.b.0.4. H.Q. NEUVILLE-VITASSE.

12th. Infantry Brigade N.27.b.0.4. to N.22.a.5.3.

10th. Infantry Brigade to the Left from N.22.a.5.3. to N.10.d.0.0. H.Q. N.8.d.5.8.

In the event of the above moves taking place, the following will be the Medical Arrangements:-

1.   No. 10 Field Ambulance will undertake the evacuation of casualties from the forward area.

The O.C. will detail 2 bearer officers and all available bearers to proceed at once to the assembly area in M.24.c.

There, 8 bearers will be sent to each Battalion of the three Brigades. The remainder will be utilized for Relay Posts, to be formed in suitable places between the A.D.Stn. and the R.A.P's.

In addition to the above personnel, the O.C. No. 10 Field Ambulance will despatch one Medical Store Cart containing sufficient equipment rapidly to form an A.D.Stn. at NEUVILLE-VITASSE.

He will also send sufficient personnel and equipment to take over the M.D.Stn. at S.2.b.7.4., (near FICHEUX).

2. MEDICAL POSTS:

R.A.Posts: Regimental Medical Officers will choose suitable places for their R.A.P's. and will notify the bearer officer or the O.C. No. 10 Field Ambulance of their exact location, immediately such sites have been determined.

Relay Posts: These will be established near the track leading from WANCOURT to NEUVILLE-VITASSE.

-2-

    <u>Advanced Dressing Station</u>:   NEUVILLE-VITASSE.

    <u>Walking Wounded Post</u>:   M.28.central. (Near MERCATEL).

    <u>Main Dressing Station</u>:   S.2.b.7.4. (Near FICHEUX).

<u>N.B.</u>   The A.D.Stn. at NEUVILLE-VITASSE may have to be abandoned as such and withdrawn to S.2.b.7.4. In that case the post will be utilized as a Bearer Post.

3. <u>EVACUATION</u>: By hand or wheeled stretchers to NEUVILLE-VITASSE, (A.D.Stn) Thence if possible, by horse or motor ambulance to the M.D.Stn. S.2.b.7.4., and from there by M.A.C. cars to Casualty Clearing Stations.

4. <u>WALKING WOUNDED POST</u>: This will be established West of MERCATEL, (M.28.central). Busses will be sent as far forward as practicable to collect Walking Wounded.

5. <u>No. 11 FIELD AMBULANCE</u>: On receipt of orders from the A.D.M.S., O.C. No. 11 Field Ambulance will send all available bearers to report to O.C. No. 10 Field Ambulance for duty at S.2.b.7.4. As many as possible of these bearers will be sent by motor ambulances. The remainder will march.

    One Tent Sub-Division less one officer, will be left at AVESNES-LE-COMTE.

    Only sufficient transport will be sent to S.2.b.7.4.

    On arrival there the O.C. No. 11 Field Ambulance will take charge of the Dressing Station.

6. <u>No. 12 FIELD AMBULANCE</u>: The Tent Division of No. 12 Field Ambulance will remain at WARLUS.

    On receipt of orders from the A.D.M.S., O.C. No. 12 Field Ambulance will send his Bearer Division to S.2.b.7.4. for duty under O.C. No. 10 Field Ambulance.

7.   Further instructions as to disposal of cases in detail will be issued later.

8.   The office of the A.D.M.S. 4th. Division will remain in its present position, unless the Division attacks East of the 3rd. system, when it will move to YORK LINES, (M.17.c.5.5.)

                                   Colonel,
                                 A.D.M.S. 4th. Division.

Issued at 12, noon.

<u>Copies to</u>:-   D.D.M.S. XVIIth. Corps.
              D.D.M.S. VIth. Corps.
              4th. Division.
              4th. Division "A".
              10th. Field Ambulance.
              11th. Field Ambulance.
              12th. Field Ambulance.
              10th. Infantry Brigade.
              11th. Infantry Brigade.
              12th. Infantry Brigade.
              Machine Gun Battalion.
              C.R.E. 4th. Division.
              O.C. 4th. Div. Signals.
              Diary. (2).
              File.

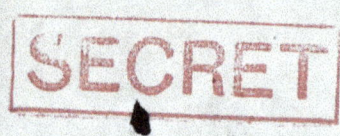 

Copy No. 29

R.A.M.C. ORDER NO. 47

by

LIEUT-COLONEL R.P.LEWIS, R.A.M.C., A/A.D.M.S. 4th. DIVISION.

6th. March, 1918.

==

1. The following move will take place forthwith:

   No. 10 Field Ambulance will take over HOPITAL ST JEAN, as 4th. Division Main Dressing Station.

2. O.C. No. 10 Field Ambulance will hand over ECOLE NORMALE to O.C. No. 47 Field Ambulance.

3. Details of reliefs to be arranged between Ambulance Commanders concerned.

4. Relief to be completed by 12, noon on 7th. inst. Completion to be reported by wire to this office.

5. Receipts will be given and taken for all stores taken and handed over respectively.

R P Lewis
Lieut-Colonel,
a/A.D.M.S. 4th. Division.

Issued at 4.30 p.m.

Distribution:
D.D.M.S. XVII Corps.   A.D.M.S. 15th. Division.
4th. Division.
4th. Division "A".
10th. Field Ambulance.
11th. Field Ambulance.
12th. Field Ambulance.
All R.M.O's.
10th. Infantry Brigade.
11th. Infantry Brigade.
12th. Infantry Brigade.
4th. Div. Signals.
C.R.E. 4th. Division.
Diary. (2).
File.

Copy No. 33

4th. DIVISION MEDICAL ARRANGEMENTS

IN CONNECTION WITH

4th. DIVISION (RESERVE DIVISION) DEFENCE SCHEME NO.2.

==

Map Refs: Sheet 51b, 1/40,000.   8th. March, 1918.

==

The 4th. Divisional Medical Arrangements produced under the above heading, dated 2nd. March, 1918 are cancelled, and the following substituted:-

I.
---

1. Should the Division be ordered to occupy the Third System between N.10.d.0.0. and the SCARPE, Brigades will be disposed as follows:-

   12th. Inf. Bde: (H.Q. N.1.a.6.5.)   N.10.d.0.0. to VINE AVENUE
                                       (exclusive), N.5.a.8.0

   11th. Inf. Bde: (H.Q. H.31.c.4.0.) N.5.a.8.0. to H.35.a.7.8.

   10th. Inf. Bde: (H.Q. H.25.d.9.5.) H.35.a.7.8. to SCARPE.

2. MEDICAL POSTS: REGIMENTAL AID POSTS.

   Left Brigade: H.28.a. and c.

   Centre Brigade: N.3.b.8.8.
                       FEUCHY CHAPEL CROSS ROADS. (N.3.b.8.1.)
                       N.4.a.5.5.

   Right Brigade: N.4.c.9.3.
                       N.4.d.3.5.

   RELAY POSTS.

   MAISON ROUGE. (N.3.a.5.7.)
   BOIS DES BOEUFS. (H.32.c.7.3.)

   ADVANCED DRESSING STATIONS.

   TILLOY.   FEUCHY.

   CORPS MAIN DRESSING STATION.

   ECOLE NORMALE, ARRAS. (47th. Field Ambulance).

3. EVACUATION: For the Right and Centre Brigades by hand and wheeled stretcher, to the Advanced Dressing Station, TILLOY. Thence by horsed and motor ambulance to the Corps M.D.Stn., ECOLE NORMALE.

   For the Left Brigade by hand and wheeled stretcher to FEUCHY. Thence by horsed and motor ambulance to Corps M.D.Stn.

4. WALKING WOUNDED POSTS: These will be at TILLOY, (H.31.c.2.5.) and ST NICHOLAS, (G.16.c.5.6.)
   Busses and lorries will be sent to these Posts to collect Walking Wounded and convey them to Cas. Clg. Stns.

-2-

The A.D.M.S. 4th. Division will reinforce these Posts if necessary, with personnel from the Division.

5.(a). NO. 10 FIELD AMBULANCE: O.C. No. 10 Field Ambulance will undertake the evacuation of casualties from the front area.
For this purpose, he will send 8 bearers per Battalion to each of the 3 Brigades.
These bearers will work between the Regimental Aid Posts and the first Relay Posts, under the orders of the Regimental Medical Officers.

O.C. No. 10 Field Ambulance will also establish an A.D.Stn. at FEUCHY, (staffed from his Unit).

Headquarters of No. 10 Field Ambulance and details will remain at the HOPITAL ST JEAN.

(b). NO. 11 FIELD AMBULANCE: On receipt of orders from the A.D.M.S. 4th. Division, O.C. No. 11 Field Ambulance will send his Bearer Division immediately to report to O.C. No. 10 Field Ambulance at the HOPITAL ST JEAN, for duty.
These will be conveyed as far as possible in motor ambulances.

One Tent Sub-Division, less one Officer will be left at AVESNES LE COMTE, together with all horse transport that is not absolutely needed at ARRAS.

The remainder of No. 11 Field Ambulance will march immediately to the HOPITAL ST JEAN.
On arrival there, the O.C. No. 11 Field Ambulance will take charge of the HOPITAL.

The two Tent Sub-Divisions of No. 11 Field Ambulance at HOPITAL ST JEAN, will be required to furnish the following parties, at the request of the D.D.M.S. XVII Corps:

1. Three M.O's. (chosen for their surgical experience), 3 N.C.O's. and 24 Other Ranks for Cas. Clg. Stns.

2. One M.O., 19 Other Ranks for Corps Main Dressing Station.

(c). NO. 12 FIELD AMBULANCE: The Tent Division of No. 12 Field Ambulance will remain at WARLUS, running the C.R.Stn.
On receipt of orders from the A.D.M.S. 4th. Division, O.C. No. 12 Field Ambulance will send his Bearer Division to the Hopital St. Jean, where they will report to the O.C. No. 10 Field Ambulance for duty.

==

II.
----

1. Should the Division be ordered to occupy the Third System North of the SCARPE, Brigades will be disposed as follows:-

12th. Inf. Bde.(H.Q. Railway Cutting).   From SCARPE to H.10.d.9.3.

10th. Inf. Bde.(H.Q. Railway Cutting).   From H.10.d.9.3. to GAVRELLE Road.

11th. Inf. Bde.(H.Q. ARRAS).

-3-

2. **MEDICAL POSTS:**   **REGIMENTAL AID POSTS.**

    <u>Left Brigade:</u>   H.9.a.5.7.
                           H.9.b.2.7.

    <u>Right Brigade:</u>   H.21.b.9.8.
                            H.15.a.2.8. (CAM VALLEY).

RELAY POST.

ATHIES.

ADVANCED DRESSING STATION.

L'ABBAYETTE.

CORPS MAIN DRESSING STATION.

ECOLE NORMALE, ARRAS.

3. **EVACUATION:** For the Right Brigade, by hand or wheeled stretcher along FAMPOUX Road to L'ABBAYETTE.

     For Left Brigade by hand or wheeled stretcher via ATHIES to L'ABBAYETTE.

     Thence by horsed or motor ambulance to the M.D.Stn. at ECOLE NORMALE.

4. **WALKING WOUNDED POSTS:** These will be at TILLOY and ST NICHOLAS, as in 4, above.

5. As in 5, above, A.D.S. at L'ABBAYETTE.

===

The following paras. will apply in both (I) and (II) above:-

1. **DISPOSAL OF CASES IN DETAIL:**

    All sick (via HOPITAL ST JEAN)) to WARLUS, via Walking Wounded
    Trivial Wounds.   )   Posts, in lorries and busses.
    N.Y.D.N.   )
    N.Y.D. Gas.   )

    Wounded, other than trivial, and Walking Wounded, to the Corps M.D.Stn.

    Eye, Throat, Nose, Ear and Dental cases will not be sent unless extremely urgent.

2. **TRANSPORT:**

    (a). <u>Motor Ambulances</u>: Four motor ambulances additional to those of the Field Ambulances of the Division, will be at the disposal of the A.D.M.S., and will be sent when urgently required.
        More may be obtained on receipt by the A.D.M.S. of a wire from the Ambulance Commander.

    (b). <u>LORRIES</u>: 8 Lorries per Division will be placed at the disposal of A.D.M.S. to clear Walking Wounded Posts.

(c). **LIGHT RAILWAYS**: These will be used whenever they are found practicable.

(d). **LAUNCHES AND BARGES**: If it is found by O.C. No. 10 Field Ambulance that the launches and barges are still working on the SCARPE, he will send notification to that effect to the A.D.M.S., in order that arrangements may be made for the craft to be met at the QUAI DU RIVAGE by motor ambulances, and the cases conveyed to the C.M.D.Stn.

3. **CLERICAL**:

(a). O.C. No. 11 Field Ambulance will detail two reliable clerks to proceed to each of the Walking Wounded Posts at TILLOY and ST NICHOLAS.
   They will record in A. & D. Books all casualties of the 4th. Division passing through those Posts.
   They will submit to the A.D.M.S. 4th. Division daily, at 6 a.m. and 6 p.m., the usual 'Casualty Wires'.
   They will also submit the ~~daily wire of Wounded Prisoners of War Admitted~~ and the Daily State. The last return to reach the Office of the A.D.M.S. by 1 p.m. daily.

(b). O.C. No. 10 Field Ambulance will send three reliable clerks, including one N.C.O. to the Corps M.D.Stn.
   They will record all 4th. Divisional casualties passing through that Unit.
   They will submit all returns detailed in (a) above.

(c). All cases sent to the Corps Rest Station, WARLUS, will be shown as transfers to the Field Ambulance running the C.R.S., and will be shown as such.

(d). German wounded ~~other than Walking Wounded~~ will be entered in A. & D. Books of the Unit administering the C.M.D.Stn., as will Corps Troops.

(e). A.F., W.3210 when no longer required will be used as notification to Units.

(f). If it is absolutely necessary to send any very urgent case direct from the A.D.Stn. to Cas. Clg. Stns., the Field Medical Card must be made out, and it is to be noted thereon 'Direct Admission to Cas. Clg. Stn.', in order that the C.C.S. may enter it as such.

4. **DUMPS**: Corps Dumps of stretchers and blankets are held at ~~soldiers~~ the HOPITAL ST JEAN, where 150 stretchers and 500 blankets are available. If any more are required, notification must be sent to the A.D.M.S.

5. **ANTI-TETANIC SERUM**: Anti-Tetanic Serum will be given and Field Medical Cards made out at Walking Wounded Posts and Corps Main Dressing Station.
   Amount of A.T.S. given must be clearly stated on the F.M.Card.

6. The Office of the A.D.M.S. 4th. Division will remain in its present position.

Issued at 1.30 a.m.

Captain,
for A.D.M.S. 4th. Division.

Distribution: D.D.M.S. XVIIth. Corps.
A.D.M.S. Guards' Division.
A.D.M.S. 15th. Division.
4th. Division.
4th. Division "A".
10th. Field Ambulance.
11th. Field Ambulance.
12th. Field Ambulance.
10th. Infantry Brigade.
11th. Infantry Brigade.
12th. Infantry Brigade.
All R.M.O's.
C.R.E. 4th. Division.
O.C. 4th. Signal Coy.
4th. Divisional Train.
Diary. (2).
File.

AMENDMENT NO.1

to

4th. DIVISION MEDICAL ARRANGEMENTS, IN CONNECTION WITH 4th. DIVISION DEFENCE SCHEME.

==

The following amendment will be made to Medical Arrangements as above, dated 7th. March, 1918:

Section I, Para.5 (b), sub-paras. 1 and 2 are cancelled, and the following substituted:

1.   2 Medical Officers, (chosen for their surgical experience), 3 N.C.O's. and 24 men, (including at least 4 Nursing Orderlies), to No. 8 Casualty Clearing Station.

2.   1 Medical Officer to No. 19 Casualty Clearing Station.

8th. March, 1918.

J.G. McCutcheon Captain,
for A/A.D.M.S. 4th. Division.

Copies to all recipients of above Medical Arrangements.

Ref: 4th. DIVISION MEDICAL ARRANGEMENTS
No.2, IN CONNECTION WITH
4th. DIVISION (RESERVE DIVISION) DEFENCE SCHEME.

===

1. AMENDMENT: Amendment No. 1 to the above Arrangements, dated 8th. inst. is cancelled, and the following substituted:-

    Section I, Para. 5(b):-

    1. 1 Medical Officer, (chosen for his surgical experience), 3 N.C.O's. and 24 men, (including at least 4 Nursing Orderlies), to No. 8 Casualty Clearing Station.

    2. On receipt of orders from the A.D.M.S., Captain C.T.Mc.L.PLOWRIGHT, R.A.M.C., M.O. 4th. M.G.Bn., will report to O.C. No. 11 Field Ambulance and proceed with the party mentioned in para. 1, above. The Senior Medical Officer will take charge of the party.

    3. O.C. No. 11 Field Ambulance will detail one Officer to proceed immediately on receipt of orders from the A.D.M.S., to take over Medical Charge of XVIIth. Corps Musketry and Reinforcement Camp.

---

2. ADDENDUM: The following will be added after para. 5 (c) of Section I:

    (d). HOLDINGS OF SICK: To be disposed of on "P" day.

i.	Hospital St Jean.	Not more than 50.
ii.	Avesnes le Comte.	Not more than 50.
iii.	Corps Rest Station, WARLUS.	Down to 400.

    i, by M.A.C. and Field Ambulance cars to C.C.S.Group at AGNEZ. O.C., M.A.C. will arrange for this evacuation.

    ii, by motor ambulance cars of No. 11 Field Ambulance direct to C.C.S.Group at AGNEZ.

    iii, by motor ambulance cars of No. 12 Field Ambulance, assisted by M.A.C. cars if necessary, to C.C.S. Group at AGNEZ.

    O's.C. Nos. 10 and 11 Field Ambulances will wire the numbers thus evacuated to the A.D.M.S. at once, to enable him to inform the D.D.M.S., who will arrange for train accommodation at AGNEZ.

H.Q. 4th. Division.
9th. March, 1918.

J.S.McCutcheon
Captain,
for a/A.D.M.S. 4th. Division.

Copies to all concerned.

Copy No. 33

4th. DIVISION MEDICAL ARRANGEMENTS NO.1

IN CONNECTION WITH

RESERVE DIVISION DEFENCE SCHEME.

(Cancelling 4th. Division Medical Arrangements, dated 16th. Feb., 1918).

===

Map Refs: Sheet 51b. 1/40,000.   10th. March, 1918.

===

1.   The Division is to be prepared to take over at short notice the centre portion of the XVIIth. Corps Front.

   (a). SOUTHERN DIVISIONAL BOUNDARY:

   'P' Sap (to right Division) - MONCHY Trench as far as junction with CURB RESERVE (to centre Division) - 'G' Post (to right Division) - Old trench H.35.c.6.3.(to right Division) - Thence a straight line to meet the CAMBRAI Road, H.32.d.3.3. - Thence the CAMBRAI Road (to right Division).

   (b). NORTHERN DIVISIONAL BOUNDARY:

   I.14.a.50.15 - Junction of CROW ALLEY and CORONA SUPPORT - Railway crossing at I.13.c.95.85 - COLT RESERVE at I.13.a.0.1. (all to left Division) - QUARRY at H.18.a.2.5. - Machine-gun emplacement at H.17.b.2.5. - Trench junction, H.16.d.5.8. - CAM Trench as far as H.16.a.0.0. (all to centre Division) - Thence straight line to FEUCHY LOCK - Thence the River SCARPE.

   The Division will take over this portion of the line with two Brigades in the Front Line and one in Reserve.

2. (a). NO. 10 FIELD AMBULANCE:

   On receiving orders from the A.D.M.S., O.C. No. 10 Field Ambulance will take over from a Field Ambulance of the left Division the Medical Posts of their Right Sector North of the SCARPE, and from a Field Ambulance of the right Division their Medical Posts South of the SCARPE, within the Divisional Boundary.
   His Headquarters will be established at BLANGY, and he will be responsible for the evacuation of casualties from the Front Area, to the Corps Main Dressing Station.
   He will at once send 8 bearers per Battalion to the 10th. and 12th. Infantry Brigades, and will send sufficient personnel to form Relay Posts, and to open A.D.S's. at FAMPOUX LOCK and FEUCHY.
   The latter will only have sufficient personnel to act as reserve A.D.S.
   He will evacuate all sick unfit for duty from the HOPITAL ST JEAN to C.C.S.

   (b). NO. 11 FIELD AMBULANCE:

   O.C. No. 11 Field Ambulance will take over the HOPITAL ST JEAN from No. 10 Field Ambulance on receipt of orders from the A.D.M.S.
   He will at once send all his available bearers to report to O.C. No. 10 Field Ambulance for duty. As many as possible of these

bearers will be despatched by motor ambulances going up to the A.D.S., - the remainder proceeding by road.

One Tent-Sub-Division less one Officer will be left at AVESNES LE COMPTE.

The remainder of R.A.M.C. personnel, and Headquarters will be stationed at the HOPITAL ST JEAN.

Only sufficient transport will be taken to ARRAS, the remainder of the transport and attached personnel being left at AVESNES LE COMTE, under the charge of the O.C. Tent Sub-Division.

(c). NO. 12 FIELD AMBULANCE:

The Tent-Division of No. 12 Field Ambulance will remain at WARLUS, running the C.R.S.

On receipt of orders from the A.D.M.S., O.C. No. 12 Field Ambulance will send his Bearer Division to the HOPITAL ST JEAN, where they will be at the disposal of O.C. No. 10 Field Ambulance.

3. MEDICAL POSTS: (a). FIRST SYSTEM.

R.A.P's:

Right Brigade.	Left Brigade.
H.30.d.2.8.(2).	H.24.b.8.2.
H.36.c.1.9.	H.24.a.5.7.(2),TRIPLE ARCH.

RELAY POSTS:

H.29.c.5.4.	H.24.a.5.7.
H.24.c.2.8.	H.18.d.2.2., SINGLE ARCH.

A.D.S.: FAMPOUX LOCK, H.23.a.9.5.
FEUCHY, H.21.c.9.5.

Walking Wounded Collecting Post:(Divisional Post).

ATHIES LOCK, H.21.a.2.6.

CORPS WALKING WOUNDED POST:

ST NICHOLAS.
TILLOY.

C.M.D.S.:

ECOLE NORMALE.

EVACUATION:

(a). RIGHT BRIGADE:(i). By hand and wheeled stretcher from H.36.c.1.9. to Relay Post at H.29.c.5.4. Thence to FEUCHY.

(ii). From R.A.P. at H.30.d.2.8. via CHINSTRAP LANE to Relay Post at H.24.c.2.8. Thence to FAMPOUX LOCK.

(b). LEFT BRIGADE: From R.A.P's. at H.18.d.2.2. and H.14.b.8.2. by hand carriage to H.24.a.5.7. Thence by wheeled stretcher to FAMPOUX LOCK.

(c). From FAMPOUX LOCK and FEUCHY by barge (if practicable) and motor ambulance to C.M.D.S.

(b). SECOND SYSTEM.

R.A.P's: Right Brigade.   Left Brigade.

        H.29.c.5.4.   H.24.a.5.7. (2).
        H.36.c.1.9. (2).   FAMPOUX LOCK.

RELAY POSTS:

        H.29.c.5.4.   FAMPOUX LOCK.
                                 H.23.c.0.6.

A.D.S: FEUCHY.

W.W.C.P: ATHIES LOCK, H.21.a.2.6.

C.W.W.P: ST NICHOLAS.
         TILLOY.

C.M.D.S: ECOLE NORMALE.

EVACUATION:

(a). RIGHT BRIGADE: From H.36.c.1.9. by hand and wheeled stretcher to Relay Post at H.29.c.5.4. Thence to FEUCHY.

(b). LEFT BRIGADE: From R.A.P. at H.24.a.5.7. and FAMPOUX LOCK by hand and wheeled stretcher to Relay Post at H.23.c.0.6. Thence to FEUCHY.

(c). From FEUCHY by motor and horsed ambulance, (sent as far up as possible if unable to reach FEUCHY), to C.M.D.S.

(c). THIRD SYSTEM.

R.A.P's: Right Brigade.   Left Brigade.

        H.28.a. and c.   H.21.b.9.9.
                                 H.15.d.2.8.

RELAY POSTS:

        H.33.d.9.9.   FEUCHY.
        H.32.c.8.3.   ATHIES MILL.

A.D.S: Cellars at 52 and 57 Rue de DOUAI, ARRAS.
        Railway Embankment. (If practicable).

C.W.W.P: ST NICHOLAS.
         TILLOY.

C.M.D.S: ECOLE NORMALE.

EVACUATION:

(a). RIGHT BRIGADE: (i). From R.A.P. at H.33.d.9.9. by hand and wheeled stretcher to Relay Post at H.32.c.8.3. Thence TILLOY.

(ii). R.A.P's. at H.28.a. and c. to Relay Post at FEUCHY. Thence to the Railway Embankment, or Car Post at H.19.b.4.5. Thence to C.M.D.S.

(b). LEFT BRIGADE: From R.A.P's. at H.21.b.9.9. and H.15.d.2.8. by hand and wheeled stretcher to ATHIES MILL. Thence A.D.S. or Car Post and C.M.D.S.

4. DISPOSAL OF CASES IN DETAIL: As in Medical Arrangements No. 2 dated 7th. March, 1918.
C.C.S. Group, Nos. 7, 8 and 19, AGNEZ LES DUISANS.

5. CLERICAL.

6. DUMPS:

7. ANTI-TETANIC SERUM: As in Medical Arrangements No. 2 dated 7th. March, 1918.

8. HOLDINGS OF SICK:

9. TRANSPORT:

(a). Motor Ambulances: Field Ambulances will utilize their own Ambulance cars as far as possible.
Additional cars will be obtained by the A.D.M.S. on receipt of a wire asking for them, from Field Ambulance.

(b). LORRIES: 8 lorries per Division will be placed at the disposal of the A.D.M.S. to clear W.W.P's.
Rendezvous for lorries for this Division will be in the PLACE DE LA PREFECTURE, ARRAS.

(c). LIGHT RAILWAYS: Will be used whenever practicable.

(d). BARGES and LAUNCHES: As in Medical Arrangements No. 2 dated 7th. March, 1918.

10. FIELD MEDICAL CARDS: F.M.Cards will be clearly marked 'AGNEZ' or 'WARLUS'. They will on no account be marked 'C.R.S.' or 'C.C.S.'

11. The Office of the A.D.M.S. will remain in its present position.

Maichnie.
Lieut.-Colonel,
a/A.D.M.S. 4th. Division.

Issued at 7.45 p.m.

Copies to:
D.D.M.S. XVIIth. Corps.
A.D.M.S. Guards' Division.
A.D.M.S. 15th. Division.
4th. Division.
4th. Division "A".
10th. Field Ambulance.
11th. Field Ambulance.
12th. Field Ambulance.
All R.M.O's.
10th. Infantry Brigade.
11th. Infantry Brigade.
12th. Infantry Brigade.
C.R.E. 4th. Division.
O.C. 4th. Div. Signals.
4th. Divisional Train.
Diary, (2).
File.

F

A.D.M.S. 4th. Division No.31/126.

all
Bn. MO's.

During active operations you will arrange that each Regimental stretcher has 2 blankets, which will be used to cover patients.

You will form an Exchange Dump, if possible at your R.A.P., which will be replenished by the Field Ambulances' Bearers from the Advanced Dressing Station.

In addition to the above, you will use the patients' ground-sheets.

J.G. McCutcheon

Headquarters,
4th. Division.
11-3-1918.

Captain, for
a/A.D.M.S. 4th. Division.

[SECRET] [URGENT]

STAND TO.

G

Stand to, to execute all moves detailed in Medical Arrangements No. 2, dated 7th. inst., from 6 a.m. on 12th. March, 1918.

ACKNOWLEDGE.

Headquarters,
4th. Division.
11-3-1918.

J.E. McCutcheon
Capt. for
Lieut.-Colonel,
a/A.D.M.S. 4th. Division.

SECRET

ADDENDUM NO. 2

to

4th. DIVISION MEDICAL ARRANGEMENTS NO.2
IN CONNECTION WITH RESERVE DIVISION DEFENCE SCHEME.

==

Sections I and II.

The following will be added to paras. 4:

"In addition, a 4th. Divisional Walking Wounded Post will be formed in cellars at billets Nos. 52 and 57 Rue de DOUAI, ARRAS. This Post will be staffed by a Tent Sub-Division from No. 10 Field Ambulance, with necessary clerks, who will render all returns detailed in Para.3 below".

H.Q. 4th. Division.
11th. March, 1918.

Captain, for
a/A.D.M.S. 4th. Division.

Copies to all concerned.

A.D.M.S. 4th. Division No. 17/12.

1. The XVIIth. Corps Main Dressing Station, ECOLE NORMALE, ARRAS, will open to receive all wounded cases from 9 a.m. on 11th. inst.

2. Sick will continue to be treated Divisionally, and when Defence Arrangements come into force, Corps Main Dressing Station will deal with cases only in accordance with Medical Arrangements 1 or 2, issued from this office.

3. No clerks will be detailed to the C.M.D.S. till defence arrangements come into force.

4. O.C., C.M.D.S. will render a nominal roll to A.D.M.S. 4th. Division daily, from 11th. inst. of all wounded cases of this Division passing through the C.M.D.S. These will be passed through the A. & D. Books of No. 10 Field Ambulance and shown on their Daily State.
Corps Troops and Other Formations will be shown on the books and States of the Field Ambulance running the C.M.D.S.

Captain, for
a/A.D.M.S. 4th. Division.

H.Q. 4th. Division.
11-3-1918.

A.D.M.S. 4th. Division No.31/126.

All
Bn. M.O.'s.

Draw at once from No. 10 Field Ambulance, at HOPITAL ST JEAN, ARRAS, the following splints:

1. Two Thomas' Leg Splints.
2. Two Thomas' Arm Splints.

Headquarters,
4th. Division.
11-3-1918.

J G McCutcheon
Captain, for
a/A.D.M.S. 4th. Division,

K

Copy No. 32

4th. DIVISION MEDICAL ARRANGEMENTS NO.3(a).

IN CONNECTION WITH

4th. DIVISION (RESERVE) DEFENCE SCHEME, AND

4th. DIVISION, G.A.4/73/G.

==

Map Refs: Sheet 51b, 1/40,000.   11th. March, 1918.

==

1. In the event of a hostile attack against the Southern portion of the Third Army front which does not involve this Corps, the Division in Corps Reserve will be prepared to march to the GOMIECOURT area to replace the Division now in Reserve to the VIth. Corps.

2. If this order is received, Brigade Groups will be ordered by 4th. Division to move as under.
    Field Ambulances are to move with Brigade Groups as shown under the orders of the respective Brigade Commanders.

    (a). 10th. Field Ambulance will move with 10th. Inf. Bde. Group to the ERVILLERS - HAMELINCOURT area.
    Route: Main ARRAS-BAPAUME Road.

    (b). 11th. Field Ambulance will move with 11th. Inf. Bde. Group to the BLAIREVILLE area.
    Route: BERNEVILLE - WAILLY - BRETENCOURT.

    (c). 12th. Field Ambulance will move with 12th. Inf. Bde. Group to the MERCATEL and BOISLEUX-AU-MONT area.
    Route: BERNEVILLE - WAILLY - FICHEUX.

    Field Ambulances will march in rear of their Brigade Groups and pick up sick. These will be disposed of by evacuation to the nearest C.C.S.

    C.C.S. Group for VIth. Corps is as follows:-

    No. 20 C.C.S.   BOISLEUX-AU-MONT.
    No. 43 C.C.S.   BAC-DU-SUD.
    Nos. 45 and 49 C.C.S. ACHIET-LE-GRAND.
    Nos. 3 and 29 C.C.S. GREVILLERS.

3. No. 12 Field Ambulance will move less the Tent-Division, which will remain at WARLUS until relieved. Then it will proceed by forced march to the MERCATEL and BOISLEUX-AU-MONT area under the command of the senior officer, and join the remainder of the Unit.
    Enough transport will remain at WARLUS with the Tent-Division to carry the remainder of No. 12 Field Ambulance equipment to the new area.

4. On arrival in the VIth. Corps Reserve Division Area, Field Ambulances will collect and dispose of by evacuation, the sick of their respective Brigade Groups.

5. (a).   O.C. No. 10 Field Ambulance will be prepared on receipt of orders from A.D.M.S., to undertake evacuation of casualties from the forward area, should the Division go into the line. (See para. 1 of Med. Arrts. No. 3, dated 3rd. March, 1918).

(b).   O.C. No. 11 Field Ambulance will be prepared to take over the M.D.S., and send his bearers to No. 10 Field Ambulance for duty. (See para. 5 of same Arrts.).

(c).   O.C. No. 12 Field Ambulance will be prepared to send his bearers to No. 10 Field Ambulance for duty. (See para. 6 of same Arrts.).

[signature]

Captain, for
a/A.D.M.S. 4th. Division.

Issued at 9.45 p.m.

Copies to: D.D.M.S. XVIIth. Corps.
D.D.M.S. VIth. Corps.
A.D.M.S. 40th. Division.
4th. Division.
4th. Division, "A".
No. 10 Field Ambulance.
No. 11 Field Ambulance.
No. 12 Field Ambulance.
All R.M.O's.
10th. Infantry Brigade.
11th. Infantry Brigade.
12th. Infantry Brigade.
C.R.E. 4th. Division.
O.C. 4th. Div. Signals.
4th. Divisional Train.
Diary, (2).
File.

Copy No. 96

R.A.M.C. ORDER NO.48

by

LIEUT.-COLONEL N.FAICHNIE, R.A.M.C., A/A.D.M.S. 4th. DIVISION.

==

Map Refs: Sheet 51b, 1/40,000.   18th. March, 1918.

==

The 4th. Division is to relieve the Guards' Division in the Left Sector of the XVIIth. Corps front.
The relief will commence on 19th. March, 1918.

1. **RELIEF OF MEDICAL UNITS:**

    (a). <u>NO. 10 FIELD AMBULANCE</u>: No. 10 Field Ambulance will relieve No. 9 Field Ambulance for the purpose of carrying out the evacuation of casualties from the Right Sector of the Divisional front.
    The relief will commence on 19th. inst., and must be completed by 6 p.m. on 29th. inst.
    Details of reliefs of Medical Posts to be arranged between O's.C. concerned.
    Headquarters, No. 10 Field Ambulance will remain at HOPITAL ST JEAN.

    (b). <u>NO. 12 FIELD AMBULANCE</u>: No. 12 Field Ambulance will relieve No. 4 Field Ambulance for the purpose of carrying out the evacuation of casualties from the Left Sector of the Divisional front.
    The relief will commence on 19th. inst., and must be completed by noon, 20th. inst.
    The Bearer Division of No. 12 Field Ambulance and the necessary staff for the A.D.S. at TANK DUMP will march on 19th. inst. to the Headquarters of No. 4 Field Ambulance at ST NICHOLAS, (G.16.c.4.8.).
    The reliefs of the Medical Posts will take place on the night of 19th/20th. March, and will be arranged between the O's.C. concerned.
    On relief at the Corps Rest Station, WARLUS, the remainder of No. 12 Field Ambulance will march to Ambulance Headquarters, at ST NICHOLAS, G.16.c.4.8.

    (c). <u>NO. 11 FIELD AMBULANCE</u>: No. 11 Field Ambulance will march on 20th. inst. to ST NICHOLAS, (G.16.d.0.9.) where Ambulance Headquarters will be established.
    A billetting party of 1 N.C.O. and 10 Other Ranks will report to the Town Major, ST NICHOLAS on the morning of the 19th. inst.
    A guard of 1 N.C.O. and 2 men will be left at AVESNES-LE-COMTE, where they will remain until relieved or told to rejoin their Unit.

    (d). Completion of all moves and reliefs to be reported by wire to the A.D.M.S. 4th. Division.

2.   Office of the A.D.M.S. 4th. Division will remain at No.1 RUE DE LA PREFECTURE, ARRAS.

3.   ACKNOWLEDGE.

Issued at 1.30 p.m.

J.G.McCutcheon
Capt`t`/ʳ Lieut-Colonel,
a/A.D.M.S. 4th. Division.

Copies to:-   D.D.M.S. XVIIth. Corps.
A.D.M.S. Guards' Division.
A.D.M.S. 15th. Division.
No. 10 Field Ambulance.
No. 11 Field Ambulance.
No. 12 Field Ambulance.
4th. Division.
4th. Division "A".
R.M.O's.
10th. Infantry Brigade.
11th. Infantry Brigade.
12th. Infantry Brigade.
C.R.E. 4th. Division.
4th. Div. Signals.
4th. Divisional Train.
Diary,(2).
File.
Town Commandant St Nicholas
Area   Avenes Le Comte
15 A A6
06 C A D S
XVII Corps Inland Water Transport

SECRET

4th. DIVISION.

MEDICAL ARRANGEMENTS IN CONNECTION WITH R.A.M.C. ORDER 48.

Map Refs: Sheet 51b, 1/40,000.   18th. March, 1918.

The following Medical Arrangements will come into force on the relief of the Guards' Division by 4th. Division:

1. **POSITIONS OF MEDICAL POSTS:**

    (a). **R.A.P's:** Battns. in Line:
    - Right: SINGLE ARCH, H.18.d.2.2.
    - Centre: QUARRY, I.13.a.1.2.
    - Left: HUSSAR TRENCH, H.5.d.9.1.

    Battns. in Support:
    - Right: H.23.a.9.0.
    - Centre: PUDDING TRENCH, H.16.b.7.7.
    - Left: NORTHUMBERLAND AVE., H.11.a.6.2.

    Battns. in Reserve:
    - Right: GORDON CAMP.
    - Centre: STIRLING CAMP.
    - Left: ST LAURENT BLANGY.

    (b). **RELAY POSTS:**
    - TRIPLE ARCH.
    - FAMPOUX, H.17.d.3.6.

    (c). **A.D.S's:**
    - Right Sector: FAMPOUX, H.23.a.8.6.
      FEUCHY, H.21.a.0.7. (Reserve A.D.S.).
    - Left Sector: TANK DUMP, H.11.a.5.3.
      L'ABBAYETTE, H.14.b.5.1. (Reserve A.D.S.)

    (d). **FIELD AMBULANCES:**
    - No. 10 Field Ambce: HOPITAL ST JEAN, ARRAS.
    - No. 11 Field Ambce: ST NICHOLAS, G.16.d.0.9.
    - No. 12 Field Ambce: ST NICHOLAS, G.16.c.4.8.

    (e). **CORPS MAIN DRESSING STATION:**
    - ECOLE NORMALE, ARRAS. (No. 47 Field Ambulance).

    (f). **CORPS REST STATION:**
    - WARLUS. (No. 4 Field Ambulance).

    (g). **C.C.S's:** Nos. 7, 8 and 19 at AGNEZ LES DUISANS.

2. **EVACUATION OF WOUNDED:**

    (a). **Wounded from Right Sector:** By hand and wheeled stretcher from R.A.P's. to the A.D.S. FAMPOUX. Thence by ambulance car and hospital barge to C.M.D.S., (in the case of evacuation by barge via QUAI DU RIVAGE).

(b). **Left Sector**: By hand and wheeled stretcher from R.A.P's. to the A.D.S. at TANK DUMP. Thence by ambulance car to the C.M.D.S.

(c). **Urgent Cases**: Urgent cases requiring immediate evacuation will be sent by motor ambulance car from the A.D.S's. to the C.M.D.S. direct. A car for this purpose will be demanded from Ambulance Headquarters by wire from the A.D.S.

(d). **Barges**: The following is the normal time-table of barges operating on the SCARPE:

Leaves FAMPOUX LOCK.	Arrives ARRAS.
7.20 a.m.	8.50 a.m.
11.20 a.m.	12.50 p.m.
3.20 p.m.	4.50 p.m.
7.20 p.m.	8.50 p.m.

An ambulance car will be stationed by O.C. No. 11 Field Ambulance at the QUAI DU RIVAGE, for the purpose of conveying patients to the C.M.D.S. from barges.

A party of 1 N.C.O. and 4 men will also be stationed at the QUAI DU RIVAGE from the same Unit to unload cases from the barges and load them on to the motor ambulance.

3. **SICK**:
(a). **From the Line**: Sick will be evacuated from the line in the same way as wounded. All sick will however, be sent from Field Ambulances to No. 10 Field Ambulance at the HOPITAL ST JEAN.

(b). **Local Sick**: Local sick from Units not in the line will be collected as follows:

From SCHRAMM BARRACKS)
     COLLEGE COMMUNALE)   by No. 10 Field Ambulance.

From GORDON CAMP)
     RIFLE CAMP)   by No. 11 Field Ambulance.
     RAILWAY TRIANGLE)

From STIRLING CAMP)
     ST LAURENT BLANGY)   by No. 12 Field Ambulance.

(c). **Evacuation**: No. 10 Field Ambulance will evacuate sick as under:
  (1). **Ordinary Sick for C.C.S.**: To 7, 8 and 19 C.C.S. in M.A.C. cars.

  (2). **Sick for C.R.S.**: Sick likely to be fit for duty in 14 days will be sent to C.R.S.

  (3). **Sick Detained**: Sick up to the number of 50, who are likely to be fit in 7 days will be detained and treated by No. 10 Field Ambulance.

  (4). **Sick to Duty**: Sick discharged to duty, (except men of 4th. Divisional Train) will be sent to 4th. Divisional Wing of the "H" Corps Musketry & Reinforcement Camp. Nominal rolls should accompany the cases stating the period of detention at the Camp recommended.

4. SPECIAL CASES:

   (a). <u>Infectious Cases</u>: To 12 Stationary Hospital, ST POL.

   (b). <u>Self-Inflicted Wounds</u>: To 6 Stationary Hospital, FREVENT.

   (c). <u>N.Y.D.N. Cases</u>: Officers: to Officers' Hospital, LUCHEUX.
                              <u>Oth.Rks</u>: 3 Can. Sty. Hpl., DOULLENS.

   (d). <u>Eye Cases</u>: To be sent from No. 10 Field Ambulance to No. 3 C.C.S., GREVILLERS, to arrive by 9 a.m. No more than 6 cases per week. Day for 4th. Division, FRIDAY.

   (e). <u>Ear, Throat and Nose Cases</u>: From No. 10 Field Ambulance to No. 12 Sty. Hpl. by 10 a.m. on Mondays.

   (f). <u>Dental Cases</u>: At No. 10 Field Ambulance at 9 a.m. on Mondays.

5. ADDITIONAL PERSONNEL: O.C. No. 11 Field Ambulance will detail 2 Medical Officers to proceed on 20th. March, 1918 to No. 10 Field Ambulance for temporary duty with that Unit.

6. <u>CLERICAL</u>: No. 10 Field Ambulance will be responsible for the whole of the records of sick and wounded of the 4th. Division, less cases at the C.R.S.

   (a). No. 10 Field Ambulance will enter in A.& D.Books all sick of the Division, both from the line and from Camps.

   (b). Wounded of 4th. Division will be taken in at the C.M.D.S., but no record of them will be kept there. The A.F's. W.3210 for cases of 4th. Division will be sent daily at 10 a.m. and 5 p.m. from C.M.D.S. to office of A.D.M.S. 4th. Division, and from there to No. 10 Field Ambulance.

   (c). From the data collected as in (a) and (b) above, No. 10 Field Ambulance will compile the Daily State and "6 to 6" wires and forward them to the office of the A.D.M.S. at the usual hours.

   (d). No. 10 Field Ambulance will also submit all routine returns in connection with sick and wounded as heretofore.

   (e). No. 12 Field Ambulance will leave 1 clerk at C.R.S. WARLUS, to assist in the clerical work there.
   He will submit to the A.D.M.S. 4th. Division daily, the Daily State of the 4th. Divisional Details who are patients at the C.R.S. as rendered hitherto by No. 12 Field Ambulance.

   (f). Wounded of 4th. Division will be entered in the A.& D.Books of No. 10 Field Ambulance.

Headquarters,
4th. Division.

Lieut-Colonel,
a/A.D.M.S. 4th. Division.

Copies to all recipients of R.A.M.C. Order No. 48.

REFERENCE 4th. DIVISION MEDICAL ARRANGEMENTS IN CONNECTION WITH R.A.M.C. ORDER NO. 48, DATED 18-3-18.

1. **AMENDMENT**:

    Para. 2, sub-para.(d) is cancelled, and the following substituted:

    (d). Barges: The following is the present Time-Table of launches and barges operating on the SCARPE:-

Leave FAMPOUX LOCK.	Arrive ARRAS BASIN.
6.00 a.m.	7.30 a.m.
9.00 a.m.	10.30 a.m.
11.00 a.m.	12.30 p.m.
1.00 p.m.	2.30 p.m.
3.00 p.m.	4.30 p.m.
4.30 p.m.	6.00 p.m.

2. **ADDENDUM**:

    The following will be added to para.4, sub-para.(f):-

    "and Thursdays."

Headquarters,
4th. Division.
20th. March, 1918.

Mackie
Colonel,
A.D.M.S. 4th. Division.

Copies to all recipients of Medical Arrangements dated 18-3-18.

SECRET

4th. DIVISION MEDICAL ARRANGEMENTS.

IN CONNECTION WITH

THE LEFT DIVISION DEFENCE SCHEME

Map Ref's: Sheet 51b, 1/40,000.　　　　　　　　　21st. March, 1918.

The 4th. Division is now in line as the Left Division of the XVIIth. Corps.

The Divisional Front will be defended in three systems, as follows:

1st. System:
　Present front line.

2nd. System:
　Front line of this system corresponds roughly with line CLYDE AVENUE - COLT RESERVE - CORDITE TRENCH.

3rd. System:
　Front line corresponds roughly to line LINCOLN LANE - LOGIC TRENCH - DINGWALL TRENCH - ITALIAN TRENCH.

---

1. POSITION OF MEDICAL POSTS:

(a). **For 1st. System:** Medical posts for the first system will all be situated as shown in "4th. Division Medical Arrangements in Connection With R.A.M.C. Order" dated 18th. March, 1918.

(b). **For 2nd. and 3rd. Systems:**

(i). R.A.P's.

2nd. System.	3rd. System.
Front line R.A.P's. will move back to:	Front line R.A.P's. will move back to:
TANK DUMP.	H.9.b.2.7.
Aid Post at H.16.b.7.7.	EFFIE TRENCH, (H.9.d.)
TRIPLE ARCH.	CAM VALLEY, (H.15.d.2.8.)
A.D.S. FAMPOUX.	

The R.A.P's. of the Support and Reserve Battalions will be in close proximity to their respective Battalion Headquarters, and R.M.O's. will notify the O.C., A.D.S. of their exact locations when established.

(ii). RELAY POSTS.

2nd. System.	3rd. System.
H.17.c.3.5.	L'ABBAYETTE.

Other Relay Posts may be formed at the discretion of the O.C. Field Ambulance evacuating the area. If such Posts are formed this office must be notified of their location.

(iii). A.D.S's.

2nd. System.	3rd. System.
FEUCHY.	FEUCHY.
L'ABBAYETTE.	L'ABBAYETTE.

Should these Posts be rendered untenable they will be moved back as follows:

(a). FEUCHY to Cellars at 52 and 57 Rue de DOUAI, ARRAS.
(b). From L'ABBAYETTE to ST NICHOLAS, (12th. Fd. Amb. H.Q.).

(iv). C.M.D.S.

For 2nd. and 3rd. Systems: ECOLE NORMALE. (47th. Fd. Amb.)

(v). W.W.P.

For 2nd. and 3rd. Systems: ST NICHOLAS. (11th. Fd. Amb.)

(vi). C.C.S.

Nos. 7, 8 and 19 at AGNEZ LES DUISANS.

(vii). C.R.S.

WARLUS.

2. DISPOSAL OF CASES IN DETAIL:

(a). Lying wounded, and severe gas cases by hand and wheeled stretchers to the A.D.S's.
Thence by motor ambulance, barge or Decauville to C.M.D.S.

(b). Walking wounded, sick, N.Y.D.(N) and N.Y.D.(Gas) cases will be directed to the W.W.P. at ST NICHOLAS.
Both 10 + 11 Field Ambulance will keep one horsed ambulance wagon continually plying between L'ABBAYETTE and ST. NICHOLAS, the horses being changed as often as necessary.
From the W.W.P. these cases will be disposed of as follows:-

Wounded by bus or lorry (supplied by A.D.M.S. on request), to 7, 8 and 19 C.C.S.

N.Y.D.(N), N.Y.D.(Gas) and sick, by bus or lorry (supplied by A.D.M.S. on request) to C.R.S.

Trivial wounded fit for duty will, after receiving a dose of Anti-Tetanic Serum, be handed over to the M.M.P. for despatch to their Units.

Tallies must be clearly marked "WARLUS" or "AGNEZ", not "C.R.S." or "C.C.S.".

3. (a). NO. 10 FIELD AMBULANCE:

(i). O.C. No. 10 Field Ambulance will be responsible for the evacuation of the Right Sector of the Divisional Front.
Should more bearers be required, they will be sent on receipt of a wire from O.C. No. 10 Field Ambulance by the A.D.M.S.

(ii). All local sick will be seen at the HOPITAL ST JEAN.

(iii). O.C. No. 10 Field Ambulance will evacuate all sick, remaining from the HOPITAL ST JEAN at once, to C.C.S. in M.A.C. cars.

(iv). He will arrange for the sick of the 4th. M.G.Battn. to be seen daily.

(b). NO.11 FIELD AMBULANCE:

(i). O.C. No. 11 Field Ambulance will open the Walking Wounded Post at ST NICHOLAS.

(ii). He will detail 3 N.C.O's. and 24 men (including 4 Nursing Orderlies) for duty at 8 C.C.S.
This party will stand to until the arrival of Captain C.T.M.PLOWRIGHT, R.A.M.C., M.O. 4th. M.G.Battn., when that officer will take charge of the party and conduct them to 8 C.C.S.

(iii). He will detail 10 men for duty at the C.R.S.

(iv). He will despatch 1 officer and 22 other ranks to C.M.D.S. This party will include 3 clerks.

(v). He will despatch 2 N.C.O's. and 8 men to the QUAI DU RIVAGE, to assist in unloading barges and the Docauville on the opposite side of the Basin.

(vi). He will station two motor ambulances at the QUAI DU RIVAGE to convoy cases to the C.M.D.S.

(c). NO. 12 FIELD AMBULANCE:

O.C. No. 12 Field Ambulance will be responsible for the evacuation of the Left Sector of the Divisional Front.

4. CLERICAL:

(a). At the Corps Main Dressing Station. The clerks detailed by No. 11 Field Ambulance will take with them an A.& D. Book, marked "No.11 Field Ambulance", supplies of Field Medical Cards, A.F.'s. W.3210 and necessary stationery.
They will record in the A.& D.Book all wounded of 4th. Division admitted to the C.M.D.S. and will render the usual wires and returns including Daily State to this office.
A.F's. W.3210 when no longer required will be sent to Units as notification of disposal of patients.

(b). At the Walking Wounded Post; All cases admitted will be entered in the A.& D.Books of No. 11 Field Ambulance.
Field Medical Cards and A.F's. W.3210 will be made out for all cases. The usual wires and returns will be rendered to this office. A.F's. W.3210 will be used as in (a) for notification.

(c). At HOPITAL ST JEAN: A.&.D.Books will be kept for sick admitted to the HOPITAL ST JEAN by No. 10 Field Ambulance.
Notification to Units of disposal of all cases will be made.
The usual wires and returns will be rendered to this office by No. 10 Field Ambulance, including Daily State.

(d). If it is absolutely necessary to send any very urgent cases direct from the A.D.S. to C.C.S., a Field Medical Card will be made out at the A.D.S., and "Direct Admission to C.C.S." will be noted thereon in order that the C.C.S. may enter it as such.

5. <u>ANTI-TETANIC SERUM</u>: Anti-Tetanic Serum will be given to all wounded admitted to the W.W.P. before despatch to C.C.S.
Anti-Tetanic Serum will not be given at the A.D.S. except to trivial wounded returned to duty.

6. <u>STRETCHERS & BLANKETS</u>: Dumps of stretchers and blankets will be formed at ST NICHOLAS and HOPITAL ST JEAN.
75 stretchers and 250 blankets may be used from each dump and more will be supplied on receipt of a message in this office.

7. <u>EYE, EAR & DENTAL CASES</u>: Only very urgent cases will be sent to specialists during operations.

8. These Arrangements will come into force at once.

9. ACKNOWLEDGE.

[signature]

Colonel,
A.D.M.S. 4th. Division.

Issued at 8.30 p.m.

Copies to:
D.D.M.S. XVIIth. Corps.
A.D.M.S. 15th. Division.
No. 10 Field Ambulance.
No. 11 Field Ambulance.
No. 12 Field Ambulance.
4th. Division.
4th. Division "A".
All R.M.O's.
10th. Infantry Brigade.
11th. Infantry Brigade.
12th. Infantry Brigade.
C.R.E. 4th. Division.
4th. Div. Signals.
4th. Divisional Train.
XVIIth. C.M.D.S.
XV M.A.C.
Inland Water Transport.
Diary (2).
File.

SECRET **URGENT**

R.A.M.C. ORDER NO. 42.

by

LIEUT-COLONEL N.FAICHNIE, R.A.M.C., A.D.M.S. 4th. DIVISION.

Map Refs: Sheet 51b, 1/40,000.   23rd. March, 1918.

1. Nos. 10, 11 and 12 Field Ambulances will move all Horsed Transport, with the exception of the Horsed Ambulance-wagons, at once to STEWART CAMP, G.13.d. (On ARRAS-ST POL Road).

    Route: Via ST CATHERINE - ST VAAST Road, as far as G.8.c.3.7. Thence over ST VAAST Bridge, and along road from ST VAAST to ARRAS-ST POL Road, through G.7.d., G.13.b. and G.13.d. to STEWART CAMP.

2. Equipment at all Forward Posts as at present established will remain "In situ".

    Enough equipment will be left at respective Ambulance Headquarters to run Posts set forth for the Third System in "4th. Division Medical Arrangements in Connection With Left Division Defence Scheme" dated 21st. March, 1918, that is:-

    No. 10 Field Ambulance.   A.D.S.   FEUCHY or Cellars, 52 and 57 Rue de DOUAI.

    No. 12 Field Ambulance.   A.D.S.   **L'ABBAYETTE or ST NICHOLAS.**

    No. 11 Field Ambulance.   M.M.P.   ST NICHOLAS.

    The whole of the remaining Field Ambulance equipment will be taken with Transport to STEWART CAMP.

3. Report completion of moves to this office by two successive runners.

4. ACKNOWLEDGE BY BEARER.

                                                Colonel,
                                                A.D.M.S. 4th. Division.

Issued at 1.0 a.m.

Copies to: No. 10 Field Ambulance.
             No. 11 Field Ambulance.
             No. 12 Field Ambulance.
             Diary.
             File.

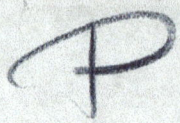

AMENDMENTS TO
4th. DIVISION MEDICAL ARRANGEMENTS IN CONNECTION WITH LEFT
DIVISION DEFENCE SCHEME.

Map refs: 1/40,000   51b.
                            51c.   24th. March, 1918.

1.   The Corps Rest Station, WARLUS, having been closed from 9 a.m. to-day, 24th. March, the terms "WARLUS" and "C.R.S." will be deleted wherever occurring in the above-named Medical Arrangements, and "46 Field Ambulance, HAUTE AVESNES" substituted.

2.   No. 46 Field Ambulance opens at 9 a.m. to-day, 24th., at HAUTE AVESNES, E.28.b. as a Sick Section, C.M.D.S.

       Para. 2, sub-para. (b) is cancelled accordingly, and the following substituted:-

(b). Walking wounded, sick, N.Y.D.(N) and N.Y.D.(Gas) cases will be directed to the W.W.P. at ST NICHOLAS.
       Both 10 and 12 Field Ambulances will keep one horsed ambulance wagon continually plying between L'ABBAYETTE and ST. NICHOLAS, the horses being changed as often as necessary.
       From the W.W.P. cases will be disposed of as follows:-

       Wounded by bus or lorry (supplied by A.D.M.S. on request) to 7, 8 and 19 C.C.S.

       N.Y.D.(N), N.Y.D.(Gas), all sick, trivial wounded, and infectious cases to No. 46 Field Ambulance, HAUTE AVESNES.

       Trivial wounded fit for duty at once will be given A.T.S. and handed over to M.M.P. for return to their units.

       Tallies must be marked "HAUTE AVESNES" or "AGNEZ" not "Sick M.D.S." or "C.C.S.".

3.   After para.2, sub-para.(b) add:-

(c). <u>Mustard Gas Cases.</u>
       These will all be treated at the ECOLE NORMALE, and will be directed there, without unloading, if they arrive at any other Unit.

6.   The following will be added to para.4, "Clerical":-

(e). Cases sent to HAUTE AVESNES will be admitted to the A.&.D. Books of the Field Ambulance sending them, and will be shown as "Transferred to 46th. Field Ambulance".

7.   ACKNOWLEDGE.

                                                Captain,

Issued at 8.15 a.m.   for A.D.M.S. 4th. Division.

Copies to all concerned.

Army Form C. 2118.

MEDICAL

WAR DIARY
or
INTELLIGENCE SUMMARY.

(Erase heading not required.)

CONFIDENTIAL

WAR DIARY

of

A.D.M.S. 4th DIVISION

for period

APRIL 1st 1918 to APRIL 30th 1918

Instructions regarding War Diaries and Intelligence Summaries are contained in F. S. Regs., Part II. and the Staff Manual respectively. Title pages will be prepared in manuscript.

Place	Date	Hour	Summary of Events and Information	Remarks and references to Appendices

WAR DIARY or INTELLIGENCE SUMMARY

Army Form C. 2118.

Place	Date	Hour	Summary of Events and Information	Remarks and references to Appendices
ETRUN	1/4/17	6am	Battle casualty sent to D.D.M.S. XVII Corps	1
		7.30am	R.A.M.C. roster casualty sent "	2
		4pm	Prisoners B war sent "	3
		"	R.A.M.C. roster casualty sent to "A"	4
		"	Battle casualty sent to D.D.M.S. XVII Corps	5
		6.30pm	1st Lieut. ADAMS, S.H. MORCUSA proceeded here treating for injury duty. Was 1st Lieut. LITTLE MORCU S.A. who reported to with ord	A
			DADMS rated 16 to 6nl hospital steam ARRAS	
			R.A.M.C. operation orders to S 2.	
			1st Lieut ADAMS, S.H. MORCUSA reported 10th ord. 1st Lt LITTLE reported same times this Office	
2/4/17	4am	Battle casualty sent to D.D.M.S. XVII Corps	6
		7.30am	R.A.M.C. roster casualty went " "	4/6
		4pm	R.A.M.C. " "	
		4.30pm	Prisoners B war " " " A	9
		6.30pm	Battle casualty sent " " "	10
		"	R.A.M.C. operation order to 53 with medical arrangements attached	B

WAR DIARY
or
INTELLIGENCE SUMMARY

Army Form C. 2118.

Place	Date	Hour	Summary of Events and Information	Remarks and references to Appendices
ETRUN	2/4/18 contd		Capt. J.B. LOW R.A.M.C. (T.C) proceeded to 1st Bn. King's Own Royal Lancs. Regt. for duty vice Capt. W.S. MIDDLETON. M.O.R.C.U.S.A. who returned to American army.	11
"	3/4/18	11.30am	Battle casualty sent to D.D.M.S. XVII Corps	12
"	"	"	R.A.M.C. Battle casualty sent to D.D.M.S. XVII Corps	13
"	"	4pm	R.A.M.C. troops casualty sent to 4 Sdn "A"	14
"	"	"	Prisoners of war sent to D.D.M.S. XVII Corps	15
"	"	6pm	Battle casualty sent to D.D.M.S. XVII Corps	16
"	"		Reinforcements. 3 Medical Officers posted as follows	
"	"		BROWN. W.E. T/c to 10 Fd. Amb.	
"	"		COOKE. A.B. T/c to 11 Fd. Amb.	
"	"		EARLE. A.B. T/c to 12 Fd. Amb.	
"	4/4/18	4pm	R.A.M.C. casualty sent to D.D.M.S. XVIII Corps	17
"	"	4.30pm	R.A.M.C. Battle casualty sent to D.D.M.S. XVIII Corps R.A.M.C. Battle casualty sent to "A"	18 / 19

Army Form C.² 2118.

WAR DIARY
or
INTELLIGENCE SUMMARY.
(Erase heading not required.)

Instructions regarding War Diaries and Intelligence Summaries are contained in F. S. Regs., Part II. and the Staff Manual respectively. Title pages will be prepared in manuscript.

Place	Date	Hour	Summary of Events and Information	Remarks and references to Appendices
ETRUN	4/4/18	4.30 p.m	Prisoners of war sent to D.D.M.S. XVII Corps	20
"	Contd	6.40 pm	Battle casualty return to DDMS XVIII Corps	21
			ADMS needed 11 staff and transport for 98 M⁰ field ambulances	
	5/4/18	9.15 am	Battle casualty return to DDMS XVIII Corps	22
		9.30 am	RAMC battle casualty return to DDMS XVII Corps	23
		4 pm	Prisoners of war return to DDMS XVII Corps	24
		4 pm	R/true battle casualty return "A"	25
		6 pm	Battle casualty return to DDMS XVIII Corps	26
	6.4.18	9.15 am	Battle casualty return to DDMS XVII Corps	27
	"	"	Battle casualty return to DDMS XVIII Corps	28
	"	4 pm	" " " " "A"	29
	"	"	Prisoners of war return to DDMS XVII Corps	30
	"	6 pm	Battle casualty return to DDMS XVIII Corps	31
			ADMS + DADMS attended conference of ADMS attached J × VII Corps D.D.M.S	None

Army Form C. 2118.

WAR DIARY
or
INTELLIGENCE SUMMARY.
(Erase heading not required.)

Instructions regarding War Diaries and Intelligence Summaries are contained in F. S. Regs., Part II. and the Staff Manual respectively. Title pages will be prepared in manuscript.

Place	Date	Hour	Summary of Events and Information	Remarks and references to Appendices
ETRUN	4/4/18	7.30am	Battle casualty wire to DDMS XVII Corps	32
"	"	"	RAMC battle casualty wire to DDMS XVII Corps	33
"	"	1pm	Prisoners of war wire to DDMS XVII Corps	34
"	"	"	" " " to DDMS XVII Corps	35
"	"	4.30pm	Battle casualty wire to DDMS XVII Corps	36
"	"	"	RAMC order no 54 re relief of 4 Div by 1st Canadian Division	C
"	"	"	ADMS attended a conference of ADsMS at DMS Office 1st Army	
"	5/4/18		T/Capt. LAMBERT. A.C. RAMC posted to 10 Fd Amb for duty. Division relieved by 1st Canadian. Divisional Headquarters moved to FOSSEUX.	
"	"	4am	Battle casualty wire to DDMS XVIII Corps	37
"	"	"	RAMC battle casualty wire to DDMS XVIII Corps	38
"	"	6pm	Battle casualty wire to XVIII Corps	39
"	"		1st/Lieut LITTLE. L. MORCUSA posted for permanent duty with 2nd Rams Fus. from 10 Fd Amb.	
			Addendum No 1 to RAMC order 54. "C" above.	

A5834. Wt. W4973/M687. 750,000 8/16 D. D. & L. Ltd. Forms/C.2113/13.

Army Form C. 2118.

WAR DIARY
or
INTELLIGENCE SUMMARY.
(Erase heading not required.)

Instructions regarding War Diaries and Intelligence Summaries are contained in F.S. Regs., Part II. and the Staff Manual respectively. Title pages will be prepared in manuscript.

Place	Date	Hour	Summary of Events and Information	Remarks and references to Appendices
FOSSEUX	9.4.18		Routine ADMS visited ADMS XV Division. 4 O.R. R.A.M.C. reinforcements arrived and posted to 10 Fd Amb.	(Sgd)
"	10.4.18		A.D.M.S. visited 12 Fd Ambulance AVESNES-LES-COMTE. 10 Fd Amb. moved from J. Putnik's to HERMAVILLE. DADMS visited 10 Fd Amb & 11 Fd Amb. Division under orders to move in 4 hours.	Sgd
"	11.4.16		Moved to BAS. RIEUX (HAZEBROUCK S-A) Porhoi J wilds. 10 Fd Amb by lorry transport by road to BUSNETTES 11 " " " " " 6 " L'ECOUFFE (Unid 67) 12 Fd " " " " " (CHATEAU BUSNES) ADMS visited DDMS 1st Corps	Sgd
BAS. RIEUX	12.4.18		ADMS & DADMS visited ADS of 10 Fd Amb & Car post in GONNEHEM. also ADMS 3rd Division making arrangements for relief of 3rd Amb. by the 4th Div also chose a site for M.D.S. at V.24.a.02. (Pont du - REVEILLON) There was conference & die the line of ambulances in ADMS Office. 10 Fd Amb relieved 142 Fd Amb. & 11 Fd Amb both over found posts & of the Ambulance	Sgd

Army Form C. 2118.

WAR DIARY
or
INTELLIGENCE SUMMARY.
(Erase heading not required.)

Instructions regarding War Diaries and Intelligence Summaries are contained in F. S. Regs., Part II. and the Staff Manual respectively. Title pages will be prepared in manuscript.

Place	Date	Hour	Summary of Events and Information	Remarks and references to Appendices
BAS. RIEUX.	10.4.18	1.45pm	Went to 12th Bde and to see a tent Subdivision to form a Main Dressing Station at PONT DU REVEILLON.	40
			11th Bde (1st Somersets and 1st Hampshire R) attacked and retook the village of RIEZ DU VINAGE. Wounded were evacuated by 10 tet amb. They were collected quickly, first lying cases arriving one hour after Zero at No. 4 A.D.S. Total casualties men Bigles (106) 65% were walking wounded	
			Medical arrangements for the attack	D
		11am	DA DMS visited A.D.S. & proposed M.D.S.	
		9pm	ADMS visited ADS.	
	11.4.18	7.30am	Acre to 070 12th Bd and to adjust M.O. for forward amb with 11th Warwicks, the Ox&Warwick & England.	Ofrc
			ADMS visited all 7th ambulances and ADSs.	41
		5.15pm	10 Bde. (2nd Duke of Wellingtons & 1st R. Hampis) attacked BOIS DE FAUCAUT.	
		9pm	Division between DADMS visited ADS & MDS. Large number of wounded were coming through at Maingil. 246 OR & 5 Offrs had passed through MDS. Evacuation very satisfactory.	
		10pm	1st A/Doyce W.H. MOR.CUSA. proceeded to 1st R Warwicks for adjt.	
		2:20pm	Medical arrangements in connection with 10th Bde attack	Ofrc

WAR DIARY or INTELLIGENCE SUMMARY

Army Form C. 2118.

Place	Date	Hour	Summary of Events and Information	Remarks and references to Appendices
BAS. RIEUX.	16.4.18	1.30pm	Visit to 10th & 2nd Fd. Ambls. for arr. with 2nd Cdn Fanlins. rec. Capt LITTLE. M.O. R.C.U.S.A. (sick)	42
		4pm	R.A.M.C. Happr. moving over to 2nd W "A".	43
			A.D.M.S. visited all Fd. Ambulances A.D.Ss & M.D.S. also 21st mot forks.	
			R.A.M.C. order no. 34.	
			R.A.M.C. reserve arrangements in connection with Reserve order no. 34, position of A.D.Ss & M.D.S. & evacuation	F
			Arrangements for relation to rest in forward area	G
			Visiting & ensuring fresh air supply, demands casualties were ordinary.	H
		17/4/18	Front much quieter. Total wounded Off. 2 O.Rs. 41. Capt. LITTLE M.O.R.C.U.S.A. & evacuated to No 1 hospital sick. Amendment arrangements A.D.M.S. visited A.D.S. & 10th & 2nd Fd. Ambulance. DADMS evacuated to hospital. Formed lines out 12 with Col M D.S.	J

gsm-2

WAR DIARY or INTELLIGENCE SUMMARY

Army Form C. 2118.

Place	Date	Hour	Summary of Events and Information	Remarks and references to Appendices
BAS. RIEUX.	18.4.18.	4pm	RAMC Voltee casualties to H DS "A"	44
		11am	ADMS visited ADS's and MDS	
		10pm	DADMS	
			In the early morning #15am a strong enemy attack was launched	
			against divisional front 10 ques heavy shell burst & it	
			Heavy fighting continued until 9 a.m.	
			Total casualties for 4 a.m. to 6 p.m. 4 Officers 1335 O.R.s	
			Evacuation so far 1000 & and toped	
		10.0 P.M.	RAMC annex 8.6.12 : 1.6.10" 1 k 11th Ambulance	
	19.4.18.		ADMS visited ADS's of 10th & 11th Ambulances	June
			10 OR RAMC arrived all 6 11th Ambulance	
			Fighting not so severe 11 Hy Bde received 10" Hy Bde.	June
	20.4.18.	11am	ADMS visited ADS's of 11 Fd Amb and R.A.P.'s of Regtl Sector	
			been to 10 Fd Amb to detail a M.O. for duty with 2 - 4 J.	
		6pm	dept RAMC's nee 1st Lieut HAYES CK MORCUSA sick in	
			hospital	
			ADMS's DADMS visited MDS 17 Fd Ambulance front Sirret	
		(2:30pm)	Entrance of front Sirret wounded for 24 hours 1 Off. + 63 O.Rs	

Army Form C. 2118.

WAR DIARY
or
INTELLIGENCE SUMMARY.
(Erase heading not required.)

Instructions regarding War Diaries and Intelligence Summaries are contained in F.S. Regs., Part II. and the Staff Manual respectively. Title pages will be prepared in manuscript.

Place	Date	Hour	Summary of Events and Information	Remarks and references to Appendices
BAS. RIEUX	20.4.18 cont	2/pm	HQrs & 10 Fd Ambulance with transport moved from BUSNETTES to LE TAILLY (V.19.L.r.d) owing JGMc	
"	21.4.18		to shelling. Office routine; front line quiet.	JGMc
"	22.4.18	3.15am	N Boche with Tanks attacked and crossed the canal and captured 1 off & 60 O.Rs. The situation was not restored. He was driven back through PACAUT wood when he was completely to our lines and LA PANNERIE. LA PANNERIE x the road to LA PANNERIE. shelled intermittently from 9am - 6pm. off S. O.Rs 133.	
	23.4.18	6pm 4.30am	ADMS walked L'ECCLEME area. 12 K by Bac (James Fairbairn) advanced their line. Canadians for the day. division rather heavy owing to severe shelling Pall Arras.	JGMc
		1am 2pm	DDMS & XIII Corps visited ADS & RAPs left sector AD.MS visited ADS & RAPs. left sector Ns becoming under his administration.	JGMc

WAR DIARY or INTELLIGENCE SUMMARY

Army Form C. 2118.

Place	Date	Hour	Summary of Events and Information	Remarks and references to Appendices
BAS. RIEUX	24.4.18	12 Noon	Division transferred to XIII Corps for administration	
		6.0 pm	Maj K 12 Fd Amb detailed as M.O. forthwith for duty with 1st Somerset L.I. (Lieut A.B. EARLE RAMC T.F. to proceed vice 1st Bn J.A.B. LOWRY MC CUSA sick. Fighting on divisional front not to be severe	
		3 pm	ADMS & DADMS visited Rfgfil & Left Bde H.Qrs. and ADSs & relay posts.	JAE
"	25.4.18	10 am	ADMS visited 10 Fd Amb Ft Qrs	
		2 pm	ADMS " MDS 12th Ambulance LETAILLY	
		6 pm	ADMS again visited 10 Fd Amb H.Qrs	
			Col Col AHERN 11 Fd and & Lt Col LEWIC 10 Fd Amb attended conference with ADMS at 7.30 pm re alteration of evacuation from forward area	
		11.15 pm	R AMC operation order no 3·8.	
	26.4.18	9 am	Medical arrangements in connection with RAMC Op order no 38	JAE
		11 am	ADMS & DADMS visited Advanced H.Qrs at GONNEHEM and CENSE. LA. VALLEE. Also H.Qrs 32nd Bde RFA at BELLERIVE.	
		4 pm	ADMS visited H.Qrs 10 Fd Amb. DADM 3 " 11 " "	

WAR DIARY or INTELLIGENCE SUMMARY

Army Form C.2118.

(Erase heading not required.)

Instructions regarding War Diaries and Intelligence Summaries are contained in F. S. Regs., Part II. and the Staff Manual respectively. Title pages will be prepared in manuscript.

Place	Date	Hour	Summary of Events and Information	Remarks and references to Appendices
BASRIEUX	26.4.18		Lighting much less severe.	
			Capt D.S. CAMPBELL R.A.M.C. assumed command R and B.M.C.	
			4 Div R.O. 26 April 1918.	gone
		27.4.18 7pm	Little time to have relay posts at present W1 d 13	gone
			from S.Y.O.H. D.M.S. visited A.D.S. B.H. & Ambulance at EDNEHEM	gone
		28.4.18 9/11am	DDMS XIII Corps accompanied by ADMS and DADMS visited	
			all ADSs Relay posts and RAPs.	
			RAMC battle casualty nil to 2 am A.	44
		29.4.18 3pm	ADMS visited MOS (113th Ambulance)	gone
		6/6 pm	RAMC operation order no 39	gone L
		30.4.18 8pm	DADMS accompanied by Br.Gl. AHERN visited Château DE WYERPPE with	
			the view of forming an A.D.S. there	
		2 pm	ADMS visited 3 mobile laboratory PERNES after going round and	
			inspecting the divisional and brigade reply[?] points	gone

Josephine[?]
Col ADMS
ADMS & Div.

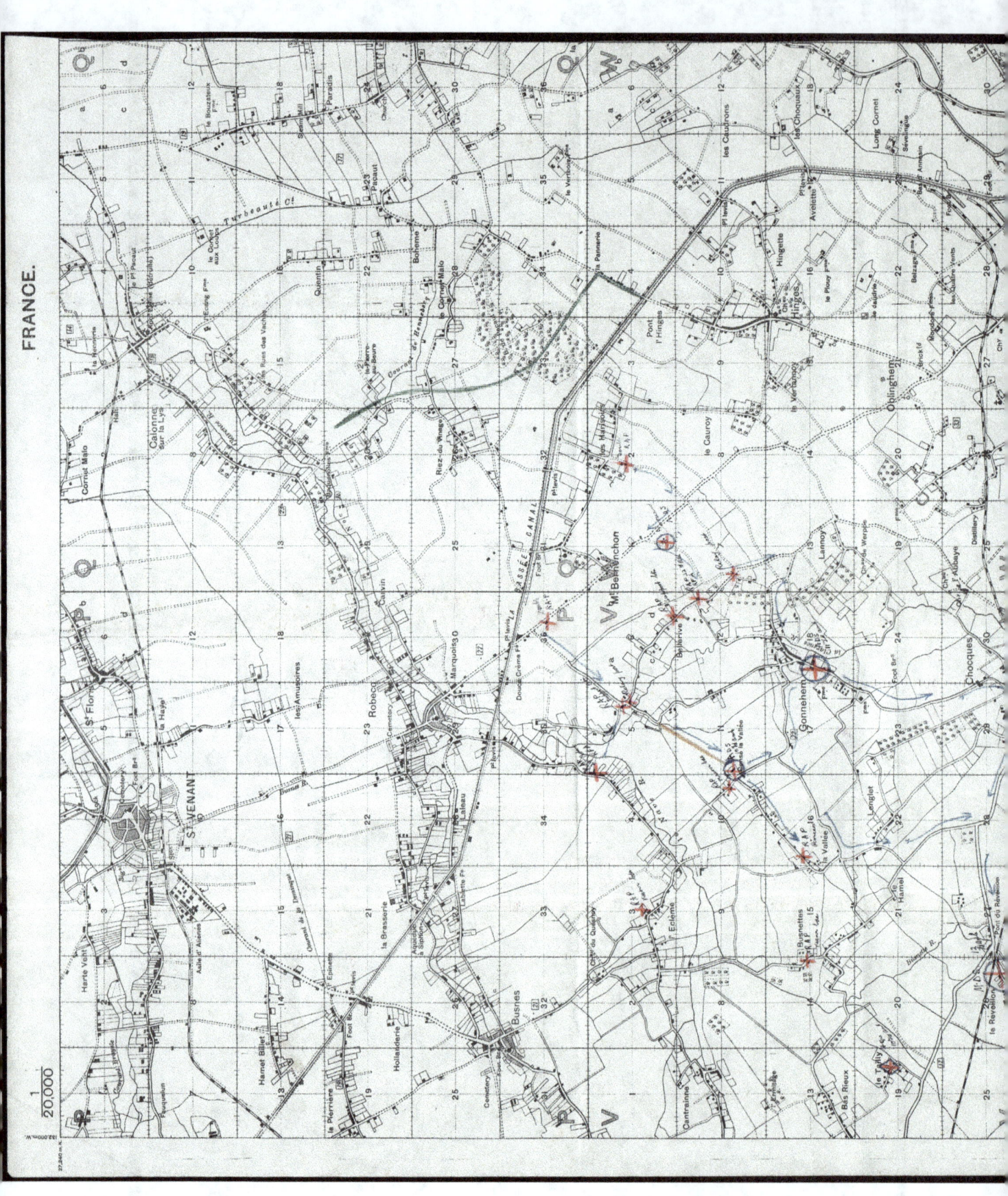

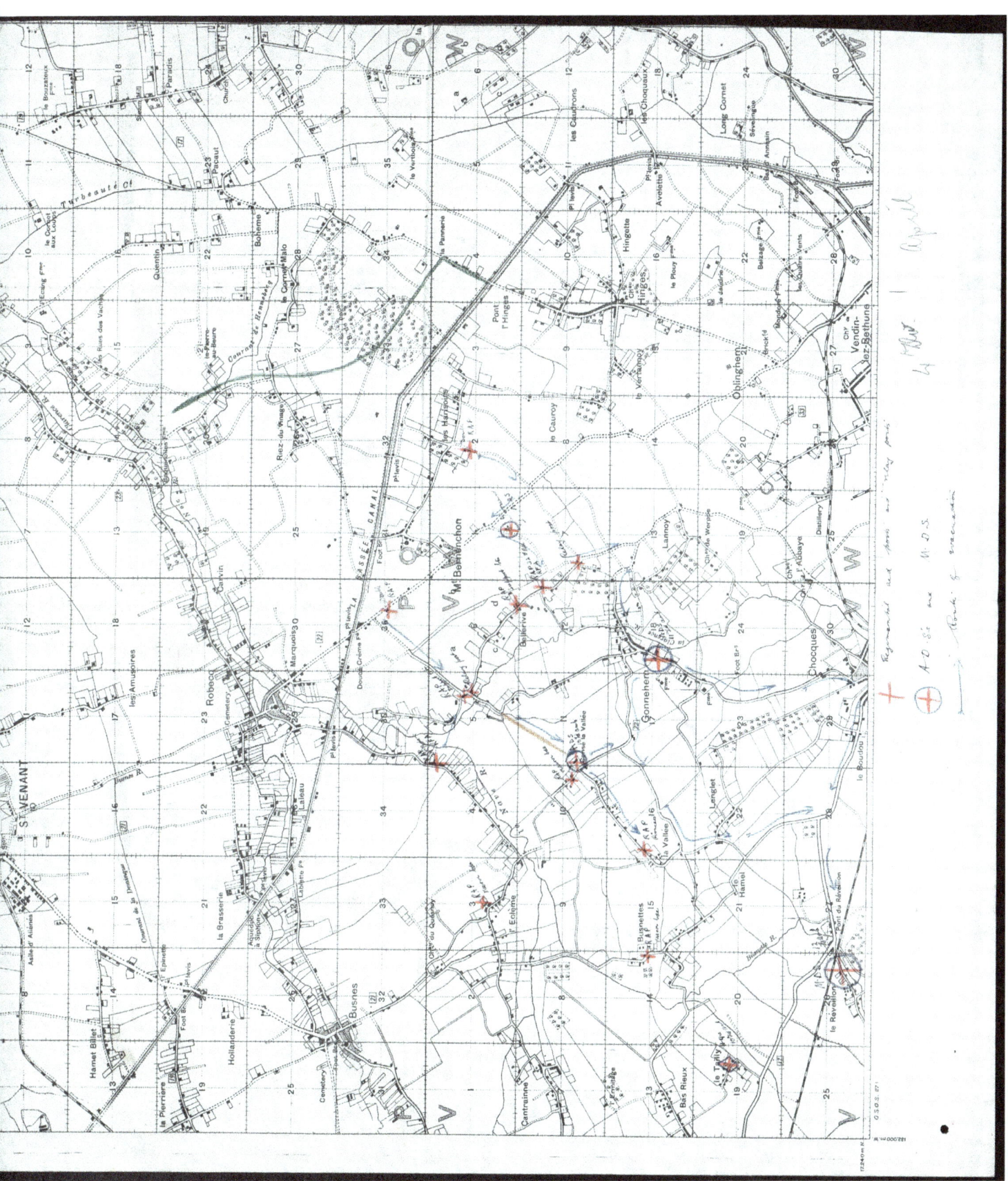

SECRET

A

Copy No. 6

Diary.

R.A.M.C. ORDER NO. 52

by

COLONEL N. FAICHNIE, A.M.S., A.D.M.S., 4th DIVISION.

Map Refs: Sheet 51c, 1/40000.   1st. April, 1918.

1.   Each Field Ambulance Commander will detail 1 Officer, 1 N.C.O. and 8 men to proceed forthwith to the huts vacated by 19 C.C.S. at L.1.c.5.5.

2.   Each party will have sufficient stores and equipment, rapidly to form Dressing Stations if necessary.

3.   Parties may be relieved by equal numbers at the discretion of Field Ambulance Commanders.

4.   Completion of moves to be reported to the office of A.D.M.S.

5.   Acknowledge.

Faichnie
Colonel
A.D.M.S. 4th. Division.

Issued at 8.0 p.m.

Distribution: D.D.M.S. XVII Corps.
10th. Field Ambulance.
11th. Field Ambulance.
12th. Field Ambulance.
Diary (2).
File.

Copy No. 31

R.A.M.C. ORDER NO. 53

by

COLONEL N. FAICHNIE, A.M.S., A.D.M.S. 4th. DIVISION.

Map Refs: Sheet 51c, 1/40,000. 2nd. April, 1918.

1. MOVES:

(a). O.C. No. 10 Field Ambulance will withdraw his party from L.1.c.5.5. to the HOPITAL ST JEAN, ARRAS, where the Unit will remain less transport, (at HAUTE AVESNES).

(b). O.C. No. 11 Field Ambulance will detail 1 Officer and 40 bearers forthwith for duty with No. 12 Field Ambulance.

The remainder of No. 11 Field Ambulance, less transport, (at HAUTE AVESNES), will proceed to L.1.c.5.5., where the Unit will remain closed in the huts vacated by No. 19 C.C.S.

(c). No. 12 Field Ambulance less transport, (at HAUTE AVESNES), will remain at ST NICHOLAS, (G.16.c.4.8.)

2. Completion of moves detailed above to be reported to A.D.M.S. 4th. Division.

Faichnie
Colonel,
A.D.M.S. 4th. Division.

Issued at 12, noon.

Distribution:
D.D.M.S., XVII Corps.
10th. Field Ambce.
11th. Field Ambce.
12th. Field Ambce.
4th. Division.
4th. Division "A".
10th. Infantry Brigade.
11th. Infantry Brigade.
12th. Infantry Brigade.
C.R.E. 4th. Division.
4th. Div. Signals.
A.R.M. 4th. Division.
4th. Div. Train.
A.D.M.S. 15th. Divn.
A.D.M.S. 1st. Can. Divn.
R.M.O's.
Diary (2).
File.

4th. DIVISION MEDICAL ARRANGEMENTS

IN CONNECTION WITH

R.A.M.C. ORDER NO. 53, DATED 2-4-18.

Map Refs: Sheets 51b and 51c, 1/40,000.   2nd. April, 1918.

1. DUTIES:

   (a). No. 10 Field Ambulance: O.C. No. 10 Field Ambulance will be responsible for the evacuation of casualties from the Divisional front South of the SCARPE, (Right Sector).

   (b). No. 12 Field Ambulance: O.C. No. 12 Field Ambulance will be responsible for the evacuation of casualties from the Divisional front North of the SCARPE, (Left Sector).

   (c). No. 11 Field Ambulance: O.C. No. 11 Field Ambulance will be prepared to function rapidly as a Main Dressing Station, at L.1.c.5.5. should occasion arise.

2. LOCATION OF MEDICAL POSTS:

   (a). R.A.P's.: R.A.P's. will be established in suitable places near Battalion Headquarters, and Regimental Medical Officers will notify O.C. 10 and 12 Field Ambulances respectively of any change in their location from time to time.

   (b). Relay Posts:

Right Sector.	Left Sector.
H.19.c.2.6.	H.15.d.2.8. (CAM VALLEY).
G.24.c.2.9.	H.9.c.50.25. (For use in alternative route if necessary).
G.22.b.6.2.	

   (c). A.D.S's:

   | HOSPICE ST JEAN. | L'ABBAYETTE. |

   (d). M.D.S's.:

   | HOSPICE ST JEAN. | ST NICHOLAS, (G.16.c.4.8.) |

3. DISPOSAL OF CASES:

(a). Lying wounded and severe gas cases to the A.D.S's. Thence by car to 8 C.C.S. at AGNEZ.

(b). Walking wounded will be collected and sent to No.8 C.C.S.
Should there be large numbers of these, lorries can be requested from No. XV M.A.C. to assist in evacuating them to C.C.S.

(c). N.Y.D.N., N.Y.D.Gas, Sick and Infectious cases will be sent by lorry or car to No. 46 Field Ambulance at HAUTE AVESNES.

(d). Trivial wounded after receiving Anti-Tetanic Serum, will be handed over th the M.M.P. for return to their Units.

4. CLERICAL:

(a). Field Medical Cards will be clearly marked 'AGNEZ' or 'HAUTE AVESNES'.

(b). 10th. and 12th. Field Ambulances will render the Daily State and usual wires connected with operations.
All routine reports and returns will also be rendered by these units as well as by No. 11 Field Ambulance.

(c). All cases sent to HAUTE AVESNES will be shown as 'Transfers' to No. 46 Field Ambulance.

5. SPECIAL CASES:

Cases for the Ophthalmic and Aural Specialists and for the Dentist will only be sent if very urgent.

Colonel,
A.D.M.S. 4th. Division.

Copies to all recipients of R.A.M.C. Order No. 53.

SECRET

Copy No. 16

R.A.M.C. ORDER NO. 54.

by

COLONEL N. FAICHNIE, A.M.S., A.D.M.S. 4th. DIVISION.

==

Map Refs: Sheets 51b and 51c, 1/40,000.   7th. April, 1918.

==

1.   The 4th. Division will be relieved by the 1st. Canadian Division.

          G.O.C. 4th. Division hands over command of the Divisional front to G.O.C. 1st. Canadian Division at 7 p.m. on 8th. inst.

2. MOVES OF FIELD AMBULANCES:

(a). No. 11 Field Ambulance: No. 11 Field Ambulance will stand fast, transport remaining as at present.

     1 Officer and 40 Other Ranks, at present attached to No. 12 Field Ambulance will rejoin No. 11 Field Ambulance to-night.

(b). No. 12 Field Ambulance: No. 12 Field Ambulance will be relieved by No. 1 Canadian Field Ambulance.
     The relief of the Forward Posts including the A.D.S. at L'ABBAYETTE will commence on 7th. inst.
     The relief of the whole Unit, including M.D.S. at ST. NICHOLAS, to be complete by noon, 8th. inst.
     Details of relief to be arranged between Ambulance Commanders concerned.

     On relief, No. 12 Field Ambulance will march to 'C' Block, 'Y' Hutments.

     Personnel for which there is no accommodation at ST NICHOLAS can be sent to 'Y' Hutments to-night.

     Transport will move to 'Y' Hutments on 8th. inst.

(c). **No. 10 Field Ambulance:** No. 10 Field Ambulance will be relieved by 2nd. Canadian Field Ambulance.

Forward Posts will be handed over on 8th. inst.

The A.D.S. and the M.D.S. at HOPITAL ST JEAN, will be handed over by noon on 9th. inst.

Reliefs of all Posts will be arranged between Ambulance Commanders concerned.

On relief No. 10 Field Ambulance will march to a destination which will be notified later.

3. Completion of Ambulance reliefs will be notified to this office by wire.

4. Office of A.D.M.S. 4th. Division will close at ETRUN at 7 p.m. on 8th. inst. and re-open at FOSSEUX at the same hour.

Mackenzie
Colonel,
A.D.M.S, 4th. Division.

Issued at 5.0 p.m.

Distribution:- No. 1 to D.D.M.S. XVIIth. Corps.
           2   A.D.M.S. 1st. Canadian Division.
           3   No. 10 Field Ambulance.
           4   No. 11 Field Ambulance.
           5   No. 12 Field Ambulance.
           6   4th. Division.
           7   4th. Division A/Q.
           8   10th. Infantry Brigade.
           9   11th. Infantry Brigade.
          10   12th. Infantry Brigade.
          11   C.R.E. 4th. Division.
          12   4th. Div. Train.
          13   4th. Div. Signals.
          14   D.A.D.V.S. 4th. Division.
      15,16   Diary.
          17   File.

ADDENDUM NO.1
to
R.A.M.C. ORDER NO. 54, DATED 7-4-18.

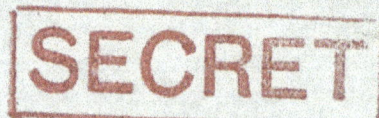

Reference para. 2, (c):

The destination of No. 10 Field Ambulance will be "Y" Hutments.

8th. April, 1918.

Colonel,
A.D.M.S. 4th. Division.

Copies to all recipients of R.A.M.C. Order No. 54.

Copy No. 12

MEDICAL ARRANGEMENTS

In Connection With

4th. DIVISION ORDER NO. 108 of 14-4-18.

Map Refs: Sheet 36a, 1/40,000.   14th. April, 1918.

The enemy hold RIEZ DU VINAGE as far West as Road through Q.26.c.& d. inclusive, aalso farm and enclosure in Q.33.a.

The 1st. Som. Lt. Inf. and 1st. Hants. R. will retake RIEZ DU VINAGE on the evening of 14th. April, 1918.

1. O.C. No. 10 Field Ambulance will be responsible for the evacuation of casualties from the line and will at once reinforce his forward posts and the A.D.S. at GONNEHEM with cars and personnel.

   He will keep in touch with 11th. Inf. Bde. H.Q. where he will be informed of the location of casualties.

2. Each Field Ambulance Commander will at once, (if not already done), send 8 bearers to each Battalion in their respective Brigade Groups.

3. Evacuation will be carried out by hand and wheeled stretcher, and ambulance car if possible to the A.D.S. at GONNEHEM.

   Thence casualties will be evacuated to M.D.S. at BUSNETTES, by Field Ambulance cars.

   From M.D.S. evacuation will be carried out to C.C.S. by cars of No. 12 M.A.C.

4. Registration of all casualties will be carried out by No. 10 Field Ambulance at the M.D.S.

   Field Medical Cards will also be filled in there, and A.T.S. administered.

5. ACKNOWLEDGE.

Ritchie
Colonel,
A.D.M.S. 4th. Division.

Issued   p.m.
Copies to all concerned.

SECRET

E

Copy No. 10

R.A.M.C. ORDER NO. 56.

by

COLONEL N. FAICHNIE, A.M.S., A.D.M.S. 4th. DIVN.

Map Refs: Sheet 36a, 1/40,000.   15th. April, 1918.

      The 10th. Infantry Brigade will this afternoon clear the enemy out of BOIS DE PACAUT and occupy the line W.10.b.9.6.- Q.28.d.9.2.-Road junction Q.28.a.7.4.-Q.27.b.3.1., where the 11th. Infantry Brigade will join them.

1.   O.C., No. 11 Field Ambulance will be responsible for the evacuation of casualties from the line, and will reinforce his forward posts and the A.D.S. at GONNEHEM with personnel and cars.
      He will keep in touch with 10th. Infantry Brigade H.Q.

2.   Evacuation will be carried out by hand and wheeled stretchers, and cars if possible, from the R.A.P's. to the A.D.S. and thence to the M.D.S. at BUSNETTES, (10th. Field Ambulance).
      From the M.D.S. wounded will be evacuated in M.A.C. cars to C.C.S.

3.   Registration of wounded will continue to be carried out at the M.D.S. by No. 10 Field Ambulance.
      Field Medical Cards will also be made out there, and A.T.S. administered.

                                                            Faichnie
                                                           Colonel,
                                       A.D.M.S. 4th. Division.

Issued at 2.50 p.m.
Copies to all concerned.

F

COPY No. 28

R.A.M.C. ORDER NO. 57.

by

COLONEL N. FAICHNIE, A.M.S., A.D.M.S. 4th. DIVISION.

Map Refs: Sheet 36a, 1/40,000.   16th. April, 1918.

(Ref. 4th. Division Order No. 110. dated 15-4-18).

The 12th. Infantry Brigade is to relieve the 11th. Infantry Brigade in the Left Sector of the Divisional Front to-day.

1. MAIN DRESSING STATION.

The present M.D.S. at BUSNETTES will close as such at 12, noon, to-day, and O.C. No. 12 Field Ambulance will open the new Divisional Main Dressing Station at PONT DU REVEILLON, (V.28.d.7.7.) at the same hour.

Casualties will be registered, Field Medical Cards filled in and A.T.S. administered at the new M.D.S.

Field Ambulance cars will evacuate from the A.D.S's. to PONT DU REVEILLON.

M.A.C. cars will evacuate from PONT DU REVEILLON to C.C.S's.

2. FORWARD EVACUATION.

From this date inclusive, the Left and Right Sectors of the Divisional Front will be evacuated by Nos. 10 and 11 Field Ambulances respectively.

3. PERSONNEL.

The eight bearers attached to each Battalion will remain with the Battalions to which they are attached, and proceed with them on relief.

/4.

4. AMBULANCE CARS.

One Ford Car of No. 12 Field Ambulance will remain with each of 10 and 11 Field Ambulances to assist in the evacuation of casualties from the R.A.P's.

[signature]
Colonel,
A.D.M.S. 4th. Division.

Issued at 11.15 p.m.

Distribution:-

1 to	D.M.S. First Army.
2	D.D.M.S. I Corps.
3	4th. Division.
4	4th. Division A/Q.
5	10th. Field Ambulance.
6	11th. Field Ambulance.
7	12th. Field Ambulance.
8	10th. Infantry Brigade.
9	11th. Infantry Brigade.
10	12th. Infantry Brigade.
11	C.R.E. 4th. Division.
12	4th. Div. Train.
13	4th. Div. Signals.
14	D.A.D.V.S. 4th. Division.
15-31	All R.M.O's.
32	Diary.
33	
34	File.

SECRET

4th. DIVISION.

MEDICAL ARRANGEMENTS IN CONNECTION WITH R.A.M.C. ORDER 57.

G

1. **POSITION OF MEDICAL POSTS.**

    (a). **R.A.P's:**   LEFT SECTOR.   RIGHT SECTOR.

           Left Bn. V.5.d.3.7.   W.9.d.7.3.
           Rt. Bn.   W.2.a.8.2.   W.9.d.1.0.
           Res. Bn. V.18.c.1.2.   V.6.d.8.2.

    (b). **Car and Relay Posts:**

           W.15.a.5.9.   W.7.c.5.6.
                                                   V.5.b.3.0.

    (c). **A.D.S's:**   GONNEHEM, V.18.a.1.6.   GONNEHEM, V.18.a.3.7.

    (d). **M.D.S.:**   PONT DU REVEILLON, V.26.d.6.7.

    All Forward Posts and the A.D.S's. will be equipped as lightly as possible, so as to render them perfectly mobile. This factor is very important.

2. **EVACUATION:**

    From Left and Right Sectors of Divisional front by 10th. and 11th. Field Ambulances respectively.

    Line of evacuation will be as follows:-
    From R.A.P's. by hand and wheeled stretchers and by Ford Car as far as practicable, to the A.D.S's. at GONNEHEM. Thence in cars of Field Ambulances to the M.D.S. at V.26.d.6.7. From the M.D.S. cars of 12 M.A.C. evacuate cases to the C.C.S. Groups.

Headquarters,
4th. Division,
16th. April, 1918.

Fraichine
Colonel,
A.D.M.S. 4th. Division,

Copies to all recipients of R.A.M.C. Order 57.

 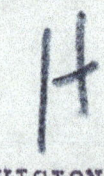 A.D.M.S. 4th. Division 17/12.

4th. DIVISION.

ARRANGEMENTS FOR COLLECTION OF SICK.

1. **AREAS OF COLLECTION.**

    The areas of collection of the Field Ambulances will be as follow:-

    No. 10 Field Ambulance: From Group of Brigade occupying Left Sector.

    No. 11 Field Ambulance: From Group of Brigade occupying Right Sector.

    No. 12 Field Ambulance: From Reserve Brigade Group.

    In addition, Field Ambulances will see the sick of such Divisional Troops as are nearest to them.

2. **DISPOSAL OF SICK.**

    All sick from Nos. 10 and 11 Field Ambulances will be sent to the M.D.S. in the same way as wounded.

    Sick likely to be fit for duty in 48 hours will be detained at the M.D.S. and treated there.

    Those likely to be fit for duty in from 2 to 10 days will be sent by 12th. Field Ambulance from the M.D.S. to the C.R.S.

    More serious cases will be evacuated to C.C.S. from the M.D.S.

Headquarters,
4th. Division.
16th. April, 1918.

J.E. McCutcheon
Captain,
for A.D.M.S. 4th. Division,

Copies to all concerned.

AMENDMENT NO.1,

to

4th. DIVISION MEDICAL ARRANGEMENTS OF 16-4-18.

Map Refs: Sheet 36a, 1/40,000.

Ref. Medical Arrangements of 4th. Division, dated 16th.April, 1918:-

Para. 1 (a), "R.A.P's." is cancelled and the following substituted:-

1. (a). R.A.P's:

	Left Sector.		Right Sector.
Left Bn.	P.36.a.7.8.	Left Bn.	W.9.d.1.0.
Right Bn.	W.2.a.8.2.	Right Bn.	W.9.d.7.7.
Res. Bn.	W.2.a.8.2.	Centre Bn.	W.9.d.7.9.

Para.1 (b). "Car and Relay Posts" is cancelled and the substituted:-

1. (b). Car and Relay Posts:

Left Sector.	Right Sector.
V.5.b.5.1.	W.8.b.9.7.
W.7.c.5.6.	W.8.d.8.2.

'th. April,1918.

Colonel,
A.D.M.S. 4th. Division.

Copies to all recipients of Med. Arrts. of 16-4-18.

SECRET.
Copy No. 34

R.A.M.C. ORDER NO. 58

by

COLONEL N. FAICHNIE, A.M.S., A.D.M.S. 4th. DIVISION.

==

Map Refs: Sheet 36a, 1/40,000.   25th. April, 1918.
==

      On the night 26/27th. inst. the 9th. Infantry Brigade, 3rd. Division, will take over the portion of the line now held by the 11th. Infantry Brigade as far West as W.4.a.8.8. (road junction inclusive to the 3rd. Division), and W.4.a.0.0. on the Canal.

      The point of boundary in the front line between 11th. and 10th. Infantry Brigades will be Q.29.c.0.5.

1.   To conform with this re-adjustment of Divisional front the following alterations of the Medical Posts will be necessary:

(a). In the Left Sector, No. 10 Field Ambulance will establish the following posts:-

    Relay and Car Post   V.5.b.5.1.
    A.D.S.   V.18.c.4.9.

(b). In the Right Sector No. 11 Field Ambulance will establish the following posts:-

    Relay and Car Post   W.7.c.1.9.
    A.D.S.   V.18.c.3.9.

2.   O.C. No. 10 Field Ambulance will be responsible for the evacuation of casualties from the Left Sector, and O.C. No. 11 Field Ambulance from the Right Sector of the Divisional Front.

3.   All moves necessary in connection with the formation of Posts enumerated above will take place on the evening of 26/27th. inst. and will be completed before midnight.

      Completion to be reported to this office by Despatch Rider.

4.   The M.D.S. will continue to be staffed by No. 12 Field Ambulance and will remain at LE REVEILLON.

Issued at 11.15 p.m.
                                      Colonel,
                              A.D.M.S. 4th. Division.

Distribution:-

No.	1	to	D.M.S. First Army.
	2		D.D.M.S. XIIIth. Corps.
	3		A.D.M.S. 3rd. Division.
	4		A.D.M.S. 61st. Division.
	5.		4th. Division.
	6.		4th. Division A/Q.
	7.		10th. Field Ambulance.
	8.		11th. Field Ambulance.
	9.		12th. Field Ambulance.
	10.		10th. Infantry Brigade.
	11.		11th. Infantry Brigade.
	12.		12th. Infantry Brigade.
	13.		C.R.E. 4th. Division.
	14.		4th. Divisional Train.
	15.		4th. Division Signals.
	16.		D.A.D.V.S. 4th. Division.
	17-32.		R.M.O's.
	33,34.		Diary.
	35.		File.

SECRET.

4th. DIVISION.

MEDICAL ARRANGEMENTS IN CONNECTION WITH

R.A.M.C. ORDER NO.58.

1. POSITION OF MEDICAL POSTS:

    (a). R.A.P's: Left Sector.   Right Sector.

    Combined for   P.36.d.3.9.   W.2.a.8.2.
    L. and R.Bn.

    (b). Relay and Car Posts:

                               V.5.b.5.1.   W.7.c.1.9.

    (c). A.D.S's:

                               GONNEHEM,V.18.c.4.9. GONNEHEM,V.18.c.3.9.

    (d). M.D.S.:   No. 12 Field Ambulance, LE REVEILLON,
                               V.26.d.6.7.

2. All Posts forward of the A.D.S's. and the A.D.S's. themselves will be equipped as lightly as possible, and will be perfectly mobile.

3. EVACUATION: From the R.A.P's. of the Left and Right Sectors of the Divisional Front by hand and wheeled stretchers and Ford Car to the A.D.S's. at GONNEHEM.
    Thence in cars of Field Ambulances to the M.D.S. at V.26.d.6.7. M.A.C. cars will evacuate from M.D.S. to C.C.S.

4. BEARERS: The 8 bearers at present attached to each Battalion will remain with the Battalion to which they are attached, and will proceed with the Unit on relief.
    They are for carrying between the R.A.P's. and the Relay Posts.
    They will be relieved at the discretion of the Field Ambulance Commanders.

5. SICK: The areas for collection of sick will be as follow:-

    (a). From Brigade Group of Left Sector: 10th. Fd. Amboe.
    (b). From Brigade Group of Right Sector: 11th. Fd. Amboe.
    (c). From Reserve Brigade Group: 12th. Fd. Amboe.

    Sick collected by 10 and 11 Field Ambulances will be sent to 12th. Field Ambulance in the same way as wounded.
    Sick likely to be fit for duty in 48 hours will be treated at the M.D.S.
    Those likely to be fit in from 2 to 10 days will be sent to the C.R.S. from M.D.S.
    More serious cases will be evacuated to C.C.S.

/6.

6. BLANKETS & STRETCHERS: A small dump of blankets and stretchers has been formed at the M.D.S. from which Nos. 10 and 11 Field Ambulances can draw after reference to this office.
   There should be no wastage of these stores if care is taken that the same number of blankets and stretchers are received in exchange when patients are being handed over from one unit to another.

7. REGISTRATION OF CASUALTIES: No.12 Field Ambulance at the M.D.S. will be responsible for the registration of all casualties passed through that unit.
   Nos. 10 and 11 Field Ambulances will keep no A.& D.Books, and will send patients to the M.D.S. with tallies properly filled in.
   Field Medical Cards will be completed for each case at the M.D.S.
   A.T.S. will also be administered there.

Colonel,
A.D.M.S. 4th. Division.

H.Q. 4th. Division.
26th. April, 1918.

Copies to all recipients of R.A.M.C. Order No. 50.

Copy No. 30

R.A.M.C. ORDER NO. 59,

by

COLONEL N. FAICHNIE, A.M.S., A.D.M.S. 4th. DIVISION.

29th. April, 1918.

===

1. O's.C. Nos. 10, 11 and 12 Field Ambulances will withdraw their bearers at present attached to Battalions, forthwith.

2. O's.C. Nos. 10 and 11 Field Ambulances will continue to be responsible for the evacuation of casualties from the R.A.P's. of the Left and Right Sectors respectively, and will send forward as many bearers as they consider necessary to evacuate casualties from the R.A.P's. to the Bearer Posts.

3. O.C. No. 12 Field Ambulance will hold 40 bearers in readiness to reinforce the bearers in the Right and Left Sectors if required.

Faichnie
Colonel,
A.D.M.S. 4th. Division.

Issued at 6 p.m.
Distribution:-

No.		
1	to	D.M.S. First Army.
2		D.D.M.S. XIIIth. Corps.
3		A.D.M.S. 3rd. Division.
4.		A.D.M.S. 31st. Division.
5		4th. Division.
6		4th. Division A/Q.
7		10th. Field Ambulance.
8		11th. Field Ambulance.
9		12th. Field Ambulance.
10		10th. Infantry Brigade.
11		11th. Infantry Brigade.
12		12th. Infantry Brigade.
13-28		R.M.O's.
29		Diary.
30		File.

4th Division

Medical

A. D. M. S.

May to August

1918

140/9912

COMMITTEE FOR THE
MEDICAL HISTORY OF THE WAR
Date 9 JUL 1916

Army Form C. 2118.

A.D.M.S. 4th Div.
Month of May 1918.

MEDICAL

WAR DIARY
or
INTELLIGENCE SUMMARY.
(Erase heading not required.)

Place	Date	Hour	Summary of Events and Information	Remarks and references to Appendices
BAS. REVX.	1.5.18	10am	DDMS XVII Corps & ADMS visited and inspected MDS and transport	
			& 10, 11 & 12 FA ambulances	
		2pm	ADMS visited transport lines of 10th & 11th Bde. paying particular attention to the issuing of the rations	JSMc
"	2.5.18	11am	ADMS visited ADS 10th FA and CENSE-LA-VALLEE.	
		2.30pm	DMS first army called accompanied by DDMS XIII Corps	
			DMS accompanied by ADMS visited MDS 12 the Rnf. Bmt. du REVEILLON	
		4pm	ADMS visited DDMS XIII Corps	JSMc
"	3.5.18	10am	ADMS visited ADS at CENSE-LA-VALLEE and looked around canal bank area for a RAP for Support Battalion & left brigade.	
		2pm	ADMS visited MDS 22 CCS LOZINGHEM and 4 CCS (Canadian) PERNES investigating the large numbers of PUO occurring in the division.	JSMc
"	6.5.18	4pm	ASMS visited 1st Royal Warwicks Reg. at BUSNETTES.	JSMc

Army Form C. 2118.

WAR DIARY
or
INTELLIGENCE SUMMARY.
(Erase heading not required.)

Instructions regarding War Diaries and Intelligence Summaries are contained in F. S. Regs., Part II. and the Staff Manual respectively. Title pages will be prepared in manuscript.

Place	Date	Hour	Summary of Events and Information	Remarks and references to Appendices
BAS RIEUX	5.3.18	10 am	DADMS XIII Corps accompanied by DADMS 4 Div visited all RAPs & ADSs.	
"		2.35 pm	ADMS & DADMS visited Corps Rest Station (30 CCS) investigating the large number of sick to the division than	gone
"	6.3.18	11 am	ADMS visited 10 Fd Amb HQrs LE TAMEY.	
"		1 pm	ADMS visited MDS (12 Fd Amb)	gone
"		2 pm	ADMS inspected 10 " " " Baer Transport	gone
"	7.3.18	9 am	ADMS visited ADS left sector and RAPs of the two front batteries. Also recce to cause with a view to having a large post across to shelter work of evacuation	gone
"	8.3.18	10 am	ADMS & DADMS attended conference in office of DDMS XIII Corps	gone
"	9.3.18	-	Throughout the day large amount of gas shelling (mustard) by the enemy, causing about 80 casualties	
"	10.3.18	10.15 am	Visit 15 11 " & 12 " Fd Ambulances to collect each of the MO. for duty with 2nd Seaforths & 1st Royal Mo's Recce Horse, M.O.'s passed, vacancies respectively.	1

WAR DIARY
or
INTELLIGENCE SUMMARY

Army Form C. 2118.

Place	Date	Hour	Summary of Events and Information	Remarks and references to Appendices
BAS RIEUX	10.5.18 a.m	10.30 am	Visit to DDMS XIII Corps re gassing of Capt D.H. HALL RAMC (TC) and 1/Lt W.H. JOYCE. MORGUSA	2
		12.15 PM	Seen 1/c DDMS X IIIth Corps re gassing of Lieut W.E. BROWN RAMC (TC)	3
		4 pm	RAMC further casualty owing to 4 Bn A during the night 8.9/10. The enemy shelled all the forward areas including SONNE HEM [?] very heavy with mustard gas shells. Considerable number of casualties resulting to divisional troops and leaving primary total force about 90.	4
			ADMS visited ADS Right sector and RAPs right sector and MDS	
		6 pm	Lt Colonel RAMC order to CO	[A]
	11.5.18	10.30 am	ADMS met DDMS XIII Corps at No MDS re to 10 Lpl and to detail Capt T.H. HARKER RAMC (TC) for temporary duty, and 2nd West Ridings and Lieut W.E. BROWN passed to 4 Can CCS	5
	12.5.18	11 am	ADMS visited to 6 CCS at PERNES	

WAR DIARY
or
INTELLIGENCE SUMMARY

Army Form C. 2118.

Place	Date	Hour	Summary of Events and Information	Remarks and references to Appendices
BAS. RIEUX	13.5.18	11 am	A.D.M.S. visited A.D.S. at CONNEHEM y Hqrs of 12th Can. Inf Bde at BUSNETTES	
		12 noon	D.A.D.M.S. accompanied A.D.M.S. and D.A.D.M.S. of 3rd Canadian Div to H.Qrs of 10 7d and M.D.S. Post of PERNION	6
		4 pm	LE TAILLY H.Qrs of 11th and at BUSNETTES and M.D.S. Post of gassed Wm 6th 4th and 2 Ranks or gassed	
"	14.5.18	3 pm	A.D.M.S. visited A.D.S. CENSE LA VALLEE and H.Qrs 10 7d and 8 LE TAILLY. Revised medical arrangements in connection with R.A.M.C. orders 3/8.39 y 60.	B
	15.5.18	11.15 am	Col HUME A.M.S. consulting physician 1st army for a lecture on Poison gas at A.D.S. VIII.C.I.B. at which D.D.M.S. XIII corps , A.D.M.S. of Div. were present and about 40 Medical Officers from the division & Corps troops.	
			Capt McCutchon R.A.M.C. proceeded on special leave to Athens 16-5-18 624.5+18 to U.K. Major BORDERO A.T.M.E. acting DADMS during his absence.	
		2.0 pm	A.D.M.S. left round and visited artillery units in BUSNETTES and L'ECLEME noting their sanitary arrangements.	HR sht.
	16.5.18		Routine work	
	17.5.18		A.D.M.S. spent all morning looking over the ground north of canal with C.O.'s in establishing a R.A.P. in neighborhood of CARVIN, & visited all Medical posts. This proceeded to start work of new R.A.P. at Battalion H.Q. in P24d65. which will clear left Bn of left sector (Q.20.c-D) and the Centre & right Batt RAP not mined (C's are at P56d.39)	

A.5834. Wt.W4973/M687. 750,000 8/16 D.D.&L. Ltd. Forms/C.2118/13.

WAR DIARY
INTELLIGENCE SUMMARY

Army Form C. 2118.

Place	Date	Hour	Summary of Events and Information	Remarks and references to Appendices
BRS. RIEUX	17.5.18		The RAP's of right sector have also been altered. The Battle aid post at LES HARRISONS is more being used as a Stretcher — an Advanced Dressing Station for Casualties from the front areas — One MO + his staff are now for casualties from the front areas. One MO + his staff is sufficient to cope with casualties of which Btn. (3 Bns in line) the second & third MO are at W1 d.13 & V12 b 23 respectively in reserve. And can reach in minutes any time. Div R.O. dated 17.5.18 announces the award of M.C. to Capt. Walker R.A.M.C. att. 1st Hampshire Regt. It thoroughly deserves it — as he has seen that Dr. Long and Will Aper Am attention in Med. Posts. An arrangement was made to even the "Arrangement" No. 1 to Retired Medical arrangements on 18.5.18 BELLEGRAVE	C
	18.5.18		The ADMS made a thorough inspection of the right sector mainly BELLEGRAVE LES HARISONS & CENSE LA VALLEE. Capt. BROWN G.H. R.A.M.C. arrived as a reinforcement and was posted to be MO of 2nd Seaforths with whom he has seen Sype in this Div. CAPT. RHO CONNOR R.A.M.C. arrived 17.5.18 and was posted to 11 R.Fus. It is with great regret that the deaths of Capt. HALL R.A.M.C. LIEUT BROWN R.A.M.C. and LIEUT JOYCE MORTCUSR are received — They were killed in action respectively & wered HB garns on 10.5.18.	

WAR DIARY or INTELLIGENCE SUMMARY

Army Form C. 2118.

Place	Date	Hour	Summary of Events and Information	Remarks and references to Appendices
BUS RIEUX	23.5.18		ADMS visited 1 Corps Section Baths - where there are now Funkers fits	
	24.5.18	9.30am	Our Corps D.S.Officer went to Mt BERNENCHON to see the pumps & wells there & two field MDS. ADMS went to improvements of ERS. In the afternoon ADMS went to see O.C. 2. Mobile Lab. at PIRES	gone
	25.5.18		ADMS went to RIEZ DU VINAGE to inspect all water supply	gone
	26.3.18		Capt J.G. McCutcheon DADMS returned from leave. ADMS & DADMS visited 6 Mobile [Laundry] in the afternoon. ADMS visited 10 FA and 8 FA	gone
	27.5.18		ADMS & DDMS visited ADS VRAPs left sector in the morning. In the evening ADMS & DADMS visited CENSE-LE-VALLE (21st West Yorks & Somersets)	gone
	28.5.18		DMS 1st Army DDMS XIII Corps & ADMS visited all medical units. The division & also M.D.S. Everything was found satisfactory. The whole day until 4.30 pm was spent by them in looking them over. Lieut S.ADAMS MORCUS attached 2nd Hants Fusiliers awarded M.C.	gone

Army Form C. 2118.

WAR DIARY
or
INTELLIGENCE SUMMARY.

(Erase heading not required.)

Instructions regarding War Diaries and Intelligence Summaries are contained in F. S. Regs., Part II. and the Staff Manual respectively. Title pages will be prepared in manuscript.

Place	Date	Hour	Summary of Events and Information	Remarks and references to Appendices
B.H.S. RIEUX	29.5.16		DADMS visited HQrs 1st Tes and BUSNETTES. ADS right sector and RAPs right sector also 32nd Bde HQrs in the former. In the afternoon the ADMS visited all gun positions of the 32nd Bde.	
"	30.5.16		DADMS visited Divisional wing of Corps reinforcement camp. ADMS visited D.M.S. 1st army in the morning and in the afternoon he visited Headquarters of the D.A.C. and inspected some of the nature done drivers	
"	31.5.16		In the morning the ADMS attended conference of ADsMS in the office of the DDMS XVII Corps. In the afternoon ADMS & DADMS visited 109 Field Amb and 195 Colours Coy and had arrangements for their sick to be seen daily. In the evening ADMS visited 29 Bde RFA HQrs and inspected their gun positions	

During the month the heaviest work and evacuation remained the same as for both B Apll. excepting the R.A.P for left bearer ? left Sector (Vimage sector) which was moved to P 24 d 6.5. (CHAVIN) All R.A.Ps were strengthened by sandbags, cement and sand bags.

N Hay Greene
Col ADMS
4th Division

Copy No. 24

4th. DIVISION R.A.M.C. ORDER NO. 60.

10th. May, 1918.

1. No. 12 Field Ambulance will relieve No. 11 Field Ambulance, and take over the evacuation of casualties from the Right Sector of the Divisional Front, on the night of 10th/11th. May, 1918.

   No. 11 Field Ambulance on relief, will take over the Main Dressing Station at EN REVEILLON.

2. All details of the reliefs to be arranged between Ambulance Commanders concerned.

3. Transport of Nos. 11 and 12 Field Ambulances will remain as at present.

4. Completion of reliefs to be reported to this office.

J.G. McCutcheon
Captain,
for A.D.M.S. 4th. Division.

Issued at 8.0 p.m.
Distribution:

1. to D.D.M.S. XIIIth. Corps.
2. A.D.M.S. 3rd. Division.
3. A.D.M.S. 31st. Division.
4. 4th. Division.
5. 4th. Division 'A/Q'.
6. 10th. Fd. Ambc.
7. 11th. Fd. Ambc.
8. to 12th. Fd. Ambc.
9. 10th. Inf. Bd.
10. 11th. Inf. Bd.
11. 12th. Inf. Bd.
12-26. R.M.O's.
27,28 Diary.
29 File.

SECRET.

4th. DIVISION

REVISED MEDICAL ARRANGEMENTS IN CONNECTION WITH
R.A.M.C. ORDERS NOS. 58, 59 & 60.

Map Refs: Sheet 36a, 1/40,000.   14th. May, 1918.

4th. Division Medical Arrangements dated 26th. April, 1918 are cancelled.

1. **POSITION OF MEDICAL POSTS:**

    (a). R.A.P's: Left Sector.   Right Sector.

                               P.36.d.3.9. (Double).   W.2.a.8.2.(Triple).
                               V.4.b.4.2.

    (b). Relay & Car Posts:

                               V.5.b.5.1.   W.7.c.3.7.
                               V.4.b.4.2.   (W.1.d.1.3.)

    (c). A.D.S's: CENSE LA VALLEE,   GONNEHEM,
                               (V.11.c.1.8.)   (V.18.c.3.9.)

    (d). M.D.S.:   No. 11 Field Ambulance, LE REVEILLON,
                               (V.26.d.6.7.)

2. **EQUIPMENT OF POSTS:**

    All Posts forward of the A.D.S's. and the A.D.S's. themselves, will be equipped as lightly as possible, and will be as mobile as possible.

3. **EVACUATION:**

    From the R.A.P's. of the Left and Right Sectors of the Divisional front by hand and wheeled stretchers and Ford car to the A.D.S's. at GONNEHEM and CENSE LA VALLEE.
    Thence in cars of Field Ambulances to the M.D.Stn. at V.26.d.6.7. and from M.D.S. to C.C.S. in cars of 22 M.A.C.

4. **COLLECTION OF SICK:**

    Areas for collection of sick will be as follow:-

    (a). From Brigade Group of Left Sector: 10th. Fd. Ambce.
    (b). From Brigade Group of Right Sector: 12th. Fd. Ambce.
    (c). From Reserve Brigade Group and such other Units as are
         notified from time to time: 11th. Fd. Ambce.

    Nos. 10 and 12 Field Ambulances will, in addition to the above, see the sick of such Corps and Army Troops as are nearest to them.

5. **BLANKETS & STRETCHERS:**

    A small dump of stretchers and blankets has been formed at the M.D.S. from which Nos. 10 and 12 Field Ambulances can draw after reference to this office.

6. REGISTRATION OF CASUALTIES:

    No. 11 Field Ambulance at the M.D.S. will be responsible for the registration of all casualties from the Divisional front.

    Nos. 10 and 12 Field Ambulances will keep no A.& D. Books, and will send patients to the M.D.S. with tallies properly filled in.

    Field Medical Cards will be completed for each case, and A.T.S. administered at the M.D.S.

7. INSTRUCTIONS FOR SPECIAL CASES:

    These have been issued from this office from time to time, to all concerned.

H.Q. 4th. Division.
14th. May, 1918.
U.

                                           Colonel,
                           A.D.M.S. 4th. Division.

Copies to all recipients of R.A.M.C. Orders 58, 59, 60.

AMENDMENT NO. 1

to

REVISED MEDICAL ARRANGEMENTS DATED 14-5-18.

Map Refs: Sheet 36a, 1/40,000.

1. Para. 1 (a) is cancelled and the following substituted:

   1 (a). R.A.P's: Left Sector.   Right Sector.

       Rt. Bn.) P.36.d.3.9.   For) W.2.a.8.2.
       Cent.Bn.)   Bde.) W.1.d.1.3.
       Left Bn. P.24.d.6.5.   Front) V.12.b.2.3.
                              to)
                              rear.)

   N.B. R.A.P. at P.35.c.1.3. will remain in use until that at P.24.d.6.5. is ready.

2. Para. 1 (b). Delete "V.4.b.4.2." from Left Sector.

3. Para. 3, "Evacuation", is cancelled, and the following substituted:

3. EVACUATION:

   (a). Right Sector: By hand carriage to the R.A.P. and thence by hand and wheeled stretcher to A.D.S. at GONNEHEM.

   (b). Left Sector: From Right and Centre Battalion by hand, wheeled stretcher and light-railway (as soon as available), from RIEZ DU VINAGE to P.36.d.3.9. Thence by wheeled stretcher to A.D.S. CENSE LA VALLEE.
       From Left Battalion by hand to P.24.d.6.5. and thence to A.D.S. CENSE LA VALLEE.

   From both A.D.S's. to M.D.S. in Field Ambulance Cars, and from M.D.S. to C.C.S. by M.A.C. cars.

                                          Colonel,
17th. May, 1918.   A.D.M.S. 4th. Division.

Copies to all recipients of Revised Med. Arrts. of 14-5-18.

Army Form C. 2118.

WAR DIARY
or
INTELLIGENCE SUMMARY.
(Erase heading not required.)

June 1918

War Diary
of
A.D.M.S. Headquarters 4th Division
for period
from 1st June 1918

3/7/18

140/3093.

COMMITTEE 3rd June 1918
MEDICAL HISTORY OF THE WAR
Date 7 AUG 1918

Macleine
Colonel
A.D.M.S 4th Division

Medical
Army Form C. 2118.

WAR DIARY
or
INTELLIGENCE SUMMARY.
(Erase heading not required.)

Instructions regarding War Diaries and Intelligence Summaries are contained in F. S. Regs., Part II. and the Staff Manual respectively. Title pages will be prepared in manuscript.

Place	Date	Hour	Summary of Events and Information	Remarks and references to Appendices
BAS. RIEUX	1.6.18		ADMS accompanied by DADMG visited 4 Canadian CCS to see a boy averted and delivered in the morning. In the afternoon ADMS & DADMS visited 1st Corps scabies station and delivered and disinfector there. In the evening ADMS & DADMS visited Bde HQrs & RAPs of the brigades not in BUSNETTES, CENSE-LE-VACLE and L'ECLEME.	done
"	2.6.18		In the morning ADMS visited 10th Tm and H. Qrs forming of a car part for divisional artillery. In the afternoon ADMS & DADMS visited 3 mobile Laboratory divisional pond PERNES. Still quiet.	done done

Army Form C. 2118.

WAR DIARY
or
INTELLIGENCE SUMMARY.
(Erase heading not required.)

Instructions regarding War Diaries and Intelligence Summaries are contained in F.S. Regs., Part II. and the Staff Manual respectively. Title pages will be prepared in manuscript.

Place	Date	Hour	Summary of Events and Information	Remarks and references to Appendices
BUS RIEUX	3.6.18		In the morning DADMS visited H.Qrs 3 & 12th Fd Ambulance & in the afternoon DADMS visited H.Qrs 8, 10 & 11 Fd Amb. Arrangements for presentation by Divisional rural retreats by the Army Corps Commander.	one
	4.6.18	2.30 pm	The Army Corps Commander accompanied by S.O.C. division and Staff presented ribbons to RE's & RAMC. There were 18 O. R's & 2 Officers RAMC recipients. Officers Battery M.C.'s & O.R.'s M.M.	
		5 pm	ADMS & DADMS visited dugouts at CANTRAINE & H.Qrs of 2nd Lancs Fusiliers in rest there.	
		6.30 pm	ADMS & DADMS visited H.Qrs 8, 10 & Fd Amb.	one
	5.6.18		ADMS visited H.Qrs 10 Fd Amb. In the morning. DADMS visited ADS Hyppolite in the evening ADMS & DADMS visited 3y Sunday Rector	one

Army Form C. 2118.

WAR DIARY
or
INTELLIGENCE SUMMARY.
(Erase heading not required.)

Place	Date	Hour	Summary of Events and Information	Remarks and references to Appendices
BAS RIEUX	6.6.18	—	In the morning the ADMS & DADMS visited 12th Bde HQrs to investigate what seemed to be an attack of mild influenza. In the afternoon the ADMS accompanied by Bacteriologist from No 3 Mobile Laboratory again visited 12 Bde HQrs. In the evening DADMS visited 12 Bde And HQrs.	
"	7.6.18	—	In the morning the ADMS & DADMS searched the area of the right sector (PACAUT) for a second ADS HARRISONS provided decided on a house in RES TREES strengthened by the DADMS visited 4 Cm CCS to view the ele- trainer.	
"	8.6.18		In the morning ADMS attended a conference of DMS, DDsMS & ADsMS first army with the DGMS France at 4 Cm CCS, re-orgn? Evacuation and Sanitation of Hospitals relative to bombing by enemy delivery of troops, sanitation, & mustard gas cases.	

WAR DIARY
INTELLIGENCE SUMMARY

Army Form C. 2118.

Place	Date	Hour	Summary of Events and Information	Remarks and references to Appendices
BAS RIEVY	9.6.18	—	In the morning the A.D.M.S. & D.A.D.M.S. visited Left Brigade H.Qrs (112 Bde) and all Battalion H.Qrs & R.A.Ps in the left Sector (Vanage Sector). In the evening the A.D.M.S & D.A.D.M.S visited H.Qrs 11 Bde and A.D.S.	
	10.6.18		D.A.D.M.S inspected billets & sanitation. In the evening A.D.M.S & D.A.D.M.S visited H.Qrs of all Batteries & 65" A 174 in the Vanage Sector. Gas are chiefly annual. Anse-lon-vallee. Visited also 17 —Bd and 8 H.Qrs BUSNETTES. Gone.	
	11.6.18		DDMS & DADMS XIIIth Corps accompanied by ADMS & DADMS 4th Div visited LES HARRISOIRS R.A.Ps and chose another site for another R.A.P and then marched along the canal bank to P 36 d 29 (Double and got left packet) and then to ADS Corse-la-vallee. This occupied the morning. In the afternoon ADMS & DADMS inspected the area of L'ECLEME & CANTRAINE Gone	

Army Form C. 2118.

WAR DIARY
or
INTELLIGENCE SUMMARY.
(Erase heading not required.)

Place	Date	Hour	Summary of Events and Information	Remarks and references to Appendices
BAS-RIEUX	12.6.18		In the morning the ADMS & DADMS accompanied the DDMS & PADMS on XIII Corps. round the left sector including the RAP at GARVIN and the village of RIEZ au VINAGE. R.A.M.C. order No. 61.	A
"	13.6.18		In the morning ADMS & DADMS & Town Major accompanied by Town major. visited 2 R.A.C. headquarters	Gone
"	14.6.18	10 am	ADMS & DADMS visited 1st R.hamicks and investigated into a case of typhoid which they had advanced on our right on right flank about 600 yards.	Gone Gone
		11.45 pm		
"	15.6.18		In the morning ADMS & DADMS inspected CANTRAINE Latrines & particularly the lavatori traps. Capt. SIMPSON.TC proceeded then in relief of T/Capt G.H.BROWN to England on Separation of contract	Gone (1)

WAR DIARY
or
INTELLIGENCE SUMMARY

Army Form C. 2118.

Place	Date	Hour	Summary of Events and Information	Remarks and references to Appendices
BAS. RIEUX	16.6.18		In the morning ADMS & DADMS inspected M.D.S. (11th Fd Amb)	
"	14.6.18		Lieut T. Copt a/major H.E.A. BOLDERO RAMC 10 Jan Aml proceeded to 61st Div on appointment as DADMS. In the evening ADMS & DADMS visited some of the guns & bivouacs of the 52nd Bde R.G.A. accompanied by O.C. and M.O.	
			In the afternoon ADMS visited to Fd Ambulance HQrs and 11th Fd Ambulance M.D.S.	
"	18.6.18		ADMS & DADMS visited M.D.S. in the forenoon. Nothing to remark.	
	19.6.18			
	20.6.18		ADMS visited M.D.S. and arranged to increase accommodation for detention of the Spectrum Hosis' days fever which is increasing rapidly every day.	
"	21.6.18		ADMS visited 16th Fd Amb HQrs BUSNETTES BATHS & LENGLET SMC	

Army Form C. 2118.

WAR DIARY
or
INTELLIGENCE SUMMARY.
(Erase heading not required.)

Place	Date	Hour	Summary of Events and Information	Remarks and references to Appendices
BAS RIEVX	22.6.18	-	In the evening ADMS & DADMS walked thro' Hqrs and all companies of the Div. train	
"	23.6.18		In the morning the ADMS visited D.G. at HESDIN. DADMS visited 10 Fd Amb. HQrs	
"			In the evening DADMS visited 30 C.C.S.	
"	24.6.18		In the morning ADMS and DADMS visited the rest R&D (in process of creation) at LES - HARRISOIRS.	
"			In the evening ADMS & DADMS visited M.D.S. (11th & 7th Amb)	
"	25.6.18		In the afternoon DADMS visited M.D.S. & 12 Hth ambulance.	
"	26.6.18		ADMS & DADMS visited Billets in Barracks when Canad. Grays were installed and made arrangements for battalion in not Horse also 526 Field Coy & R.G.A. Hars. to go through the Sprayer on 27.6.18.	
"			In the evening ADMS & DADMS moved to Div. M.T. Coy. AUCHEL	

Army Form C. 2118.

WAR DIARY
or
INTELLIGENCE SUMMARY.
(Erase heading not required.)

Place	Date	Hour	Summary of Events and Information	Remarks and references to Appendices
BAS. RIEUX	27.6.18		In the morning ADMS. & DADMS. visited Battalion HQrs of right & centre Battalion of PACAUT sector also visited (11th Bde) Bde HQrs and HQrs of 63rd A.F.A. In the afternoon ADMS visited No 3 mobile Laboratory Peronne	
"	28.6.18		In the afternoon ADMS and DDMS XIII Corps visited MDS 4th Division and MDS 3rd Division also 3rd Division N. Qr.	June
"	29.6.18		In the afternoon ADMS watched 1st Rhe. Bde, 1 EVICK Sprayer pronounce tanks, and 376 (Durham) Field Coy and 71st & 61st Yanks (Americans) B. attack.	June
"	30.6.18		In the morning ADMS & DADMS visited reserve Brigade and chose sites for RAPs in case of an B. attack. In the evening DADMS visited L'ECLEME and selected a room there for "Verey" Sprayer station.	June

During the month No Changes in Transport Received.

Fairchild Lt Col AMS ADMS 54 Div

Copy No. 16

4th. DIVISION R.A.M.C. ORDER NO. 61.

(Vide 4th. Division Order No. 131).

Map Refs: Sheet 36a. 1/40,000.   12th. June, 1918.

The 3rd. Division are advancing their front on the night 14/15th. June.
The operation is to be carried out as a surprise, without preliminary bombardment.
The 11th. Infantry Brigade is to move forward its right so as to conform to this movement, and will establish three posts between the left of the 76th. Brigade and our present front line.

1. O.C. No. 12 Field Ambulance will be responsible for the evacuation of casualties of the 4th. Divisional Troops engaged in this operation.

2. He will reinforce the MOUND Post, (W.1.d.1.3.) with 24 bearers.
    These will carry from the R.A.P. at LES HARISOIRS, (W.2.a.8.2.) to the MOUND.
    If necessary, O.C. No. 12 Field Ambulance will so dispose these bearers as to carry from the CANAL BANK to LES HARISOIRS, and from LES HARISOIRS to the MOUND.

3.(a). Should more bearers be required they will be supplied on demand from the A.D.M.S.

   (b). Extra ambulance cars may be obtained on demand of O.C. No. 12 Field Ambulance direct to No. 11 Field Ambulance.

4. O.C. No. 12 Field Ambulance will form a small dump at LES HARISOIRS, (W.2.a.8.2.) after dark on 12th. inst., as follows:-

    20 Stretchers.
    40 Blankets.
    6 Thomas' Splints.

5. These orders will only be in force until the battlefield has been cleared of wounded.

6. Zero hour will be notified later.

7. Field Ambulances to acknowledge.

Issued at 5 p.m.

Colonel,
A.D.M.S. 4th. Division.

- 2 -

Distribution:-

Copy No.	1	to	D.D.M.S. XIIIth. Corps.
	2		A.D.M.S. 3rd. Division.
	3		10th. Field Ambulance.
	4		11th. Field Ambulance.
	5		12th. Field Ambulance.
	6		4th. Division.
	7		4th. Division A/Q.
	8		11th. Infantry Brigade.
	9		M.O. 1st. Som. Lt. Inf.
	10		M.O. 1st. Hants. Regt.
	11		M.O. 1st. Rifle Brigade.
	12		4th. Bn. M.G.Corps.
	13		22 M.A.C.
	14) 15)		Diary.
	16		File.

MEDICAL

Army Form C. 2118.

Vol 48

WAR DIARY
or
INTELLIGENCE SUMMARY.
(Erase heading not required.)

Place	Date	Hour	Summary of Events and Information	Remarks and references to Appendices
BUS RIEUX	1.7.15		Office routine.	
	2.7.15		DADMS in the morning fixed up a room for lunch. Stopped in LIERES. In the afternoon ADMS visited 10.2nd and H.Qs and transport lines of 11 Bde.	
	3.7.15		In the morning he ADMS & DADMS visited war wagon lines of all divisional artillery and arranged for fitting of four harnesses as a small hospital for knee deep fever cases.	
	4.7.15		In the afternoon ADMS visited some B battery positions of 63 AFA on the Runney. ADMS & DADMS visited 4 pm. Finn H.Qrs. Force.	
	5.7.15		In the morning ADMS accompanied by DDMS visited ADS right (Paraph) before and RAPs & have return. Col _____ HARRISON. First party of 3 officers proceeded on XIII Corps Officers Rest at PARIS PLACE. gone	

A5834 W.t.W4973/M687 750,000 8/16 D.D. & L. Ltd. Forms/C.2118/13.

Army Form C. 2118.

WAR DIARY
or
INTELLIGENCE SUMMARY.
(Erase heading not required.)

Instructions regarding War Diaries and Intelligence Summaries are contained in F. S. Regs., Part II. and the Staff Manual respectively. Title pages will be prepared in manuscript.

Place	Date	Hour	Summary of Events and Information	Remarks and references to Appendices
B.I.S. RIEUX	5.7.18		In the evening the ADMS visited 12" & 31" Bde Transport lines at ALLOUAGNE	gone
"	6.7.18		In the morning ADMS & DADMS visited Sun Section & 13th H.G. of 164 Bde R.F.A.	
	7.7.18		ADMS went to Corps H.Qs in the morning and attended a conference of ADiMS with DDMS Two O.R. R.A.M.C. wounded (12 india amb)	
	8.7.18		In the morning ADMS visited DDMS. XIII Corps.	
		6.30pm	T/CAPT. F.P. JOSCELYNE R.A.M.C. (T.C.) arrived for duty and posted to 12 Fd Ambulance.	
	9.7.18		ADMS continued the duty of A/DDMS XIII Corps during absence of DDMS on leave.	
	10.7.18		ADMS visited 22 M.A.C. in the morning. ADMS visited 12 Fd Ambulance in the evening for the sports. Efft.	gone

WAR DIARY
INTELLIGENCE SUMMARY

Army Form C. 2118.

Place	Date	Hour	Summary of Events and Information	Remarks and references to Appendices
BAS-RIEUX	11/7/18		In the evening ADMS visited Corps H.Qrs. 3 whole bat. & 6 C.C.S.	
	12.7.18		Capt J.W. BINGHAM RAMC (TC) arrived for duty and posted to 10 Field Ambulance. In the morning the ADMS visited Divisional Supply wagon lines and inspected the issuing of rations for Headquarters Company & divisional troops. In the evening ADMS visited Corps Scabies Station Corps Headquarters.	Gone. Gone.
	13.7.18		C.D. CHRISTIE Ch. Y Div RAMC arrived for duty with 12th Ambulance. In the morning ADMS visited the Baths at BUSNETTES and ADS at CENSE-LA-VALLEE. In the evening ADMS visited Corps H.Qrs.	Gone.

Army Form C. 2118.

WAR DIARY
or
INTELLIGENCE SUMMARY.
(Erase heading not required.)

Instructions regarding War Diaries and Intelligence Summaries are contained in F. S. Regs., Part II. and the Staff Manual respectively. Title pages will be prepared in manuscript.

Place	Date	Hour	Summary of Events and Information	Remarks and references to Appendices
BUS. RUEUX	15.7.18	—	2. Personal examination of lines. D.A.D.M.S. visited 10th Fd. Amb. H.Q. & No 1 Group D.A.D.M.S. visited 127th Fd. Amb. H.Q.	
	16.7.18	—	In the afternoon A.D.M.S. visited Corps M.Q. and A.D.M.S. 74th Divn.	
		—	In the morning A.D.M.S. visited the area at 1st Fd. Amb. & PENSE LA VALLEE. Talks on 18th Fd. Amb. & to tents to be in use PACANT WOOD. Medical arrangements for move on PACANT WOOD arranged. In front several area.	A
		—	In the morning A.D.M.S. visited Posts at BUSNETTES and informed the ambulance to be in use delivering clothes also Agn. 12 7d Divn.	B
	17.7.18	—	In the afternoon A.D.M.S. visited C.R.S. (3 C.C.S) and Corps H.Qrs. to inform D.A.D.M.S. visited A.D.S. & R.A.P.s including No 5.	
		night	D.A.D.M.S. (PACANT) Sector at W.26.B.3 ready for use & A.D.S. and Post at W.26.B.3 ready for use & R.A.P.s and Posts

WAR DIARY or INTELLIGENCE SUMMARY

Army Form C. 2118.

Place	Date	Hour	Summary of Events and Information	Remarks and references to Appendices
BAS RIEUX	16/7/18		ADMS visited ADS, RAPs & all Bn Hqrs in the VINAGE Sector in the morning. In the afternoon 2.30 pm 2/7 Bn Duke of Wellingtons carried out a raid on FACENT Wood. Total number of casualties were 4 officers and 49 other ranks.	
	17/7/18		In the morning ADMS went to Corps HQrs. In the evening ADMS inspected horse lines. Chambers at BUSNETTES.	Gone Gone
	18/7/18		In the evening ADMS visited Corps HQrs.	
	19/7/18		In the morning ADMS visited Corps HQrs.	
	20/7/18		In the morning ADMS visited MDS's (117th Amb) and transport of 11 Fld Amb.	gone gone
	21/7/18		In the morning DADMS visited 10th Fd Amb. HQrs.	
	22/7/18		In the morning ADMS of COMMENCHEM YCHSELE VALLEY & Bde Reception Camp HORINGHEM	gone gone

WAR DIARY
or
INTELLIGENCE SUMMARY

Army Form C. 2118.

(Erase heading not required.)

Place	Date	Hour	Summary of Events and Information	Remarks and references to Appendices
BAS RIEUX	23/7/18		In the morning ADMS visited RAPs of right sector and rety fact.	
	24.7.18		In the morning ADMS visited Corps RAPs & DMS fifth army.	
	25.7.18		In the afternoon ADMS visited Corps HQ at HQ. Conference at ADMS's.	
	26.7.18		In the afternoon ADMS accompanied the DMS fifth army. He inspected MDS and Corps Scabies Station.	
			In the morning ADMS accompanied the ADMS XXII Corps visiting schemes of reorganisation and MDS.	Apps. One.
	27.7.18		Office routine. Technical arrangements also addendum to L. of C. matters. ADMS visited Corps HQ. DADMS visited 10 K.H.W. am 11.9th now MDS	
	28.7.18		In the morning ADMS accompanied by DQ XI Division I/Room inspected the wells on left HARRODS's left & views of front water front for forward areas.	
	29.7.18		ADMS visited Corps HQs. In the evening DADMS visited one.	

A(8604) Wt. W1771/M2 31 750,000 5/17 Sch. 53 Forms/C2118/14
D. D. & L., London, E.C.

Army Form C. 2118.

WAR DIARY
or
INTELLIGENCE SUMMARY.
(Erase heading not required.)

Instructions regarding War Diaries and Intelligence Summaries are contained in F.S. Regs., Part II. and the Staff Manual respectively. Title pages will be prepared in manuscript.

Place	Date	Hour	Summary of Events and Information	Remarks and references to Appendices
BAS RIEUX	29.7.18		G.O.C. fifth army interviewed D.M.S. fifth army and ADMS fourth division under M.O.S. 11th Ord in the morning	
		11am	D.A.D.M.S with A.D.E. SOMMEHEM	
		10 am	H.Q. 10th Ord in the afternoon	
"	30.7.18		Office routine. ADMS visited Corps H.Qrs. & DADMS inspected Advanced Dump	
"	31.7.18		B. 32 Bde & 29 Bde R.F.A. also 65th Bde A.F.A. ADMS visited Corps H.Qr	
			Routine Evacuation and the same for July as for June. See Diary and forms at War 683 attached are in the 28/7/18	

J. Macpherson
Col. A.D.M.S.
ADMS - 4 Div.

SECRET

A.D.M.S. 4th. Division No. 17/12.

4th. DIVISION.

MEDICAL ARRANGEMENTS IN CONNECTION WITH 4th. DIVN.

G.A. 7/18 dated 15-7-1918.

17th. July, 1918.

The 10th. Infantry Brigade is carrying out a raid on PACAUT WOOD on the 18th. inst.

1. O.C. No. 12 Field Ambulance will be responsible for the evacuation of all casualties from this operation, which pass through the Divisional Area.

2. He will reinforce the R.A.P's. and Forward Post at W.1.d.1.3.

3. Additional motor ambulances if required, will be supplied on demand from No. 11 Field Ambulance, direct.

4. Zero hour will be notified later.

5. Field Ambulances to acknowledge.

[signature]

Major,
for A.D.M.S. 4th. Division.

Issued at 1 p.m.

Distribution:-
- 10th. Field Ambulance.
- 11th. Field Ambulance.
- 12th. Field Ambulance.
- 4th. Division."
- 4th. Division "A/Q".
- H.Q. 10th. Inf. Bde.
- M.O. 1st. R. Warwick Regt.
- M.O. 2nd. W. Riding R.
- M.O. 2nd. Seaf. Highrs.

Copy No. B Diary

4th DIVISION.
MEDICAL ARRANGEMENTS NO.2.

Map Refs.: Sheets 36a) 1/40,000.   17th July, 1918.
                     44b)

All previous Medical Arrangements are cancelled.

1. **POSITION OF MEDICAL UNITS:**

    (a). R.A.P's:

	Left Sector.		Right Sector.
Rt.Bn. Con.Bn. }	P.36.d.3.9.	Rt.Bn. Lt.Bn. }	W.2.b.8.3.
Lt.Bn.	P.24.d.6.5.	Con.Bn. }	W.2.a.8.2.

    Reserve Brigade (In defence positions).

    Rt.Bn. Con.Bn. } V.12.b.2.3.
    Lt.Bn. P.35.b.1.1.

    (b). Car & Relay Posts:

    V.5.b.5.1.   W.1.d.1.3.
    V.4.b.4.2.   W.7.c.3.7.

    (c). A.D.Stns:
    CENSE LA VALLEE,   GONNEHEM,
    (V.11.c.1.8.)   (V.18.c.3.9.)

    (d). M.D.Stn:
    No.11.Field Ambulance,LE REVEILLON, V.26.d.6.7.

    (e). H.Q.& Transport of Fd Amboes:

Headquarters.	Transport.
10th Field Ambce. LE TAILLY	LE TAILLY.
11th Field Ambce. REVEILLON.	ALLOUAGNE.
12th Field Ambce. BUSNETTES.	BUSNETTES.

2. **EQUIPMENT OF POSTS:**

    All posts forward of and including the A.D.S's. will be equipped as lightly as possible,to give them the maximum of mobility.

3. **EVACUATION:**

    (a) Right Sector: By hand carriage to the R.A.P. and thence by hand,wheeled stretcher and Ford Car to A.D.S. at GONNEHEM.

(b). Left Sector: From Right and Centre Battalions by hand, wheeled stretcher and light railway from RIEZ DU VINAGE to P.36.d.5.9.(R.A.P.). Thence by wheeled stretcher and Ford Car to the A.D.S. at CENSE LA VALLEE.

From Left Battalion by hand and wheeled stretcher to P.24.d.5.5. (R.A.P.) and thence to A.D.S. at CENSE LA VALLEE.

From both A.D.S's to M.D.S. in Field Ambulance cars, and in M.A.C. cars from M.D.S. to C.C.S.

4. COLLECTION OF SICK:

Areas for collection of sick will be as follows:-

(a). From Brigade Group of L.Sector: 10th Field Ambulance.

(b). From Brigade Group of R.Sector; and from Div Details: 12th Field Ambulance.

(c). From Reserve Brigade Group and such other Units as are notified from time to time.   11th Field Ambulance.

Nos. 10 and 12 Field Ambulances will, in addition to the above, see sick of such Corps and Army Troops, (including Artillery) as are nearest to them.

5. BLANKETS AND STRETCHERS:

A small dump of blankets and stretchers has been formed at the M.D.S. from which Nos.10 and 12 Field Ambulances can draw after reference to the A.D.M.S.

6. REGISTRATION OF CASUALTIES:

No.11.Field Ambulance at the M.D.S. will be responsible for the registration of all casualties from the Divisional Front.
Nos.10. and 12. Field Ambulances will keep no A.& D. Books but will send patients to the M.D.S. with tallies properly filled in.

Field Medical Cards and A.T.S. will be completed and administered respectively at the M.D.S.

7. INSTRUCTIONS FOR SPECIAL CASES:

(a). The following special cases will be sent to the M.D.S. direct, or to the nearest Medical Posts of the Division on the day before that on which they are due to see the Specialists.

Cases.	To be at M.D.S.	Seen by Specialist on day, and at places as shown.
Dental.	Sundays & Thursdays. (by 6 p.m.)	Mondays & Fridays at MDS.
Dental, Officers.	To be seen by appointment at No.1. Can.C.C.S. PERNES. Appointments to be made direct.	
Eye.	Off: Saturdays. O.R: Tuesdays.	Offs: Sundays.) At 22 O.R: Wednesdays) C.C.S.

| Ear, Throat and Nose. | Off: Saturdays. O.R: Thursdays. | Off: Sundays. O.R: Fridays. | 12 Sty. Hpl. |

(b). Other cases are disposed of as shown below, after leaving the Main Dressing Station.

Nature of Cases.	Disposal from M.D.S.
Self-Inflicted Wounds.	To 12 Sty. Hpl. ST POL.
N.Y.D.N. Cases.	To 1 C.C.Stn., WAVRANS.
Scabies Cases.	To XIII Corps Scabies Stn., ALLOUAGNE.
Rest Station Cases.	Oth.Rks: 30 C.C.S. WAVRANS. Officers: Officers' Rest Stn., PARIS PLAGE.

(c). Infectious cases are disposed of as shown below:

Nature of Cases.	Disposal.
Early Scarlet Fever, Enteric, Diphtheria and Infectious Jaundice.	To receiving C.C.S.
Dysentery & Suspected Dysentery.	To 39 Sty.Hpl. AIRE.
Diagnosed and Suspected C.S.M.	To 12 Sty.Hpl. ST POL.
All other infectious cases.	To 12 Sty.Hpl. ST POL.

(d). Ordinary wounded cases are evacuated to one of the C.C.Stns. in the following Group :

```
No. 6 C.C.Stn.      PERNES.
No. 22 C.C.Stn.     PERNES.
No. 1 Can. C.C.S.   PERNES.
No. 4 Can. C.C.S.   PERNES.
```

8. **SANITARY SECTION:**

No. 37 Sanitary Section with Headquarters at ALLOUAGNE, is in sanitary charge of the area.

9. **UNFITS:**

Officers and men whom the M.O. thinks unfit will be sent to the office of the A.D.M.S. at 10 a.m. on Mondays. They will be accompanied by a statement on the cases written and signed by the M.O. It must be remembered that no "Hospital" cases should be sent in for examination.

10. **MEDICAL STORES:**

For the present, No. 12 Advanced Depot of Medical Stores, PERNES, will be used by the Division.
Later, No. 1 at PERNES AIRE, will supply the Division.

11. **MOBILE LABORATORIES:**

<u>Bacteriological</u>: No. 20 Mob. Bac. Lab. AIRE.

<u>Hygiene</u>: No. 9 Mob. Hyg. Lab. THEROUANNE.

Colonel,
A.D.M.S. 4th. Division.

Copies to all concerned.

SECRET

AMENDMENTS TO
4th. DIVISION MEDICAL ARRANGEMENTS NO. 2 DATED 17th. JULY.

In Para. 7, "Instructions for Special Cases":

Sub-para. (a), table of cases:-

(1). DENTAL. Delete existing arrangements, and substitute the following:-

Cases.	To be at M.D.S.	Seen by Specialist on day, and at places shown.
Dental.	Tuesdays & Thursdays. (By 6 p.m.).	Wed. & Fridays at MDS.
Dental, Officers.	Tuesdays by 9 a.m.	Tuesday mornings at M.D.S.

(2). EAR, THROAT & NOSE. Delete existing arrangements and substitute the following:-

Ear, Throat & Nose.	Off: Saturdays. O.R: Tues.& Thurs.	Off: Sundays. O.R: Wed.& Fri.) At 51 C.C.S.

Sub-para. (b), table of cases:-

(3). Cancel the first two items on the table and substitute the following:-

Nature of Cases.	Disposal from M.D.S.
Self-Inflicted Wounds.	To 51 C.C.S., COYECQUE.
N.Y.D.N. Cases.	To 51 C.C.S., COYECQUE.

Sub-para. (c):-

(4). Cancel table of Infectious Diseases, and substitute the following:-

Nature of Cases.	Disposal.
Dysentery and Suspected Dysentery.	To 8 C.C.S., ELNES.
All other infectious cases.	To 51 C.C.S. COYECQUE.

/Over.

(5). Reference para. 10, 'Medical Stores':-

    Delete "PERNES AIRE" in last line but one, and substitute "WAVRANS-SUR-L'AA".

                                                   Colonel,
27-7-18.   A.D.M.S. 4th. Division.
U.

Copies to all recipients of 4th. Div. Med. Arrangements No. 2.

SECRET

ADDENDUM NO. 1

to

4th. DIVISION MEDICAL ARRANGEMENTS NO. 2, of 17-7-18.

==

After para.3, 'Evacuation', insert the following:-

" (c). Should the necessity arise, wounded from the Left Battn. R.A.P., Left Sector, at P.24.d.6.5. may be evacuated through the Car Post of the Division on our left, at P.24.b.3.3. to the M.D.S. of that Division."

Mackenzie
Colonel,

27-7-18.
U.

A.D.M.S. 4th. Division.

MEDICAL
Form C. 2118.

ADMS Army 4 D

WAR DIARY
or
INTELLIGENCE SUMMARY.
(Erase heading not required.)

Instructions regarding War Diaries and Intelligence Summaries are contained in F.S. Regs., Part II. and the Staff Manual respectively. Title pages will be prepared in manuscript.

Place	Date	Hour	Summary of Events and Information	Remarks and references to Appendices
BKS RIEUX	1 Aug 17		In the morning DDMS inspected the ADSs at SOMMEREM and accompanied by ADMS & DADMS to the advanced headquarters and the hutments & CENSE LA VALLE, also the huts at BUSNETTES A.D.S. 13 D.H. and at BUSNETTES.	
"	2 Aug		Received official notice that LADMS started ADMS 19th Divn.	
"	3 Aug		In the morning DADMS visited and inspected the sanatorium at CANTRAINE and LECLEME area. In the morning ADMS visited Corps HQrs. In the afternoon ADMS judged the cleanliness of the divisional cookers at divisional sanitary school.	
Ham	4 Aug		ADMS & DADMS attended divisional commemoration service.	
"	5 Aug		In the morning ADMS visited troops and Army HQrs. In the afternoon ADMS motored to over sanitary [illegible]	
			On the morning [illegible] afternoon DADMS inspected [illegible] BKS RIEUX and BUSNETTES [illegible]	

D. D. & L., London, E.C.
Wt. W4771/M2 31 750,000 5/17 Sch. 52 Forms/C2118/14
(A8004)

Army Form C. 2118.

WAR DIARY
or
INTELLIGENCE SUMMARY.
(Erase heading not required.)

Instructions regarding War Diaries and Intelligence Summaries are contained in F. S. Regs., Part II. and the Staff Manual respectively. Title pages will be prepared in manuscript.

Place	Date	Hour	Summary of Events and Information	Remarks and references to Appendices
BAS. RIEVL	6.8.18		In the morning ADMS accompanied by DADMS Sanitation Officer Army visited toks at BUSNETTES. In the afternoon DADMS visited KAP left batteries left sector and inspected latrines etc of the left sector. In the evening DADMS visited 6am HQrs.	
"	7/8/18		In the morning DADMS visited all Fd Ambs HQrs and discussed the situation arising out of the enemy withdrawal.	
			3.9. Heard centre aid post at P.36.a. right aid post Q.26.c.17 and the centre aid post at P.36 & 3.9 was made into forward A.D.S. by 10 Fd Ambl.	
"	8/8/18		In the morning ADMs visited Corps & Div. A few morning casualties. 3 O/R 4 O/Rs any Enemy withdrawal.	some

WAR DIARY
or
INTELLIGENCE SUMMARY.
(Erase heading not required.)

Army Form C. 2118.

Place	Date	Hour	Summary of Events and Information	Remarks and references to Appendices
BUSNES	2.9.18		In the morning ADMS visited 246 R.A.M.C. & Left Section also inspected H.Qrs & 14 Bde R.F.A. at PHILOMEL LODGE (near LILLERS). During afternoon ADMS visited Corps H.Qrs and completed reports re dental outbreak in BURBURE & re proposed medical arrangements in 3rd Army.	A
	10.9.18		In the morning ADMS investigated again outbreak of diarrhoea at BURBURE, also visited A.T.R.E. and 4 Div details. In the afternoon ADMS visited AIRE and saw advanced operating centre 39 Stationary Hospital and also Army Laboratory.	
	3.9.18		In the morning D.D.M.S. visited LES HARRISOIR and R.A.Ps. In the afternoon ADMS inspected 21st Lnc Yorks (Pioneers) as Gn right inspects these gone was more concerned in those work than any other arrangements to the Medical arrangements. No. 3.	B

WAR DIARY or INTELLIGENCE SUMMARY

Army Form C. 2118.

Place	Date	Hour	Summary of Events and Information	Remarks and references to Appendices
BUS. RIEUX	12.8.18		Office routine.	Some
	13.8.18		In the morning DADMS inspected Hd. Qrs. & Aid-posts of also some forward lines, visited Hqrs. 3 Battalions & 102 in LE QUESNOY and CENSE LA VALLEE. and twelve gun details chiefly looking at sanitation of these areas. In the afternoon ADMS inspected billets area for a suitable place for divisional baths.	
	14.8.18		In the morning ADMS went to BUSNETTES and inspected the recent drafts to the 1st R Warwicks, to also visited all R.A.P's right sector and chose a site for a proposed new advanced R.A.P. In the afternoon ADMS visited a Corps H.Qrs. As a result 1 gas (mustard) shelling chiefly in Vauxe sector on the 12 & 8 18. 4 Officers & 102 O.Rs. had been admitted to the M.D.S.	

Army Form C. 2118.

WAR DIARY
or
INTELLIGENCE SUMMARY.
(Erase heading not required.)

Place	Date	Hour	Summary of Events and Information	Remarks and references to Appendices
BAS RIEVX.	15/9/18		In the morning ADMS inspected the troops & the Kerr Battalions of the 10 m.g. Bde. at rest. In the afternoon DADMS accompanied by O.C. 39 Sanitary Section inspected the Stables and early estab. and general sanitation of the area & the canal bank. In the afternoon DADMS visited Porkeys horses B. the Corphses and examined the Sanatorium & employing the Sanitarian & the Portuguese battalion in CANTRAINNE. Also visited No. 2 Section D.A.C.	
		16.8.18	In the morning ADMS inspected HQ Coy and details & the hachine Gun Bttn of LA-VALLEE also the companys at LE CAUROY and LECLEME and then forward advanced HQrs in BELLERIVE. Also inspected cloths in laundry at BUSNETTES. Subsequently ADMS visited 6 CCS to see an officer suffering from paratyphoid fever.	

Army Form C. 2118.

WAR DIARY
or
INTELLIGENCE SUMMARY.
(Erase heading not required.)

Instructions regarding War Diaries and Intelligence Summaries are contained in F. S. Regs., Part II. and the Staff Manual respectively. Title pages will be prepared in manuscript.

Place	Date	Hour	Summary of Events and Information	Remarks and references to Appendices
BAS. RIEUX	19/5/18		In the morning DADMS inspected transport lines & Bn.Sisters of 10th Ind Bde. In the evening ADMS heavily examined sent drafts of 1st Kings own R.L. Regiment for the posting of Capt. A.P. O'Connor & Capt. V.F. Scott Hill RAMC to 11 & 10 Fd.Amb respectively. Capt F.P. Joscelyne (T.d) RAMC left for temporary duty with 5th Army Hqrs.	fyne fyne fyne
	20.5.18	10am	In the morning ADMS visited any Hospital (DMS). DADMS noted H.O.S staff sister. (No 39 mobile laboratory) DADMS inspected sanitation of 11 at Bde transport lines and D.I's stores. In the evening DADMS visited LECLUSE and ADMS examined the Dogs of 10 Fd.Amb. Battalions met of the two above RAMC Sisters and parts. In the afternoon DADMS visited LECLUSE and ADMS examined the Dogs of 10 Fd.Amb. Battalions met of the two above RAMC Sisters and parts & baths Hqrs arranging installation, fruits & capsules transiting to every unit C	fyne

WAR DIARY
or
INTELLIGENCE SUMMARY.

Army Form C. 2118.

Place	Date	Hour	Summary of Events and Information	Remarks and references to Appendices
BAS RIEUX	20.8.18		In the morning DADMS visited back area arranging for ambulance sites after relief	C
		3pm	RAMC meeting orders re relief	
			In the evening DADMS arrived ADMS 19th Division and arranged re taking over of medical posts	
	21.8.18		In the morning DADMS visited 10th and arranged for Div Hospital at AUCHEL to be opened by them	
			In the afternoon ADMS attended technical consulting surgeon 5th Army at M.D.S. 19th Division	D
			RAMC order No. 62 re connection and relief of division	E
			" " No. 63	F
			Medical arrangements for collection of Sick Off in back area 10th and move to AUCHEL.	
	22.8.18		DADMS visited 10th and are arranging for removal hospital and gone.	
			ambulance coach to 11 Tot and M.D.S.	
			ADMS in the morning visited RAPs of left sector & inspected the two forelements	

Army Form C. 2118.

WAR DIARY
or
INTELLIGENCE SUMMARY.
(Erase heading not required.)

Instructions regarding War Diaries and Intelligence Summaries are contained in F. S. Regs, Part II. and the Staff Manual respectively. Title pages will be prepared in manuscript.

Place	Date	Hour	Summary of Events and Information	Remarks and references to Appendices
BAS-RIEUX	22/8/18		In the evening ADMS visited ADMS 19th Division re taking over Ambulances	G
"	23/8/18		11.y.12. Fd Ambulances moved to AMETTES & WESTREHEM respectively. DADMS visited 10.y.11. Fd Ambulances in the afternoon and the foreseen to xxv H.Qrs. gave	H, I, J
BOMY	24/8/18		RAMC moving under orders from XIII Corps to XXII Corps RAMC order No 64 arranging heavier transports & cars DADMS visited all ambulances and Corps H.Qrs. ADMS visited Corps H.Qrs arranging for re-moving & see Seed etc	gone
HAUTECLOQUE	25/8/18		Davignon moved from XIII Corps to XXIII Corps area in the morning ADMS visited XIII Corps H.Qrs in the afternoon Position of Ambulances 10. HERLIN-LE-SEC. 11 TERNAS 12 CROIX. gone	

D.D. & L., London, E.C. (A8029) Wt. W1771/M231 750,000 5/17 Sch. 52 Form/C2118/14

Army Form C. 2118.

WAR DIARY
or
INTELLIGENCE SUMMARY.
(Erase heading not required.)

Instructions regarding War Diaries and Intelligence Summaries are contained in F.S. Regs., Part II. and the Staff Manual respectively. Title pages will be prepared in manuscript.

Place	Date	Hour	Summary of Events and Information	Remarks and references to Appendices
VILLERS AU BOIS	26.8.18		Division moved from HAUTECLOQUE in the evening. Ambulances moved under Brigade orders to rest positions. 10th VILLERS-AU-BOIS. 11th CHATEAU-DE-LA-HAIE. 1st AGNIERES. Off XXII Corps for Canadian Corps on from midnight 26.8/F. 28th.	
"	27.8.18		Division prepared to take over from 3rd Canadian Division. ADMS & DADMS visited ADSs & forward posns. on 3rd Canadian Divisional front.	
"			ADMS visited DDMS Canadian Corps. Lieut. WILSON J.H. MORCUSA joined for duty, posted to 11 Fd Amb. R.Amb. over Zo 65. re relief.	K
ARRAS	28.8.18		Division moved to ARRAS. 24 Brres to assembly area west of MONCHY-LE-PREUX. During night 28/29 relieved 3rd Can Division.	
"	29.8.18 2.45am		R.Amb.C order No 66 (medical arrangements for rest area). Officer i/c ADMS march to Girls School ST SAUVER. DADMS visited forward area with OC 11 Fd Amb. and arrange appointment to R.Amb order no 66. Capt WILLIAMS J.R MORCUSA posted for duty to 11 Fd Ambulance	L
"	30.8.18		on joining as a reinforcement Offr	L(A)

Army Form C. 2118.

WAR DIARY
or
INTELLIGENCE SUMMARY.

(Erase heading not required.)

Place	Date	Hour	Summary of Events and Information	Remarks and references to Appendices
ARRAS.	30.8.18		ADMS accompanied O/C N.W.R. visited A.D.S. & forward posts. DADMS visited W.W.P. & MDS (ARRAS) Divisn area and visited ETERPIGNY for Casualties sight.	
"	31.8.18		ADMS visited W.W.P. & MDS and about out post of Corps hqrs.	

J. Jacchié
Colonel
A.D.M.S.
4th Division

1/9/18

A

Copy No. 36 (diary)

4th. DIVISION
MEDICAL ARRANGEMENTS NO. 3.

Map Refs: Sheets 36a) 5/40,000.   9th. August, 1918.
                  44b)

All previous Medical Arrangements are cancelled.

1. **POSITION OF MEDICAL UNITS.**

   (a). R.A.P's: Left Sector.   Right Sector.

           Rt.Bn. Q.26.b.6.1.   Rt.Bn. W.2.b.8.3.
           Cen.Bn. Q.26.b.35.40.   Cen.Bn.) W.2.a.8.2.
           Lt.Bn. Q.20.b.1.2.   Lt.Bn.)

   (b). Forward Dressing Posts:

           P.36.d.3.9.   W.1.d.1.3.

   (c). Relay Posts:

           P.36.a.9.7.
           V.5.b.5.1.

   (d). A.D.Stns:
           CENSE LA VALLEE,   GONNEHEM,
           (V.11.c.1.8.)   (V.18.c.3.9.)

   (e). M.D.Stn:
           PONT DU REVEILLON, (V.26.d.7.7.)

   (f). Fd.Ambce.H.Q. & Transport:
                        Headqrs.   Transport.
           10th. Fd. Ambce.   LE TAILLY.   LE TAILLY.
           11th. Fd. Ambce.   REVEILLON.   ALLOUAGNE.
           12th. Fd. Ambce.   BUSNETTES.   BUSNETTES.

   (g). Office of A.D.M.S.:
           BAS RIEUX, (U.24.a.9.7.)

2. **EVACUATION.**

   (a). Right Sector: By hand carriage to the R.A.P's. and thence by hand, wheeled stretcher and Ford car to W.1.d.1.3. Thence by ambulance car to the A.D.S., V.18.c.3.9. and M.D.Stn.

   (b). Left Sector: By hand carriage to R.A.P's. and thence by wheeled stretcher and light-railway to P.36.d.3.9. Thence to the M.D.Stn. (via A.D.S. if necessary) by ambulance cars.

   (c). From M.D.Stn: To C.C.Stn. Group, PERNES in M.A.C. cars.

                                   [signature]
                                        Major,
H.Q. 4th. Division.   for A.D.M.S. 4th. Division.
U.

-2-

4th. DIVISION

Distribution:- Copy No. 1 D.M.S. Fifth Army.
                        2   D.D.M.S. XIII Corps.
                        3   10th. Field Ambulance.
                        4   11th. Field Ambulance.
                        5   12th. Field Ambulance.
                        6. 4th. Division.
                        7   4th. Division "A/Q".
                        8   10th. Inf. Bde.
                        9   11th. Inf. Bde.
                       10   12th. Inf. Bde.
                       11   C.R.E. 4th. Division.
                       12   4th. Div. Train.
                       13   O.C. 4th. Sigs Coy.
                    14-28   R.M.O's.
                       29   A.D.M.S. 19th. Divn.
                       30   A.D.M.S. 74th. Divn.
                       31   22nd. M.A.C.
                    32,33   Diary.
                       34   File.

AMENDMENTS TO
4th. DIVISION MEDICAL ARRANGEMENTS No.3.

1. Para. 1 (a) is cancelled and the following substituted:

   1. (a). R.A.P's.

	Left Sector.		Right Sector.
Outpost Bn.	P.26.b.5.1.	Outpost Bn.)	W.2.a.8.2.
Lt.Sup.Bn.	P.24.d.7.4.	Lt.Sup.Bn.)	
Rt.Sup.Bn.	P.36.d.3.9.	Rt.Sup.Bn.	W.2.b.8.3.

2. In para.1 (b). Heading to be amended to read:

   "Forward Dressing Posts and Car Posts:"

3. To para. 1 (c), 'Relay Posts', add the following to list of such posts in Left Sector:

   Q.26.c.1.7.

                                        Colonel,
                                   A.D.M.S. 4th. Division.

11th. August, 1918.
U.

Distribution as before.

AMENDMENTS (2) TO

4th. DIVISION MEDICAL ARRANGEMENTS No.3.

1. Ref. Amendments dated 11th. August, para.1:

    Left Sector, Outpost Bn.: for 'P.26.b.5.1.' read 'Q.26.b.5.1.'

2. Ref. Medical Arrangements No. 3:

    Under the heading 'Relay Posts, Right Sector', should be included:
    "Q.33.c.3.3."

                                                          Colonel,
11th. August, 1918.   A.D.M.S. 4th. Division.
U.

Distribution as before.

SECRET

C

Diary

Copy No. 10

4th. DIVISION.

R.A.M.C. WARNING ORDER, In Connection with 4th. Div. WARNING

ORDER, Dated 20th. August, 1918.

Map Refs: 36a. 1/40000.   20th. August, 1918.

1. The 4th. Division is being relieved by 74th. & 19th. Divisions.
   The 74th. Division is taking over that portion of the present 4th. Divisional Front North of a line running approximately U.6.central - Q.22.d.2.3. - R.24.c.0.5., and the 19th. Division, that portion South of that line.

2. On relief, the Division will be located in the AUCHEL area, AMES Staging Area and FLECHIN Sub-area.

3. Relief by 74th. Division is to be completed by 6 a.m. 23rd. August, and that by 19th. Division, by 6 a.m. 24th. August.

4. Detailed instructions regarding reliefs of Field Ambulances will be notified later.

5. Field Ambulances acknowledge.

Issued at 2.0 p.m.
U.

Colonel,
A.D.M.S. 4th. Division.

Distribution:-

    Copy 1 to   D.D.M.S. XIIIth. Corps.
         2.   A.D.M.S. 19th. Division.
         3.   A.D.M.S. 74th. Division.
         4.   10th. Field Ambulance.
         5.   11th. Field Ambulance.
         6.   12th. Field Ambulance.
         7.   4th. Division.
         8.   4th. Division 'A/Q'.
         9 & 10. War Diary. ✓
         11.   File.

SECRET

Copy No. 33

4th. DIVISION R.A.M.C.

ORDER NO. 62.

(In Connection with 4th. Div.G.A.6/8).

Map Refs: HAZEBROUCK, 5a.   21st. August, 1918.

1. O.C., No. 12 Field Ambulance will take over from No. 10 Field Ambulance all Medical Posts in the Left Section which he considers necessary, and will assume charge of the evacuation of all casualties from the Divisional Front forthwith.

    Other Medical Posts in the Left Section will be closed forthwith.

2. O.C., No. 10 Field Ambulance will return all his personnel forthwith to LE TAILLY on relief by 12th. Field Ambulance, and will proceed by march route to AUCHEL on the evening of 21st. August.

    The parties of 10th. Field Ambulance on agricultural work will complete the work for the 21st. August, and then proceed independently to AUCHEL, where they will rejoin their Unit.

    O.C., No. 10 Field Ambulance will open up the HOTEL DE VILLE, AUCHEL, as a Divisional Hospital and Diarrhoea Centre. He will be ready to receive sick from the Division by 6 a.m. on 23rd. inst.

    All surplus Medical Stores, and B.R.C.S. Stores held by No. 10 Field Ambulance will be returned to the Main Dressing Station, and receipts obtained.

    O.C., No. 10 Field Ambulance will arrange to send a Medical Officer with a large car daily, to all villages in the new area which accommodate Billeting Parties, in order to pick up any sick they may have.

3. Registration of all sick from the Division in new area, will at present be carried out by No. 10 Field Ambulance at AUCHEL. Cases will be detained until Medical Arrangements are issued.

    The Main Dressing Station will continue to work as at present until further orders.

4. Completion of reliefs, and arrival in new area of No. 10 Field Ambulance, will be notified to this office by D.R.

5. Field Ambulances acknowledge.

                                             Colonel,
                                      A.D.M.S. 4th. Division.

Issued at 11.0 a.m.
U.

- 2 -

Distribution:-

Copy No. 1 to D.D.M.S. XIIIth. Corps.
2. A.D.M.S. 19th. Division.
3. A.D.M.S. 74th. Division.
4. 10th. Field Ambulance.
5. 11th. Field Ambulance.
6. 12th. Field Ambulance.
7. 4th. Division.
8. 4th. Division 'A/Q'.
9. 10th. Infantry Brigade.
10. 11th. Infantry Brigade.
11. 12th. Infantry Brigade.
12. C.R.E. 4th. Division.
13. H.Q. 4th. Div. Arty.
14. 4th. Div. Sigs.
15. 4th. Divisional Train.
16. D.A.D.V.S. 4th. Division.
17,to) R.M.O's.
31.)
32, 33. Diary.
34. File.

SECRET E

4th. DIVISION R.A.M.C.

ORDER NO. 63.

(In connection with 4th. Div. Order 147).

Copy No. 16

Map Refs: Hazebrouck, 5a.
36a. 1/40000.

21st. August, 1918.

1. No. 11 Field Ambulance will hand over the Main Dressing Station to No. 57 Field Ambulance on 23rd. inst.

2. No. 12 Field Ambulance will hand over the evacuation of the forward area to No. 58 Field Ambulance on 23rd. inst.

3. Both reliefs to be complete by 12, noon.

4. All stores above mobilization equipment, and all B.R.C.S. Stores to be handed over and receipts obtained.

5. On relief, Field Ambulances will proceed by march route to the following destinations:-

   No. 11 Field Ambulance to AMETTES.
   No. 12 Field Ambulance to WESTREHEM.

6. Completion of reliefs and arrival in new area to be notified to this office by D.R.

7. Office of A.D.M.S. 4th. Division closes at BAS RIEUX at 6 a.m. on 24th. inst. and re-opens at BOMY at the same hour.

8. Field Ambulances acknowledge.

Issued at 2.40 p.m.
U.

Colonel,
A.D.M.S. 4th. Division.

Distribution:-   Copy No. 1 to D.D.M.S. XIII Corps.
                        2.   A.D.M.S. 19th. Division.
                        3.   A.D.M.S. 74th. Division.
                        4.   10th. Field Ambulance.
                        5.   11th. Field Ambulance.
                        6.   12th. Field Ambulance.
                        7.   4th. Division.
                        8.   4th. Division 'A/Q'.
                        9.   10th. Infantry Brigade.
                        10.   11th. Infantry Brigade.
                        11.   12th. Infantry Brigade.
                        12.   C.R.E. 4th. Division.
                        13.   4th. Div. Arty.
                        14.   4th. Div. Signals.
                        15.   4th. Div. Train.
                        16.17. Diary.
                        18.   File.

A.D.M.S. 4th. Division No. 17/154.

No. 10 Field Ambulance,
No. 11 Field Ambulance,
No. 12 Field Ambulance.

ARRANGEMENTS FOR COLLECTION & REGISTRATION
OF SICK IN NEW AREA.

1. The daily sick of the Division will be collected in the new area as follows:-

(a). **No. 10 Field Ambulance:**

No. 10 Field Ambulance will make arrangements to see the daily sick of the Company of the 4th. Divisional Train in AUCHEL. These can be seen at their M.I. Room or at 10th. Field Ambulance Headquarters, whichever is more convenient.

In addition to this, the following villages will be toured daily, in the morning, for sick of 4th. Divisional Units billetted therein:-

| AUCHEL. | RAIMBERT. | LOZINGHEM. |
| FLORINGHEM. | | CAMBLAIN CHATELAIN. |

(b). **No. 11 Field Ambulance:**

No. 11 Field Ambulance will send a motor ambulance daily to the Headquarters of the 4th. Div. Amm. Col. This car will be at the disposal of the M.O., 4th. D.A.C. on his daily round. It will return to No. 11 Field Ambulance with the daily sick of the 4th. Div. Amm. Col.

In addition, sick of the Division from the following villages will be collected daily:-

AMETTES.	LIERES.	FAUCQUENHEM.
AMES.	BELLERY.	NEDONCHELLE.
BAILLEUL.		PALFART.

(c). **No. 12 Field Ambulance:**

No. 12 Field Ambulance will collect sick daily from 4th. Divisional Units in the following villages:-

FEBVIN PALFART.	WESTREHEM.	AUCHY AU BOIS.
LIGNY LES AIRES.	BOMY.	RELY.
	FLECHIN.	

2. **Divisional Hospital & Diarrhoea Centre:**

No. 10 Field Ambulance will function as the Divisional Hospital and Diarrhoea Centre, at AUCHEL.
Sick for evacuation will be sent to the PERNES Group from this Unit.
All Divisional sick will be sent to No. 10 Field Ambulance from Nos. 11 and 12 Field Ambulances.
Ambulances must arrange with their respective M.O's. to collect the daily sick in such time as will allow of all sick being admitted to No. 10 Field Ambulance daily, before 11 a.m.

3. Registration of Sick:

(a). No. 11 Field Ambulance will function as the M.D.S. until 12, noon, 23rd. inst. At this hour, the A. & D. Books of this Unit will close.

(b). In the new area, No. 10 Field Ambulance will show all Divisional sick as direct admissions to the A.&.D. Book of that Unit.

The Daily State (A.F., W.3185) will be sent in from that Unit to reach this office at 9 a.m. daily. Period, 9 a.m. to 9 a.m.

No. 10 Field Ambulance will render the first Daily State to this office at 9 a.m. on 22nd. inst.

Other returns will be rendered in accordance with this office number 38/68, dated 16-7-18.

Major,
for A.D.M.S. 4th. Division.

21st. Aug.1918.
U.

Copies to all concerned.

SECRET.   "G"   A.D.M.S. 4th. Division No. 17/154.
----------   ------------------------------------

O.C.,
No. 10 Field Ambulance.
No. 11 Field Ambulance.
No. 12 Field Ambulance.

With reference to this office number as above, dated 21st. inst;

Owing to alterations in the Billeting List, the following villages will be added to those from which No. 12 Field Ambulance collects daily sick:-

    ERNY ST JULIEN.   ENQUIN LES MINES.

The following village will be deleted from the same list:-

    FLECHIN.

                                                  Major,
22-8-1918.   for A.D.M.S. 4th. Division.
U.

Distribution as before.

SECRET.   Copy No. 12

4th. DIVISION R.A.M.C.
WARNING ORDER.
(In connection with 4th. Division Warning Order d/24-8-18).

==

1.   The 4th. Division is to be prepared to entrain, commencing at 7 a.m. on 25th. inst. for a destination that will be communicated later.

2.   Personnel only of Infantry Brigade Groups will be moved by train.
   Field Ambulances will move with their respective Brigade Groups.

   Transport will move by road with respective Brigade Transport Groups.
   Transport will start moving about 8 p.m. 24th. inst.

3.   Detailed orders will be issued later.

4.   Field Ambulances acknowleddge.

Issued at 1.0 p.m. 24-8-1918.

                                    Colonel,
                            A.D.M.S. 4th. Division.

Distribution:- 1. D.D.M.S. XIII Corps.
               2. 4th. Division.
               3. 4th. Division 'A/Q'.
               4. 10th. Field Ambulance.
               5. 11th. Field Ambulance.
               6. 12th. Field Ambulance.
               7. 10th. Infantry Brigade.
               8. 11th. Infantry Brigade.
               9. 12th. Infantry Brigade.
              10. 4th. Divisional Train.
              11.)
              12.) Diary.
              13. File.

Copy No. 14

4th. DIVISION R.A.M.C. ORDER NO.64.

(In connection with 4th. Division Orders Nos. 148 and 149).

Map Refs: LENS 11.
HAZEBROUCK 5a.

24th. August, 1918.

1. In continuation of R.A.M.C. Warning Order of even date. The 4th. Division is being transferred from Fifth Army to First Army, (XXII Corps).

2. (a). Transport of the Division in Brigade Groups is marching on night 24th/25th. inst. in accordance with attached table 'A'.

   (b). Personnel will proceed by tactical trains on 25th. inst. as shown on attached table 'B'. *not attached*

   (c). Field Ambulances will be included in Brigade Groups as follows:-
   10th. Field Ambulance in 10th. Bde. Group.
   11th. Field Ambulance in 11th. Bde. Group.
   12th. Field Ambulance in 12th. Bde. Group.

   (d). All moves of Field Ambulances to be made under orders of Group Commander concerned.

3. Entraining and Detraining Stations, and Destinations of Groups are shown on attached table 'C'.

4. Field Ambulances to acknowledge.

Issued at 5.30 p.m.

Colonel,
A.D.M.S. 4th. Division.

Distribution:-
1. D.D.M.S. XIIIth. Corps.
2. 4th. Division.
3. 4th. Division 'A/Q'.
4. 10th. Field Ambulance.
5. 11th. Field Ambulance.
6. 12th. Field Ambulance.
7. 10th. ~~Field Ambulance~~. Inf. Bde.
8. 11th. Infantry Brigade.
9. 12th. Infantry Brigade.
10. 4th. Divisional Train.
11. C.R.E. 4th. Division.
12. 4th. Div. Signals.
13. C.R.A. 4th. Division.
14,15. Diary.
16. File.

TO ACCOMPANY
4th. DIVISION R.A.M.C. ORDER 64.

Table 'A'. Brigade Transport March Table. Night 24/25th.

Unit.	Route.	Instructions.
12th. Inf. Bde. Group.	FIEFS - SAINS LES PERNES - TANGRY - HESTRUS - WAVRANS- CROIX.	March to be completed 4.30 a.m. 25-8-18.
11th. Inf. Bde. Group.	AUMERVAL - PERNES - VALHOUN- BRYAS - OSTREVILLE - ST MICHEL	To be clear of PERNES 10 p.m.
10th. Inf. Bde. Group.	PERNES - ST POL - X Roads just N. of HERLIN LE SEC - BUNEVILLE	Not to enter PERNES before 10 p.m.

Table 'C'. Entraining and Detraining Stations & Destinations.

Unit.	Entrain at.	Detrain at.	Destination.
10th. Bde. Group.	PERNES.	PT HOUVIN.	BUNEVILLE, (Sub-Area).
11th. Bde. Group.	LILLERS.	BRYAS.	ST MICHEL, (Sub-Area).
12th. Bde. Group.	BERGUETTE.	WAVRANS.	CROIX, (Sub-Area).
Div. Headqrs.	HAUTECLOQUE.		

A.D.M.S. 4th. Division No. 17/154.

O.C.,
No. 10 Field Ambulance.
No. 11 Field Ambulance.
No. 12 Field Ambulance.

COLLECTION & REGISTRATION OF SICK.

1. This office number as above, dated 21st. inst. is cancelled.

2. On arrival in the new area, Field Ambulances will collect the sick from the Brigade Group with which they are moving.

3. Sick will be taken to the nearest Cas. Clg. Stn. or Stationary Hospital.

4. Daily States willbe forwarded to this office by each Field Ambulance daily.

5. Detailed arrangements will be issued in the new area.

McCutcheon
Major for Colonel,
A.D.M.S. 4th. Division.

24th. Aug. 1918.
U.

K

Copy No. 53

4th. DIVISION R.A.M.C. ORDER NO. 65.

(Issued in conjunction with 4th. Division Order No. 153).

Map Refs: Sheet 51b.　　　　　　　　　27th. August, 1918.

The 4th. Division has been transferred to the Canadian Corps, and is to relieve the 3rd. Canadian Division.
On 28th. inst., the Division is moving to places of assembly E. of ARRAS.

1. Field Ambulances will move on 28th. inst. by march route to destinations shown below. Moves to start before 12,noon.

   (a). No. 10 Field Ambulance to the HOPITAL ST JEAN, ARRAS, where it will be held in readiness to relieve 10th. Can. Fd. Ambce. as Main Dressing Station.

   (b). No. 11 Field Ambulance to GIRLS' SCHOOL ST SAUVEUR, (G.29.c.6.4.), ready to relieve 9th. Can. Fd. Ambce. in the forward area.

   (c). No. 12 Field Ambulance to the ECOLE DES JEUNES FILLES, ARRAS; (Opposite HOTEL DU COMMERCE) ready to relieve 8th. Can. Fd. Ambce. as Walking Wounded Post.

2. No. 10 Field Ambulance will send 2 M.O's. and 12 Field Ambulance 1, for temporary duty to No. 11 Field Ambulance. These Officers will be despatched to arrive at No. 11 Field Ambulance by 9 a.m. on 28th. inst.

3. Bearers will be despatched to Battalions in the Division on 28th. inst., to arrive by 9 a.m. as follows:

   (a). No. 10 Field Ambulance:

To each Battn. in 10th. Inf. Bde.	2 squads.
To 1st. Som. Lt. Inf.	2 squads.
To 1st. Hants. Regt.	1 squad.

   (b). No. 12 Field Ambulance:

To 1st. Hants. Regt.	1 squad.
To 1st. Rifle Brigade.	2 squads.
To each Battn. in 12th. Inf. Bde.	2 squads.

   These bearers will carry two days' rations with them, and will be at the disposal of their respective R.M.O's. until further orders. They will carry casualties from the R.A.P's. to the first Field Ambulance Bearer Posts.

4. Field Ambulances to acknowledge.

Issued at 9.30 p.m.

for A.D.M.S. 4th. Division.
Major,

Distribution:-

```
No. 1 to  D.D.M.S. Can. Corps.
    2.    A.D.M.S. 3rd. Can. Division.
    3.    No. 10 Field Ambulance.
    4.    No. 11 Field Ambulance.
    5.    No. 12 Field Ambulance.
    6.    4th. Division.
    7.    4th. Division 'A/Q'.
    8.    10th. Infantry Bde.
    9.    11th. Infantry Bde.
    10.   12th. Infantry Bde.
    11.   C.R.A. 4th. Division.
    12.   C.R.E. 4th. Division.
    13.   4th. Divisional Train.
    14.   D.A.D.V.S. 4th. Division.
    15.   4th. Div. Signals.
    16.   A.P.M. 4th. Division.
    17-31. R.M.O's.
    32,33. Diary.
    34.   File.
```

SECRET.
                                                    Copy No. 84

4th. DIVISION R.A.M.C. ORDER NO.66.

(In connection with 4th. Division Order No. 154 of 27-8-18).

Map Refs: Sheet 51b, 1/40,000.   29th. August, 1918.

The 4th. British Division is relieving 3rd. Canadian Division to-night, (28th/29th. August, 1918).

The boundary between the 4th. British Division and 1st. Canadian Division on our Right will be the centre of the ARRAS-CAMBRAI Road.

The 4th. British Division will take over the front from the ARRAS - CAMBRAI Road as far North as the grid line running East and West between I.36. and O.6, with the 10th. Infantry Brigade on the Right and the 11th. Infantry Brigade on the Left.
The 12th. Infantry Brigade will be in reserve in the old trenches East of MONCHY.
Boundary between 10th. and 11th. Inf. Bdes. as follows:-

LONG WOOD inclusive to 11th. Inf. Bde. - ETERPIGNY inclusive to 10th. Inf. Bde. - Trench junction in DROCOURT - QUEANT line at P.15.d.2.8.

1. **RELIEFS:** The reliefs detailed in para 1, R.A.M.C. Order No. 65 dated 27th. inst. will be carried out at once.
    Completion to be reported to this office by D.R.

2. **DISPOSITIONS:**

    (a). No. 11 Field Ambulance: O.C. No. 11 Field Ambulance will be responsible for the evacuation of all wounded from the Divisional front. For this purpose he will take over such existing posts as he considers necessary for his scheme of evacuation. He will form his A.D.Stn. at O.13.b.8.8. Car Posts and Relay Posts will be formed at his discretion, and always in touch with R.A.P's. as changes in the position of these occur.
    He will report changes in the locations of his Posts to this office from time to time at his earliest convenience.

    He will form a Walking Wounded Collecting Post on the ARRAS-CAMBRAI Road at N.12.a.0.4. This will be pushed forward as circumstances permit. Lorries will be stationed there and will convoy walking wounded and slightly sick to the Walking Wounded Post at No. 12 Field Ambulance, ECOLE DES JEUNES FILLES, ARRAS.
    In the event of the Walking Wounded Collecting Post being pushed forward, a guide will be left on the previous site to direct lorries to the new position.

    Lying wounded and sick will be carried by hand and wheeled stretchers to the Relay and Car Posts. Thence by Ford Cars to the A.D.Stn., and thence by Ambulance cars to the M.D.Stn. HOPITAL ST JEAN, ARRAS; (10 Fd. Ambce).

                                                    /(b).

(b). No. 10 Field Ambulance: O.C. No. 10 Field Ambulance will have charge of the C.D.Stn. at the HOPITAL ST JEAN, ARRAS. He will receive all lying wounded and lying sick from No. 11 Field Ambulance cars, and will evacuate them to Nos. 7, 33 and 1 C.C.Stns. at LIGNY ST FLOCHEL.

M.A.C. Cars from Nos. 8, 12 and 51 M.A.C's. will be at the disposal of No. 10 Field Ambulance for this purpose.

(c). No. 12 Field Ambulance: O.C. No. 12 Field Ambulance will be in charge of the Walking Wounded Post at the ECOLE DES JEUNES FILLES, ARRAS. He will receive all walking wounded and walking sick from No. 11 Field Ambulance, and evacuate them to No. 42 C.C.Stn., MINGOVAL, in lorries provided for this purpose.

NOTE: For the purpose of classification, lightly gassed cases will be treated as walking wounded, and seriously gassed as lying cases.

3. PERSONNEL:

(a). O.C. No. 11 Field Ambulance will employ his own bearers and officers to the fullest extent in the forward area.

(b). He will place one officer and four Other Ranks at the W.W.C.P. mentioned in para. 2,(a) above.

(c). O's.C. Nos. 10 and 12 Field Ambulances will each hold in readiness 50 bearers with the necessary N.C.O's. to be sent to augment the bearers of No. 11 Field Ambulance in the forward evacuation.

These will be sent on receipt of orders from this office.

(d). O.C. No. 12 Field Ambulance will hold in readiness, one Medical Store Cart with necessary equipment, and a party consisting of 1 N.C.O. and 6 Nursing Orderlies. These will be moved forward on receipt of orders from this office, to form an Advanced Dressing Post on a site to be selected by O.C. No. 11 Field Ambulance, and will function pending the arrival of personnel of No. 11 Field Ambulance to form the new A.D.Stn. This party will be at the disposal of O.C. No. 11 Field Ambulance until he has formed the new A.D.Stn., when they will rejoin their Unit.

4. TRANSPORT:

(a). O's.C. Nos. 10 and 12 Field Ambulances will send all their ambulance cars with the exception of one large car each, to report at once to H.Q. No. 11 Field Ambulance at C.29.c.6.4. They will then be at the disposal of O.C. No. 11 Field Ambulance for work in the forward area.

(b). O's.C. Nos. 10 and 12 Field Ambulances will send their horsed ambulance wagons to report at the H.Q. of No. 11 Field Ambulance at 7.30 a.m. on 29th. inst. These will be used by O.C. No. 11 Field Ambulance on the ARRAS-CAMBRAI Road, forward of the W.W.C.P., to which Post they will convoy walking wounded and sick. Horses and personnel of these wagons will be relieved every 6 hours.

5. ANTI TETANIC SERUM: FIELD MEDICAL CARDS: A.T.S. will be administered, and F.M.C. made out at the W.W.P. and M.D.S. only.

/(6).

6. CLERICAL:

(a). O's.C. Nos. 10 and 12 Field Ambulances will keep A.& D. Books at the M.D.S. and W.W.P. respectively. Separate Books will be kept for British & Canadian Troops.

(b). Daily States will be rendered by these Units, for period ending 12. noon.

(c). A wire will be sent to this office every 6 hours,(at 6 a.m., 12 noon, 6 pm. and 12 midnight), showing the numbers of wounded, by Formations, admitted since the previous wire. First Wire due at 6 a.m. 29th. inst.

7. GENERAL:

(a). O's.C. Nos. 10 and 12 Field Ambulances will each hold in readiness two Water Carts filled with chlorinated water, and having the necessary personnel. These will be sent forward on receipt of request from O.C. No. 11 Field Ambulance, through this office, for more water.

(b). Arrangements will be made at the W.W.P. and M.D.S., for every wounded man to receive a hot meal before he is evacuated to the C.C.Stns.

(c). Five sets of pack-saddlery are at the disposal of O.C. No. 11 Field Ambulance for use at his discretion in the forward area. Nos. 10 and 12 Field Ambulances may be asked to supply horses in relief of those of No. 11 Field Ambulance.

8. Office of A.D.M.S. is now open at No. 21 Boulevard VAUBAN, ARRAS.

9. Field Ambulances to acknowledge.

Issued at 2.45 a.m.

Major,
for A.D.M.S. 4th. Division.

Distribution: No. 1 to D.D.M.S. Canadian Corps.
2. A.D.M.S. 3rd. Can. Division.
3. A.D.M.S. 1st. Can. Division.
4. 10th. Field Ambulance.
5. 11th. Field Ambulance.
6. 12th. Field Ambulance.
7. 10th. Inf. Brigade.
8. 11th. Inf. Brigade.
9. 12th. Inf. Brigade.
10. 4th. Division.
11. 4th. Division 'A/Q'.
12. C.R.A. 4th. Division.
13. C.R.E. 4th. Division.
14. 4th. Div. Signals.
15. 4th. Divisional Train.
16. D.A.D.V.S. 4th. Division.
17. A.P.M. 4th. Division.
18-32. All R.M.O's.
33,34. Diary.
35. File.

AMENDMENTS TO
R.A.M.C. ORDER NO. 66.

1. In para. 6,(c): Times at which wires are due will be amended to read as follows:-

    (c). Wires showing numbers of wounded admitted, by Formations from 8 a.m. to 4 p.m. and from 4 p.m. to 8 a.m., will be rendered to this office daily. They should be sent punctually.
    First wire to be sent at once, covering period 8 a.m. to 4 p.m. 29th. inst.

    This para. will be substituted for para. 6,(c) of R.A.M.C. Order No. 66.

2. In para. 8: For 'No. 21 Boulevard VAUBAN' substitute 'Girls' School, ST SAUVEUR, G.29.c.6.4.'.

Colonel,
A.D.M.S, 4th. Division.

29th.Aug.1918.
U.

Distribution as before.

4th Division

Medical

A. D. M. S.

September to December
1918

140/3262

A.D.M.S. Div IX

September 1916

MEDICAL HISTORY OF THE
COMMITTEE FOR THE
Date -5 NOV 916

ADMS 4

WAR DIARY
INTELLIGENCE SUMMARY

Army Form C. 2118.

WO 95 50 A

Place	Date	Hour	Summary of Events and Information	Remarks and references to Appendices
ARRAS	1/9/18		A.D.M.S. Lt. Colonel Montgomery A.D.M.S. visited H.W.P. & M.D.S. (ARRAS) and attended Corps conference. R.M.O. orders no 69. in connection with operation 2/9/18.	A
	2/9/18		In the afternoon visited and moved forward to LF Spre	
		296.5am	FOSSE FARM. 11th Divⁿ attacked and succeeded in penetrating DROCOURT-QUÉANT line. Casualties fairly heavy, but evacuation was rapid owing to excellent aviation of roads, motors & ford Cars from shells posts. Chief wounds were machine gun wounds. M.D.S. H.W.P. and A.D.S. (VIS-EN-ARTOIS) D.M.S. First Army & visitors from Zero 9am to 8pm A.D.M.S. stayed the whole day the wounded A.D.S.	
			D.A.D.M.S. visited on & afternoon H.W.P. & M.D.S. Photographs taken in action Spre	

Capt. J. STEEL. MC. R.A.M.C.

A 584 Wt. W4973/M687 750,000 8/16 D.D.&L.Ltd. Forms/C.2118/13.

Army Form C. 2118.

WAR DIARY
or
INTELLIGENCE SUMMARY.
(Erase heading not required.)

Instructions regarding War Diaries and Intelligence Summaries are contained in F. S. Regs., Part II. and the Staff Manual respectively. Title pages will be prepared in manuscript.

Place	Date	Hour	Summary of Events and Information	Remarks and references to Appendices
ARRAS	2/9/18		Division advanced. Captured ETAING. Casualties few. Again encountered heavy smoke. Lt Col D AHERN DSO O/C 11 Fd Amb slightly wounded but remained at duty. D.A.D.M.S. in the morning at ZERO 4.35 am proceeded to forward area marked AOS & car & may park & Thqrs 11 Fd Amb. In the afternoon Lt Col Major R L RITCHIE RAMC arrived for duty as DADMS. In the evening Offices of A.D.M.S. moved to 21 BOULEVARD VAUBAN ARRAS.	
"	3/9/18		Division ordered to move. 10 & 11 Fd Amb to CHELERS & CAUCOURT area respectively. Divisions Hqrs VILLERS CHATEL & MINGOVAL	

D. D. & L., London, E.C.
(A8004) Wt. W1771/M2/31 750,000 5/17 **Sch. 52** Forms/C2118/14

WAR DIARY or INTELLIGENCE SUMMARY

Army Form C. 2118.

Place	Date	Hour	Summary of Events and Information	Remarks and references to Appendices
ARRAS	4/9/18	—	Lieut Col Major R.L. RITCHIE R.A.M.C. assumed duties of D.A.D.M.S. in relief of Capt. Maguire J.G. McCUTCHEON R.A.M.C. (SR) as Officer Commanding.	
	contd		10th Field Amb.	
			A.D.M.S & D.A.D.M.S visited 23 CCS	
VILLERS CHATEL	6/9/18	—	Move of Division to Rest area complete. A.D.M.S Office VILLERS CHATEL. 10th Field Amb. 11th 2nd Aust. GAVCHIN LEGAL. 12th H.Q. Amb. ORLENCOURT. Total casualties of Division passing through the Addn. Officers 67. Other Ranks 1749. during period Aug 28th – Sept 5th.	J.S.M.C
VILLERS CHATEL	7/9/18		A.D.M.S proceeded on leave to the U.K.	J.S.M.C
"	8.9.18		O.H.D.M.S visited 10th & 12th Field Ambulances	J.S.M.C
"	10.9.18		R.A.M.C Sports held with 2nd. Field Ambulance S.S. No 164.	J.S.M.C
"	12.9.18		R.M.O's Conference at H.Q. subject of Extra Medical at R.A.P. during an advance.	J.S.M.C

WAR DIARY
or
INTELLIGENCE SUMMARY.
(Erase heading not required.)

Army Form C. 2118.

Place	Date	Hour	Summary of Events and Information	Remarks and references to Appendices
VILLERS CHATEL	12.9.18	-	DADMS visited 1st Fd Ambces & 2nd Bn Duke of Wellington & 10th Fd Amb.	June
"	13.9.18		DADMS visited bams at FREVILLERS and MAGNICOURT. 2nd Lancashire Fusiliers also visited.	June
"	14.9.18		DADMS visited baths at TINCQUES also SAA Supp Sec at DAINON	June
"	15.9.18		11th Fd Amb moved from GAUCHIN LEGAL to CAMBLIGNEUL. DADMS visited 4th Bn MGC. DADMS visited 11th Fd Amb.	June
"	16.9.18		ADMS attended Corps Conference	June
"	17.9.18		RAMC order No. 69. In connection with relief of 11th Division by 4th Division. ADMS visited ADMS 11th Division.	June
"	18.9.18		ADMS visited M.D.S. ADMS 4th Division. No 10 Fd Amb moved from LA NEUVILLE PLANQUETTE to BLANGY (Sheet S.B. G 24 6 2 3) No 14 ADS at Sheet S.B. O 4 c O 8. Amendment to RAMC order No 69 issued.	G1
"	19.9.18		No 11 Fd Amb. moved from CAMBLIGNEUL to Bat & Divnl hostels ARRAS. to form the MDS. Amendment No 2 to RAMC order No 69 issued.	June
ARRAS	20.9.18		ADMS Office moved from VILLERS CHATEL to PLACE ST CROIX ARRAS. 12 Field Amb moved from ORLENCOURT to HOSPICE ST JEAN ARRAS.	June 2
"	21.9.18		Amendment No 3 to RAMC order No 69 issued. M.A.A Arrangement No 1 issued 16.9.18	June 3 D.

Army Form C. 2118.

WAR DIARY
or
INTELLIGENCE SUMMARY.
(Erase heading not required.)

Place	Date	Hour	Summary of Events and Information	Remarks and references to Appendices
ARRAS	22.9.18		DMS/DMS visited R+L Brigades in line, both ADSs, all car and relay posts also RAP 2nd Warwickshire Regt.	
"	23.9.18		ADMS returned from 14 days leave to UK	
"	24.9.18		ADMS attended DMS Conference at Agnez les Duisans	
"	"		ADMS visited rounds in R+L front Brigade area, also RAPi Clarkes + Cave Post - Announcement to No 1 Canadian to No 1 Indian encampment 12.9.18 and DDRMS visited en route day leave to UK - myon Durach from II F.A. acting	
"	25.9.18		ADMS visited the Boulevier Front & CCS.	
"	26.9.18		ADMS visited rounds the left front Brigade unitting also RSO, relay posts and the ADS	
"	27.9.18		ADMS visited hospital huts of 10th Field Ambt. and to Col HQ and visited the Agnez les Duisans Grand J CCS.	
"	28.9.18		ADMS visited rounds the ulterior Brigade to Brigade HQ and also the DRC	
"	29.9.18		A.D.M.S inspected the Divisional reception camp and Details attended the No 6 bathing arrangements. He also went down to look into from No 70 Casual British Labour Coy, about the adequate supply of water from let Coloured corps - R.A.M.C. also No 70 Casual Divisional subsidiary units for R.A.M personnel received to No. Force from N.B a. 1 West S.I.B. AOMS - the class in Corps of Dorchester	
1st Force Form	30.9.18		Tribunal Survey of Corps farm at Draw-Roads to No.11 Filter Centre	

Lieu COMMR RAMC

SECRET. A Copy No. 34

4th. DIVISION.
R.A.M.C. ORDER NO. 67.

Map Refs: Sheet 51b, 1/40,000.   1st. Septr. 1918.

INTENTION:

The 4th. Division is attacking the enemy's positions opposite its front at a time, and on a date to be notified.

The 4th. Canadian Division will be on the right and the 11th. Division on the left of the 4th. British Division.

Divisional boundaries will be as shown on attached tracing marked 'A'.**

Objectives assigned to the 4th. Division (British) are three in number, named as follows:

    1st. Objective   RED LINE.
    2nd. Objective   GREEN LINE.
    3rd. Objective   BLUE LINE.

The limits of those objectives are as shown on attached tracing 'A'. **

The Yellow line on tracing 'A' indicates the line from which the attacking troops of the 4th. British Division will step off.

1. POSTS: O.C. No. 11 Field Ambulance will be responsible for the evacuation of casualties from the Divisional Front.
    By Zero plus 3 hours he will be prepared to establish Car or Relay Posts as follows, to ensure a line of evacuation from the new Divisional Line:

(a). One in ETERPIGNY, (P.14.a.).
(b). One near DURY, (P.21.a.).

As soon as he considers conditions favourable, he will open the Post already established at O.22.b.4.6. in VIS EN ARTOIS as the new A.D.Stn.

2. EVACUATION: Evacuation will be by hand and wheeled stretcher from the R.A.P's. to the Posts at ETERPIGNY and DURY.
    Thence by Ford Car to the new A.D.Stn. at O.22.b.4.6.
Thence as laid down in R.A.M.C. Order No. 66 dated 29th. ult.

3. The positions of all other Medical Posts will remain at the discretion of O.C. No. 11 Field Ambulance as laid down in R.A.M.C. Order No. 66. In the event of any post in the forward area being pushed forward, O.C. No. 11 Field Ambulance will inform the A.D.M.S. of its new location at once.

4. Field Ambulances acknowledge.

                              Colonel,
Issued at 5.0 p.m.   A.D.M.S. 4th. Division.

** Not attached.

Distribution:-

    No. 1. D.D.M.S. Can. Corps.
        2. A.D.M.S. 11th. Division.
        3. A.D.M.S. 4th. Canadian Division.
        4. 10th. British Field Ambulance.
        5. 11th. British Field Ambulance.
        6. 12th. British Field Ambulance.
        7. 10th. British Infantry Brigade.
        8. 11th. British Infantry Brigade.

        9. 12th. British Infantry Brigade.
      10. 4th. British Division.
      11. 4th. British Division 'A/Q'.
      12. C.R.A. 4th. British Division.
      13. C.R.E. 4th. British Division.
      14. 4th. British Division Signals.
      15. 4th. British Divisional Train.
      16. D.A.D.V.S. 4th. British Division.
      17. A.P.M. 4th. British Division.
    18-32 All Reg. Med. Officers.
    33,34 Diary.
    35 File.

SECRET.   **B**   Copy No. 34

4th. DIVISION.

R.A.M.C. ORDER NO. 68.

(In connection with 4th. Division No. G.S.164.)

Map Refs: 51b, 1/40,000.   3rd. Sept. 1918.

The 4th. British Division is being relieved by the 1st. British Division on 3rd. inst. and during night 3/4th. inst.

1. **RELIEFS:**

    (a). No. 10 Field Ambulance: The 4th. Divisional Section of the Main Dressing Station will be handed over to No. 141 Field Ambulance.

    No. 10 Field Ambulance will march on relief to the billets vacated by 141st. Field Ambulance in the RUE DE JUSTICE, ARRAS.

    (b). No. 11 Field Ambulance: O.C. No. 11 Field Ambulance will hand over the evacuation of the forward area to O.C. No. 1 Field Ambulance, together with all posts.

    On relief, No. 11 Field Ambulance will march to the GIRLS' SCHOOL, ST SAUVEUR.

    (c). No. 12 Field Ambulance: No. 12 Field Ambulance will hand over the 4th. Divisional Section of the Walking Wounded Post to No. 2 Field Ambulance.

    On relief, No. 12 Field Ambulance will march to the HOSPICE DES VIEILLARDS, ARRAS.

2. **STORES:** All stores will be handed over, except those carried by Field Ambulances as Mobilization Equipment. Receipts will be obtained.

3. **PERSONNEL:TRANSPORT:** Bearers, Horsed ambulances, and cars will return to their own Units at once.

    Bearers attached to Regimental Units will remain with them until further orders.

4. **REPORTS:** Reliefs will take place at once. Reports on completion will be forwarded to the office of the A.D.M.S. Ambulance Commanders will arrange all details mutually.

5. Office of A.D.M.S. 4th. Division will close at ST SAUVEUR at 5 p.m. and re-open at No. 21 BOULEVARD VAUBAN, ARRAS at the same hour.

6. Field Ambulances to acknowledge.

                                              J.S. McCutcheon
                                              Major for
                                              Colonel,
                                              A.D.M.S. 4th. Division.

Issued at 4.30 p.m.

Distribution :-

No. 1. to D.D.M.S. Can. Corps.
2. A.D.M.S. 4th. Can. Division.
3. A.D.M.S. 1st. Brit. Division.
4. 10th. Brit. Field Ambulance.
5. 11th. Brit. Field Ambulance.
6. 12th. Brit. Field Ambulance.
7. 10th. Brit. Inf. Bde.
8. 11th. Brit. Inf. Bde.
9. 12th. Brit. Inf. Bde.
10. 4th. Brit. Division.
11. 4th. Brit. Division 'A/Q'.
12. C.R.A. 4th. Brit. Division.
13. C.R.E. 4th. Brit. Division.
14. 4th. Brit. Division Signals.
15. 4th. Brit. Divisional Train.
16. D.A.D.V.S. 4th. Brit. Division.
17. A.P.M. 4th. Brit. Division.
18.)
32.) Reg. Med. Officers.
33.)
34. Diary.
35. File.

SECRET.   4th. DIVISION   Copy No. 35

R.A.M.C. ORDER NO. 69.

(In connection with 4th. Division Order No.157).

Map Refs: Sheet 51 B, 1/40,000.   17th. Sept. 1918.

The 4th. Division is to relieve the 11th. Division and the left Brigade of the 56th. Division in the line. The relief commences on 18th. inst, and is to be completed by 10 a.m. on 20th. inst.

On completion of the relief, boundaries will be as follow:

(a). Between 4th. Division, (10th. Inf. Bde.) and 56th. Division, K.27.central - P.12.central - P.11.c.8.4. - P.15.central - thence due West along grid line to ARRAS - CAMBRAI road.

(b). Between 10th. Inf. Bde. and 11th. Inf. Bde., J.28.c.0.0. - R.SENSEE at P.3.a.5.4. to its junction with R.COJEUL - thence R.COJEUL to O.10.d.0.0. - thence cross roads O.13.b.8.8.

(c). Between 4th. Division, (11th. Inf. Bde.) and 49th. Division, the R.SCARPE.

1. **MOVES OF FIELD AMBULANCES:**

    Field Ambulances will move with their respective Brigade Groups, under orders of the Brigades.

2. **RELIEFS:** On arrival in the new area, Field Ambulances will carry out the following reliefs:

    (a). No. 10 Field Ambulance: No. 10 Field Ambulance will relieve No. 35 Field Ambulance, and Post of 2/2nd. London Field Ambulance in the new Divisional Area, on night 18th/19th. inst.
    O.C., No. 10 Field Ambulance will be responsible for the evacuation of casualties from the front. Ambulance H.Qrs. at G.24.a.9.2.

    (b). No. 11 Field Ambulance: No. 11 Field Ambulance will relieve No. 33 Field Ambulance on 19th. inst. Hd.Qrs. DEAF & DUMB INSTITUTE, ARRAS.
    O.C., No. 11 Field Ambulance will run the Divisional M.D.Stn.

    (c). No. 12 Field Ambulance: No. 12 Field Ambulance will take over billets at present occupied by No. 34 Field Ambulance, and will be in reserve. Hd.Qrs., H.20.b.1.7

3. **POSTS:** On completion of reliefs, the following will be the scheme of Posts in the Divisional Area:

    (a). Forward Posts:

    Car Loading Post,   O.4.c.8.3.
    Relay Posts,   I.34.c.1.1., I.27.d.4.4., O.9.a.3.9., O.2.c.4.4., O.1.a.6.2.

    Adv. Drg. Stn.,   O.4.c.0.8.

-2-

    (b). **M.D.Stn:**   DEAF AND DUMB INSTITUTE, ARRAS. G.22.b.3.2.

4. **EVACUATION:** From R.A.P's. by hand carriage, wheeled stretcher, trolley and Ford car, to A.D.Stn. at O.4.c.0.8. Thence by light railway to Detraining Point near M.D.Stn. From M.D.Stn. to C.C.S. in M.A.C. cars.

    Alternative route from A.D.Stn. by ambulance cars to ARRAS-CAMBRAI road at O.14.a.0.6. Thence ARRAS-CAMBRAI road to M.D.S.

5. **PERSONNEL:**

    (a). O.C. No. 10 Field Ambulance will send 4 bearers to each of the Battalions in the 10th. and 11th. Inf. Bdes. These bearers will remain under the command of O.C. No. 10 Field Ambulance, and will be rationed by him. They will be used to clear from R.A.P's. to the Relay Posts only, and will not be employed in front of the R.A.P's.

    (b). O.C., No. 11 Field Ambulance will arrange to have an Unloading Party with sufficient cars at the Detraining Point, for the purpose of unloading and conveying wounded to the M.D.Stn.

6. **FORD CARS:** Nos. 11 and 12 Field Ambulances will send a Ford Car each to No. 10 Field Ambulance, to assist in evacuation in the forward area. These cars will be despatched on 19th. inst., before 12. noon.

7. **REGISTRATION. A.T.S.:** All registration of casualties will be carried out at the M.D.Stn. Field Medical Cards will also be made out there, and Anti-Tetanic Serum administered.

8. **STORES:** All surplus stores will be taken over from outgoing Field Ambulances, and receipts given.

9. Reliefs to be arranged in detail between Ambulance Commanders concerned. Completion to be reported to this office.

10.   The Office of the A.D.M.S. 4th. Division will close at VILLERS CHATEL at 10 a.m. on 20th. inst., and re-open at PLACE ST. CROIX, ARRAS, at the same hour.

11.   Field Ambulances to acknowledge.

                                          Lieut-Colonel,

Issued at 6.45 p.m.   a/A.D.M.S. 4th. Division.

Distribution:-

No. 1	to	D.D.M.S. XXII Corps.	No. 13	to	4th. Division.
2	to	A.D.M.S. 11th. Division.	14	to	4th. Division 'A/Q'.
3	to	A.D.M.S. 56th. Division.	15	to	C.R.E. 4th. Division.
4	to	A.D.M.S. 49th. Division.	16	to	4th. Division Sigs.
5	to	10th. Field Ambulance.	17	to	4th. Divl. Train.
6	to	11th. Field Ambulance.	18	to	D.A.D.V.S. 4th. Divn.
7	to	12th. Field Ambulance.	19	to	A.P.M. 4th. Division.
8	to	10th. Infantry Bde.	20-34		R.M.O's.
9	to	11th. Infantry Bde.	35, 36		Diary.
10	to	12th. Infantry Bde.	37		File.

SECRET.

AMENDMENTS

to

4th. DIVISION R.A.M.C. ORDER NO. 69.

Map Refs: 51b, 1/40,000.

In para. 3, (a), 'Forward Posts': Delete 'Car Loading Post, O.4.c.8.3.' and substitute the following:

Car Loading Posts: Left Bde: O.4.c.8.3.

        Right Bde: P.13.d.2.7.
             P.21.b.3.5.

At end of Para. 3, (a), add the following note:

" An A.D.S. for the Right Bde. will be established in one of the following sites, as soon as the A.D.M.S. 56th. Division can hand them over: O.23.d.7.5., O.15.d.2.5."

                Lieut-Colonel,
                a/A.D.M.S. 4th. Division.

18th. Sept. 1918.
U.

Distribution as before.

SECRET.

AMENDMENTS NO. 2

to

4th. DIVISION R.A.M.C. ORDER NO. 69.

Map Refs: 51b, 1/40,000.

The second amendment dated 18th. inst. is cancelled, and the following substituted:

"Para. 3,(a), 'A.D.Stn. , 0.4.c.0.8.' is cancelled, and the following substituted:"

Adv.Drg.Stns: Left Bde: 0.4.c.0.8.
                Right Bde: 0.15.d.2.5. (ST ROHART FACTORY).

Para. 2,(c) is cancelled and the following substituted:

(c). No. 12 Field Ambulance: No. 12 Field Ambulance will take over the portion of the HOPITAL ST JEAN, ARRAS, at present held by 9th. Canadian Field Ambulance, and will be in reserve.

                                               Lieut-Colonel,
                                       a/A.D.M.S. 4th. Division.

19th.Sept.1918.
U.

Distribution as before.

S E C R E T.

AMENDMENTS NO. 3
to
4th.Div.R.A.M.C. ORDER NO. 69, DATED 17-9-18.

Map Refs: 51b, 1/40,000.

In para. 2,(a), line 6:-

    Delete, "G.24.a.9.2." and substitute, "ST ROHART FACTORY, O.15.d.2.5."

                                         Lieut-Colonel,
                                       a/A.D.M.S. 4th. Division.

20th.Sept.1918.

Distribution as before.

SECRET.

4th. DIVISION

MEDICAL ARRANGEMENTS NO. 1.

Map Refs: Sheets 51b, 51c, LENS 11.   21st. Sept. 1918.

1. **MEDICAL POSTS:**

	Right Sector.		Left Sector.
(a). R.A. Posts.	P.10.b.1.9.	-Rt.Bn.-	O.5.c.25.85.
	P.9.a.6.8. d.50	-Lt.Bn.-	I.33.b.55.20.
	P.13.d.6.4.	-Sup.Bn.-	O.2.d.1.5.
(b). Relay Posts.	P.21.b.5.5.		I.33.d.8.0.
	P.13.d.2.8.		I.27.d.4.4.
			D.9.a.3.9.
			O.2.c.4.4.
(c). Car Posts.	P.21.a.7.2.		O.4.c.6.2.
	P.13.d.2.8.		
(d). Adv. Dr. Stns.	O.15.d.2.5.		O.4.c.0.6.
(e). Car Relay Post.	N.12.d.4.8.		

   (f). **Field Ambulance Headquarters.**

      10 Fd. Ambce.   O.15.d.2.5. (ST ROHART FACTORY.)
      11 Fd. Ambce.   G.22.b.3.3. (DEAF & DUMB INSTITUTE).
      12 Fd. Ambce.   G.21.d.6.4. (HOPITAL ST JEAN).

   (g). **Main Dressing Station.**

      No. 11 Field Ambulance, G.22.b.3.3.

   (h). **Field Ambulance Transport.**

      10 Fd. Ambce.   G.17.c.7.6.
      11 Fd. Ambce.   G.22.b.2.6.
      12 Fd. Ambce.   G.22.a.8.9.

2. **EVACUATION:**

   (a). **From Right Brigade:** From Right and Left Battalions by hand carriage and wheeled stretcher to Relay Post. Thence to Car Post and by car to A.D.Stn.
      From Support Battalion by hand carriage to Relay post, thence to A.D.Stn. by car.

   (b). **From Left Brigade:** From Right Battalion by hand carriage & wheeled stretcher to A.D.Stn. From Left Battalion by hand carriage to Relay Post. Thence by hand and wheeled stretcher to A.D.Stn.
      From Support Battalion to Relay Post O.2.c.4.4. by hand. Thence to Car Relay Post by wheeled stretcher.

   (c). **From A.D.Stns:** From Right A.D.Stn. to M.D.Stn. by car. From Left A.D.Stn. to M.D.S. by light railway.(Failing railway, by car).

   (d). **From M.D.Stn:** To C.C.Stns. and Special Hospitals in Field Ambulance and M.A.C. Cars.

3. CASUALTY CLEARING STATIONS:

Nos. 23, 1 Can. and 4 Can. C.C.Stns. receive cases, (sick and wounded) in rotation. Cases are evacuated to C.C.Stn. in M.A.C. cars.

4. CORPS REST STATION:

No. 2 C.C.Stn., ANVIN, is Corps Rest Station. Notification will be sent daily to M.D.Stn. of the numbers of beds vacant. Cases will be transferred in M.A.C. cars.
Only cases which are likely to recover in from 6 to 14 days should be sent to the C.R.S.

5. MOTOR AMBULANCE CONVOY:

No. 42 M.A.C. works the XXIInd. Corps. It is situated at ACQ.

6. SPECIAL CASES:

(a). Gassed Cases. Lightly gassed cases will be sent to the Corps Rest Station.
Gassed cases of a more severe nature will be transferred to the Corps Gas Centre, (2/1st. Highland Fd. Ambce.) at ECOIVRES, F.13.b.3.2., in M.A.C. cars.

(b). "S.I." Cases. These will be evacuated to No. 12 Sty. Hpl. ST POL, with full particulars regarding the case.

(c). "N.Y.D.N." Cases. To 12 Sty. Hpl, ST POL.

(d). Infectious Cases. Infectious cases, including Dysentery, will be evacuated to No. 12 Sty. Hpl. ST POL.

(e). Ear, Throat and Nose Cases. To No. 12 Sty. Hpl. ST POL. Urgent cases will be taken in at any time.
Ordinary cases will be sent to 12 Sty. Hpl. in Field Ambulance cars from the M.D.Stn., to arrive ST POL at 9 a.m. as under. Not more than 6 cases to be sent on any one day:-

Officers: SUNDAYS.   Other Ranks: WEDNESDAYS.
                                         FRIDAYS.
Patients will be in possession of kits and A.B. 64. One day's rations will be carried by all personnel and patients proceeding. Nominal roll in duplicate as hitherto.

(f). Ophthalmic Cases. To No. 12 Sty. Hpl. ST POL. Urgent cases will be received at any time. Ordinary cases will proceed as under:-

Officers: SATURDAYS.   Other Ranks : THURSDAYS.

Ordinary cases will be sent from the M.B.Stn. in Field Ambulance cars, to arrive at 9 a.m. Not more than 15 cases per day to be sent. Nominal roll in duplicate to accompany patients. A.B. 64 to be in possession. One day's rations to be carried.

(g). Dental Cases. Dental cases will be collected to the number of 30, at No. 12 Field Ambulance each Tuesday. They will be seen by the Dental Surgeon from No. 57 C.C.Stn., under arrangements to be notified later.
The Dental Surgeon will forward his reports to the A.D.M.S.

/Men.

Men whose mouths are ready, and who have been seen by a Dental Surgeon, and who require dentures, will be evacuated to No. 57 C.C.Stn.

(h). <u>Chinese Labourers</u>: These will be evacuated to 11 C.C.Stn., MOULLE.

7. <u>SANITARY SECTIONS</u>: For the Town of ARRAS, No. 1 Can. San. Sec. ST SAUVEUR.
    For the Forward Area, No. 63 San. Sec., MAROEUIL.

8. <u>MOBILE LABORATORIES</u>:

    No. 6 Hygiene, AGNEZ LES DUISANS.
    No. 2, LIGNY ST FLOCHEL.

9. <u>ADVANCED DEPOT, MEDICAL STORES</u>:

    No. 33, SAVY.

10. <u>MOBILE X-RAY UNIT</u>:

    No. 6, AUBIGNY.

11. <u>BRITISH RED CROSS STORES</u>:

    Advanced Stores, Central Area, HAM EN ARTOIS.

    <u>Postal Address</u>:   B.R.C.S. Advanced Stores,
                            Central Area, B.E.F.

= * = * = * = * = * =

21st.Sept.1918.
U.

D. Ahern Lt.Col.
A.D.M.S. 4th. Division.

Copies to all concerned.

S E C R E T.

AMENDMENTS NO. 1

to

4th. DIVISION MEDICAL ARRANGEMENTS NO. 1 DATED 21-9-1918.

Map Refs: Sheet 51b, 1/40,000.

1. R.A.P.   Delete "P.10.b.1.9" in para. 1 (a), and substitute "P.16.b.2.9.".

    At end of Para. 1 insert the following:

    Note: Alterations of Medical Posts will be published from time to time in Disposition Reports of Medical Posts.

2. Dental Arrangements: Delete para. 6, (g), and substitute the following:

    (g). Dental Cases: The Dental Surgeon from 22 C.C.S. will live at No. 12 Field Ambulance, HOPITAL ST JEAN. He will see cases from the Division and Corps Troops in the vicinity at 9a.m. on Mondays, Wednesdays and Fridays. Medical Units sending in cases will arrange for their attendance at the prescribed hour. Not more than 30 cases to be brought before D.S. in one day. Officers to attend at times stated or by appointment with D.S.

[signature]
Major,
for A.D.M.S. 4th. Division.

24th. Sept. 1918.
U.

Distribution as before.

SECRET.   Copy No. 27

4th. DIVISION

R.A.M.C. ORDER NO. 70.

(In connection with 4th. Division Order No. 161).

Map Refs: 51b, 1/40,000.   29th. September, 1918.

The 4th. Division is extending its front on the night 29th/30th. Sept.1918, taking over the front held by the 167th. Infantry Brigade.

On completion of the relief of 167th. Bde., boundaries will run as follow:

(a). Left Divisional Boundary as before.
(b). Inter-Brigade Boundary as before.
(c). Right Divisional Boundary, Q.10.central - Q.10.d.5.4. - along HIRONDELLE RIVER to P.30.b.7.5. - along stream to SAUDEMONT CHAPEL, (P.30.a.7.8.) - P.24.c.0.0. - thence along grid line, West to ARRAS-CAMBRAI road.

1. O.C., No. 10 Field Ambulance will establish such new Posts as he considers necessary, in sites chosen by himself, to ensure evacuation of casualties from the new front.

2. He will report to the A.D.M.S. when those Posts have been established, giving map references of new Posts, and line of evacuation.

3. Office of A.D.M.S. 4th. Division will close at PLACE STE. CROIX at 12, noon on 30th. Sept. and re-open at LES FOSSES FARM at the same hour.

4. Field Ambulances to acknowledge.

                                        Faichnie
                                        Colonel,
                                A.D.M.S. 4th. Division.

Issued at 6.0 p.m.

Distribution:

Copy No.		
1	to	D.D.M.S. XXIInd. Corps.
2		No. 10 Field Ambulance.
3		No. 11 Field Ambulance.
4		No. 12 Field Ambulance.
5		A.D.M.S. 56th. Division.
6		4th. Division.
7		4th. Division 'A/Q'.
8		10th. Infantry Brigade.
9		11th. Infantry Brigade.
10		12th. Infantry Brigade.
11		4th. Div. Signals.
12-26		R.M.O's.
27,28		Diary.
29		File.

4th. Division No. A.3222/282.
A.D.M.S. 4th. Division No. 34/52.

A.D.M.S.,
4th. Division.

Under authority granted by His Majesty the King, the Corps Commander has awarded the Military Medal to the following Other Ranks, as shown:-

MILITARY MEDAL.

M2/134059	Pte.	G.M.LEWIS.	A.S.C.M.T. att.	No. 11 Fd.Ambce.
105129	—	C.E.BROADHEAD.	R.A.M.C.	No. 11 Fd.Ambce.
90447	—	L.JORDAN.	R.A.M.C.	No. 11 Fd.Ambce.
32732	—	O.J.COXHEAD.	R.A.M.C.	No. 11 Fd.Ambce.
63579	—	J.T.COOLE.	R.A.M.C.	No. 11 Fd.Ambce.
20469	a/L.Cpl.	J.T.STEWART.	R.A.M.C.	No. 10 Fd.Ambce.

Please convey the G.O.C's. congratulations to the recipients.

29-9-18.

sd/D.M.DURHAM. Lieut.,
A/D.A.A.G. 4th. Division.

A.D.M.S. 4th Division

Army Form C2118.

Vol 50

WAR DIARY
or
INTELLIGENCE SUMMARY.
(Erase heading not required.)

Instructions regarding War Diaries and Intelligence Summaries are contained in F.S. Regs, Part II. and the Staff Manual respectively. Title pages will be prepared in manuscript.

Place	Date	Hour	Summary of Events and Information	Remarks and references to Appendices
La FOSSE FARM	1.10.18		A.D.M.S. visited the Headquarters of No 10 Field Ambulance and found many improvements since work done. Also in the afternoon he saw the Town Major of Arras about sanitation. No 2 Field Ambulance arrangements.	A. DP.
"	2.10.18		A.D.M.S. went round the forward area to inspect the new Relay Post & Aid Post of the Somerset L.I. Former to west the extension of the divisional line to the right. He visited also the new A.D.S. at DURY.	DP.
"	3.10.18		No change in forward or medical arrangements. Casualties in the division continue few. A.D.M.S. conferred with 'Q' on the following of the troops.	DP
"	4.10.18		A.D.M.S. went to 63 Sanitary Sect. with reference to contacts of a suspected case of C.S.M. visited No 11, 12 Field Ambulances – inspected No 12 transport. R.A.M.C. order No 71 issued.	B. DP
"	5.10.18.		A.D.M.S. visited the R.D.M.S. XXII Corps. Made arrangements for move of the Field Ambulances. R.A.M.C. order No 72 issued, also A.D.M.S. No 17/1354.	DP
"	6.10.18		A.D.M.S. went to Agny. Gd. Duisans.	C. D. DP
WARLUS	7.10.18		Divisional H.Q. moved from La Fosse Farm to WARLUS. A.D.M.S. Office opened at WARLUS at 10.00. A.D.M.S. went round to see the new billets of all Field Ambulances.	DP
"	8.10.18		A.D.M.S. visited 12th Field Amb.	DP

Army Form C. 2118.

WAR DIARY
or
INTELLIGENCE SUMMARY.
(Erase heading not required.)

Instructions regarding War Diaries and Intelligence Summaries are contained in F. S. Regs., Part II. and the Staff Manual respectively. Title pages will be prepared in manuscript.

Place	Date	Hour	Summary of Events and Information	Remarks and references to Appendices
Wadus	9.10.18		A.D.M.S. went to D.M.S. forma H.Q. over No 10 Field Amb. to take over XXII Corps Rlwy station at MINORAL R.A.M.C. order No 73	E.
"	10.10.18		A.D.M.S. circled 62nd Brigade billeting area & inspected same	
"	11.10.18		D.A.D.M.S. returned from 14 days leave to U.K. Durain moved to BOURLON AREA. A.D.M.S. Officer at BOURLON. (Ref. Sqr. E.12.d.8.9.) (10th F.A. moved to QUEANT. 22nd Corps M.D.S.)	
"	12.10.18		D.A.D.M.S. visited 11th Field Ambulance.	
"	13.10.18		Division moved to ESCAUDOEUVRES Area. 12th Field Ambulance placed at Inpost at A.D.M.S. H.Q. Durain with 16th F.A. Rte. to Snarty Corch. about R.147 S.T. 11 F.A. 12 F.A. A.D.M.S. Office located at Skot S.g.c. T.25.b.6.39, 11 FA - T.25.c.5.5, 12 FA A.S.6.3.0.	
ESCAUDOEUVRES	17.10.18		4th Division relieving 49th Division in the line. R.A.M.C. order No 76 issued and had med arrangements there to.	F. & F.1.
"	18.10.18		Ve6 Med Arrangement No 77 issued regarding move of 10 F.A. to CAMBRAI from Queant	G.
NAVES	19.10.18		4th Div. H.Q. moved to NAVES. A.D.M.S. Office head Qr. R.A.M.C. order No 78 issued	H. & H.1.
"	20.10.18		and Medical arrangements here to issued. Div. Captured HASPRES & SAULZOIR.	
"	21.10.18		Addendum No 1 to R.A.M.C. order No 78 issued. Casualties by W. in Yorksbury H... Operation	

M.S. McIntire
Major R.A.M.C.
A.D.M.S. 4th Div

Army Form C. 2118.

WAR DIARY
or
INTELLIGENCE SUMMARY.
(Erase heading not required.)

Instructions regarding War Diaries and Intelligence Summaries are contained in F. S. Regs., Part II. and the Staff Manual respectively. Title pages will be prepared in manuscript.

Place	Date	Hour	Summary of Events and Information	Remarks and references to Appendices
AVESNES LE SEC	23.10.18		Div HQ moved to AVESNES LE SEC. Med arrangements in connection with 4th Division order No 169 issued.	I.
"	24.10.18		Division attacked this morning on a 2 Brigade front and made considerable progress. Capturing the villages of VERCHAIN + MONCHAUX. About 600 prisoners + 2 guns taken. Our casualties were light. ADMS visited 12 F.A.	
"	25.10.18		Operations continued on high ground and machine gun posts cleared. ADMS visited MDS. DADMS visited CCWP	
"	26.10.18		Village of QUERENAING + ARTRES captured. Casualties light in spite of a counter-attack under enemy barrage. DADMS visited MDS CCWP + HQ 12 FA. Push has secured our new RHONELLE and crossed also. MATHAULIN MARECUSA + Capt W.F.R. SIMPSON struck off strength of 49th Div. ADMS visited CWP DADMS visited MDS. (27th RAMC Adv. orders to 80 hours)	J.
"	27.10.18			
"	28.10.18		10 Field Ambulance closed MDS at NAVES + reopened it at VILLERS - EN - CAUCHIE. ADMS visited 11 Field Ambulance.	
"	29.10.18		ADMS visited CCWP and DADMS visited 12 Field Ambulance. ADS moved from VERCHAIN to QUERENAING. CCWP moved to HASPRES.	
"	30.10.18		ADMS visited 12 Field Ambulance and W.W.C.P.	
"	31.10.18		DADMS visited 12 Field Ambulance + ADS. CCWP MDS.	

M Mulchey DSO
Major RAMC
(a)

SECRET.

4th. DIVISION.

MEDICAL ARRANGEMENTS NO. 2.

Map Refs: Sheets 51b, 51c, LENS 11.   1st. October, 1918.

1. **MEDICAL POSTS:**

    (a). R.A.P's.

		Right Sector.	Left Sector.
	Rt.	Q.13.c.1.9.	O.5.c.25.85.
	Cen.	P.16.b.2.9.	
	Lt.	P.9.d.5.0.	I.33.b.55.20.
	Sup.	P.13.d.6.4.	O.2.d.1.5.

    (b). Relay Posts.   P.25.b.2.6.   I.33.d.8.0.
                                       I.27.d.4.4.
                                       O.9.a.3.9.
                                       O.2.c.4.4.

    (c). Car Posts.   P.21.a.7.2.
                       P.15.d.2.8.   O.4.c.6.2.

    (d). A.D.Stns.   O.15.d.2.5.   O.4.c.8.8.

    (e). Car Relay Post.   N.12.d.4.8.

    (f). Main Dressing Station.
            No. 11 Field Ambulance, G.22.b.3.3.

    (g). Ambulance Headquarters.
            No. 10 Field Ambce. O.15.d.2.5. (ST. ROHART FACTORY).
            No. 11 Field Ambce. G.22.b.3.3. (DEAF & DUMB INST.).
            No. 12 Field Ambce. G.21.d.6.4. (HOPITAL ST JEAN).

    (h). Ambulance Transport.
            No. 10 Field Ambce. G.17.c.7.6.
            No. 11 Field Ambce. G.22.b.2.6.
            No. 12 Field Ambce. G.15.d.6.1.

2. **EVACUATION:**

    (a). RIGHT BRIGADE:
        From Centre and Left Battns. by hand and wheeled stretcher to Car Post, and by car to A.D.S.
        From Right Battn. by wheeled stretcher and light railway to Relay Post, P.23.b.2.6., and by car to A.D.S.
        From Support Battn. by hand carriage to Relay Post, and to A.D.S. by car.

    (b). LEFT BRIGADE:
        From Right Battn. by hand and wheeled stretcher to A.D.S.
        From Left Battn. by hand to Relay Post, and by wheeled stretcher to A.D.S.
        From Support Battn. by hand to Relay Post, O.2.c.4.4. by hand, and wheeled stretcher to Car Relay Post.

    (c). FROM A.D.STNS.
        From Right A.D.S. to M.D.S. by ambulance cars.
        From Left A.D.S. to M.D.S. by light railway. (Failing light railway, by ambulance cars).

/d.

-2-

(d). FROM M.D.S: To C.C.S. and Special Hospitals in M.A.C. Cars.

3. **CASUALTY CLEARING STATIONS:**
Nos. 33, 1 Can. and 4 Can. C.C.Stns., all at AGNEZ LES DUISANS, receive sick and wounded in rotation. Cases are evacuated to C.C.S. in M.A.C. cars.

4. **MOTOR AMBULANCE CONVOY:**
No. 43 M.A.C. At ETRUN.

5. **SPECIAL CASES:**

   (a). GASSED CASES. Lightly gassed cases will be sent to the Corps Rest Station when that Unit is again open. Until then, they will be evacuated as follows.
   Severer cases will be transferred to the Corps Gas Centre, at ECOIVRES, (F.15.b.5.2.) in M.A.C. cars.

   (b). "S.I." CASES. To No. 12 Sty. Hpl., ST POL.

   (c). "N.Y.D.N." CASES. To No. 12 Sty. Hpl.

   (d). Infectious Cases. No. 12 Sty. Hpl. This includes Dysentery and Suspected Dysentery.

   (e). EAR, THROAT & NOSE CASES. To No. 12 Sty. Hpl. Only urgent cases to be sent for the present. Sent from M.D.S. in Field Ambulance cars, to arrive at ST POL at 9 a.m.
   OFFICERS: Sundays.   OTHER RANKS: Wednesdays & Fridays.
   Previous instructions regarding rations, etc., hold good.

   (f). OPHTHALMIC CASES. To No. 12 Sty. Hpl. Only urgent cases to be sent. Sent from M.D.S. in Field Ambulance cars to arrive ST. POL at 9 a.m. as follows.
   OFFICERS: Saturdays.   OTHER RANKS: Thursdays.
   Previous instructions regarding rations, etc., hold good.

   (g). DENTAL CASES: Dentist from 22 C.C.S. lives at 12 Field Ambulance. Days for 4th. Division and neighbouring Corps Troops, Mondays, Wednesdays and Fridays. Officers to attend at times stated or by appointment direct. Dentist commences at 9 a.m. daily. Not more than 50 cases per diem to attend.

   (h). Chinese Labourers: To 11 C.C.S., MOULLE.

7. **SANITARY SECTION:** No. 63, MAROEUIL.

8. **MOBILE LABORATORIES:**
No. 6 Hygiene, AGNEZ LES DUISANS.
No. 2, LIGNY ST. FLOCHEL.

9. **ADVANCED DEPOT OF MEDICAL STORES:** No. 33, SAVY.

10. **MOBILE X-RAY UNIT.** No. 6, AUBIGNY.

11. **BRITISH RED CROSS STORES:** HAM EN ARTOIS.
Postal Address: B.R.C.S. Advanced Stores,
Central Area,
B.E.F.

Medical Arrangements No. 1, dated 21-9-18, are cancelled.

L. Pascall Major,
for A.D.M.S. 4th. Division.

Distribution as before.

B

SECRET.   Copy No.

4th. DIVISION

R.A.M.C ORDER NO. 71.

(Issued in conjunction with 4th. Division Order No. 162).

4th. October, 1918.

The 4th. Division is to be relieved by 1st. Canadian Division between 5th. and 7th. inst.

On completion of relief the 4th. (British) Division will remain in XXII Corps, and will be withdrawn into Army Reserve, in the area HABARCQ - WANQUETIN - WARLUS.

Divisional Headquarters will be at WARLUS.

Relief will be carried out as under:-

(i). On 5th. October.

    (a). 10th. (British) Inf. Bde. less one Battalion will march to the new area, after 12, noon.

    (b). A and B Brigade Groups of 1st. Canadian Division arrive by 12, noon in the neighbourhood of HAUCOURT and GUEMAPPE respectively.

(ii). On 6th. October and night 6/7th. October.

    A and B Brigades 1st. Canadian Division relieve the 11th. and 12th. (British) Inf. Bdes. respectively.

(iii). The Reserve Brigade of 1st. Canadian Division will be accommodated in GUEMAPPE area. It will not arrive in this area before 12 noon, 7th. Octr.

1. RELIEFS: Field Ambulances will be relieved independantly of their respective Brigade Groups, under orders of the A.D.M.S., which will be issued later.

2. Field Ambulances acknowledge.

                                            Colonel,
Issued at 1900.   A.D.M.S. 4th. Division.

Distribution:-

1	to D.D.M.S. XXII Corps.	8.	to 10th. (Brit) Inf. Bde.
2	A.D.M.S. 1st. Can. Division.	9	11th. (Brit) Inf. Bde.
3	10th. Field Ambulance.	10	12th. (Brit) Inf. Bde.
4.	11th. Field Ambulance.	11)	
5.	12th. Field Ambulance.	12)	Diary.
6	4th. (British) Division.	13	File.
7.	4th. (British) Division A/Q.		

SECRET.   Copy No. 32

4th. DIVISION
R.A.M.C. ORDER NO. 73.

Map Refs: Sheets 51b, LENS 11.   5th. October, 1916.

In continuation of 4th. Division R.A.M.C. Order No. 72:

1. RELIEFS:

   (a). No. 10 Field Ambulance will be relieved by No. 2 and 3 Canadian Field Ambulances as follows:-
      (i). No. 2 Canadian Field Ambulance will take over the Posts of the Right Brigade, and Ambulance Headquarters at ST ROHART FACTORY.
      (ii). No. 3 Canadian Field Ambulance will take over the Posts of the Left Brigade.
         Reliefs to be complete by midnight, 6/7th. October.

   (b). No. 11 Field Ambulance will be relieved by No. 1 Canadian Field Ambulance at the Main Dressing Station, DEAF & DUMB INSTITUTE, ARRAS.
         Relief to be completed by 6 p.m. on 6th. October.

   (c). No. 12 Field Ambulance will be relieved by part of No. 3 Canadian Field Ambulance at the HOPITAL ST JEAN, ARRAS, to be complete by midnight 6/7th October.

   (d). Advance Parties of the Canadian Units will arrive on the evening of to-day, preparatory to taking over from their respective opposite numbers.

   (e). Details of Reliefs to be arranged between O's.C. concerned.

   (f). Completion of Reliefs will be reported to the office of the A.D.M.S. 4th. (Brit) Division by D.R.

2. MOVES: Field Ambulances will move by march route on relief, to the following destinations:
      No. 10 Field Ambulance   WANQUETIN.
      No. 11 Field Ambulance   BERNEVILLE.
      No. 12 Field Ambulance   MONTENESCOURT.

   Brigades are arranging billeting accommodation for the Field Ambulances in the new area. O's.C. Field Ambulances will send a billeting party under an officer to report to the Staff Captains of their respective Brigades, before the arrival of their Units in the new area.

3. STORES: Surgical and Medical Equipment held over mobilization equipment and that authorised by G.R.O., will be handed over to incoming Units and receipts obtained. These will be forwarded to the office of the A.D.M.S. in duplicate.

4. Office of A.D.M.S. will close at LES FOSSES FARM at 10 a.m. on 7th. October, and re-open at WARLUS at the same hour.

5. Field Ambulances to acknowledge.

                                                    Colonel,
                                                    A.D.M.S. 4th. Division.

Issued at 1800.

                                                    /Distribution.

Distribution:

```
Copy No.   1 to D.D.M.S. XXII Corps.
           2    A.D.M.S. 1st. Canadian Division.
           3    No. 10 Field Ambulance.
           4    No. 11 Field Ambulance.
           5    No. 12 Field Ambulance.
           6    4th. Division.
           7    4th. Division "A/Q".
           8    10th. Infantry Brigade.
           9    11th. Infantry Brigade.
          10    12th. Infantry Brigade.
          11    4th. Div. Arty.
          12    C.R.E. 4th. Division.
          13    4th. Div. Signals.
          14    4th. Divisional Train.
          15    D.A.D.V.S. 4th. Division.
       16-31    R.M.O's.
       32,33    Diary.
          34    File.
```

SECRET.   A.D.M.S. 4th. Division No. 17/154.

COLLECTION OF DIVISIONAL SICK.

1.   On 6th. inst., No. 12 Field Ambulance will collect the morning sick of the 10th. Infantry Brigade Group in the new area.
       Other sick will be sent in on that day as usual.

2.   After 6th. inst., the following will be the distribution of Units for purposes of sick collection:

   (a). No. 10 Field Ambulance:

       10th. Inf. Bde. Group.
       9th. Field Coy. R.E.

   (b). No. 11 Field Ambulance:

       11th. Inf. Bde. Group.
       Divisional Headquarters.
       526th. Fd. Coy. R.E.
       21st. W. Yorks. R.
       H.Q. 4th. Div. Arty.
       4th. Bn. M.G.Corps.
       4th. Div. Amn. Col.

       In addition, No. 11 Field Ambulance will send a car daily, with a M.O., to see the sick of the 4th. Divisional Train, and convey any cases to No. 11 Field Ambulance.

   (c). No. 12 Field Ambulance:

       12th. Inf. Bde. Group.
       406th. Fd. Coy. R.E.
       4th. Div. Recep. Camp.

3.   The following Units will send their sick and wounded to the nearest Medical Unit in their locality:

       29th. Bde. R.F.A.
       32nd. Bde. R.F.A.
       4th. Mobile Vety. Section.
       207th. Employment Coy.

                                               Ritchie
                                               Colonel,
                                               A.D.M.S. 4th. Division.

5th. October, 1918.
U.

Copies to:-   D.D.M.S. XXII Corps.
                Field Ambulances.
                Reg. Med. Officers.
                4th. Division "A/Q".
                A.D.M.S. 1st. Can. Division.
                Infantry Brigades.
                4th. Divl. Train.
                H.Q. 4th. Div. Arty.
                207th. Emp. Coy.
                Field Companies.

SECRET.   Copy No. 27

4th. DIVISION,

R.A.M.C. ORDER NO. 73.

Map Refs: LENS, 11.   9th. October, 1918.

1. No. 10 Field Ambulance will take over forthwith, the XXIInd. Corps Rest Station, MINGOVAL.

2. An Advance Party of 1 Officer and 10 Other Ranks will proceed at once, to commence taking over from 1/1 W.Riding Field Ambulance, who are at present running the Rest Station.

3. Relief details to be arranged between Ambulance Commanders concerned. Relief to be complete by 10.a.m. on 10th. inst.

4. All stores and equipment above establishments to be taken over and receipts given.

5. Completion of relief to be notified to this office by wire.

6. Field Ambulances acknowledge.

                                                    Maichine
                                                    Colonel,
                                              A.D.M.S. 4th. Division.

Issued at 1500 hours.

Distribution:- 1 D.D.M.S. XXII Corps.
               2 A.D.M.S. 4th. Division.
               3 No. 10 Field Ambulance.
               4 No. 11 Field Ambulance.
               5 No. 12 Field Ambulance.
               6 4th. Division.
               7 4th. Division 'A/Q'.
               8 10th. Inf. Bde.
               9 11th. Inf. Bde.
              10 12th. Inf. Bde.
              11- R.M.O's.
              26
              27 4th. Div. Train.
              28) Diary.
              29)
              30 File.

SECRET.   Copy No. 26

4th. DIVISION.

R.A.M.C. ORDER NO. 74.

(In conjunction with 4th. Division Order No. 164.)

11th. October, 1918.

The 4th.(British) Division is moving on 11th. October, from the WARLUS area to the BOURLON - FONTAINE NOTRE DAME area.

Personnel will move by bus in three Brigade Groups as under :-
    10th. Infantry Brigade Group.
    11th. Infantry Brigade Group.
    12th. Infantry Brigade Group.

Transport will move by road, in similar groups to those indicated in the above. It will stage at WANCOURT on night 11/12th. October.

1. For all purposes connected with this move, Field Ambulances will move with their respective Brigade Groups; viz:

    10th. Field Ambulance with 10th. Brigade Group.
    11th. Field Ambulance with 11th. Brigade Group.
    12th. Field Ambulance with 12th. Brigade Group.

2. All details of moves will be arranged between Ambulance Commanders and Brigades concerned.

3. Office of A.D.M.S. 4th. Division will close at WARLUS at 15.00 hours and re-open in the new area, (location to be notified later), at the same hour.

4. Field Ambulances to acknowledge.

                                            D. Purcell.
                                                    Major,
Issued at 01.00 hours.   for A.D.M.S. 4th. Division.

Distribution:- 1 to D.D.M.S. XXII Corps.
                2   10th. Field Ambulance.
                3   11th. Field Ambulance.
                4   12th. Field Ambulance.
                5   4th. Division.
                6   4th. Division 'A/Q'.
                7   10th. Infantry Brigade.
                8   11th. Infantry Brigade.
                9   12th. Infantry Brigade.
                10   4th. Div. Train.
                11-26 R.M.O's.
                27,28 Diary.
                29   File.

SECRET.   Copy No. 35

4th. DIVISION
R.A.M.C. ORDER NO. 76.
(Issued in conjunction with 4th. Division Order No. 166.)

Map Refs: Sheets 51a. and 57b.   17th. October, 1918.

The 4th. Division will relieve the 49th. Division between 17th. and 19th. October, 1918.

The 11th. Infantry Brigade will relieve the 148th. Infantry Brigade in the Left Section on 17th. and 17/18th.

The 10th. Infantry Brigade will relieve the 147th. Infantry Brigade in the Right Section on 18th. and 18/19th.

The 12th. Infantry Brigade will relieve the 146th. Infantry Brigade in Divisional Reserve on 18th.

1. **RELIEFS OF MEDICAL UNITS:**

    (a). No. 12 Field Ambulance will relieve the 1/2nd. W.Riding Field Ambulance in the forward area, and will be responsible for evacuation of Divisional casualties.
    H.Q. at T.25.a.9.1. Other Posts will be taken over in situ. Advanced Party of 12 Field Ambulance to report to 1/2 W.Riding Field Ambulance at 17.00 hours on 17th. inst.
    Relief to be complete by 18.00 hours on 18th. inst.

    (b). No. 11 Field Ambulance will relieve the 1/3 W.Riding Field Ambulance at the XXII Corps Walking Wounded Post, the CHURCH, ESCAUDOEUVRES, (T.25.a.4.4.) and the Light Railway Entraining Point, (S.24.c.3.3.).
    Relief to be complete by 21.00 hours on 18th. inst.

    (c). No. 10 Field Ambulance will remain at QUEANT until further orders.

2. **COMPLETION** of above reliefs to be reported to the A.D.M.S. by D.R. Particulars of situation of all Posts, H.Q. and Transport will be forwarded when this report is sent in.

3. **STORES & EQUIPMENT** will be taken over from Field Ambulances of 49th. Division, receipts given and vouchers of stores taken over, sent to this office in duplicate.

4. **DETAILS OF RELIEFS:** will be arranged between Ambulance Commanders concerned.

5. **OFFICE OF A.D.M.S.** will close at 10.00 hours on 19th. inst. at ESCAUDOEUVRES, and re-open at NAVES at the same hour.

6. Field Ambulances acknowledge.

                                                    Major
                                                for Colonel,
Issued at 12.00 hours.   A.D.M.S. 4th. Division.

Distribution:

No.		
1	to	D.D.M.S. XXII Corps.
2		A.D.M.S. 49th. Division.
3		A.D.M.S. 51st. Division.
4		No. 10 Field Ambulance.
5		No. 11 Field Ambulance.
6		No. 12 Field Ambulance.
7		4th. Division.
8		4th. Division 'A/Q'.
9		10th. Infantry Brigade.
10		11th. Infantry Brigade.
11		12th. Infantry Brigade.
12		C.R.A. 4th. Division.
13		C.R.E. 4th. Division.
14		4th. Div. Signals.
15		4th. Div. Train.
16		D.A.D.V.S. 4th. Division.
17		D.A.P.M. 4th. Division.
18		4th. Bn. M.G.Corps.
19-34		Regimental M.O's.
35,36		War Diary.
37		File.

Copy No. 34

4th. DIVISION

MEDICAL ARRANGEMENTS IN CONNECTION WITH R.A.M.C.

ORDER NO. 76.

Map Refs: Sheets 51a, 57b, 57c.   18th. October, 1918.

1. **MEDICAL POSTS:**

    (a). R.A.P's: Right Section.   Left Section.
                    U.6.c.3.7.   O.27.d.0.1.
                    U.5.b.5.2.   O.27.d.1.1.
                    U.5.b.3.6.   O.22.c.25.35.

    (b). Car Post: O.22.c.25.35.

    (c). A.D.Stn: U.5.d.3.3.

    (d). Dressing Station H.Q.:   T.23.a.7.0.

    (e). Walking Wounded Collecting Post: T.23.a.7.9.

    (f). De-Gassing Room & Bath: T.23.a.7.0.

    (g). Corps W.W.Post: T.25.a.6.4.   Entraining Post: S.24.c.3.7.

    (h). Corps M.D.Stn: CONVENT, ESCAUDOEUVRES.

2. **EVACUATION:**

    (a). From Right Sector: From R.A.P's. by hand carriage to A.D.S. at U.5.d.3.3.

    (b). From Left Sector: From R.A.P's. by hand carriage and wheeled stretchers to the Car Post at O.22.c.25.35. Thence to the H.Q. Dressing Station, T.23.a.7.0, in ambulance cars.

    (c). From A.D.S. and H.Q.Dressing Station: Lying wounded to C.M.D.S. by ambulance cars. Walking Wounded from T.23.a.7.0. in lorry and bus to C.W.W.P. Thence by light railway to QUEANT.
    Note: During "Peacetime" warfare, walking wounded are evacuated in the same way as lying wounded.

3. **H.Q., MEDICAL UNITS:**

    No. 12 Field Ambulance. H.Q. T.23.a.7.0. Evacuation of forward area.

    No. 11 Field Ambulance: H.Q. T.25.a.6.4. Walking Wounded Post. (XXII Corps).

    No. 10 Field Ambulance: H.Q. HOPITAL GENERAL, CAMBRAI. Section of Corps Rest Station. Bearers in Reserve.

/4.

4. PERSONNEL:

(a). Officers: Two M.O's. will be sent from No. 11 Field Ambulance for temporary duty with No. 12 Field Ambulance forthwith.

(b). Other Ranks: (i). The Bearer Division of No. 10 Field Ambulance will proceed to NAVES on arrival in the CAMBRAI area on 19th. inst. They will be placed under the command of O.C., No. 12 Field Ambulance at NAVES, and will form a reserve of bearers. They will march with horsed ambulances.

(ii). O.C., No. 11 Field Ambulance will send two squads of bearers with 4 stretchers to each R.A.P. on 19th. inst. before 12 hours. These bearers will be used for evacuation between the R.A.P. and Relay Posts or Car Posts.

5. AMBULANCE CARS:

(a). Large Cars: O.C. No. 11 Field Ambulance will send four large cars to No. 12 Field Ambulance before 12 hours on 19th. inst.

(b). Ford Car: O.C. No. 10 Field Ambulance will send a Ford Car to No. 12 Field Ambulance before 12 hours on 19th. inst.

(c). Reserve: The remainder of the cars of Nos. 10 and 11 Field Ambulances will form a reserve from which O.C. No. 12 Field Ambulance may draw in case of necessity.

6. WHEELED STRETCHERS: No. 11 Field Ambulance will send 6 wheeled stretchers to No. 12 Field Ambulance in the large cars detailed in para. 5 (a) above.

7. REGISTRATION: O.C., No. 11 Field Ambulance will be responsible for the registration of all walking wounded passing through his W.W.P. He will submit the usual returns to the A.D.M.S., but will despatch the daily wire direct to all A.D's.M.S. concerned, by 08.30 daily. He will forward the daily wire for 4th. Division and that for the Corps Troops to this office at 08.30 daily.

Colonel,
A.D.M.S. 4th. Division.

Distribution as for R.A.M.C. Order No. 76.

SECRET.   Copy No. 11

4th. DIVISION
R.A.M.C. ORDER NO. 77.

18th. October, 1918.

1. No. 10 Field Ambulance will move from QUEANT to the HOPITAL GENERAL, No. 21 Rue du Petit Seminaire, CAMBRAI on 19th. inst. Move to start at 08.00 hours.

2. Nine lorries will call at H.Q. of 10th. Field Ambulance at QUEANT at 08.00 hours, to convey personnel and stores, including dump of stretchers and blankets, to the new area.
   Transport will move independently by march route. Main roads to be avoided as far as possible.

3. No. 10 Field Ambulance will take over a section of the HOPITAL GENERAL, and remain at the disposal of O.C., No. 35 Field Ambulance until further orders, less Bearer Divn.

4. Completion of move to be reported to office of A.D.M.S. by D.R.

5. Field Ambulances acknowledge.

                                                    Colonel,
Issued at 15.30 hours.   A.D.M.S. 4th. Division.

Distribution: No. 1 to D.D.M.S. XXII Corps.
                     2   10th. Field Ambulance.
                     3   11th. Field Ambulance.
                     4   12th. Field Ambulance.
                     5   4th. Division.
                     6   4th. Division 'A/Q'.
                     7   D.A.D.V.S. 4th. Division.
                     8   D.A.P.M. 4th. Division.
                     9   4th. Div. Train.
                    10   4th. Div. Signals.
                    11,12 Diary.
                    13   File.

SECRET.   Copy No. 36

4th. DIVISION

R.A.M.C. ORDER NO. 78

Map Refs: Sheets 51a, 57b.   20th. October, 1918.

      Medical Posts of XXIInd. Corps are moving to new positions on 21st. inst.

1.   No. 10 Field Ambulance will move by march route at 07.00 hours on 21st. inst. from CAMBRAI to NAVES.
      There they will take over the present H.Q. of No. 12 Field Ambulance, at T.23.a.7.2., and open those H.Q. as the 4th. Divisional Main Dressing Station.
      M.D.S. to be open and receiving casualties from No. 12 Field Ambulance by 10.00 hours.
      Advance Party of No. 10 Field Ambulance to be at T.23.a.7.2. with enough equipment to start the M.D.S., by 08.00 hours on 21st. inst.

2.   No. 11 Field Ambulance will close the Walking Wounded Collecting Post at ESCAUDOEUVRES at 23.00 hours on 20th. inst.
      The W.W.C.P. will be re-opened by No. 11 Field Ambulance at billets Nos. 5 and 6, IWUY, at 10.00 hours on 21st. inst.
      No. 11 Field Ambulance will move by march route from their present location to IWUY.
      Advance Party to be at new position by 08.00 hours on 21st. inst.

3.   No. 12 Field Ambulance will move forward their H.Q. from NAVES to VILLERS EN CAUCHIE. Equipment will be carried there on transport, which will be parked under suitable cover in or near the village. All transport must be invisible from the air. Horses may be picketed with those of No. 10 Field Ambulance at NAVES, by arrangement with O.C. No. 10 Field Ambulance.
      Move of No. 12 Field Ambulance to be complete by 10.00 hours on 21st. inst.

4.   Completion of all moves to be reported to office of A.D.M.S. with locations of all H.Q. and Posts.

5.   Field Ambulances acknowledge.

                                                         Major,

Issued at 22.00 hours.   for A.D.M.S. 4th. Division.
U.
                                                  / Distribution.

Distribution:-

No.	1	to	D.D.M.S. XXII Corps.
	2		A.D.M.S. 49th. Division.
	3		A.D.M.S. 51st. Division.
	4		No. 10 Field Ambulance.
	5		No. 11 Field Ambulance.
	6		No. 12 Field Ambulance.
	7		4th. Division.
	8		4th. Division 'A/Q'.
	9		10th. Infantry Brigade.
	10		11th. Infantry Brigade.
	11		12th. Infantry Brigade.
	12		C.R.A. 4th. Division.
	13		C.R.E. 4th. Division.
	14		4th. Div. Signals.
	15		4th. Div. Train.
	16		D.A.D.V.S. 4th. Division.
	17		D.A.P.M. 4th. Division.
	18		4th. Bn. M.G.Corps.
	19		42 M.A.C.
	20-35		Regtl. M.O's.
	36,37.		Diary.
	38		File.

SECRET.

4th. DIVISION.

MEDICAL ARRANGEMENTS IN CONNECTION WITH R.A.M.C. ORDER 78.

Map Refs: Sheets 51 a, 57 b.

1. **Medical Posts:**

   (a). R.A.P's: Locations follow.

   (b). A.D.Stn: VILLERS EN CAUCHIE.(U.5.d.3.2.).

   (c). C.W.W.C.P.: IWUY.

   (d). 4th. Div. M.D.S.: NAVES. (T.23.a.7.2.).

2. **Evacuation: Lying Wounded:**

   (a). From Right Sector: From R.A.P's. by hand, wheeled stretcher and Ford Car to A.D.S., U.5.d.3.2. Thence M.D.S. in cars.
   From Left Sector: From R.A.P's. by hand carriage and Ford Car to M.D.Stn., T.23.a.7.2. direct.
   From M.D.S.: To C.C.Stn. in M.A.C. cars of No. 42 M.A.C.

   (b). Walking Wounded: By returning transport and lorries to IWUY, by following roads:-

   AVESNES LE SEC - IWUY.   AVESNES LE SEC - VILLERS EN CAUCHIE.
   VILLERS EN CAUCHIE - NAVES to U.10.b. Thence to IWUY. Detachment of No. 11 Field Amboo. at Cross-Roads to direct walking wounded to IWUY.
   From W.W.C.P., IWUY, to 30 C.C.S., CAMBRAI, in cars of 42 M.A.C.

3. **Sick:** Sick will be sent to the nearest M.O. in the case of Units without a M.O. All cases which are for hospital will be sent to No. 10 Field Ambulance at T.23.a.7.2., or to No. 11 Field Ambulance, IWUY, for evacuation to Corps Collecting Station for sick. This Unit will be at the CONVENT, ESCAUDOEUVRE.

4. **Stretchers & Blankets:** The Corps Dump of stretchers and blankets is at the CONVENT, ESCAUDOEUVRES. Field Ambulances may draw on this dump after reference to the A.D.M.S.

5. **Registration and Returns:**

   (a). Walking Wounded Post: No registration of walking wounded will be carried out at this Post. Registration will be done at 30 C.C.Stn. Clerks will be left there.
   O.C. No. 11 Field Ambulance will however, keep a record of the cases passing through this Post, belonging to the 4th. Division. A nominal roll of officers and numbers of other ranks will be made out for the following periods, and these returns will be collected by D.R. from this office:-

   8 a.m. till 2 p.m.   8 p.m. till 8 a.m.
   2 p.m. till 8 p.m.

/b.

-2-

(b). 4th. Div. Main Dressing Stn: Registration of lying cases will be carried out at No. 10 Field Ambulance. Usual returns and reports will be rendered to this office. In addition, returns for the same periods as those rendered under para. (a) above, will be forwarded to the office of the A.D.M.S. by No. 10 Field Ambulance. Numbers of Other Ranks are by Units.

(c). Sick: A. & D. Books will not be kept by Field Ambulances of this Division. A Daily State will however be rendered to the office of the A.D.M.S. by Nos. 10 and 11 Field Ambulances, showing the numbers of cases sent to the Corps Collecting Station for Sick. Period, 8 a.m. till 8 a.m.

[signature]

Major,
for A.D.M.S. 4th. Division.

20-10-18.
U.

Distribution as for R.A.M.C. Order No. 78.

SECRET.

ADDENDUM NO. 1

to

4th. DIVISION MEDICAL ARRANGEMENTS IN CONNECTION WITH R.A.M.C. ORDER 78.

Sheet 51a.

Ref. para. 1(a) of Medical Arrangements above:

The following are the present locations of R.A.P's:-

Right Sector.	Left Sector.
P.32.b.4.5.	P.19.b.1.9.
P.32.b.4.6.	O.24.b.8.7.(Two).
U.6.d.1.6.	

[signature] Major
for Colonel,
A.D.M.S. 4th. Division.

21-10-18.
U.

Distribution as before.

SECRET.   A.D.M.S. 4th. Division No. 55/296/3.

4th. DIVISION

NO.2 PROVISIONAL MEDICAL ARRANGEMENTS.

(Issued in Conjunction with 4th. Division No. G.A.4/109.)

Map. Refs: 51a, 57b, 57c.

The rôle of the XXII Corps is to protect the left flank of the Third Army.

The 4th. Division may be ordered to support the 49th. and 51st. Divisions at short notice.

In this eventuality, the 4th. Division will occupy the following front, from which it will be prepared to counter-attack, the object being to regain the present front lines of the 49th. and 51st. Divisions:-

Along high ground about U.10.d. - U.9.central - U.2.central - across the front of IWUY about O.31.central - O.30.central - to the railway (inc.) about O.30.a.4.0.

The 10th. Infantry Brigade will be on the right, and the 11th. Infantry Brigade on the left.

Boundaries as follow:-

(a). Between 4th. Divn. and Left Divn. of XVII Corps:

    CAMBRAI - SAULZOIR road.

(b). Between 10th. and 11th. Brigades:

    Railway from T.18.a.0.0. to N.36.d.2.0. (inc.to 10th. Bde.) thence IWUY - AVESNES LE SEC road to O.22.central (inc. to 10th. Inf.Bde.) - thence line to O.12.central.

(c). Between 4th. Divn. and Right Divn. Can. Corps:

    CANAL DE L'ESCAUT exc. to N.28.d.2.0. - thence line to Railway at N.24.a.0.0. - thence N. along railway inc. to its junction with CANAL DE L'ESCAUT.

Divisional Headquarters, and H.Q. 10th. Inf. Bde. will remain in present positions.

1. EVACUATION: No. 12 Field Ambulance will be responsible for the evacuation of casualties from 10th. Inf. Bde. Sector, and No. 11 Field Ambulance from 11th. Inf. Bde. Sector.

2. POSTS: O's.C. Nos. 11 and 12 Field Ambulances will select suitable sites for A.D.Stns. in their respective Bde. Sectors. They will establish Relay and Bearer Posts to ensure evacuation of casualties in shortest time. Location of all Posts will be wired to A.D.M.S. as soon as established or moved. Constant touch will be maintained with R.A.P's. and Bde. H.Q.

3. PERSONNEL: For the purposes of evacuation, each of the above Field Ambulances will send forward 2 Bearer Sub-Divisions with the necessary Officers.

    One Tent-Sub-Division with Officers will also be sent forward to establish the A.D.Stn. of each Field Ambulance.

4. TRANSPORT: Field Ambulances will utilize their own cars for purposes of evacuation from the line. The cars of No. 10 Field Ambulance will be brought forward if necessary, and placed at the disposal of Nos. 11 and 12 Field Ambulances.

5. HEADQUARTERS: The H.Q. of the 11th. and 12th. Field Ambulances will remain in their present locations.

6. ARRANGEMENTS: All "Back" arrangements will be as laid down in "Provisional Medical Arrangements No. 1", amended on 15th. October, 1918.

7. CODE WORD: On receipt of the code word "STROKE THREE", Nos. 11 and 12 Field Ambulances will at once proceed to function in accordance with the above instructions.

8. Field Ambulances acknowledge.

Major,
for A.D.M.S. 4th. Division.

Copies to:— D.D.M.S. XXII Corps.
No. 10 Field Ambulance.
No. 11 Field Ambulance.
No. 12 Field Ambulance.
A.D.M.S. 49th. Division.
A.D.M.S. 51st. Division.
4th. Division.
4th. Division 'A/Q'.
10th. Infantry Brigade.
11th. Infantry Brigade.
12th. Infantry Brigade.
C.R.E. 4th. Division.
4th. Bn. M.G. Corps.
21st. W. Yorks. R.(P).

SECRET.   A.D.M.S. 4th. Division No. 55/296/1.

4th. DIVISION

NO.1 PROVISIONAL MEDICAL ARRANGEMENTS.

In the event of the Division going into action, the following provisional Medical Arrangements will come into force:

1. EVACUATION: From the forward area to Main Dressing Stations, ESCAUDOEUVRES. From M.D.S's. to Corps Main Dressing Station, QUEANT, in M.A.C. Cars.

    From 14th. inst. a light railway will run from ESCAUDOEUVRES to QUEANT, and will convey walking wounded only.

    A broad guage railway runs from QUEANT to MERCATEL C.C.S. Group.

2. CAS. CLG. STNS.: Nos. 1, 22, 30, 33 C.C.Stns. All at MERCATEL. these will receive all cases.

3. SPECIAL CASES: Self-Inflicted.   )
                    "N.Y.D. 'N'".   ) To receiving C.C.S. for
                    Ear, Throat, Nose.   ) No. 12 Sty. Hpl.
                    Infectious.   )

                    Eye Cases.   12 Sty.Hpl. on Tuesdays
                                              and Wednesdays. URGENT
                                              cases only.

4. (a). ANTI-TETANIC SERUM: Will be given at the A.D.S. of the Ambulances in line. "T" will be marked in indelible ink on the left wrist as hitherto.

    (b). MORPHIA: After dose of Morphia has been given, "M" will be marked on forehead in indelible ink, and time and amount of dose noted on tally or Field Medical Card.

    (c). FIELD MED. CARD: Will be made out at the A.D.S. Full particulars will invariably be entered on card, including any information which it is necessary to transfer from tally.

5. STRETCHERS & BLANKETS: Stretchers and blankets will be available at the C.M.D.S. Application for these must be made to the A.D.M.S. by Ambulance Commanders, and they will be drawn from the C.M.D.S. after authority, in returning M.A.C. cars.

6. SICK DETENTION: Nos. 11 and 12 Field Ambulances will arrange to accommodate sick cases at their present Headquarters. Only such cases as are likely to be fit in 4 days will be retained. Other sick to C.M.D.S. as usual. Only sick which are detained will be recorded by Field Ambulances. Those sent to the C.M.D.S. will be registered there.

7. **REGISTRATION:** Each Division in line has a Divisional Main Dressing Station. The wounded and sick of the Division concerned are registered there.

The only casualties registered in Field Ambulances as such will be as shown in para. 6; that is, detained cases.

No. 10 Field Ambulance will register other sick sent them by Field Ambulances of this Division.

All direct admissions from other Units, or local sick will also be registered by 10 Field Ambulance.

No. 10 Field Ambulance will render to this office, the daily wire, which will embody <u>direct</u> admissions of the Division, and Corps Troops. Separate wires will be forwarded for Divisional and Corps Troops. Army Troops will be shown on the Corps Troops wire.

No. 10, 11, 12 Field Ambulances will continue to render routine returns and states in connection with sick and wounded. Direct admissions only will figure on these returns, unless the returns are laid down as applying to transfers.

NOTE: Paras. 2,3,6 and 7 above will come into force at once.

[signature]
Colonel,
A.D.M.S. 4th. Division.

14th. October, 1918.
U.

Copies to :—
D.D.M.S. XXII Corps.
A.D's.M.S. Flank Divisions.
4th. Division.
4th. Division 'A/Q'.
Field Ambulances.
R.M.O's.
Div. Train.
4th. Bn. M.G.C.

SECRET.   Copy No. 29

4th. DIVISION

R.A.M.C. ORDER NO. 75.

(In conjunction with 4th. Division Order No.165, dated 12-10-18).

Map Refs: Sheets 51a, 51b, 57b, 57c.   12th. October, 18.

    The 4th. (British) Division will move on 13th. October to the area between R.ERCLIN - CANAL DE L'ESCAUT - CAMBRAI - SAULZOIR Road.

    The Western limit of this area will be the road from A.11.a.7.6. to PONT ROUGE Railway Bridge at A.4.b.0.4.

1. **MOVES:** Nos. 11 and 12 Field Ambulances will move to the new area under orders from the 11th. and 12th. Infantry Brigades respectively. Accommodation is being reserved in the new area for these Units, by Brigades concerned.

2.   Arrival in the new area to be notified immediately to the Office of the A.D.M.S.

3.   No. 10 Field Ambulance will remain at QUEANT, and function as XXIInd. Corps Main Dressing Station.

4.   Field Ambulances acknowledge.

                                                                       Major,
Issued at 22.30 hours.   for A.D.M.S. 4th. Division.

Distribution:- 1 to D.D.M.S. XXII Corps.
                2   No. 10 Field Ambulance.
                3   No. 11 Field Ambulance.
                4   No. 12 Field Ambulance.
                5   4th. Division.
                6   4th. Division 'A/Q'.
                7   10th. Infantry Brigade.
                8   11th. Infantry Brigade.
                9   12th. Infantry Brigade.
              10   C.R.A. 4th. Division.
              11   C.R.E. 4th. Division.
              12   4th. Div. Signals.
              13   4th. Div. Train.
          14-28   R.M.O's.
          29,30   Diary.
              31   File.

S E C R E T.	Copy No. 36

4th. DIVISION

MEDICAL ARRANGEMENTS IN CONNECTION WITH 4th. DIVISION ORDER NO.169.

Map Refs: Sheets 51a, 57b.	23rd. October, 1918.

1. POSITIONS OF MEDICAL POSTS:

   (a). R.A.P's: Right Sector.   Left Sector.

                         P.27.c.8.5.   P.19.a.15.50.
                         P.27.c.2.0.   P.13.c.3.5.
                         P.32.b.4.2.   P.13.a.80.15.

   (b). Car Posts: P.13.a.9.2.
                                P.13.c.5.7.

   (c). A.D.Stn.:   SAULZOIR. P.27.c.2.2.

   (d). Walking Wd. Lorry Post: U.5.d.3.2.

   (e). W.W.C.P.:   IWUY. N.35.d.3.1.

   (f). Div. M.D.Stn: NAVES. T.23.a.7.2.

2. EVACUATION:

   (a). Lying Wounded: From R.A.P's. by hand carriage, wheeled stretcher and Ford Car to the A.D.Stn.
       Thence to the Div. M.D.S. at NAVES by Field Ambulance cars. From M.D.S. to C.C.S. in M.A.C. cars.

   (b). Walking Wounded: From R.A.P's. along following roads:

     (i). SAULZOIR - VILLERS EN CAUCHIE, and HASPRES - VILLERS EN CAUCHIE to W.W.Lorry Post at U.5.d.3.2. Thence to W.W.C.P. IWUY, in lorries.

     (ii). HASPRES - AVESNES LE SEC and AVESNES LE SEC - IWUY to IWUY.

       From IWUY to 50 C.C.Stn. in Lorries and Busses of 42 M.A.C.

   (c). Sick: Will be directed to report to No. 11 Field Ambulance at IWUY or No. 10 Field Ambulance at NAVES. Thence to C.R.S. or C.C.S. CAMBRAI.

3. BLANKETS & STRETCHERS: Small dumps have been made in the vicinity of Car Posts and R.A.P's. on which R.M.O's may call. Field Ambulances may call on the Corps Dump through the A.D.M.S.

4. REGISTRATION:

   (a). No. 12 Field Ambulance will do no registration.

   (b). No. 10 Field Ambulance will register all sick and wounded passing through that Unit and transferred to C.R.S. or C.C.S. Daily State and usual returns to be rendered to A.D.M.S., together with Operation Casualty Wire as at present.

   (c). No. 11 Field Ambulance will register sick passed through to C.R.S. or C.C.S. and will submit Daily State and Casualty Wire as in (b) above.
   No. 11 Field Ambulance will not however, keep an A.&.D. Book of wounded, the registration thereof being carried out at the Corps W.W.C.C.S.
   Returns and reports regarding sick to be rendered to this office as usual.

5. A.T.S.: A.T.S. will be administered at the M.D.S. but not at the W.W.C.P.

6. Field Medical Cards: F.M.C. will be made out at the M.D.S. and W.W.C.P.

7. Field Ambulances acknowledge.

Issued at 19.00 hours.
U.

F. Fletcher
Major,
for A.D.M.S. 4th. Division.

Copies to all concerned.

SECRET.   Copy No. 32

4th. DIVISION.
R.A.M.C. ORDER NO. 80.

Map Refs: 51a.   27th. October, 1918.

1. No. 10 Field Ambulance will close the Divisional Main Dressing Station at T.23.a.7.2. at 10.00 hours on 28th. inst., and re-open it at VILLERS EN CAUCHIE, U.5.d.3.2., at the same hour.

2. Completion of move to be reported to A.D.M.S.

                                                        Major,
Issued at 7.30.p.m.   for A.D.M.S. 4th. Division.
U.

Distribution:-

    Copy No. 1   to D.D.M.S. XXII Corps.
              2   A.D.M.S. 51st. Division.
              3   No. 10 Field Ambulance.
              4   No. 11 Field Ambulance.
              5   No. 12 Field Ambulance.
              6   4th. Division.
              7   4th. Division "A/Q".
              8   10th. Infantry Brigade.
              9   11th. Infantry Brigade.
             10   12th. Infantry Brigade.
             11   C.R.A. 4th. Division.
             12   C.R.E. 4th. Division.
             13   D.A.D.V.S. 4th. Division.
             14   D.A.P.M. 4th. Division.
             15   4th. Divisional Train.
             16   4th. Div. Signal Coy.
          17-31   Regtl. M.O's.
          32,33   Diary.
             34   File.

MEDICAL

confidential 9 A 51

CONFIDENTIAL
Nov. 1918

War Diary
of
ADMS 4th Division

from
1-11-18 to 30-11-18

COMMITTEE FOR THE
MEDICAL HISTORY OF THE WAR
10 JAN 1919
Date

Army Form C. 2118.

WAR DIARY
or
INTELLIGENCE SUMMARY.
(Erase heading not required.)

Place	Date	Hour	Summary of Events and Information	Remarks and references to Appendices
AVESNES LE SEC.	1.11.18.		4th Division attacked this morning at 5.15. Attack successful at first, but after all objectives had been gained heavy counter attacks threw us out of the village of PRESEAU. 1st Rifle Brigade suffering severe casualties in the process. Battlefield cleared in the afternoon. 200 Shelter Cases passing through the ADS. Camp functioned smoothly. By 2 P.M. 600 walking w. had passed through. Capt P.G. Leeman RAMC, 12th Field Ambulance wounded leg. ADsMs visited 12 Field Ambulance CCWP & MDS	A
HASPRES	2.11.18.		ADMS office moved from AVESNES LE SEC to HASPRES. 4th Division attacked this morning to capture PRESEAU. Operation completely successful. 5 Guns & 3 Trench Tanks captured & held as over 600 Prisoners. RAMC order no 81 issued (re relief) ADMS & DADMS visited CWP this morning. Casualties in 2 days operation very light. Lieut. P.R. Shannon (11th FA) died of wounds.	
AVESNES LE SEC.	3.11.18.		ADMS office moved from HASPRES to AVESNES LE SEC. The relief of the division by the 11th Division complete by 10 A.M. this morning. Total Casualties passed through Med. Units since 20.10.18. Offs wounded 65 OR wounded 1395 Total 1460. P of W. Offs 15 OR 247 Total 262. DADMS visited DRS. ADMS visited 10th FA.	
"	4.11.18.		ADMS visited 10th Fd B^tt at VILLERS-EN-CAUCHIE. ADMS attended funeral of Lieut. P.R. SHANNON at VILLERS-EN-CAUCHIE, & inspected billets there and at HASPRES.	B
"	5.11.18.		Division warned that a move is near. RAMC order No 82 issued (Move of 11 Fds Ambulances) 10 FA & 12 FA warned to move with their respective Brigades.	
"	6.11.18		No 10 Field Ambulance moved from VILLERS EN CAUCHIE to PRESEAU. No 11 FA moved DRS from ESCAUDOEUVRES to HASPRES. No 12 FA from SAULZOIR to ARTRES.	

Army Form C. 2118.

WAR DIARY
or
INTELLIGENCE SUMMARY.
(Erase heading not required.)

Place	Date	Hour	Summary of Events and Information	Remarks and references to Appendices
MESNES LE SEC	7.11.18		ADMS visited No 10 Field Ambulance. All Ambulances were established at their new locations by 18.00 hrs 6.11.18. Ceremonial Parade at VALENCIENNES.	
"	8.11.18		DADMS visited 10th Field Ambulance at PRESEAU. also 10th Brigade HQre. Town in a very unsanitary condition. Several dead Germans lying about.	
"	9.11.18		ADMS visited 11th Field Ambulance.	
"	10.11.18		ADMS & DADMS visited 12th Field Ambulance. RAMC order No 83 issued.	
PRESEAU	11.11.18		ADMS office closed at MESNES LE SEC. and opened again at PRESEAU. ADMS visited 12 F.A.	
"	12.11.18.		ADMS visited 10 Field Ambulance and 11 Field Ambulance. DADMS visited 11 F.A.	
"	13.11.18		ADMS visited 11 Field Ambulance and attended GOC's Conference in afternoon. ADMS also visited DDMS in morning. DADMS visited 10 Field Ambulance. Lieut SHEARER.A. joined 12.11.18 for duty and was posted to 12 Field Ambulance.	C
"	14.11.18		DADMS visited 11 Field Ambulance and 1st Som Light Infantry.	
"	15.11.18		DADMS visited 10 Field Ambulance, also 2nd Duke of Wellington's Regt and 1st Royal Warwickshire Regt. Billets fair. Excellent work has been done in spite of the filthiness of the Village. Grease traps few in number, but latrines good. Regtl Pioneers working at Cookhouses and latrines. Billets rather overcrowded.	

WAR DIARY
INTELLIGENCE SUMMARY

Army Form C. 2118.

Instructions regarding War Diaries and Intelligence Summaries are contained in F. S. Regs., Part II. and the Staff Manual respectively. Title pages will be prepared in manuscript.

(Erase heading not required.)

Place	Date	Hour	Summary of Events and Information	Remarks and references to Appendices
PRESEAU	16.11.18.		DADMS visited 2nd Seaforth Highlanders in Company with M.O. Billets good and extremely tidy. No-foot lying about. Rations of high standard system, in fair condition. Water carts & cookers excellent. Inconveniences in course of construction. Food varied and of good quality. Billets slightly overcrowded owing to return of inmates. ADMS fractured ceremonial parade with No 10 Field Ambulance.	
"	17.11.18.		ADMS visited first to CURGIES and 1st Hampshires. Billets clean but ill-ventilated and damp. DADMS visited 10th Field Ambulance.	
"	18.11.18.		Trial Ceremonial parade of all three Field Ambulances this morning. (In Thurston)	
"	19.11.18		Div HQ. including ADMS office moved today from PRESEAU to VALENCIENNES. No 10 Field Ambulance moving from PRESEAU to VALENCIENNES and No 12 Field Ambulance from ARTRES to ST. SAULVE. DADMS visited 10th Inf. Bde. in VINCENT BARRACKS VALENCIENNES and found them in a filthy and insanitary condition. No latrine accommodation and tons of manure and filth left lying about. Measures suggested and steps taken to improve the condition. CAPT SHEARER evacuated to CCS. Influenza.	
VALENCIENNES	20.11.18.		Divisional Parade & Church past held at SAULTAIN this morning. All Field Ambulances represented. DADMS visited 10th Bde. again this afternoon and found conditions much improved. 72 hrs of manure removed before 12 noon.	

Army Form C. 2118.

WAR DIARY
INTELLIGENCE SUMMARY.
(Erase heading not required.)

Instructions regarding War Diaries and Intelligence Summaries are contained in F. S. Regs., Part II. and the Staff Manual respectively. Title pages will be prepared in manuscript.

Place	Date	Hour	Summary of Events and Information	Remarks and references to Appendices
VALENCIENNES	21.11.18.		ADMS visited and inspected 12th Field Ambulance, No 4 Coy ASC Div Train also the Base Reft. No 57 CCS was also visited. In afternoon ADMS visited No 10 Field Ambulance. DADMS visited Div. Railheads at BOUCHAIN and 4th Div. Reception Camp. Keit Sanitation has been left in a very bad state. Nearly 50 tons of liquid excreta having been left behind by the Germans. No attempt has since been made to remove them. The i/c has done Excellent work, but much still remains to be done. O.C. No 8 San Sec has the matter in hand.	
"	22.11.18.		ADMS and DADMS visited and inspected Barracks in VALENCIENNES occupied by 12 & 10th Inf. Bde. Billets clean and tidy, but although much has been done in the way of cleaning up, much repair still remains. Latrines of a proper type are being erected. Bathing facilities are also available. In afternoon DADMS inspected Nos 10 & 11 Field Ambulances. In the former case with the ADMS 4th Division. Everything satisfactory.	
"	23.11.18.		ADMS visited DMS' Office, 1st Army. DADMS visited in morning 2nd D'Northumbrian Fd Amb. In afternoon DADMS visited No 8 Sanitary Section at ESCAUDOEUVRES.	
"	24.11.18		ADMS visited 12 Field Ambulance + 10th Rifle with DADMS (Man.) 1st Army in afternoon. + 12th Brigade. DADMS visited 10 Field Ambulance.	
"	25.11.18.		DDMS Conference in morning. DADMS inspected Sanitation of Rifle Range + Found Scenery very Satisfactory. 12 Field Ambulance has also visited at ST SAULVE.	

SECRET.   Copy No. 34

4th. DIVISION

R.A.M.C. ORDER NO. 81.

Map. Refs: Sheet 51a.   2nd. November, 1918.

The 4th. Division is being relieved in the line by the 11th. Division, on the 2nd. and night 2/3rd. November, 1918.

1. **RELIEFS:**

   (a). No. 12 Field Ambulance will hand over all forward posts to No. 33 Field Ambulance on night 2/3rd. Nov. Relief to be completed by 05.00 hours on 3rd. Nov.
   On completion of relief, No. 12 Field Ambulance will be stationed at SAULZOIR, P.32.c.2.2, and will be responsible for collection of the sick of the 10th. Inf. Bde. Group at SAULZOIR.

   (b). No. 10 Field Ambulance will close the Div. M.D.S. at 05.00 hours on 3rd. inst., after which that unit will not receive wounded.
   The M.A.C. cars will be directed to No. 35 Field Ambulance at HASPRES, which will be the M.D.S. of 11th. Division. On their last journey up, the M.A.C. cars will convey all extra equipment to No. 35 Field Ambulance.
   No. 10 Field Ambulance will, after closing M.D.S., remain at VILLERS EN CAUCHIES, & collect sick of the Groups at VILLERS & HASPRES.
   The Div. Rest Station will remain open there, until such time as arrangements are made for the transfer of the patients to No. 11 Field Ambulance at ESCAUDOEUVRES.

   (c). No. 11 Field Ambulance will hand over the Corps W.W.P. at HASPRES to No. 34 Field Ambulance. The two clerks of 4th. Division will remain at the Post until no further casualties of 4th. Division arrive to be registered. They will then return to their Unit.
   No. 11 Field Ambulance will take over the CONVENT, ESCAUDOEUVRES, as 4th. Divisional Rest Station, from No. 34 Field Ambulance.
   Advance party to proceed to-night.
   Reliefs to be completed at 10.00 hours on 3rd. inst.

2. **STORES:** All stores and equipment above that authorised in W.E. and G.R.O. will be handed over to incoming or relieving Units. Receipts will be obtained, and forwarded to this office in duplicate.

3. **COMPLETION OF RELIEFS & MOVES** to be reported to this office.

4. **OFFICE OF A.D.M.S.** 4th. Division will close at HASPRES at 10.00 hours on 3rd. Nov. and re-open at AVESNES LE SEC at the same hour.

5. **RETURN OF TRANSPORT, EQUIPMENT & PERSONNEL** will be arranged between Ambulance Commanders concerned.

                                                   Major,
Issued at 09.30 hours.   for A.D.M.S. 4th. Division.
U.

Distribution:-

Copy No.	1 to	D.D.M.S. XXII Corps.
	2	A.D.M.S. 11th. Division.
	3	A.D.M.S. 49th. Division.
	4	A.D.M.S. 61st. Division.
	5	No. 10 Field Ambulance.
	6	No. 11 Field Ambulance.
	7	No. 12 Field Ambulance.
	8	4th. Division.
	9	4th. Division "A/Q".
	10	10th. Infantry Brigade.
	11	11th. Infantry Brigade.
	12	12th. Infantry Brigade.
	13	C.R.A. 4th. Division.
	14	C.R.E. 4th. Division.
	15	D.A.D.V.S. 4th. Division.
	16	D.A.P.M. 4th. Division.
	17	4th. Divisional Train.
	18	4th. Signal Company.
	19-33	Regimental Medical Officers.
	34,35	Diary.
	36	File.

SECRET.   Copy No. 32

4th. DIVISION.

R.A.M.C. ORDER NO. 82.

Map Refs: Sheet 51a.   5th. November, 1918.

1. No. 11 Field Ambulance will close the 4th. Divisional Rest Station at the CONVENT, ESCAUDOEUVRES, on 6th. November, and re-open it at HASPRES on the same date, at P.19.a.2,3.

2. Personnel will move by march route.
   Arrival of Unit in new location will be notified to A.D.M.S.
   No restrictions as to time of move.
   M.A.C. Cars will convey patients of 4th. Division to new location, and cars of Nos. 10 and 12 will assist by arrangement between O's.C. concerned.
   Sick of Other Formations than 4th. Division will be sent to 22 C.C.S., (Corps Rest Station).

3. Nos. 10 and 12 Field Ambulances will not send any sick to No. 11 Field Ambulance until 7th. inst.

4. No. 11 Field Ambulance will leave a guard behind to look after the Corps Dump at the CONVENT. This Dump will be moved forward in M.A.C. cars to HASPRES, as soon as No. 11 Field Ambulance is established there. O.C., No. 11 Field Ambulance will notify this office when the Dump has been completely moved forward.

Issued at 19.00 hours.   Major,
                                          for A.D.M.S. 4th. Division.

Distribution:

    Copy No. 1   to   D.D.M.S. XXII Corps.
              2   No. 10 Field Ambulance.
              3   No. 11 Field Ambulance.
              4   No. 12 Field Ambulance.
              5   4th. Division.
              6   4th. Division "A/Q".
              7   10th. Infantry Brigade.
              8   11th. Infantry Brigade.
              9   12th. Infantry Brigade.
             10   C.R.A. 4th. Division.
             11,   C.R.E. 4th. Division.
             12   D.A.D.V.S. 4th. Division.
             13   D.A.P.M. 4th. Division.
             14   4th. Divisional Train.
             15   4th. Signal Company.
          16-30   Regtl. M.O's.
          31,32   Diary.
             33   File.

SECRET.   Copy No. 33

4th. DIVISION

R.A.M.C. ORDER NO. 83.

Map Refs: Sheet 51a.   10th. November, 1918.

The 11th. Infantry Brigade Group is moving on 11th. inst. to the area CURGIES – SAULTAIN.

1. No. 11 Field Ambulance will move up from HASPRES to CURGIES or SAULTAIN with the 11th. Brigade, on 11th. and 12th. November.

2. O.C., No. 11 Field Ambulance will arrange direct with the Staff Captain, 11th. Brigade, for billets for the 11th. Field Ambulance, and the sick in the Divisional Rest Station.

3. A suitable proportion of the transport and personnel of No. 11 Field Ambulance will move forward to the new location on 11th. inst., and prepare the accommodation there for the reception of the patients.
   These will be moved to the new location during the afternoon of 11th. inst. and on 12th. inst.
   When the last of the patients have been moved forward, the remainder of the personnel and transport of No. 11 Field Ambulance will move forward also.
   A guard of 1 N.C.O. and 2 men will be left with the Corps Dump at HASPRES.

4. Completion of move will be notified to A.D.M.S. 4th. Division.

5. O.C., No. 11 Field Ambulance will arrange to hold in readiness, two horsed ambulance wagons to march in rear of 11th. Brigade should the Staff Captain demand them.
   Sick of the 11th. Brigade in the new area will be collected by No. 11 Field Ambulance.

6. Office of A.D.M.S. 4th. Division closes at 10.00 on 11th. inst. at AVESNES LE SEC, and re-opens at PRESEAU at the same hour.

7. Field Ambulances acknowledge.

                                            Faichnie
                                            Colonel,
                                    A.D.M.S. 4th. Division.

Issued at 19.00 hours.
U.

/Distribution.

Distribution:-

Copy No.		
1	to	D.D.M.S. XXII Corps.
2		No. 10 Field Ambulance.
3		No. 11 Field Ambulance.
4		No. 12 Field Ambulance.
5		4th. Division.
6		4th. Division "A/Q".
7		10th. Infantry Brigade.
8		11th. Infantry Brigade.
9		12th. Infantry Brigade.
10		C.R.A. 4th. Division.
11		C.R.E. 4th. Division.
12		D.A.D.V.S. 4th. Division.
13		D.A.P.M. 4th. Division.
14		4th. Divisional Train.
15		4th. Signal Company.
16-30		Regtl. M.O's.
31		42nd. W.A.C.
32		Dental Surgeon, 22 C.C.Stn.
33,34		Diary.
35		File.

Army Form C. 2118.

WAR DIARY
or
INTELLIGENCE SUMMARY.
(Erase heading not required.)

Instructions regarding War Diaries and Intelligence Summaries are contained in F. S. Regs., Part II. and the Staff Manual respectively. Title pages will be prepared in manuscript.

Place	Date	Hour	Summary of Events and Information	Remarks and references to Appendices
VM-ERQUENNES	1.12.16		ADMS visited 10th Infantry Brigade and 1st Royal Warwickshire Regt. In afternoon ADMS + DADMS visited 11th Field Ambulance and the 1st Rifle Brigade.	
"	2.12.16		ADMS Spent day in BINCHE took walk OC 11 F.A. inspecting site for DRS. DADMS visits 1st E Machine Gun Batt.	
"	3.12.16		ADMS visited 10 Field Ambulance, also 1st Hants + 1st Somerset L.I.	
"	4.12.16		ADMS visited 10th R.F.C in VINCENT BARRACKS, also M.G. R.E. in RONZIER BARRACKS. DADMS visited 2nd Iron Regt. 2nd Lan. Fusiliers, & 1st King's Own Regt.	
"	5.12.16		ADMS visited 10th Brigade and 10th Field Ambulance. Lt Col J.G. McCUTCHEON departs this day for duty in U.K. and is struck off the strength. DADMS visited 12 Field Ambulance and Div. Reception Camp.	
"	6.12.16		ADMS visited 11th Field Ambulance. DADMS visited 4th Div. Train and 4th Batt. M.G. Corp.	
"	7.12.16		DADMS inspected 11th Field Ambulance at CURGIES also 1st Som L.I. & 1st R. Brigade. ADMS visited DMS First Army	
"	8.12.16		DADMS visited 10 Field Ambulance.	

Army Form C. 2118.

WAR DIARY
or
INTELLIGENCE SUMMARY.
(Erase heading not required.)

Instructions regarding War Diaries and Intelligence Summaries are contained in F. S. Regs., Part II. and the Staff Manual respectively. Title pages will be prepared in manuscript.

Place	Date	Hour	Summary of Events and Information	Remarks and references to Appendices
VALENCIENNES	9.12.18		DADMS visited PRESEAN and inspected 21st & York Regt and 1st Hampshire Regt.	
"	10.12.18		BADMS visited 16th Field Ambulance BINCHE & LA LOUVIERE. ADMS visited 16 Field Ambulance and inspected the depôt du Armées in Afternoon. Inspected Machine Gunners at ROZIER BARRACKS. DADMS visited 1st Royal Warwickshire Regt & 2nd Seaforth Highlanders at VINCENT BARRACKS, also the Mobile Veterinary Section at MARLY.	
"	11.12.18		ADMS attended DMS conference with Ambulance Commander. DADMS visited 11 Field Ambulance.	
"	12.12.18		ADMS visited 12th Brigade and 12th Field Ambulance. DADMS visited 10th Brigade → A. Patrns promise of No 11 Field Ambulance to La Louvière and found 12 Field Ambulance DADMS visited DDMS at MONS.	
"	13.12.18		ADMS visited DDMS at MONS. Football to know Cup. RAMC beat 32nd FAR (3-1)	
"	14.12.18		ADMS accompanied DMS to station with a view to selecting site for Civilian Sedan Centre	
"	15.12.18		ADMS and DADMS visited all Field Ambulances.	
"	16.12.18		ADMS visited 10th Brigade at VINCENT BARRACKS. DADMS visited 4th Div. Royal Engineers. 11 Field Ambulance moved to La Louvière area (ref A above)	

Army Form C. 2118.

WAR DIARY
or
INTELLIGENCE SUMMARY.
(Erase heading not required.)

Instructions regarding War Diaries and Intelligence Summaries are contained in F. S. Regs., Part II. and the Staff Manual respectively. Title pages will be prepared in manuscript.

Place	Date	Hour	Summary of Events and Information	Remarks and references to Appendices
VALENCIENNES	17.12.18		DADMS visited 12th Field Ambulance, and 2nd Essex Regiment.	
"	18.12.18		ADMS visited 11th Brigade. DADMS visited 10th Brigade & 1st Royal Warwickshire Regt.	
"	19.12.18		ADMS visited DMS office. DADMS visited 10th Field Ambulance.	
"	20.12.18		ADMS proceeded on 14 days leave to U.K. Lt Col Ahern DSO assuming duties of ADMS	
"	21.12.18		DADMS visited 12th Brigade and 12th Field Ambulance, also Renfrew Field Company.	
"	22.12.18		DADMS visited 9 Field Coy R.E. and Durham Field Coy. also Mob. Vet. Sec.	
"	23.12.18		DADMS visited 11th Brigade, 1st Somersets & 1st Rifle Brigade, in afternoon visited 1st Hampshire Regt at SEBORG.	
"	24.12.18		DADMS visited 10 Field Ambulance and ADMS 11th Division.	
"	26.12.18		DADMS visited 10th Brigade, 1st Warwickshire Regt & 2nd Duke of Wellington in aftn. noon visited 2nd Seaforth Highlanders	
"	27.12.18		DADMS visited inspection 4th Div Sig Coy R.E. & 207 Employment Coy.	
"	28.12.18		DADMS visited 1st King's Own Regt & 2nd Lancashire Fusiliers also 12th Field Ambulance	

Army Form C. 2118.

WAR DIARY
or
INTELLIGENCE SUMMARY.
(Erase heading not required.)

Instructions regarding War Diaries and Intelligence Summaries are contained in F. S. Regs., Part II. and the Staff Manual respectively. Title pages will be prepared in manuscript.

Place	Date	Hour	Summary of Events and Information	Remarks and references to Appendices
VALENCIENNES	29.12.18		ADMS visited 2/5 W. York Regt at PRESEAU. also 11th Brigade.	B
"	30.12.18		DADMS visited 1st Field Ambulance and 1st M G Battn. (ADMS 1/250 round - now.)	
"	31.12.18		DADMS visited 2nd Seaforth Highlanders + 2nd Duke of Wellington Regt.	

M J McIntire
DADMS
Major LE Div

31.12.18.

A.D.M.S. 4th. Division No. 23/33.

O.C.,
No. 11 Field Ambulance.

1. The unit under your command will close at CURGIES on 15th. inst. and move to the new area, occupying the reserved billets for the Divisional Rest Station at LA LOUVIERE, as follows:-

   (a). Transport will move by march route, starting from CURGIES at 10.00 hours on 15th. inst.
   It will stage the night 15/16th. inst. at BOISSU, arrangements for billets there being made with the Burgomaster.

   Transport will proceed to LA LOUVIERE on 16th. inst.

   (b). Seven lorries will call at your present Headquarters on the morning of 16th. inst., to move personnel and stores to LA LOUVIERE. Time at which lorries will call at CURGIES will be notified later.

2. On arrival at LA LOUVIERE, you will proceed to prepare the reserved premises, (particulars of which can be obtained from the Burgomaster) for use as the Divisional Rest Station.
   Indents for material and stores, &c., will be submitted to this office and the B.R.C.S.
   The Divisional Rest Station is to be made as comfortable as circumstances permit.

3. On your arrival in the new area, you will be responsible for the collection of the sick of the Divisional Artillery. The car at present attached to them will be returned to No. 12 Field Ambulance, which Unit will report its return to this office.

4. No. 12 Field Ambulance will take over the collection of your present sick-round from you on 15th. inst. No cases will be sent to your Unit from Nos. 10 and 12 Field Ambulances after 14th. inst.

5. In your new location you will dispose of sick for C.C.Stn. to the nearest C.C.Stn.

6. No. 11 Field Ambulance to acknowledge.

                                        Colonel,
                                        A.D.M.S. 4th. Division.
12th.Decr. 1918.
U.

Copies to all concerned.

A.D.M.S., 4th. Division. No.

O.C.,
No. 10 Field Ambulance.
No. 11 Field Ambulance.
No. 12 Field Ambulance.

The 4th. Division will move to the new area E. of MONS on the 4th., 5th. and 6th. January 1919.

No. 10 Field Ambulance will move with the 10th. Infantry Brigade and 4th. Bn. M.G.C.
No. 12 Field Ambulance will move with the 12th. Infantry Brigade and 21st. West Yorks (P).
The 11th. Infantry Brigade and Divisional H.Q. will move on Jan. 5th.
Details of the move will be arranged direct with Brigades concerned.

On arrival in the new area No. 10 Field Ambulance will be billetted in BINCHE and be responsible for the collection of sick of the 10th. Inf. Brigade, 4th. Bn. M.G.Corps and 4th. Div. Am. Col.
They will establish a small Rest Station at BINCHE for the sick of the above named units.

No. 12 Field Ambulance will proceed to the Billets previously reconnoitred at LA LOUVIERE and will be responsible for the collection of sick of the 12th. Inf. Brigade, 4th. Divisional Engineers and 21st. 2ost Yorks (P).

All cases for hospital will be transferred to :-

No. 11 Field Ambulance who will remain in their present Billets and function as the Divisional Rest Station. They will also be responsible for the collection of sick of the 11th. Inf. Brigade, and 29th. and 32nd. Brigades, R.F.A.

Cases from both Rest Stations, who are not likely to be fit for duty in 14 days will be evacuated to No. 30 Cas.Clg. Stn. LA LOUVIERE.
Returned P.O.W. are to be sent to No. 1 Cas.Clg.Stn. MONS.

M.A.C. No. 42. MONS. Sanitary Section. No. 63. LA LOUVIERE.
Adv.Dep.Med.Stores. MONS.   Mobile Laboratory No. 2 MONS.

Dental arrangements will remain as at present.

Major,
for A.D.M.S., 4th. Division.

30-12-1918.

Copies to all concerned

BEF

4 DIVISION

ADMS

1919 JAN – 1919 FEB

BOX-1141

MEDICAL

96 53

140/34/89

CONFIDENTIAL

Jan. 1919

WAR DIARY.

OF

A.D.M.S. 4TH. DIVISION.

FROM

1-1-1919 TO 31-1-1919.

BOX 1140

WAR DIARY
or
INTELLIGENCE SUMMARY.

Army Form C. 2118.

Place	Date	Hour	Summary of Events and Information	Remarks and references to Appendices
BINCHE	20.1.19		ADMS & Staff attended photograph of 2nd Div RAMC at LA LOUVIERE. ADMS inspected No 2 Field Ambulance.	Appx
"	21.1.19		ADMS van Corps visited ADMS at BINCHE. + inspected 10 Field Ambulance.	Appx

ADMS
Jul 54

31
CONFIDENTIAL.
WAR DIARY.
&
MEDICAL
HQrs
4th DIVISION. Feb 18 —
FEBRUARY Feb 6 1919

Army Form C. 2118.

WAR DIARY
or
INTELLIGENCE SUMMARY.
(Erase heading not required.)

Instructions regarding War Diaries and Intelligence Summaries are contained in F. S. Regs., Part II. and the Staff Manual respectively. Title pages will be prepared in manuscript.

Place	Date	Hour	Summary of Events and Information	Remarks and references to Appendices
BINCHE	1.2.19		ADMS attends DDMS Conference at MONS in morning. In afternoon DADMS visited	
BINCHE	2.2.19		1st Som L I & 1st R B.	
			ADMS went to La Louvière to make arrangements about Belgian civil general hospital for women. DADMS visited 1st Field Ambulance.	
	3.2.19		ADMS & DADMS attended Bacteriological lecture at MONS in afternoon.	
			[illegible handwritten entries]	
	16.2.19		[illegible]	
	17.2.19			
	18.2.19			

Army Form C. 2118.

WAR DIARY
or
INTELLIGENCE SUMMARY.
(Erase heading not required.)

Place	Date	Hour	Summary of Events and Information	Remarks and references to Appendices
BINCHE	19.2.19		ADMS held conference of the three Ambulance Commanders at this office at 9.30 and afterwards attended	
			NTO's conference at 10 OPS	
	20.2.19		ADMS visited 11 Field Ambulance Stables and in afternoon	
	21.2.19		DADMS visited 9 Stationary hospital for this own B.K. & Inoculation. DADMS visited 12 & 16 Lieutfjeld & 9 St Pass by	
	22.2.19		ADMS visited 12 & Field Ambulance & La Louvriere	
	23.2.19		ADMS visited DDMS & OMS	
	24.2.19		ADMS & DADMS visited DMS	
			ADMS & DADMS visited Sound 2.9.	
	25.2.19		ADMS visited 11 Field Ambulance Major R.Z. RITCHIE Returned from leave	
	26.2.19		ADMS & DADMS attended XXII Corps race meeting at MONS	
	27.2.19		DADMS visited 11 Field Ambulance ADMS conferred with Ambulance Commanders	
	28.2.19		ADMS & DADMS visited 10 Field Ambulance	

M MKutchie
Major DADMS
4th Division

Army Form C. 2118.

WAR DIARY
or
INTELLIGENCE SUMMARY.
(Erase heading not required.)

Instructions regarding War Diaries and Intelligence Summaries are contained in F. S. Regs., Part II. and the Staff Manual respectively. Title pages will be prepared in manuscript.

Place	Date	Hour	Summary of Events and Information	Remarks and references to Appendices
VALENCIENNES	1.1.19		DADMS visited 10 Field Ambulance.	ADMS
"	2.1.19		DADMS visited 12 Field Ambulance and 2nd Essex Regt. In afternoon visited 2nd Duke of Wellingtons Regt. and 1st Royal Warwickshire Regt.	ADMS
"	3.1.19		DADMS visited 2nd Lancashire Fusiliers and 1st Kings Own Regt. Also 12th Brigade. R.A.M.C. football team defeated in Lucas Cup Competition by 2nd Duke of Wellingtons (4-3)	ADMS
"	4.1.19		12th Brigade + 12 Field Ambulance moved to La Louviere area.	ADMS
"	5.1.19		11th Brigade + Div. HQ moved to new area. ADMS Office closed at VALENCIENNES at 0800 hrs and opened at BINCHE on arrival.	ADMS
BINCHE	6.1.19		DADMS visited 11 Field Ambulance and 12 Field Ambulance at LA LOUVIERE. ADMS returned from 14 days leave to U.K.	ADMS
"	7.1.19		ADMS visited 11 FA at ZALOUVIERE, and conferred with local authorities as to means of stamping out venereal disease	ADMS
"	8.1.19		ADMS visited 10 Field Ambulance. DADMS visited 2nd Duke of Wellingtons Regt. and 1st Royal Warwickshire Regt.	ADMS

Army Form C. 2118.

WAR DIARY
or
INTELLIGENCE SUMMARY.
(Erase heading not required.)

Instructions regarding War Diaries and Intelligence Summaries are contained in F.S. Regs., Part II. and the Staff Manual respectively. Title pages will be prepared in manuscript.

Place	Date	Hour	Summary of Events and Information	Remarks and references to Appendices
BINCHE.	9-1-19.		DADMS visited units of 10th Bde. 1st R Warwickshires. 2nd Dof Wrs & 2nd Seaforth Highlanders. Temporary latrines have been erected on the pit system. Cookhouses poor.	AST/u
"	10-1-19.		ADMS visited 11th Field Ambulance.	AST/u
"	11-1-19.		DADMS visited 29th & 32nd Bdes RFA. in afternoon 4th DAC.	AST/u
"	12-1-19.		DADMS visited 4th Div Train at MANAGE. In afternoon 2nd Seaforth Highlanders	AST/u
"	13-1-19.		ADMS visited 10 Field Ambulance. DADMS visited 2nd Suffolk Regt 1st King's Own Regt.	AST/u
"	14-1-19.		ADMS attended GOC's Conference. DADMS visited 11 Field Ambulance.	AST/u
"	15-1-19.		ADMS visited 10 Field Ambulance	AST/u
"	16-1-19.		ADMS visited units of 12th Brigade. 1st King's Own. 2nd Essex Rt. and inspected their Sanitary arrangements.	AST/u
"	17-1-19.		DADMS visited 1st R Warwickshire Regt. and 1st Hampshire Regt.	AST/u
"	18-1-19.		ADMS interviewed Area Commandant LA LOUVIERE. also 12th Field Ambulance. also attended meeting of Corps Medical Society at MONS in afternoon.	AST/u

Army Form C. 2118.

WAR DIARY
or
INTELLIGENCE SUMMARY.
(Erase heading not required.)

Instructions regarding War Diaries and Intelligence Summaries are contained in F. S. Regs., Part II. and the Staff Manual respectively. Title pages will be prepared in manuscript.

Place	Date	Hour	Summary of Events and Information	Remarks and references to Appendices
BINCHE	19.1.19		ADMS visited 10 Field Ambulance. DADMS visited 12 Field Ambulance	ASM
"	20.1.19		Civic reception at Binche in honour of 3rd Division	ASM
"	21.1.19		ADMS & DADMS visited and inspected 29th Bde RFA (+ Batteries)	ASM
"	22.1.19		ADMS & DADMS visited 10 Field Ambulance. Afternoon visited 1st R.B & 1st Bn L.I.	ASM
"	23.1.19		ADMS & DADMS visited & inspected the 32nd Bde RFA. Everything satisfactory	ASM
"			ADMS visited 15th Royal Irish Rifles Regt. and 2nd Duke of Wellington Regt. DADMS	ASM
"	24.1.19		visited 2nd Sussex Regt & 2nd Lancashire Fusiliers.	ASM
"	25.1.19.		ADMS visited 12 Field Ambulance. Inspected billets & transport	ASM
"	26.1.19		DADMS visited 1st Kings Own Regt and 3 Field Coys RE in MORLANWELZ.	ASM
"	27.1.19.		ADMS attended XXII Corps Conf. at BRUSSELS. DADMS visited 11 & 12 Field Ambulances	ASM
"	28.1.19		DADMS visited 2nd Seaforth Highlanders and - in afternoon - Mob. Vet. Section.	ASM
"	29.1.19		ADMS and DADMS visited and inspected 4th Div Reception Camp at FAYT-LE-SENEFFE and 4th Div Train at MANAGE	ASM

www.ingramcontent.com/pod-product-compliance
Lightning Source LLC
Chambersburg PA
CBHW080821010526
44111CB00015B/2590